Advances and Applications of Soft Computing

Advances and Applications of Soft Computing

Guest Editor

Michael Voskoglou

MDPI

Basel • Beijing • Wuhan • Barcelona • Belgrade • Novi Sad • Cluj • Manchester

Guest Editor
Michael Voskoglou
School of Engineering
University of Peloponnese
(Ex Graduate Technological
Educational Institute of
Western Greece)
Patras
Greece

Editorial Office
MDPI AG
Grosspeteranlage 5
4052 Basel, Switzerland

This is a reprint of the Special Issue, published open access by the journal *Mathematics* (ISSN 2227-7390), freely accessible at: https://www.mdpi.com/journal/mathematics/special_issues/CVV73STHDQ.

For citation purposes, cite each article independently as indicated on the article page online and as indicated below:

Lastname, A.A.; Lastname, B.B. Article Title. *Journal Name* **Year**, *Volume Number*, Page Range.

ISBN 978-3-7258-3453-2 (Hbk)
ISBN 978-3-7258-3454-9 (PDF)
https://doi.org/10.3390/books978-3-7258-3454-9

Contents

About the Editor

Michael Voskoglou

Michael Voskoglou (B.Sc., M.Sc., M.Phil. and Ph.D. in Mathematics) is an Emeritus Professor of the Graduate Technological Educational Institute (T.E.I.) of Western Greece in Patras. From 1987 to 2010, he held the position of Full Professor at the same Institute. Prior to that, he served as an instructor at the Hellenic Open University, at the Mathematics Department of the University of Patras, at the Schools of Primary and Secondary In-Service Teachers' Training in Patras, and as a teacher of mathematics at the Greek Public Secondary Education systems from 1972 to 1987. He has held visiting researcher positions at the Bulgarian Academy of Sciences (1997-2000), University of Warsaw (2009), University of Applied Sciences in Berlin (2010), and National Institute of Technology of Durgapur (2016). Professor Voskoglou has authored and edited 20 books and has published approximately 650 papers, with over 2500 citations. He has reviewed for the American Mathematical Society and has edited numerous mathematical journals. He has supervised many student dissertations and served as an external examiner of Ph.D. dissertations at universities in Egypt, India, and Saudi Arabia. His research interests include algebra, fuzzy logic, Markov chains, artificial intelligence, and mathematics education.

Preface

Conversely, soft computing methods do not rely on symbolic logical reasoning or numerical modelling. Instead, they utilize approximate reasoning and processes to address complex real-life problems that are difficult to model mathematically or are not adequately represented by conventional methods. Soft computing integrates several computing paradigms mainly including probabilistic reasoning, fuzzy logic, artificial neural networks and genetic algorithms. These paradigms are complementary to each other and can be utilized concurrently to solve specific problems. Soft computing emerged during the 1980s and has since been successfully applied in many domestic, commercial, and industrial settings, making it a significant research area in automatic control engineering.

The present reprint contains 10 of the total 31 articles submitted that were accepted and published in the Special Issue "Advances and Applications of Soft Computing" of the MDPI *Mathematics* journal. This Special Issue can be regarded as a continuation of the Special Issue "Fuzzy Sets, Fuzzy Logic and their Applications" of the same journal containing, which contained a total of 57 papers and was also published in the form of a book in three volumes (2020, 2021, and 2023). It is my hope that all these 67 articles, which cover a wide range of the theory and applications of soft computing, will provide useful feedback for all those working in this area.

The ten papers of the present book are listed in the order that they were accepted and published in *Mathematics* during the years 2023 and 2024. The first paper, authored by Anushree Bhattacharya and Madhumangal Pal, presents an application of fuzzy graph theory to the facility location problem with a case study in the Indian banking system.

The second paper, authored by Said Broumi, Raman Sundareswaran, Marayanagaraj Shanmugapriya, Prem Kumar Singh, Michael Voskoglou, and Mohamed Talea, attempts a multi-criteria decision analysis of faculty performance using interval-valued Fermatean neutrosophic sets.

The subsequent paper, authored by Na Chen, Shengling Gentg, and Yonming Li, presents a novel approach for modeling and verifying uncertain cyber-physical systems. This approach utilizes decision processes and employs fuzzy linear time properties.

The fourth paper, authored by Abdulaziz M. Alanaz, Gulam Muhiuddin, Bashair M. Alenazi, Tonmoy Maharatra, and Madhumangal Pal, utilizes m-polar fuzzy saturation graphs to solve optimal allocation problems.

The fifth paper, authored by Zanyar A. Ameen and Mesfer Algahtani, studies some classes of soft functions defined by soft open sets modulo soft sets of the first category.

The subsequent paper, authored by Ahmed Al-Omari and Wafa Agurashi, introduces the concept of soft ideal dense sets and examines their fundamental properties, with a focus on hyperconnectedness and resolvability of soft ideal topological spaces.

In the seventh paper, authored by De Andres Sanchez, an intuitionistic fuzzy chain ladder method is used to calculate insurance claim reserves.

In their subsequent paper, Hao Guan, Waheed Ahmed Khan, Amna Fida, Jana Shafi, and Aysha Khan introduce some new types of dominations in intuitionistic fuzzy directed graphs. These new types of domination are based on certain types of strong arcs. The authors discuss various useful characteristics of these dominations and examine existing relations among them.

In the ninth paper, Dina Abuzaid, Samer Al-Ghour, and Monia Naghi introduce a novel class of soft sets is introduced, called "soft $\omega\delta$ – open sets". This class constitutes a soft topological space, and the authors prove some related decomposition theorems.

In the final paper, the authors Panagiotis Mangenakis and Basil Papadopoulos present a formula that, under specific conditions, produces new classes of strong fuzzy negations, fuzzy implications, and copulas.

As the Guest Editor, I would like to express my gratitude to the authors and reviewers, as well as the administrative staff of MDPI, for their support in completing this project. I would also like to extend my special thanks to the Managing Editor, Ms. Grace Du, for her excellent collaboration and assistance over the past five years (2018-2024).

Michael Voskoglou
Guest Editor

mathematics MDPI

Article

A Fuzzy Graph Theory Approach to the Facility Location Problem: A Case Study in the Indian Banking System

Anushree Bhattacharya † and Madhumangal Pal *,†

Department of Applied Mathematics with Oceanology and Computer Programming, Vidyasagar University, Midnapore 721102, India; rsmo_ anumath96@mail.vidyasagar.ac.in
* Correspondence: mmpalvu@mail.vidyasagar.ac.in
† These authors contributed equally to this work.

Abstract: A fuzzy graph G is stated to have a set of trees as its tree cover if all the vertices of G are in their union. The maximum weight tree in the tree cover is assumed to be the cost of a tree cover for a fuzzy graph. For an integer $\beta > 0$, finding a set of trees to cover all the vertices of a graph with minimum cost and at most β number of spanning trees is known as the β-tree cover problem. Combining the tree-covering concept and facility location problem in a fuzzy environment for solving critical real-life problems in the recent era is a more fruitful approach. This issue strongly inspires us to develop a model with a practical algorithm. This paper provides an algorithm and complexity analysis to determine the number of rooted trees s covering the given fuzzy graph. In addition, a model is constructed with three optimization programming problems in the facility location problem and a tree covering fuzzy graphs. The model includes two types of the facility location problem, simultaneously addressing a variable covering radius and a fixed covering radius. A numerical example is provided to further describe the model, then, in the application part of the paper, the proposed model is applied to solve the real-life problem of maximizing demand saturation by minimizing the number of small denominations in the Indian banking system. This problem involves the data input of different indicators in the banking system along with details of the denominations of banknotes.

Keywords: fuzzy graph; tree covers; covering problem; tree covering number; fuzzy optimization

MSC: 05C72

Citation: Bhattacharya, A.; Pal, M. A Fuzzy Graph Theory Approach to the Facility Location Problem: A Case Study in the Indian Banking System. *Mathematics* **2023**, *11*, 2992. https://doi.org/10.3390/math11132992

Academic Editor: Michael Voskoglou

Received: 15 June 2023
Revised: 1 July 2023
Accepted: 2 July 2023
Published: 4 July 2023

1. Introduction

Most of the problems with uncertainties in our daily life can be modelled by fuzzy graphs. Fuzzy graph theory plays a salient role in making real connections between various objects in a system, with applications in network routing, wireless sensor networks, computer science, medical science, operations research, and more. In this introductory situation, the concept of fuzzy graphs provided by Rosenfield [1] is presented as an interesting fuzzy mathematical tool in graph theory.

A tree cover of a fuzzy graph $G = (V, \sigma, \mu)$, denoted by $\tau(G)$, is the set of the minimum number of fuzzy trees as induced subgraphs that cover all the vertices of G. For a crisp graph, the tree cover number is approximated as the maximum positive semi-definite nullity as a conjecture. Although this graph parameter was first introduced as an essential tool in 2011, there is very little information in the existing literature.

For minimizing the maximum cost of a tree cover, we are interested in finding a tree covering of a fuzzy graph with at most s number of trees which span the whole graph, as it is known that constant factor approximations to travelling salesperson tracks can be used to find the minimum number of spanning trees.

The actual purpose of the facility location problem is to decide which node to allocate to a set of facilities in order to provide full coverage to the service needed for several demand nodes in a system in the most efficient way. In addition, a customer or demand point may decide on the location of their facility nodes to cover the demand needed by every customer in the fuzzy network. Nowadays, one of the crucial problems is the placement of servers or data objects in any communication network to ensure that the latency of access is optimized. However, the primary purpose of the problem is always the same; the aim is to maximize the profit, that is, to minimize the allocation costs of different facility nodes in the system.

Many facility location problems include possible locations for facility nodes to be built on or opened at already-built facilities. In this case, information about the building or opening cost for a facility in that location is supplied. A set of demand nodes or customers can be considered, with detailed information about the amount to be covered and the connection cost between the demand point and a certain facility point. On the other hand, many conditions or restrictions in a facility's location problem need to be satisfied. An objective function which needs to be optimized is always present in such problems. One objective function is generally based on the cost, which includes all types of costs, such as demand, ordering, transportation, etc., for all system facilities.

In certain facility location problems, a profit can be associated with the assignment, then the objective profit function is optimized. One critical way of characterizing the facility location problem is on the basis of whether the facilities in the system are of variable-covering radius or fixed-covering radius in terms of how many demand nodes are to be covered by a facility within its covering radius. This kind of facility location problem is difficult to solve; we handle such problems in this article.

Now, we have to go through the rich literature on covering problems, which is the main topic of work within this article. The tree covering problems modelled and solved in this article are closely associated with the works of Arkin, Hassin, and Levin [2], who have dealt with various covering problems, including coverage of vertices for a crisp graph and a subset of edges of a graph with a partition in walks, paths, or stars. There are a variety of studies on approximation algorithms to minimize the number of objectives for covering purposes (such as paths) by satisfying some restrictions on the cost of each covering object.

An efficient feasible solution includes k-tours for covering the vertices of a crisp graph in the k-traveling salesperson problem. The main objective in this model is to minimize the total tour length. It is possible to partition all vertices of a graph into several clusters, and the weight of a star or low-cost spanning trees in the cluster is considered the weight of the cluster in that graph. Rana et al. [3] worked on unweighted interval graphs with conditional covering problems (CCP). In addition, Bhattacharya and Pal have presented works on different types of covering problems involving fuzzy graphs [4–7].

Mordeson and Peng [8] discussed concepts around various operations on fuzzy graphs. Samanta and Pal [9] have provided results on the fuzzy colouring of fuzzy graphs and fuzzy tolerance graphs. Fuzzy planar graphs with m-polarity are discussed in the work of Ghorai and Pal in [10]. Cardinal and Hoefer [11] have worked on various types of covering games. Chang and Zadeh handled fuzzy mappings and control techniques in [12]. Chaudhry introduced new heuristics for solving CCP in [13]. Chen and Chen [14] have provided a new method of finding similarity measures between two fuzzy numbers. Ghorai and Pal [15] have studied faces and dual m-polar fuzzy graphs. Jurji and Borut combined research on the facility location and covering problems in [16]. Fuzzy graphs were used in network optimization by Koczy [17]. In a similar way, Hakimi [18] worked on communication networks. The problem of emergency service facility location was handled by Toregas et al. [19]. Related problems on fuzzy graphs were studied and solved by Bhattacharya and Pal in [20].

Nayeem and Pal [21] solved the shortest path problem on a network. Ni [22] worked on a research area involving covering problems of edges having minimum weights. Pal et al. [23] detailed new ideas with respect to modern trends in fuzzy graph theory. Pramanik et al. [24] discussed interval-valued fuzzy planar graphs. A study on bipolar fuzzy graphs was revealed by Rashmanlou et al. in [25]. The research area of Samanta et al. in [26] included vague graphs and their strengths.

The motivation for the present article arises from the "Doctor station location" problem. Consider the problem of a hospital that requires s doctors to be located in the campus area for total coverage. A single doctor can be assigned to a particular number of patients, and the doctors make their rounds in shifts during the morning. The purpose of the problem is to find suitable locations for doctor stations and determine how to cover the requirement of treating every patient in such a way that the time for completing the entire process is minimized. Similar types of real-life problems motivate us to use the concept of tree covering in a modelled graph.

The "doctor station location" problem is similar to the problem of covering a graph with at most k number of tours while maintaining the minimum value of the maximum length of a tour. A constant factor approximation for a minimum number of trees spans the whole graph of travelling salesperson tours. We are interested in finding a covering of the graph with at most k number of spanning trees and the minimum value of the maximum weight of those trees. When a doctor must return to their station to pick up necessary supplies without first visiting every patient, a variation occurs in the considered problem. At such a point, the problem of covering the graph is formulated with the help of stars in the graph. In addition, we can consider the possibility of the hospital already having been built with all required doctor stations, in which case we only need to find the best possible way of assigning patients to doctors. Thus, these problems are transformed into the problem of finding rooted trees that covering the graph.

The idea described above inspires us to deal with tree-covering problems; for a realistic level of imprecision, we include the flavour of fuzzy graphs in this article. In addition, we chose the banking system as a case study in the application part, keeping in mind the importance of a developed model in solving real-life problems involving a combination of the facility location problem and tree covering of fuzzy graphs. The need to address such circumstances and situations influence our construction of a model with three optimization programming problems.

The main contributions in the sense of covering problems and real-life implications are organized in this portion. There are two variations of the facility location problems, one in which the covering radius is fixed for all facility vertices and one in which the covering radius differs for the vertices of different facilities. Earlier works have addressed covering radius variations and solved related problems involving a particular type of covering radius. However, it is more practical to have the number of demand points be saturated by a particular facility vertex of a fuzzy network depending on the covering radius type.

The contributions of this paper can be summarized as follows:

(i) This paper is the first to handle the two cases of a fixed covering radius and variable covering radius simultaneously in one model. The concept behind our proposed model is intended to cover all demand vertices. In this paper, we solve such complex facility location problems by minimizing the number of facility vertices, minimizing the total cost for all demand vertices, and maximizing the demand saturation of facility vertices. All fuzzy solutions for the model are determined using 'LINGO' mathematical software 18.0.44.

(ii) We introduce new definitions of tree cover and tree covering numbers for a fuzzy graph, design an efficient algorithm to determine the number of rooted trees s needed to cover a fuzzy graph, and present the algorithm's complexity analysis.

(iii) In the application part, we analyze the Indian banking system using our developed model and algorithm. As an outcome of this real-life application, the conclusion is reached that the number of small denominators (up to INR 100) is minimized. The cost required to maintain the flow of denominations for the Indian banking system is thereby minimized. Lastly, the demand saturation of denominations at the bottom level is assessed in the interest of economic freedom.

This article includes the following sections, excluding the present introduction. In Section 2, necessary definitions and concepts are provided. The covering problem considered in this article is described in Section 3 with the mathematical formulation. Section 4 illustrates the mathematical formulation of the developed model. Section 5 illustrates the model with a suitable example. A real-life application involving emergency aircraft landing situations is analyzed using the proposed model in Section 6. Finally, our overall conclusions are provided in Section 7.

2. Preliminaries

Several basic definitions and necessary aspects are provided in this portion of the paper. These parameters are beneficial in developing the model for a fuzzy graph with a facility location concept.

Here, all the components of a triangular fuzzy number (TFN) are normalized, i.e., between 0 and 1. Different types of scaling are used for the normalization process in different situations. Additionally, the format of the TFN with the representation of its components as in Definition 1 is followed throughout the article.

Definition 1 ([4])**.** *Let $\tilde{P} = (p_1, p_2, p_3)$ be a TFN that has the following function as its membership function:*

$$\mu_{\tilde{P}}(x) = \begin{cases} 0 & if \;\; x \leq p_1 \\ \dfrac{x - p_1}{p_2 - p_1} & if \;\; p_1 < x \leq p_2 \\ 1 & if \;\; x = p_2 \\ \dfrac{p_3 - x}{p_3 - p_2} & if \;\; p_2 < x \leq p_3 \\ 0 & if \;\; x \geq p_3. \end{cases}$$

Then, the defuzzified form of $\tilde{P}$ is denoted by $|\tilde{P}|$, defined as

$$|\tilde{P}| = \frac{1}{6}|(p_1 + 4p_2 + p_3)|.$$

Definition 2 ([8])**.** *A fuzzy graph $G = (V, \sigma, \mu)$ is a non-empty set which carries two functions, $\sigma : V \to [0,1]$ and $\mu : V \times V \to [0,1]$, for all $x, y \in V$, where σ is the vertex-membership function and μ is the edge-membership function satisfying $\mu(x,y) \leq min\{\sigma(x), \sigma(y)\}$.*

Definition 3 ([4])**.** *A set of vertices $\tilde{V_C}(G)$ of a fuzzy graph $G = (V, \sigma, \mu)$ is said to be a fuzzy vertex cover of G if each vertex of $G = (V, \sigma, \mu)$ is incident to every edge of G within a fuzzy covering radius $\tilde{R^g}$.*

Definition 4. *Consider a fuzzy graph $G = (V, \sigma, \mu)$. A coverage radius $\tilde{R^g}$ of G is defined as a predefined number which reflects a distance in G. If $\tilde{d}(u, v) \leq \tilde{R^g}$ for an arbitrary vertex u of G, then this vertex v is covered by u in fuzzy graph G.*

Definition 5. *Let G be a crisp graph and let $F_G = \{G_1, G_2, \ldots.., G_n\}$ be a collection of subgraphs of G where G_i is a tree for all $i = 1, 2, \ldots., n$. If $G_i \in F_G$ exists for every edge $e \in E(G)$ such that $e \in E(G_i)$, then F_G is a tree cover of G.*

Definition 6. *The tree covering number for a crisp graph G is provided by*

$$t_C(G) = min\{|F_G| : F_G \text{ is a tree cover of } G\}.$$

Definition 7. *Let $G = (V, \sigma, \mu)$ be a fuzzy graph and let $\tau(G) = \{T_1, T_2, \ldots.T_n\}$ be a collection of subgraphs of G where T_i is a fuzzy tree for all $i = 1, 2, \ldots., n$. If there exists $T_i \in \tau(G)$ for every* *edge uv with $\sigma(uv) \neq 0$ in G such that $\sigma(uv) \neq 0$ in T_i, then $\tau(G)$ is a tree cover of fuzzy graph $G = (V, \sigma, \mu)$.*

Definition 8. *The tree covering number of a fuzzy graph $G = (V, \sigma, \mu)$ is provided by*

$$T_C(G) = min_{T_i \text{ in } \tau(G)} \Big\{ \sum \frac{\sigma(u)\sigma(v)}{\mu(uv)} : u, v \in V(T_i), \mu(uv) \neq 0 \Big\}.$$

2.1. Notations and Symbols

This part clarifies all the necessary notations to signify the quantities used in the entire paper in deducing the theories. The symbols and their meanings are provided in tabular form in Table 1.

Table 1. Notations and their meanings.

Symbol	Meaning
G	fuzzy graph.
V	non-empty vertex set for fuzzy graph G.
σ	vertex membership function.
μ	edge-membership function.
T_{C_i}	i-th tree cover in any fuzzy graph.
$M_\mu(G)$	spanning tree with minimum size with respect to edge-membership function for a fuzzy graph G.
F_i	i-th forest present in a fuzzy graph.
$d(T, x)$	distance of the tree T from any arbitrary vertex x.
A	considered fixed bin capacity of the proposed algorithm FUZZY-BIN-PACK.
$c(T)$	cost of the tree T.
$\tau(G)$	tree-cover set for a fuzzy graph.
$I = \{1, 2, ..., m\}$	the set of possible choices of demand locations in a fuzzy graph.
$J = \{1, 2, ..., n\}$	the collection of possible choices of facility locations.
y_j	fuzzy variable for indicating demand saturation for demand point j.
c_{ij}	the approximate number of days to saturate demand by a facility vertex i to a demand vertex j, which is a fuzzy number.
δ_{ij}	it is 1, if the cost is paid by demand node j to facility node i, 0 otherwise.
f_i	the fuzzy cost (fuzzy) paid in facility node i for transportation.
d_j	fuzzy cost paid for demand ordering by demand point j.
K	maximum number of possible vertices (locations) which will be allocated in a fuzzy graph G.
M	maximum limit of the total amount of facility supplied in a fuzzy system for the developed model.
$\tilde{R}g$	fuzzy covering radius.
$T_C(G)$	tree covering number.
F	set of facility points of the fuzzy graph.
D	set of demand points of the fuzzy graph.
x_i	fuzzy variable denoting the point for placing facility.
F_n	total number of facility nodes in a fuzzy graph.
Z_c	total cost involved in the fuzzy system.
D_s	demand saturation of fuzzy system.
$w(u, v)$	weight associated to an arbitrary edge (u, v) of fuzzy graph G.
w_i or, $w(i)$	weight associated to an arbitrary vertex i.
$c(u, v)$	fuzzy cost associated to an arbitrary edge (u, v).
$c(u)$	fuzzy cost associated to an arbitrary vertex u.

2.2. Problem under Consideration

Consider a fuzzy graph $G = (V, \sigma, \mu)$, where V is the set of vertices. There are three types of vertices in the graph: facility vertices, demand vertices, and free vertices. The free vertices are neither demand vertices nor facility vertices. The graph is assumed to contain some demand and facility vertices, while the free vertices may or may not exist.

The facility vertices can store commodities (such as food, water, weapons, etc.) required for emergency or regular distribution. These vertices may be hospitals, military camps/offices, ration shops, or distribution centres. Demand vertices take such commodities for use, and generally represent people, organizations, etc. Free vertices are neither demand vertices nor facility vertices. Thus, new facility vertices may be initiated with respect to any free vertices. Because these vertices have no demand, free vertices cannot be considered demand vertices.

There are two possible cases. The first is that all the demand vertices are covered by at least one facility vertex (i.e., the required demand is fulfilled by any one of the facility vertices), regardless of the cost or distance to reach the facility. In the second case, certain demand vertices are not covered by facility vertices (as the demand vertices may be far away from facility vertices, or transport or other costs may be too high).

In both situations, we insert more facility vertices to reduce the cost, distance, etc. It is assumed that each facility vertex may cover all the demand vertices within a specific circular region (i.e., provide the commodities to the demand vertices). The radius of this circular region is called the covering radius. This radius may be the same for all facility vertices (i.e., fixed) or different for different ones. In this case, the covering radius is variable or dynamic.

Many parameters or situations may arise with respect to constructing new facility vertices. Here, we select the free vertices as facility points under different assumptions, objectives, and constraints.

The main assumptions are:

(a) The building cost for a facility point at an arbitrary vertex (say, i) can be taken as c_i (a fuzzy number).
(b) If a customer at vertex k has decided to take services from a facility point (at i), then a cost δ_{ik} (a combination of the establishment cost, ordering cost, and transportation cost) is imposed on the demand point.
(c) There are two types of covering radius: the first is a variable covering radius in which each facility serves unlimited customers, i.e., the covering radius is flexible depending on the situation, while the second is a fixed covering radius in which each facility can serve a maximum (say, u) number of demand points.

The objectives of our model are as follows:

(a) Minimize the total number of facilities.
(b) Minimize the total cost for all demand points.
(c) Maximize demand saturation by the facilities.

We use the following constraints or restrictions:

(a) The total number of facility nodes must be less than or equal to the maximum number of locations allocated in the fuzzy graph.
(b) The sum of the value of supplying a service by an arbitrary facility point i to a customer at demand point j is assumed to take a fixed value (say, M).
(c) The total demand cost in a certain period (say, t_1) is less than or equal to the total servicing cost in the fuzzy network.
(d) The servicing cost paid by an arbitrary demand point i is always a positive amount.
(e) The upper limit of the covering demand cost is the product of K and c_{ij}, where K is the maximum number of possible vertices (locations) allocated in a fuzzy graph G and c_{ij} is the approximate number of days needed by a facility vertex i to saturate demand with respect to a demand vertex j, with j being a fuzzy number.
(f) The flexibility of a facility point j in terms of providing facilities is less than or equal to the amount of the covering demand.
(g) There should always be a non-zero day for ordering demand and providing facilities from a facility point.

3. Problem Description

In this portion, the considered covering problem in a facility location model is described in a broader sense. A simple connected fuzzy graph is taken as an example throughout this article. The covering radius for the facility points is taken as a fuzzy number. In a system with fuzziness, distances and other types of costs are taken as fuzzy numbers as well.

Our model assumes that the resulting fuzzy system has two types of facility nodes.

(i) Facility location problem with variable covering radius. For the variable covering radius case, the following problem is considered: let $N = \{1, 2, ..., n\}$ be a possible set of locations, and let d_{ij} for $i, j = 1, 2, ..., n$ be the distances between them. For possible choices of points to open a facility, for each location $j \in D$, a subset $F \subseteq N$ is supplied, while for opened facility points a subset $D \subseteq N$ is assigned to the demand points. Corresponding to every location $i \in F$, the non-negative cost f_i is assumed at location i. In addition, δ_{ij} is the cost of demand location j assigning an opened facility point at i per unit of demand.

It is assumed that these costs are symmetric and non-negative fuzzy numbers and that they satisfy the following triangular inequality:

$\delta_{ij} = \delta_{ji}$ for all $i, j \in N$ and $\delta_{ij} + \delta_{jk} \geq \delta_{ik}$ for all $i, j, k \in N$.

To minimize the total cost, finding a feasible assignment to an open facility point of every location in the set D is required.

(ii) Facility location problem with fixed covering radius. In this case, we consider the situation where every existing facility point produces a total demand less than or equal to a positive integer. It is interesting to investigate whether we can prove that the adaptive covering radius in our developed algorithm affects the capacity of the facility location problems for finding the tree cover of a fuzzy graph and solving facility location problems with a fixed covering radius.

When the optimal value of the total demand is given in the variable covering radius type, the trivial problem is finding the corresponding facility points for the fuzzy graph. In this case, anyone can assign each location $j \in D$ to the location i such that δ_{ij} provides the minimum value among all possibilities ensuring that $y_i = 1$.

There is sufficient capacity for the fixed covering radius to saturate the total demand occurring in a fuzzy system. Two variants of facility location problems exist in our consideration. The situations are selected depending on the demand condition for each vertex of the fuzzy graph. An arbitrary facility point is allocated for only one demand point, or the facility point is fractionally split among more than one demand point in the system.

First, we must determine the type of the problem, i.e., whether it is of variable or fixed covering radius type. Then, we need to find an arrangement to ensure that there is a route to a facility point by optimizing all parameters. For example, we can take the amount of demand at each demand point together with an integer value representing the upper bound of demand for a particular problem. A minimum cost assignment is determined if the optimum value for total demand is supplied. In every problem, the presumption is that corresponding weights (edge weights and vertex weights) for facility points are provided.

To solve the considered problem, one crucial task is to find a tree cover of a fuzzy graph with an optimized cost different from the problem. In the next portion, we design an algorithm for finding such a tree cover.

3.1. Algorithm to Find Rooted Trees Covering Fuzzy Graph G

The bin packing problem is an optimization problem in which items of different sizes must be packed into a finite number of bins or containers, each of a fixed capacity and depending on the covering radius, in a way that minimizes the number of bins used. Generally, a BIN-PACK Algorithm refers to an approximation algorithm used to solve the above bin packing problem.

In this portion of the paper, we modify an existing BIN-PACK algorithm designed for crisp graphs for use with fuzzy graphs. We briefly describe the FUZZY-BIN-PACK Algorithm used to find a tree cover for the fuzzy graph $G = (V, \sigma, \mu)$ with an optimized cost of at most $4A$. It should be noted here that the set of vertices for locating the facility/demand points is treated as a collection of elements in our modified algorithm.

In Algorithm 1, we take a fuzzy graph $G = (V, \sigma, \mu)$ with vertex and edge costs as input. We provide a fixed capacity A for a fixed covering radius case of facility vertices (i.e., bin capacity) for the given graph. We aim to find a tree cover of G with an optimized cost of at most $4A$. In the first step, we compare the cost of any arbitrary vertex with A. If the cost is higher than A, we remove it from the vertex set of G. Next, we find a spanning tree with a minimum size in G, a transformed version of G when the roots in a given sample set S of vertices to be either facility or demand nodes are contracted to a single vertex. Then, we collect all uncontracting from the minimum spanning tree and obtain forests $\{F_i\}_i$ for $i = 1, 2, ..., z$. Now, to decompose the edges of each forest, we can find trees and an individual component such that the cost of the obtained trees must belong to $[A, 2A)$ and the cost of the other portion must be less than the fixed bin capacity A. In the next step, if the distances from the obtained trees to an arbitrary vertex of G are less than or equal to A, we check whether the trees are subgraphs or not for all possible cases. If all trees are not subgraphs of G, then we can conclude that the considered bin capacity is too low in cost; in this case, the process is repeated after modifying the value. On the other hand, if every tree is a subgraph of G, a success statement is returned for the choice of this bin capacity in obtaining an optimized tree cover of G. Finally, we obtain a set of trees which are all subgraphs of G for which the number of roots of these trees is finite, i.e., a tree covering with optimized bin capacity for the facility and demand vertices of the given fuzzy graph with finite size.

Algorithm 1: FUZZY-BIN-PACK.

Input:	A fuzzy graph $G = (V, \sigma, \mu)$ with associated costs to the vertices and edges. Also, a fixed bin capacity 'A' and a sample set S of vertices for choosing as facility and demand vertex are given.
Output:	A tree cover for the fuzzy graph $G = (V, \sigma, \mu)$ with the optimized cost at most $4A$.
Step 1:	If $c(u) > A$, then $V(G) = V(G) \backslash u$ for any arbitrary $u \in V(G)$.
Step 2:	For a fuzzy graph $G = (V, \sigma, \mu)$, find $M_\mu(G)$ (spanning tree with minimum size) of G which is a transformed version of G when the roots in S are contracted to a single vertex.
Step 3:	In S, un-contracting roots from $M_\mu(G)$; obtain a forest $\{F_i\}_i$ for $i = 1, 2, ..., z$.
Step 4:	Decompose edges of each tree F_i into trees $\{T_j^i\}_j + N_i$ such that $c(T_j^i) \in [A, 2A)$, for every j and $c(N_i) < A$.
Step 5:	If $d(T_j^i, x) \leq A$ for any arbitrary vertex $x \in V(G)$. Check whether T_j^i is a sub-graph of G for all j.
Step 6:	If not all trees are sub-graph of G, then Return failure: "A is a too low cost".
Step 7:	If every tree is a sub-graph of G, then Return to success and go to step 8.
Step 8:	Get a set of trees where each tree consists of T_j^i, a sub-graph of G, the number of roots is s, and the tree N (if any) in leftover, which contains the fuzzy root graph G, denoted by r.

3.2. Complexity Analysis of the Proposed Algorithm

We next explore the complexity analysis of our proposed FUZZY-BIN-PACK algorithm. In this algorithm, we fix the bin capacity to cover the whole fuzzy graph with the help of trees by limiting the cost to most four times the bin capacity, as per our previous considerations. If there are n number of vertices with non-zero membership values in the fuzzy graph, then the cost verification for the total number of vertices takes $O(n)$ times. In the next step, if there are m numbers of contracting roots in S to find a connected tree it takes $O(mn)$ times, as this is the most generalized possibility for finding trees to make a tree cover. For other situations, every tree needs to be checked to determine whether it is a subgraph of the considered fuzzy graph G by verifying the tree's distance from any arbitrary vertex of the main graph. For this purpose, the required time is $O(mn)$. Therefore, the total time required to perform the proposed algorithm is $O(n) \times O(mn) \times O(mn) = O(m^2n^3)$. Thus, the time complexity of our proposed FUZZY-BIN-PACK algorithm is $O(m^2n^3)$.

3.3. Advantages of Proposed Algorithm

In brief, the approximation algorithm known as BIN-PACK can be used to solve problems related to precise data. This algorithm helps to find the minimum number of total bins needed to assign each item to a bin when considering a finite number of items of different weights and a fixed capacity of bins in the system. This is useful in finding the minimum number of facility vertices needed to saturate all the demand in a system with crisp data and parameters, i.e., it is helpful for crisp graph scenarios under a graph-theoretical approach.

Practically, however, such crisp models have little relation ro real-life problems which involve several imprecise data types. Suppose that the number of the bins is not fixed; in this scenario, the existing algorithm is not applicable, as it cannot find any parameter with fuzziness. More clearly, it is obvious that in any network the accessible amount of facilities and order of demand are uncertain, and depend on various circumstances within the system. Therefore, it is notable that fuzzy graphs are a more practically justified tool for modeling realistic problems. In these cases, the existing BIN-PACK algorithm fails to compute the solution due to the need to handle fuzzy parameters. These more complex situations motivate us to modify the BIN-PACK algorithm for fuzzy environments and develop our proposed FUZZY-BIN-PACK algorithm. A complexity analysis of the proposed modified algorithm is provided in Section 3.2.

4. Mathematical Formulation

In this article, we consider fuzzy systems modeled as fuzzy graphs. If any uncertain or vague parameters are present in any system, it can be described as a fuzzy environment. Vertices are chosen as facility or demand vertices based on the relevant information of a particular case. It is obvious that in real life the available facilities and possible demand must be imprecise. Thus, the vertices are fuzzy with regard to their respective membership functions. Here, x_i represents the number of fuzzy vertices that are facility vertices; on the other hand, y_j represents the amount of demand saturation by facility nodes. It is assumed in the model that the maximum possible number for allocating demand or facility nodes is K. The other notations and their proper meaning in the proposed model are provided in Table 1. Next, we move through the mathematical formulation of objective functions subject to all conditions in the model to find the solution of the problem described in Section 2.2.

The main objectives of the developed model are as follows:

(i) To construct the first objective function, we multiply the number of facilities n by the corresponding fuzzy variable x_i representing potential locations of facility vertices. Meanwhile, several demand points m are multiplied by the fuzzy variable y_j to represent demand saturation of the demand vertices. The operational cost is incorporated in the calculation of the facility vertices through multiplication by the parameter δ_{ij}. In this way, the total number of facility and demand nodes provided by

$$Min\ F_n = \sum_{j \in J} \delta_{ij} y_j m + \sum_{i \in I} \delta_{ij} x_i n$$

is minimized.

(ii) The second objective function related to total fuzzy cost is constructed by taking the difference between two quantities, the first representing the product of the minimum number of days among c_{ij} needed to saturate demand in the fuzzy network based on the amount of fuzzy cost f_i paid by the facility node for transportation and the second representing the product of the fuzzy cost d_j paid for demand ordering, where the maximum possible number for allocating demand or facility nodes in the network is K. Therefore, we seek to minimize the total cost, which is represented by

$$Min\ Z_c = \sum_{i \in I} min_{j \in J} c_{ij} f_i - K(max_{j \in J} d_j).$$

(iii) The last objective function seeks to maximize the total demand saturation of the fuzzy network. The demand saturation of the network depends on the tree covering number corresponding to the tree coverage of the network, the fuzzy transportation and ordering costs, the fuzzy weights associated with demand, and the number of facility points M for facilities available in the network. Thus, this objective function involves four expressions: the first for fuzzy cost, the second for tree covering number $T_C(G)$, the third corresponding to the fuzzy weights w_i, and the last for the available facilities. Therefore, we seek to maximize the demand saturation, as follows:

$$Max\ D_s = \sum_{i \in I} \sum_{j \in J} c_{ij} \delta_{ij} + \sum_{j \in J} d_j y_j T_C(G) - \sum_{i \in I} w_i (\sum_{j \in J} \delta_{ij}) - M \times f_i.$$

The above-described functions are optimized in our model subject to certain conditions that need to be satisfied. The constraints subjected to these objective functions are as follows:

(a) The total number of facility nodes must be less than or equal to the maximum number of locations that can be allocated in the fuzzy graph

$$1 \leq \sum_{j \in J} y_j \leq K.$$

(b) The sum of the value of supplying services from an arbitrary facility node i to a customer at demand point j is assumed to be a fixed value (say, M):

$$\sum_{j \in J} \delta_{ij} n \leq M \text{ for } i \in I.$$

(c) The amount of total demand cost in a certain period (say, t_1) is less than or equal to the total servicing cost in the fuzzy network:

$$\sum_{j \in J} (\max d_j) c_{ij} \leq \sum_{j \in J} \sum_{i \in I} f_i y_j m.$$

(d) The servicing cost paid by an arbitrary demand node i is always a positive amount:

$$0 \leq f_i \leq 1.$$

(e) The upper limit of the covering demand cost is the product of K and c_{ij}:

$$T_C(G) \times (max_{j \in J} d_j) \times f_i \leq K \times \sum_{j \in J} c_{ij}$$

for $i \in I$.

(f) The flexibility amount when a facility node j provides facilities is less than or equal to the amount of the covering demand

$$\sum_{j \in J} \sum_{i \in I} c_{ij} y_j \leq \sum_{j \in J} d_j T_C(G)$$

(g) There should always be a non-zero day for ordering demand and for a facility node to provide facilities:

$$0 \leq c_{ij} \leq 1.$$

5. Example Illustration

This section illustrates use of the proposed model for the fixed covering radius case of the fuzzy graph $G = (V, \sigma, \mu)$ in Figure 1 along with its vertices and corresponding edges. In this section, the parameters taken as fuzzy numbers in the description of the problem, such as the covering radius, distances, weights, and the costs corresponding to the vertices and edges of the fuzzy graph, are triangular fuzzy numbers. The proposed model can be illustrated using other types of fuzzy numbers as well.

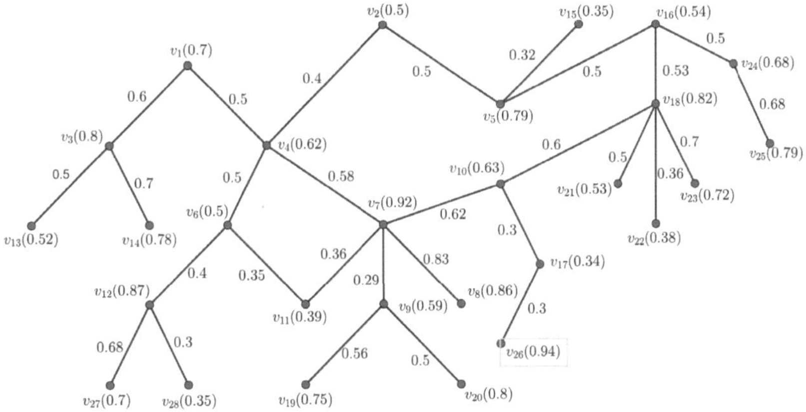

Figure 1. Considered fuzzy graph for illustration with the grey boxed value is the highest vertex-membership value.

In this example, the fuzzy graph $G = (V, \sigma, \mu)$ in Figure 1 with 26 vertices and 29 edges and their corresponding membership values, weights, and fuzzy costs is taken as an example. All of the weights and costs are triangular fuzzy numbers. We assume that all required data are supplied in Table 2.

To assign the edge membership values in the fuzzy graph, it is maintained that

$$\mu(u, v) \leq min\{\sigma(u), \sigma(v)\},$$

$$w(u, v) \leq min\{w(u), w(v)\},$$

$$c(u, v) \leq min\{c(u), c(v)\},$$

for any arbitrary vertices u and v in $V(G)$.

Using our developed algorithm, we can find a tree cover for the considered fuzzy graph as follows:

$$\tau(G) = \{T_1, T_2, T_3, T_4\}$$

where

$$T_1 = \{v_1, v_3, v_4, v_6, v_7, v_{12}, v_{13}, v_{14}, v_{27}, v_{28}\},$$

$$T_2 = \{v_8, v_9, v_{10}, v_{11}, v_{19}, v_{20}\},$$

$$T_3 = \{v_{17}, v_{18}, v_{21}, v_{22}, v_{23}, v_{26}\},$$

$$T_4 = \{v_2, v_2, v_5, v_{15}, v_{16}, v_{24}, v_{25}\}.$$

Table 2. Details of vertices for this illustration.

Vertices (v_i)	Membership Value ($\sigma(v_i)$)	Weights ($w(v_i)$)	Costs ($c(v_i)$)
v_1	0.7	$(0.6, 0.8, 0.9)$	$(0.2, 0.5, 0.7)$
v_2	0.5	$(0.3, 0.4, 0.7)$	$(0.4, 0.5, 0.8)$
v_3	0.8	$(0.9, 0.97, 0.99)$	$(0.4, 0.52, 0.78)$
v_4	0.62	$(0.7, 0.83, 0.88)$	$(0.3, 0.48, 0.57)$
v_5	0.79	$(0.27, 0.35, 0.48)$	$(0.7, 0.82, 0.9)$
v_6	0.5	$(0.4, 0.57, 0.63)$	$(0.6, 0.73, 0.85)$
v_7	0.92	$(0.4, 0.6, 0.7)$	$(0.32, 0.46, 0.53)$
v_8	0.86	$(0.2, 0.37, 0.42)$	$(0.49, 0.58, 0.67)$
v_9	0.59	$(0.3, 0.42, 0.59)$	$(0.5, 0.63, 0.78)$
v_{10}	0.63	$(0.49, 0.56, 0.64)$	$(0.3, 0.5, 0.78)$
v_{11}	0.39	$(0.53, 0.68, 0.72)$	$(0.79, 0.82, 0.93)$
v_{12}	0.87	$(0.48, 0.53, 0.6)$	$(0.2, 0.37, 0.42)$
v_{13}	0.52	$(0.3, 0.42, 0.53)$	$(0.4, 0.5, 0.7)$
v_{14}	0.78	$(0.5, 0.7, 0.9)$	$(0.9, 0.95, 0.98)$
v_{15}	0.35	$(0.7, 0.72, 0.8)$	$(0.3, 0.34, 0.43)$
v_{16}	0.54	$(0.2, 0.32, 0.45)$	$(0.7, 0.81, 0.9)$
v_{17}	0.34	$(0.4, 0.57, 0.62)$	$(0.6, 0.72, 0.84)$
v_{18}	0.82	$(0.6, 0.8, 0.9)$	$(0.32, 0.46, 0.54)$
v_{19}	0.75	$(0.4, 0.53, 0.67)$	$(0.5, 0.62, 0.79)$
v_{20}	0.8	$(0.3, 0.42, 0.53)$	$(0.4, 0.5, 0.7)$
v_{21}	0.53	$(0.5, 0.62, 0.73)$	$(0.2, 0.35, 0.48)$
v_{22}	0.38	$(0.6, 0.72, 0.83)$	$(0.42, 0.57, 0.6)$
v_{23}	0.72	$(0.47, 0.52, 0.68)$	$(0.53, 0.68, 0.74)$
v_{24}	0.68	$(0.52, 0.68, 0.79)$	$(0.3, 0.4, 0.7)$
v_{25}	0.79	$(0.58, 0.62, 0.84)$	$(0.35, 0.48, 0.57)$
v_{26}	0.94	$(0.39, 0.46, 0.79)$	$(0.82, 0.87, 0.94)$
v_{27}	0.7	$(0.28, 0.37, 0.42)$	$(0.58, 0.62, 0.78)$
v_{28}	0.35	$(0.45, 0.51, 0.67)$	$(0.32, 0.48, 0.55)$

The programming problem denoted as Problem 1 of the constructed model with three objective functions and associated conditions is provided as follows:

Problem 1. $Min\ F_n = \sum_{j\in J} \delta_{ij} y_j m + \sum_{i\in I} \delta_{ij} x_i n$

$Min\ Z_c = \sum_{i\in I} min_{j\in J} c_{ij} f_i - K(max_{j\in J} d_j)$

$Max\ D_s = \sum_{i\in I} \sum_{j\in J} c_{ij}\delta_{ij} + \sum_{j\in J} d_j y_j T_C(G) - \sum_{i\in I} w_i(\sum_{j\in J} \delta_{ij}) - M \times f_i$

Subject to constraints

$1 \leq \sum_{j\in J} y_j \leq K$

$\sum_{j\in J} \delta_{ij} n \leq M\ for\ i \in I$

$\sum_{j\in J} (maxd_j) c_{ij} \leq \sum_{j\in J} \sum_{i\in I} f_i y_j m$

$0 \leq f_i \leq 1$

$T_C(G) \times (max_{j\in J} d_j) \times f_i \leq K \times \sum_{j\in J} c_{ij}$

$for\ i \in I$

$\sum_{j\in J} \sum_{i\in I} c_{ij} y_j \leq \sum_{j\in J} d_j T_C(G)$

$0 \leq c_{ij} \leq 1$

We assume the following for this example:

$\delta_{ij} = 1$ *for the payment situation of demand point j with respect to facility point i.*

$minc_{ij}$ *is the approximate number of days needed by facility node i to saturate the demand of demand node j=(0.58, 0.65, 0.79).*

f_i *is the fuzzy amount to be determined; it is the approximated cost paid at facility node i for transportation.*

$K = \sigma(v_1) + \sigma(v_7) + \sigma_{10} + \sigma_{18} = 0.7 + 0.92 + 0.63 + 0.82 = 3.07$

$max_{j\in J} d_j$ *is the fuzzy cost paid for demand ordering by demand point j = (0.79, 0.82,0.95).*

x_i *is a fuzzy variable used to identify many facility nodes in a fuzzy network, which is a fuzzy number.*

y_j *is a fuzzy variable used to identify many demand nodes in a fuzzy system.*

It is defined that $T_C(G) = min\{T_{C_1}, T_{C_2}, T_{C_3}, T_{C_4}\}$.

Now, we have to evaluate the values $T_{C_1}, T_{C_2}, T_{C_3}, T_{C_4}$ *corresponding to the trees* T_1, T_2, T_3, T_4, *respectively, in the tree covering set of G.*

$T_{C_1} = \{\sigma(v_1) + \sigma(v_3) + \sigma(v_4) + \sigma(v_6) + \sigma(v_7) + \sigma(v_{11}) + \sigma(v_{12}) + \sigma(v_{13}) + \sigma(v_{14}) + \sigma(v_{27}) + \sigma(v_{28})\} = 7.15$

$T_{C_2} = \sigma(v_7) + \sigma(v_{11}) + \sigma(v_9) + \sigma(v_8) + \sigma(v_{10}) + \sigma(v_{19}) + \sigma(v_{20}) = 4.96$

$T_{C_3} = \sigma(v_{10}) + \sigma(v_{17}) + \sigma(v_{18}) + \sigma(v_{21}) + \sigma(v_{22}) + \sigma(v_{23}) + \sigma(v_{26}) = 4.36$

$T_{C_4} = \sigma(v_2) + \sigma(v_4) + \sigma(v_5) + \sigma(v_{15}) + \sigma(v_{16}) + \sigma(v_{10}) + \sigma(v_{24}) + \sigma(v_{25}) = 4.9$

$T_C(G) = min\{7.15, 4.96, 4.36, 4.9\} = 4.36$, *which corresponds to the tree* T_{C_3}. *Thus, we have to calculate the total summed weight of the tree for the tree covering number of G.*

Therefore, $\sum_{i\in I} w_i = w(v_{10}) + w(v_{17}) + w(v_{18}) + w(v_{21}) + w(v_{22}) + w(v_{23}) + w(v_{26}) = (0.49, 0.56, 0.64) + (0.4, 0.57, 0.62) + (0.6, 0.8, 0.9) + (0.5, 0.62, 0.73) + (0.6, 0.72, 0.83)$
$+(0.47, 0.52, 0.63) + (0.39, 0.46, 0.79) = (3.45, 4.25, 5.14)$.

In addition, the maximum fuzzy limit of the total amount of facilities supplied in the fuzzy system is $M = (8.92, 9.95, 10.98)$.

By solving the programming problems of the model with the help of the mathematical software 18.0.44 'LINGO', the variables to be determined are f_i, x_i, y_j, m and n. These are all fuzzy parameters, and are taken as triangular fuzzy numbers in this illustration. Then, Problem 1 is reduced to Problem 2 below.

Problem 2. *Min* $F_n = \sum_{j\in J} y_j m + \sum_{i\in I} x_i n$

Min $Z_c = (0.58, 0.65, 0.79) f_i - 3.07 \times (0.79, 0.82, 0.95)$

Max $D_s = (0.58, 0.65, 0.79)m - (0.79, 0.82, 0.95) \times 4.36 y_j - \{(3.45, 4.25, 5.14)$
$-(8.92 f_1, 9.95 f_2, 1.98 f_3)\}$

Subject to conditions

$$1 \leq \sum_{j\in J} y_j \leq 3.07$$

$$(n_1, n_2, n_3) \leq (8.92, 9.95, 10.98)$$

$$(0.79, 0.82, 0.95) \times (0.58, 0.65, 0.79) \leq \sum_{j\in J}\sum_{i\in I} f_i y_j m$$

$$0 \leq f_i \leq 1$$

$$4.36 \times (0.79, 0.82, 0.95) \times f_i \leq 3.07 \times (0.58, 0.65, 0.79)$$

$$\sum_{j\in J} (0.58, 0.65, 0.79) y_j \leq 3.07 \times (0.79, 0.82, 0.95)$$

Using 'LINGO' mathematical software, we obtain the following solutions for these programming problems.

$f_i = (0.78, 0.84, 0.97)$, $x_i = (2.84, 3.59, 4.01)$, $y_j = (0.98, 1.29, 3.02)$, $m = (3.12, 4.39, 5.74)$, $n = (1.05, 2.71, 3.23)$. *The minimum number of approximate choices for facility nodes is* $MinF_n = (2.97, 3.28, 5.72)$, *the minimized total fuzzy cost for the fuzzy network is* $Min\ Z_c = (4.43, 5.12, 5.78)$, *and the maximized demand saturation concerning weights and fuzzy costs is* $Max\ D_s = (0.94, 2.37, 10.92)$.

6. Example Application

The recent COVID-19 pandemic has caused an abnormal situation for the global economy due to complicated circumstances such challenges within of the banking system and other financial institutions. In the Indian banking system. there is an ongoing revolution in the operations and services of banks and financial institutions due to the incorporation of new and updated technologies.

The Reserve Bank of India functions as a sunshade for the entire Indian banking industry, being responsible for the central banking system and regulatory processes. There are two types of banks in the Indian banking system, namely, commercial banks and co-operative banks.

At present, different opportunities and challenges are faced by the Indian banking system. According to the Annual Report of the RBI, the main opportunities and challenges of the banking industry lie in continued development of the banking process to sustain the Indian banking system while reducing bankruptcies and other negative parameters.

Compared to the previous year, the level of consumer awareness is significantly higher. Today, consumers need internet banking, mobile banking, and ATM services with high frequency and reliability.

In the banking system, the optimal number of banknotes per denomination is not certain, and varies per year according to the annual report of the Reserve Bank of India. Any banknote denomination can be represented with the help of many other banknotes, a relation that is imprecise and varies over time. Thus, a great deal of vagueness and uncertainty exist in the banking system, and problems related this can be represented and solved with the help of fuzzy graphs. To construct a fuzzy graph related to this system, it is first necessary to choose proper vertices and edges; this selection process is described in the next portion.

6.1. Construction of Fuzzy Graph

In the last part of 2020–2021, the number of soiled banknotes needing to be disposed of was severely affected by the COVID-19 pandemic, a phenomenon that was expedited slowly in order to maintain a stable economic structure. Thus, there was a 32% decline in the disposal process of soiled banknotes in that financial year compared to the previous year.

Following the annual report of the Reserve Bank of India at the end of March 2021, here we consider the denominations of banknotes as vertices of a fuzzy graph. To assign vertex membership values, we first observed the denomination of banknotes from 2019 to 2021. Then, we took the average as the mean value of a triangular fuzzy number (TFN). The fuzzy graph uses these triangular fuzzy numbers as vertex membership values. On the other hand, if other banknotes can represent any banknote, then an edge exists between those vertices corresponding to the same banknotes. For example, there is an edge between the vertices corresponding to banknotes with values of INR 100 and 500. In addition, the vertex membership values are used to assign edge membership values in the fuzzy graph.

First, we must find the average percentage of parameters which affect the banking system, then turn this into a triangular fuzzy number. These TFNs are used to find similarity measures with the vertex membership values in order to determine the corresponding fuzzy weights for each vertex in the constructed fuzzy graph. The cost is taken as a fuzzy number representing the difference between denominations in the year 2021 and the denominations' averages corresponding to their vertices. Here, the facility points are assumed to be the smaller denominations and the demand points are to be taken as larger denominations. The edge membership values in the fuzzy graph must maintain the following:

$$\mu(u,v) \leq min\{\sigma(u),\sigma(v)\}.$$

After constructing the fuzzy graph, we have to find a fuzzy tree cover and its tree covering number, then proceed to find the objectives and constraints of this particular part of the example. We aim to find the minimum number of smaller banknote denominations, minimize the fuzzy cost in the Indian banking system, and maximize demand saturation with respect to banknote circulation.

6.2. Case Study

At 21.4 percent of GDP for the end of December 2020, India's external debt remained lower than that of its emerging-market peers. The external vulnerability indicators at the end of March of 2021 are listed in Table 3, which reflect the approximate percentage unless indicated otherwise.

Table 3. Details of approximate percentage of parameters in the banking system.

Indicator	2013	2019	2020	End-March, 2021
Debt service ratio (debt service to current receipts)	5.9	6.4	6.5	9.0
Ratio of concessional debt to total debt	11.1	8.7	8.8	9.1
Ratio of short-term debt to reserves	33.1	426.3	22.4	17.7
Reserve cover of imports	7.0	9.6	12.0	18.6
External Debt to GDP ratio	22.4	19.9	20.6	21.4
Ratio of short-term debt to total debt	23.6	20.0	19.1	18.4

The number of frauds reported during the financial year 2020–2021 decreased by 15% in terms of number and 25% in terms of value. There was a decrease in the share of PSBs in terms of both value and number among the total number of frauds concerning private sector banks during the corresponding period.

Banknotes in Circulation

During 2020–2021, there were increases of 16.8% and 7.2% in the value and volume, respectively, in the circulation process of banknotes. The highest share in volume terms is for the INR 500 denomination, whereas the lowest is for INR 10 banknotes, as of 31 March 2021. Table 4 shows the details on banknotes in circulation to the end of March of 2021.

Table 4. Approximate number of banknotes in circulation (end March, 2021) as vertices of a fuzzy graph.

Denomination (Rs.) of Banknotes	2019	2020	2021	Average	v_i	$\sigma(v_i)$
2 and 5 Rs. notes	10.4	9.7	9.0	9.7	v_1	$(9.5, 9.7, 10.2)$
10 Rs. notes	28.7	26.2	23.6	26.16	v_2	$(25.53, 26.16, 28.7)$
20 Rs. notes	8.0	7.2	7.3	7.5	v_3	$(6.73, 7.5, 8.25)$
50 Rs. notes	7.9	7.4	7.0	7.43	v_4	$(6.32, 7.43, 8.63)$
100 Rs. notes	18.5	17.2	15.3	17	v_5	$(16.38, 17, 18.72)$
200 Rs. notes	3.7	4.6	4.7	4.33	v_6	$(3.89, 4.33, 5.76)$
500 Rs. notes	19.8	25.4	31.1	25.43	v_7	$(23.81, 25.43, 26.95)$
2000 Rs. notes	3.0	2.4	2.0	2.46	v_8	$(2.37, 2.46, 3.54)$

The fuzzy graph constructed using all these data is shown in Figure 2.

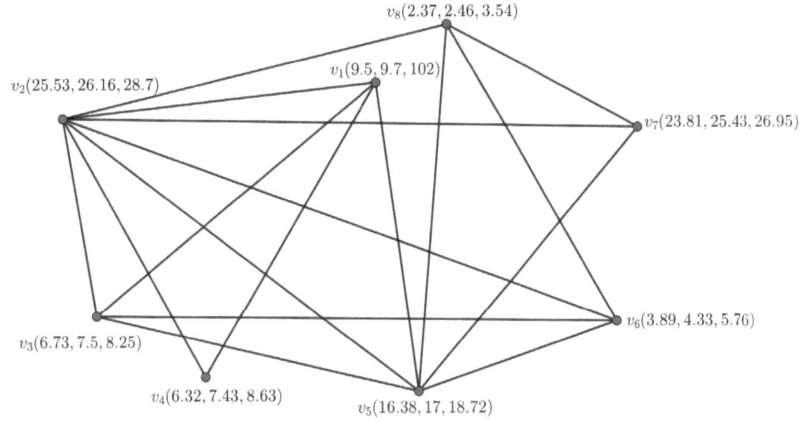

Figure 2. Fuzzy graph G for this application.

6.3. Formulation of the Problem

In this application area of our developed model, we have taken the Indian banking system as a fuzzy network, considering banknote denominations as items to be supplied from the facility to the demand vertices. The tree-like flow of denominations from the Reserve Bank of India to the common people helps in modeling such a system using the concept of tree cover in a fuzzy graph. The main problem is to minimize the number of small denominations without affecting the flow of demand in the lower layer related to the market level. For this purpose, we can use our proposed model with appropriate assumptions related to the Indian banking system to find all the solutions to the problem. The specific assumptions and considerations are described in the following portion.

Our objective for this application using the proposed model is to minimize the approximate number of smaller denominators (**Obj 1**), minimize the approximate total fuzzy cost in the Indian banking process concerning the corresponding weights mentioned earlier (**Obj 2**), and maximize demand saturation with respect to the economic need of the people through circulation of banknotes in the Indian economic system while accounting for external vulnerability indicators (**Obj 3**).

For this application, the data are as follows.

$\delta_{ij} = 1$ for the payment situation of the larger denomination j with respect to the smaller denomination i.

$minc_{ij}$ is the approximate number of days needed to saturate demand using a small denomination i with respect to a larger denomination j = (8.78, 9.35, 10.59).

f_i is a fuzzy amount to be determined, representing the approximate cost of a smaller denomination i for transportation from one bank to another.

$K = \sigma(v_3) + \sigma(v_4) + \sigma(v_1) + \sigma(v_8) + \sigma(v_5) = 7.5 + 7.43 + 9.7 + 2.46 + 17 = 44.09$

$max_{j \in J} d_j$ is a fuzzy cost paid for demand ordering due to circulation of the larger denomination j = (8.29, 9.32, 12.57).

x_i is a fuzzy variable used to identify a number of smaller denominations in the fuzzy banking system, and is a fuzzy number.

y_j is a fuzzy variable used to identify the number of larger denominations in the fuzzy banking network.

It is defined that $T_C(G) = min\{T_{C_1}, T_{C_2}, T_{C_3}\}$, where

$$T_{C_1} = \{v_2, v_1, v_3, v_4, v_5\},$$

$$T_{C_2} = \{v_5, v_7, v_6, v_2\},$$

and

$$T_{C_3} = \{v_8, v_6, v_3, v_4\},$$

$T_C(G) = min\{27.52, 42.36, 24.74\} = 24.74$, which corresponds to the tree T_{C_3}. Thus, we have to calculate the total summed weight of the tree for the tree covering number of G.

Therefore, $\sum_{i \in I} w_i = w(v_8) + w(v_6) + w(v_3) + w(v_4) = (3.49, 4.16, 5.34) + (2.34, 3.82, 4.32) + (5.26, 7.18, 8.39) + (4.35, 6.73, 9.81) = (15.44, 21.89, 27.86)$.

In addition, the maximum fuzzy limit of the total amount of facilities supplied in the fuzzy system is $M = (18.79, 19.65, 20.28)$.

By solving the programming problems of the model using 'LINGO' mathematical software, the variables to be determined are f_i, x_i, y_j, m, and n. In this illustration, all of these fuzzy parameters are taken as triangular fuzzy numbers.

6.4. Solution of Programming Problems

Then the problem Problem 1 is reduced to the problem, namely Problem 3 given by the following.

Problem 3. $Min\ F_n = \sum_{j \in J} y_j m + \sum_{i \in I} x_i n$

$Min\ Z_c = (5.82, 6.35, 7.39) f_i - 26.23 \times (7.39, 8.42, 9.92)$

$Max\ D_s = (5.82, 6.35, 7.39)m - (8.72, 8.92, 9.25) \times 24.69y_j - \{(12.45, 14.73, 15.48) - (18.79f_1, 19.65f_2, 20.28f_3)\}$

Subject to conditions

$$1 \leq \sum_{j \in J} y_j \leq 33.947$$

$$(n_1, n_2, n_3) \leq (18.62, 19.25, 22.84)$$

$$(7.39, 8.42, 9.92) \times (5.82, 8.57, 9.91) \leq \sum_{j \in J} \sum_{i \in I} f_i y_j m$$

$$0 \leq f_i \leq 1$$

$$24.66 \times (7.39, 8.42, 9.92) \times f_i \leq 33.947 \times (5.82, 6.35, 7.39)$$

$$\sum_{j \in J} (5.82, 6.35, 7.39) y_j \leq 3.07 \times (7.39, 8.42, 9.92).$$

Using the mathematical software 'LINGO', we have the following solutions for these programming problems.

f_i = (5.78, 6.84, 8.97), $x_i = (4.68, 5.79, 8.31)$, $y_j = (7.28, 9.89, 10.52)$, $m = (8.16, 8.53, 9.24)$, $n = (10.35, 12.92, 14.23)$. *The minimum number of approximate choices for facility nodes is Min* $F_n = (9.27, 9.86, 9.23)$, *the minimum total fuzzy cost for the fuzzy network of the banking system is Min* $Z_c = (14.38, 15.72, 16.98)$, *and the maximum demand saturation concerning the weights and fuzzy costs is Max* $D_s = (3.84, 4.37, 5.62)$.

6.5. Insightful Analysis

Based on the solutions obtained by the model in this application scenario, we can conclude the following:

(i) The minimized number of total small denominations (i.e., banknotes of INR 2, 5, 10, 20, 50, and 100) provide a total coverage in the RBI banking system of $(9.27, 9.86, 9.23)$, which is a fuzzy volume, i.e., in lakh; that is, a minimum total number of new banknotes of 9.27 lakh to 9.23 lakh per year in denominations of INR 2 to 100 need to be supplied for a smooth flow of denominations in the optimized sense, with the best results occurring for the case of 9.86 lakh.

(ii) The minimized total fuzzy cost in the fuzzy system representing the banking process is $(14.38, 15.72, 16.98)$ (in volume, i.e., INR notes in lakh) for smooth circulation of banknotes in the coming financial year to sustain the economic development of India. This objective function reflects the minimum denomination number needed to calculate cost for maintaining flow in the Indian banking system per year, and ranges from 14.38 lakh to 16.98 lakh, with 15.72 lakh being the best possibility.

(iii) The maximized demand saturation of banknote circulation in the Indian economic system with respect to external vulnerability indicators can be deduced as $(3.84, 4.37, 5.62)$, which is a fuzzy approximation. With the above-mentioned minimized objective function values in (i) and (ii), the demand for denominations (number of banknotes) at the population level is deduced as 3.84 lakh to 5.62 lakh. The best possible case is if the deduction in the number of denominations is 4.37 lakh.

7. Conclusions

In this article, we have considered the tree-covering of fuzzy graphs using tree-covering numbers. An efficient algorithm has been designed for evaluating tree cover for fuzzy graphs in two different situations involving the facility location problem: first, when the number of facility vertices in the fuzzy graph is variable, and second, when there is a fixed covering radius. As a fruitful solution to a realistic problem, we have modified the existing BIN-PACK algorithm to develop the FUZZY-BIN-PACK algorthm, which is very effective in fuzzy environments. A complexity analysis was carried out, showing its efficient performance. Most importantly, we have extended the common idea of tree cover to construct a model with a series of programming problems for solving complex versions of the facility location problem in scenarios with fuzzy characteristics. The parameters obtained by our developed algorithm can help with constructing objective functions and relevant conditions to be maintained for developing the model for solving such facility location problems involving fuzzy graphs. The useful 'LINGO' mathematical software was used with the proposed model to separately find component-wise solutions and then combine them to obtain fuzzy solutions. The model was applied to a case study involving the circulation of banknotes in the Indian banking system, showing the usefulness of this model in efficiently solving real-life problems.

In our upcoming work, we intend to develop models by combining the concepts of graphoidal coverage and domination in fuzzy graphs. In addition, it might be interesting to construct a algorithm to evaluate graphoidal covering numbers for fuzzy graphs. Graphoidal coverage is an interesting topic in graph theory that can be extended to fuzzy graphs by considering the role of vertex and edge membership functions, and may be a better covering concept for path-related models. Incorporating the idea of domination can help to model real-world decisionmaking and choose the best possibilities for any facility vertices in a productive way. Further application to real-life problems related to sustainable development goals needs to be considered in future studies as well.

Author Contributions: A.B.: Conceptualization, Methodology, Software, Data Curation, Writing—Original draft preparation. M.P.: Supervision, Visualization, Investigation, Writing—Reviewing and Editing, Validation. All authors have read and agreed to the published version of the manuscript.

Funding: Financial support of the first author was provided by the Department of Science and Technology (DST), New Delhi, India, for research through the letter No. DST/INSPIRE/03/2019/001407 and Reg. No. IF190612, and is thankfully acknowledged.

Informed Consent Statement: Before submitting this work, all co-authors and the responsible authorities have declared their consent to submit this article tacitly or explicitly at the institute/organization where the work was developed.

Data Availability Statement: All of the data in the application part were taken from the Annual Report of the Reserve Bank of India, 2020–2021, published on 24 May 2021.

Conflicts of Interest: The authors declare no conflict of interest.

References

1. Rosenfield, A. Fuzzy graphs. In *Fuzzy Sets and Their Application*; Zadeh, L.A., Fu, K.S., Shimura, M., Eds.; Academic Press: New York, NY, USA, 1975; pp. 77–95.
2. Arkin, E.; Hassin, R.; Levin, A. Approximations for minimum and min-max vehicle routing problems. *J. Algorithms* **2006**, *59*, 1–18. [CrossRef]
3. Rana, A.; Pal, A.; Pal, M. The conditional covering problem on unweighted interval graphs with non-uniform coverage radius. *Math. Comput. Sci.* **2012**, *6*, 33–41. [CrossRef]
4. Bhattacharya, A.; Pal, M. Vertex covering problems of fuzzy graphs and their application in CCTV installation. *Neural Comput. Appl.* **2021**, *33*, 1–24. [CrossRef]
5. Bhattacharya, A.; Pal, M. Optimization in business strategy as a part of sustainable economic growth using clique covering of fuzzy graphs. *Soft Comput.* **2021**, *25*, 7095–7118. [CrossRef]
6. Bhattacharya, A.; Pal, M. Fuzzy covering problem of fuzzy graphs and its application to investigate the Indian economy in new normal. *J. Appl. Math. Comput.* **2022**, *68*, 479–510. [CrossRef]
7. Bhattacharya, A.; Pal, M. Fifth Sustainable Development Goal, Gender equality in India: Analysis by Mathematics of Uncertainty and Covering of Fuzzy Graphs. *Neural Comput. Appl.* **2021**, *33*, 15027–15057. [CrossRef]
8. Mordeson, J.N.; Peng, C.S. Operation on fuzzy graphs. *Inf. Sci.* **1994**, *79*, 159–170. [CrossRef]
9. Samanta, S.; Pramanik, T.; Pal, M. Fuzzy colouring of fuzzy graphs. *Afr. Math.* **2016**, *27*, 37–50. [CrossRef]
10. Ghorai, G.; Pal, M. A study on m-polar fuzzy planar graphs. *Int. J. Comput. Sci. Math.* **2016**, *7*, 283–292. [CrossRef]
11. Cardinal, J.; Hoefer, M. Non-cooperative facility location and covering games. *Theor. Comput. Sci.* **2010**, *411*, 1855–1876. [CrossRef]
12. Chang, S.S.L.; Zadeh, L. On fuzzy mappings and control. *IEEE Trans. Syst. Man. Cyberne* **1972**, *2*, 30–34. [CrossRef]
13. Chaudhry, S.S. New heuristics for the conditional covering problem. *Opsearch* **1993**, *30*, 42–47.
14. Chen, S.J.; Chen, S.M. A new method to measure the similarity between fuzzy numbers. *IEEE Int. Conf. Fuzzy Syst.* **2001**, *3*, 1123–1126.
15. Ghorai, G.; Pal, M. Faces and dual of m-polar fuzzy planar graphs. *J. Intell. Fuzzy Syst.* **2016**, *31*, 2043–2049. [CrossRef]

16. Mihelic, J.; Borut, R. Facility location and covering problems. In *Theoretical Computer Science*; Information Society: Ljubljana, Slovenia, 2004.
17. Koczy, L.T. Fuzzy graphs in the evaluation and optimization of networks. *Fuzzy Sets Syst.* **1992**, *46*, 307–319. [CrossRef]
18. Hakimi, S.L. Optimum Distribution of Switching Centers in a Communication Network and Some Related Graph Theoretic Problems. *Oper. Res.* **1965**, *13*, 462–475. [CrossRef]
19. Toregas, C.; ReVelle, C.; Swain, R.; Bergman, L. The location of emergency service facilities. *Oper. Res.* **1971**, *19*, 1363–1373. [CrossRef]
20. Bhattacharya, A.; Pal, M. Fuzzy tree covering number for fuzzy graphs with its real-life application in electricity distribution system. *Sadhana* **2022**, *47*, 1–10. [CrossRef]
21. Nayeem, S.M.A.; Pal, M. Shortest path problem on a network with imprecise edge weight. *Fuzzy Optim. Decis. Mak.* **2005**, *4*, 293–312. [CrossRef]
22. Ni, Y. Fuzzy minimum weight edge covering problem. *Appl. Math. Model.* **2008**, *32*, 1327–1337. [CrossRef]
23. Pal, M.; Samanta, S.; Ghorai, G. *Modern Trends in Fuzzy Graph Theory*; Springer: Berlin, Germany, 2020. [CrossRef]
24. Pramanik, T.; Samanta, S.; Pal, M. Interval-valued fuzzy planar graphs. *Int. J. Mach. Learn. Cybern.* **2016**, *7*, 653–664. [CrossRef]
25. Rashmanlou, H.; Samanta, S.; Pal, M.; Borzooei, R.A. A study on bipolar fuzzy graphs. *J. Intell. Fuzzy Syst.* **2015**, *28*, 571–580. [CrossRef]
26. Samanta, S.; Pal, M.; Rashmanlou, H.; Borzooei, R.A. Vague graphs and strengths. *J. Intell. Fuzzy Syst.* **2016**, *30*, 3675–3680. [CrossRef]

Article

Faculty Performance Evaluation through Multi-Criteria Decision Analysis Using Interval-Valued Fermatean Neutrosophic Sets

Said Broumi [1,2,*], Raman Sundareswaran [3], Marayanagaraj Shanmugapriya [3], Prem Kumar Singh [4], Michael Voskoglou [5] and Mohamed Talea [1]

1. Laboratory of Information Processing, Faculty of Science Ben M'Sik, University of Hassan II, Casablanca 20000, Morocco; taleamohamed@yahoo.fr
2. Regional Center for the Professions of Education and Training (C.R.M.E.F), Casablanca 20340, Morocco
3. Department of Mathematics, Sri Sivasubramaniya Nadar College of Engineering, Chennai 603110, India; sundareswaranr@ssn.edu.in (R.S.); shanmugapriyam@ssn.edu.in (M.S.)
4. Department of Computer Science and Engineering, Gandhi Institute of Technology and Management, Visakhapatnam 530045, India; psingh@gitam.edu
5. School of Engineering, University of Peloponnese, 26334 Patras, Greece; voskoglou@teiwest.gr
* Correspondence: broumisaid78@gmail.com or s.broumi@flbenmsik.ma

Abstract: The Neutrosophic Set (N_{set}) represents the uncertainty in data with fuzzy attributes beyond true and false values independently. The problem arises when the summation of true ($\mathcal{T}r$), false ($\mathcal{F}a$), and indeterminacy ($\mathcal{I}n$) values crosses the membership value of one, that is, $\mathcal{T}r + \mathcal{I}n + \mathcal{F}a < 1$. It becomes more crucial during decision-making processes like medical diagnoses or any data sets where $\mathcal{T}r + \mathcal{I}n + \mathcal{F}a < 1$. To achieve this goal, the FN_{set} is recently introduced. This study employs the Interval-Valued Fermatean Neutrosophic Set ($IVFN_{set}$) as its chosen framework to address instances of partial ignorance within the domains of truth, falsehood, or uncertainty. This selection stands out due to its unique approach to managing such complexities within multi-decision processes when compared to alternative methodologies. Furthermore, the proposed method reduces the propensity for information loss often encountered in other techniques. IVFNS excels at preserving intricate relationships between variables even when dealing with incomplete or vague information. In the present work, we introduce the $IVFN_{set}$, which deals with partial ignorance in true, false, or uncertain regions independently for multi-decision processes. The $IVFN_{set}$ contains the interval-valued $\mathcal{T}r_{membership}$ value, $\mathcal{I}n_{membership}$ value, and $\mathcal{F}a_{membership}$ for knowledge representation. The algebraic properties and set theory between the interval-valued FN_{set} have also been presented with an illustrative example.

Keywords: Fermatean neutrosophic sets; interval-valued Fermatean neutrosophic sets; faculty performance evaluation; multicriteria decision analysis

MSC: 03E72; 05C72; 90B50

1. Introduction

The acronyms given in the following Table 1 are used throughout the entire manuscript. For the computation of linguistic words like tall or young, Zadeh proposed FS in 1965 [1]. F_{set} are used to represent the acceptance and rejection of fuzzy attributes by membership values that lie in [0, 1]. The N_{set} helps to represent the hesitant part with the independent values of $\mathcal{T}r_{membership}$, $\mathcal{I}m_{membership}$, and $\mathcal{F}a_{membership}$ such that $^-0 < \mathcal{T}r_{membership} + \mathcal{I}m_{membership} + \mathcal{F}a_{membership} < 3^+$ [2]. Later, interval-valued membership sets were introduced, which dealt with the ignorance of partial data about the membership values [3,4]. Yager [5–7] coined a new kind of F_{set} called the PF_{set} as an extension of the IF_{set}. It has many practical applications in MCDM [8,9]. It is based on the Fermatean fuzzy set [10],

Citation: Broumi, S.; Sundareswaran, R.; Shanmugapriya, M.; Singh, P.K.; Voskoglou, M.; Talea, M. Faculty Performance Evaluation through Multi-Criteria Decision Analysis Using Interval-Valued Fermatean Neutrosophic Sets. *Mathematics* 2023, 11, 3817. https://doi.org/10.3390/math11183817

Academic Editors: Gia Sirbiladze and Fuyuan Xiao

Received: 14 July 2023
Revised: 14 August 2023
Accepted: 25 August 2023
Published: 5 September 2023

Copyright: © 2023 by the authors. Licensee MDPI, Basel, Switzerland. This article is an open access article distributed under the terms and conditions of the Creative Commons Attribution (CC BY) license (https://creativecommons.org/licenses/by/4.0/).

which was recently hybridized with the N_{set} [11–13] and Fermatean fuzzy graph [14]. Rani and Mishra [15] studied the $IVFF_{set}$. The $IVFF_{set}$ [16,17] is used in several fields for the DM process because of its extensive properties [18,19].

Table 1. Acronyms.

Abbreviations	Full Phrase
Fuzzy Set	FS
Intuitionistic Fuzzy Set	IFS
Neutrosophic Set	NS
Interval valued Pythagorean neutrosophic sets	IVPNS
Interval-valued Fermatean neutrosophic set	IVFNS
Interval valued neutrosophic sets	IVNS
Pythagorean Fuzzy Set	PFS
Fermatean Fuzzy set	FFS
Interval-valued Fermatean Fuzzy numbers.	IVFFN
Interval-valued Fermatean Fuzzy sets	IVFFS
Hesitant Fermatean fuzzy sets	HFFS
Interval valued hesitant Fermatean fuzzy sets	IVHFFS
Multi-Criteria decision-making	MCDM
Technique for Order of Preference by Similarity to Ideal Solution	TOPSIS
Interval-valued Fermatean fuzzy TOPSIS	IVFFTOPSIS
Single valued neutrosophic set	SVNS
Fermatean neutrosophic graph	FN_{graph}

The N_{set} theory is introduced by Smarandache [2] as an extension of the IF_{set} theory to deal with indeterminacy. Wang [4] defined the $IVSN_{set}$ in 2010 as an extension of interval fuzzy sets [20]. Zhang et al. [21] applied the concept of Interval neutrosophic sets in multicriteria decision-making problems. Wang, T [22] introduced a projection model with unknown weight information within an interval neutrosophic environment and applied it to software quality-in-use evaluation. Another class of the N_{set} is the $IVNP_{set}$ with the dependent interval-valued Pythagorean component, proposed by Stephy and Helen [13]. Clearly, it is a generalization of the $IVPN_{set}$ and can handle more information than the IVN_{set}. Motivated by the FF_{set} Jansi [11] defined the FN_{set} and provided its various properties. Jeevaraj [16] introduced the concept of the $IVFF_{set}$s and derived mathematical operations on the class of the $IVFF_{set}$. Score functions in the $IVFF_{set}$ are introduced and their properties are studied. Recently, PalaniKumar and Iampan [17] proposed the concept of the spherical $IVFF_{soft\ set}$. Liu et al. [18] discussed Fermatean fuzzy linguistic term sets, their basic operational laws, and aggregate functions. Broumi et al. [19] proposed the $IVFN_{graph}$ and presented some basic operational laws. He also [23] introduced the FN_{graph} and RFN_{graph}, SFN_{graph}, and F_{number} product graphs.

For DM problems in the Neutrosophic context, the value of times squared of the sum of the $\mathcal{T}r, \mathcal{I}m$, and $\mathcal{F}a$ degrees does not exceed two. To deal with this issue, Sweety and Jansi introduced the FN_{set} [11]. Also, the FN_{set} is a generalization of the PN_{set} and it is characterized by the condition that the cubes of their sum of their $\mathcal{T}\mathbf{r}_{\mathbf{membership}}$, $\mathcal{F}\mathbf{a}_{\mathbf{membership}}$, and $\mathcal{I}\mathbf{m}_{\mathbf{membership}}$ degrees do not exceed them twice. Motivated by the above literature, we develop the idea of the $IVFN_{set}$ and its algebraic operations. The major findings of the present article are as follows:

- To establish and study the $IVFN_{set}$ and its algebraic operations.
- To introduce the accuracy and score functions (AF and SF) of the $IVFN_{number}$.
- To illustrate the applications of the $IVFN_{set}$.

Section 1 includes an introductory part; Section 2 deals with the basic algebraic operations related to the $IVFN_{set}$; Section 3 defines the AF and SF of the $IVFN_{set}$; and Section 4 discusses the application of the $IVFN_{set}$ and delivers recommendations for future research.

2. Prerequisites

In this section, we briefly introduce the necessary basic definitions and preliminary results.

A F_{set} [1] A on $\mathfrak{A}$ is of the form: $A_{PFS} = \{\langle \hbar, \mu_A(\hbar)\rangle | \hbar \in \mathfrak{A}\}$ where $\mu_A(\hbar) : \mathfrak{A} \to [0,1]$. A PFS [5–7] A on $\mathfrak{A}$ is of the form: $A_{PFS} = \{\langle \hbar, \mathcal{T}r_A(\hbar), \mathcal{F}a_A(\hbar)\rangle | \hbar \in \mathfrak{A}\}$, where $\mathcal{T}r_A(\hbar) : \mathfrak{A} \to [0,1]$ denotes the membership degree (***md***) and $\mathcal{F}a_A(\hbar) : \mathfrak{A} \to [0,1]$ denotes the ***non − md***, $\forall \hbar \in \mathfrak{A}$ to the set A_{PFS}, respectively, such that $0 \leq (\mathcal{T}r_A(\hbar))^2 + (\mathcal{F}a_A(\hbar))^2 \leq 1$. Corresponding to its ***mf***, the indeterminacy degree is given by $\phi_A(\hbar) = \sqrt{1 - \mathcal{T}r_A(\hbar)^2 - \mathcal{F}a_A(\hbar)^2}, \forall \hbar \in \mathfrak{A}$. A FF_{set} [11] A on $\mathfrak{A}$ is of the form as $A_{FFS} = \{\langle \hbar, \mathcal{T}r_A(\hbar), \mathcal{F}a_A(\hbar)\rangle | \hbar \in \mathfrak{A}\}$ where $\mathcal{T}r_A(\hbar) : \mathfrak{A} \to [0,1]$ represents the ***md***, and $\mathcal{F}a_A(\hbar) : \mathfrak{A} \to [0,1]$ represents the ***non − md***, $\forall \hbar \in \mathfrak{A}$ to the set A, respectively, such that $0 \leq (\mathcal{T}r_A(\hbar))^3 + (\mathcal{F}a_A(\hbar))^3 \leq 1$. Corresponding to its ***f***, the indeterminacy degree is given by $\pi_A(\hbar) = \sqrt{1 - \mathcal{T}r_A(\hbar)^3 - \mathcal{F}a_A(\hbar)^3}$, $\forall \hbar \in \mathfrak{A}$.A N_{set} [2] A on $\mathfrak{A}$ is defined by its truth $(\mathcal{T}r_A(\hbar))$, indeterminacy $(\mathcal{I}m_A(\hbar))$ and falsity membership function $(\mathcal{F}a_A(\hbar))$ such that $0^- \leq \mathcal{T}r_A(\hbar) + \mathcal{I}m_A(\hbar) + \mathcal{F}a_A(\hbar) \leq 3^+$ for all $\hbar \in \mathfrak{A}$, whose all the subset of $[0^-, 1^+]$.

In the following, Figure 1 depicted the graphical visualization between the Intuitionistic, Pythagorean, and Fermatean Fuzzy sets.

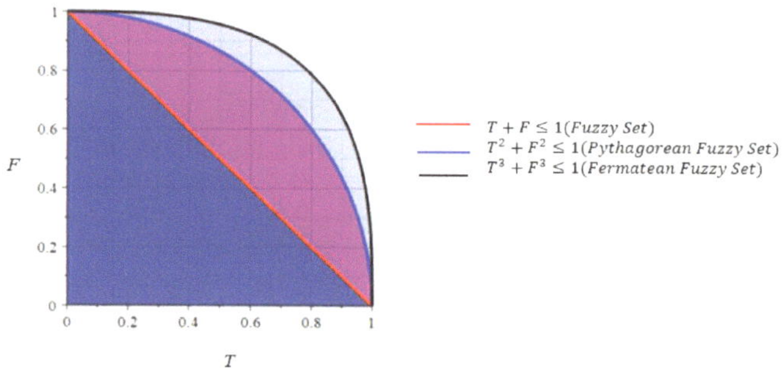

Figure 1. A graphical visualization of the Intuitionistic, Pythagorean, and Fermatean Fuzzy sets.

The SVN_{set} [3] A on $\mathfrak{A}$ is is of the form: $A_{SVNS} = \{\langle \hbar, \mathcal{T}\mathbf{r}_A(\hbar), \mathcal{I}\mathbf{m}_A(\hbar), \mathcal{F}a_A(\hbar)\rangle | \hbar \in \mathfrak{A}\}$, where $\mathcal{T}\mathbf{r}_A(\hbar) : \mathfrak{A} \to [0,1]$ represents the ***md***, $\mathcal{I}\mathbf{m}_A(\hbar) : \mathfrak{A} \to [0,1]$ represents the ***indeterminacy − md***, and $\mathcal{F}a_A(\hbar) : \mathfrak{A} \to [0,1]$ represents the ***non − md***, $\forall \hbar \in \mathfrak{A}$ to the setA, respectively, with $0 \leq \mathcal{T}r_A(\hbar) + \mathcal{I}\mathbf{m}_A(\hbar) + \mathcal{F}a_A(\hbar) \leq 3$. The PN_{set} [8] is defined as, $0 \leq (\mathcal{T}r_A(\hbar))^2 + (\mathcal{I}m_A(\hbar))^2 \leq 1$ and $0 \leq (\mathcal{F}a_A(\hbar))^2 \leq 1$ then $0 \leq (\mathcal{T}r_A(\hbar))^2 + (\mathcal{I}\mathbf{m}_A(\hbar))^2 + (\mathcal{F}a_A(\hbar))^2 \leq 2$. Sweety et al. [11] introduced the FN_{set} as: $0 \leq (\mathcal{T}\mathbf{r}_A(\hbar))^3 + (\mathcal{I}\mathbf{m}_A(\hbar))^3 \leq 1$ and $0 \leq (\mathcal{F}a_A(\hbar))^3 \leq 1$ then $0 \leq \hbar \in \mathfrak{A}$ to the set A, with $(\mathcal{T}\mathbf{r}_A(\hbar))^3 + (\mathcal{I}\mathbf{m}_A(\hbar))^3 + (\mathcal{F}a_A(\hbar))^3 \leq 2\ \forall \hbar \in \mathfrak{A}$. An IVF_{set} [19] set $\widetilde{A}$ on $\mathfrak{A}$ is a function $\widetilde{A} : \mathfrak{A} \to Int([0,1])$ and the set of all IVF_{set} on $\mathfrak{A}$ is denoted by $\hbar(\mathfrak{A})$. Suppose that $\widetilde{A} \in \hbar(\mathfrak{A}), \forall \hbar \in \mathfrak{A}, \mu_{\widetilde{A}}(\hbar) = \left[\mu^-_{\widetilde{A}}(\hbar), \mu^+_{\widetilde{A}}(\hbar)\right]$ is the ***md*** of an element $\hbar$ to $\widetilde{A}$, $\mu^-_{\widetilde{A}}(\hbar), \mu^+_{\widetilde{A}}(\hbar)$ are the least and greatest bounds of ***md***$\hbar$ to $\widetilde{A}$, where $0 \leq \mu^-_{\widetilde{A}}(\hbar) \leq \mu^+_{\widetilde{A}}(\hbar) \leq 1$. The $IVPFS$ [10] A on $\mathfrak{A}$ is of the form as: $A_{IVNP_{set}} = \{\langle \hbar, [\mathcal{T}\mathbf{r}^-_A(\hbar), \mathcal{T}\mathbf{m}^+_A(\hbar)], [\mathcal{F}a^-_A(\hbar), \mathcal{F}^+_A(\hbar)]\rangle : \hbar \in \mathfrak{A}\}$ where $0 \leq \mathcal{T}\mathbf{r}^-_A(\hbar) \leq \mathcal{T}\mathbf{r}^+_A(\hbar) \leq 1, 0 \leq \mathcal{F}a^-_A(\hbar) \leq \mathcal{F}a^+_A(\hbar) \leq 1$ and $0 \leq (\mathcal{T}\mathbf{r}^+_A(\hbar))^2 + (\mathcal{F}a^+_A(\hbar))^2 \leq 1, \forall \hbar \in \mathfrak{A}$. $IVFF_{set}$ [13] A on $\mathfrak{A}$ of the form as: $A_{IVNP_{set}} = \{\langle \hbar, [\mathcal{T}\mathbf{r}^-_A(\hbar), \mathcal{T}\mathbf{r}^+_A(\hbar)], [\mathcal{F}a^-_A(\hbar), \mathcal{F}a^+_A(\hbar)]\rangle : \forall \hbar \in \mathfrak{A}\}$ where $0 \leq \mathcal{T}\mathbf{r}^-_A(\hbar) \leq \mathcal{T}\mathbf{r}^+_A(\hbar) \leq 1, 0 \leq \mathcal{F}a^-_A(\hbar) \leq \mathcal{F}a^+_A(\hbar) \leq 1$ and $0 \leq (\mathcal{T}\mathbf{r}^+_A(\hbar))^3 + (\mathcal{F}a^+_A(\hbar))^3 \leq 1, \forall \hbar \in \mathfrak{A}$. A IVN_{set} [24] A for every point $x \in \mathfrak{A}, \mathcal{T}\mathbf{r}_A(\hbar), \mathcal{I}\mathbf{m}_A(p), \mathcal{F}a_A(\hbar) \subseteq [0,1]$.

$A_{\mathrm{IVN_{set}}} = \{\langle[\mathcal{T}\mathbf{r}_A^-(\hbar),\ \mathcal{T}\mathbf{r}_A^+(\hbar)],[\mathcal{I}\mathbf{m}_A^-(\hbar),\mathcal{I}\mathbf{m}_A^+(\hbar)],[\mathcal{F}\boldsymbol{a}_A^-(\hbar),\ \mathcal{F}\boldsymbol{a}_A^+(\hbar)]\rangle : \forall\hbar \in \mathfrak{A}\}$ with $0 \leq\ \mathcal{T}\mathbf{r}_A^+(\hbar)+\mathcal{I}\mathbf{r}_A^+(\hbar)+\mathcal{F}\boldsymbol{a}_A^+(\hbar)\ \leq 3$. An $IVNP_{set}$ [25] A on $\mathfrak{A}$ is of the form as $A_{IVNP_{set}} = \{\langle[\mathcal{T}\mathbf{r}_A^-(\hbar),\ \mathcal{T}\mathbf{r}_A^+(\hbar)],[\mathcal{I}\mathbf{m}_A^-(\hbar),\mathcal{I}\mathbf{m}_A^+(\hbar)],[\mathcal{F}\boldsymbol{a}_A^-(\hbar),\ \mathcal{F}\boldsymbol{a}_A^+(\hbar)]\rangle : \forall\hbar \in \mathfrak{A}\}$ where $\mathcal{T}\mathbf{r}_A^-(\hbar),\ \mathcal{T}\mathbf{r}_A^+ : \mathfrak{A} \to [0,\ 1]$ represents the least and greatest bounds of truth ***md***, $\mathcal{I}\mathrm{m}_A^-(\hbar),\mathcal{I}\mathrm{m}_A^+(\hbar) : \mathfrak{A} \to [0,\ 1]$ represents the least and greatest bounds of ***indeterminacy md***, and $\mathcal{F}a_A^-(\hbar),\ \mathcal{F}a_A^+(\hbar) : \mathfrak{A} \to [0,\ 1]$ represents the least and greatest bounds of ***falsity md***, $\forall\hbar \in \mathfrak{A}$ to the set A, with $0 \leq \left[\frac{\mathcal{T}\mathbf{r}_A^-(\hbar)+\mathcal{T}\mathbf{r}_A^+(\hbar)}{2}\right]^2 + \left[\frac{\mathcal{I}\mathbf{m}_A^-(\hbar)+\mathcal{I}\mathbf{m}_A^+(\hbar)}{2}\right]^2 + \left[\frac{\mathcal{F}a_A^-(\hbar)+\mathcal{F}a_A^+(\hbar))}{2}\right]^2 \leq 2$. In Zhang et al. [21], the operators of set-theoretic on the IN_{set} are defined as follows:

The IVN_{set} is contained in another $IVN_{set}\mathrm{B_{IVN_{set}}}$, $\mathrm{A_{IVN_{set}}} \subseteq \mathrm{B_{IVN_{set}}}$, $\Leftrightarrow \mathcal{T}\mathbf{r}_A^-(\hbar) \leq \mathcal{T}\mathbf{r}_B^-(\hbar),\ \mathcal{T}\mathbf{r}_A^+(\hbar) \leq \mathcal{T}\mathbf{r}_B^+(\hbar);\ \mathcal{I}\mathbf{m}_A^-(\hbar) \geq \mathcal{I}\mathbf{m}_B^-(\hbar),\mathcal{I}\mathbf{m}_A^+(\hbar) \geq \mathcal{I}\mathbf{m}_B^+(\hbar);\mathcal{F}\boldsymbol{a}_A^-(\hbar) \geq \mathcal{F}\boldsymbol{a}_B^-(\hbar)$,
$\mathcal{F}\boldsymbol{a}_A^+(\hbar) \geq \mathcal{F}\boldsymbol{a}_{\mathbf{B}}^+(\hbar), \forall\hbar \in \mathfrak{A}$.

Two IVN_{set}, $A_{\mathrm{IVN_{set}}} = B_{\mathrm{IVN_{set}}} \Leftrightarrow A_{\mathrm{IVN_{set}}} \subseteq B_{\mathrm{IVN_{set}}}$ and $B_{\mathrm{IVN_{set}}} \subseteq A_{\mathrm{IVN_{set}}}$,
That is,

$$\mathcal{T}\mathbf{r}_A^-(\hbar) = \mathcal{T}_{rB}^-(\hbar),\ \mathcal{T}\mathbf{r}_A^+(\hbar) = \mathcal{T}\mathbf{r}_B^+(\hbar)\ ;\mathcal{F}\boldsymbol{a}_A^-(\hbar) = \mathcal{F}\boldsymbol{a}_B^-(\hbar),\mathcal{F}\boldsymbol{a}_A^+(\hbar) \geq \mathcal{F}\boldsymbol{a}_B^+(\hbar),$$
$$\mathcal{I}\mathbf{m}_A^-(\hbar) = \mathcal{I}\mathbf{m}_B^-(\hbar),\mathcal{I}\mathbf{m}_A^+(\hbar) = \mathcal{I}\mathbf{m}_B^+(\hbar),\text{for all } \hbar \in \mathfrak{A}.$$

The IVN_{set} A is empty $\Leftrightarrow \mathcal{T}\mathbf{r}_A^-(\hbar) = \mathcal{T}\mathbf{r}_A^+(\hbar) = 0,\ \mathcal{F}\boldsymbol{a}_A^-(\hbar) = \mathcal{F}\boldsymbol{a}_A^+(\hbar) = 1$ and $\mathcal{I}\mathbf{m}_A^-(\hbar) = \mathcal{I}\mathbf{m}_A^+(\hbar) = 0$, for all $\hbar \in \mathfrak{A}$.

A complement of the INV_{set} is

$$A_{\mathrm{IVN_{set}^C}} = \left\{\begin{matrix} p,\ [\mathcal{T}\mathbf{r}_A^-(\hbar),\mathcal{T}\mathbf{r}_A^+(\hbar)], \\ [1-\mathcal{I}\mathbf{m}_A^+(\hbar),1-\mathcal{I}\mathbf{m}_A^-(\hbar)], \\ [\mathcal{F}\boldsymbol{a}_A^-(\hbar),\mathcal{F}\boldsymbol{a}_A^+(\hbar)] \end{matrix}\right\}, \hbar \in \mathfrak{A}$$

$A_{IVN_{set}} \cap B_{IVN_{set}}$, defined as follows:

$$A_{IVN_{set}} \cap B_{IVN_{set}} = \left\{\left\langle\begin{matrix} p, [\mathcal{T}\mathbf{r}_A^-(\hbar) \wedge \mathcal{T}\mathbf{r}_B^-(\hbar),\mathcal{T}\mathbf{r}_A^+(\hbar) \wedge \mathcal{T}\mathbf{r}_B^+(\hbar)], \\ [\mathcal{I}\mathbf{m}_A^-(\hbar) \vee \mathcal{I}\mathbf{m}_B^-(\hbar),\mathcal{I}\mathbf{m}_A^+(\hbar) \vee \mathcal{I}\mathbf{m}_B^+(\hbar)], \\ [\mathcal{F}\boldsymbol{a}_A^-(\hbar) \vee \mathcal{F}\boldsymbol{a}_B^-(\hbar),\ \mathcal{F}\boldsymbol{a}_A^+(\hbar) \vee \mathcal{F}\boldsymbol{a}_B^+(\hbar)] \end{matrix}\right\rangle\right\}, \hbar \in \mathfrak{A}$$

$A_{\mathrm{IVN_{set}}} \cup B_{\mathrm{IVN_{set}}}$, defined as follows:

$$A_{IVN_{set}} \cup B_{IVN_{set}} = \left\{\left\langle\begin{matrix} k, [\mathcal{T}\mathbf{r}_A^-(\hbar) \vee \mathcal{T}\mathbf{r}_B^-(\hbar),\mathcal{T}\mathbf{r}_A^+(\hbar) \vee \mathcal{T}\mathbf{r}_B^+(\hbar)], \\ [\mathcal{I}\mathbf{m}_A^-(\hbar) \wedge \mathcal{I}\mathbf{m}_B^-(\hbar),\mathcal{I}\mathbf{m}_A^+(\hbar) \wedge \mathcal{I}\mathbf{m}_B^+(\hbar)] \\ [\mathcal{F}\boldsymbol{a}_A^-(\hbar) \wedge \mathcal{F}\boldsymbol{a}_B^-(\hbar),\mathcal{F}\boldsymbol{a}_A^+(\hbar) \wedge \mathcal{F}\boldsymbol{a}_B^+(\hbar)] \end{matrix}\right\rangle\right\},\ \hbar \in \mathfrak{A}.$$

The difference between two $IVN_{set}A$ and $IVN_{set}\ B$ is the $IVN_{set}A_{\mathrm{IVN_{set}}} \ominus B_{\mathrm{IVN_{set}}}$, defined as A⊖B = < $[\mathcal{T}\mathbf{r}^-_{A_{\mathrm{IVN_{set}}}\ominus B_{\mathrm{IVN_{set}}}}, \mathcal{T}\mathbf{r}^+_{A_{\mathrm{IVN_{set}}}\ominus B_{\mathrm{IVN_{set}}}}]$, $[\mathcal{I}\mathbf{m}^-_{A_{\mathrm{IVN_{set}}}\ominus B_{\mathrm{IVN_{set}}}}, \mathcal{I}\mathbf{m}^+_{A_{\mathrm{IVN_{set}}}\ominus B_{\mathrm{IVN_{set}}}}]$, $[\mathcal{F}\boldsymbol{a}^-_{A_{\mathrm{IVN_{set}}}\ominus B_{\mathrm{IVN_{set}}}}, \mathcal{F}\boldsymbol{a}^+_{A_{\mathrm{IVN_{set}}}\ominus B_{\mathrm{IVN_{set}}}}]$> where

$$\mathcal{T}\mathbf{r}^L_{A_{\mathrm{IVN_{set}}}\ominus B_{\mathrm{IVN_{set}}}} = \max(\mathcal{T}\mathbf{r}_A^-(\hbar),\mathcal{T}\mathbf{r}_B^-(\hbar)),\ \mathcal{T}\mathbf{r}^+_{A_{\mathrm{IVN_{set}}}\ominus B_{\mathrm{IVN_{set}}}} = \max(\mathcal{T}\mathbf{r}_A^+(\hbar),\mathcal{T}\mathbf{r}_B^+(\hbar))$$
$$\mathcal{I}\mathbf{m}^L_{A_{\mathrm{IVN_{set}}}\ominus_2 B_{\mathrm{IVN_{set}}}} = \max(\mathcal{I}\mathbf{m}_A^+(\hbar),1-\mathcal{I}\mathbf{m}_B^+(\hbar)),\ \mathcal{I}\mathbf{m}^U_{A_{\mathrm{IVN_{set}}}\ominus_2 B_{\mathrm{IVN_{set}}}} = \max(\mathcal{I}\mathbf{m}_A^+(\hbar),1-\mathcal{I}\mathbf{m}_B^-(\hbar))$$
$$\mathcal{F}\boldsymbol{a}^L_{A_{\mathrm{IVN_{set}}}\ominus_2 B_{\mathrm{IVN_{set}}}} = \max(\mathcal{F}\boldsymbol{a}_A^-(\hbar),\mathcal{T}\mathbf{r}_B^-(\hbar)),\ \mathcal{F}\boldsymbol{a}^U_{A_{\mathrm{IVN_{set}}}\ominus_2 B_{\mathrm{IVN_{set}}}} = \max(\mathcal{F}\boldsymbol{a}_A^+(\hbar),\mathcal{T}\mathbf{r}_B^+(\hbar))$$

The scalar division of the IVN_{set}A is $A_{\mathrm{IVN_{set}}}/\mathrm{a}$, defined as follows:

$$A_{\mathrm{IVN_{set}}}/a == \left\{\left\langle\begin{matrix} \hbar, [\max(\mathcal{T}\mathbf{r}_A^-(\hbar)/a,1),\max(\mathcal{T}\mathbf{r}_A^+(\hbar)/a,1)], \\ [\min(\mathcal{I}\mathbf{m}_A^-(\hbar)/a,1),\min(\mathcal{I}\mathbf{m}_A^+(\hbar)/a,1)], \\ [\min(\mathcal{F}\boldsymbol{a}_A^-(\hbar)/a,1),\min(\mathcal{F}\boldsymbol{a}_A^+(\hbar)/a,1)] \end{matrix}\right\rangle\right\},\ \hbar \in \mathfrak{A},\ a \in R^+$$

$A_{\text{IVN}_{\text{set}}}.a$, defined as follows:

$$A_{\text{IVN}_{\text{set}}}.a = \left\{ \left\langle \begin{array}{l} p, \left[\max\left(\mathcal{T}\mathbf{r}_A^-(\hbar).a,1\right), \max\left(\mathcal{T}\mathbf{r}_A^+(\hbar).a,1\right)\right], \\ \left[\min\left(\mathcal{I}\mathbf{m}_A^-(\hbar).a,1\right), \min\left(\mathcal{I}\mathbf{m}(\hbar).a,1\right)\right] \\ \left[\min\left(\mathcal{F}\boldsymbol{a}_A^-(\hbar).a,1\right), \min\left(\mathcal{F}\boldsymbol{a}_A^+(\hbar).a,1\right)\right] \end{array} \right\rangle \right\}, \hbar \in \mathfrak{A},\ \text{a} \ \in R^+.$$

3. Interval-Valued Fermatean Neutrosophic Sets ($IVFN_{set}$)

The concept of the $IVFN_{set}$, $IVFN_{umber}$, and their basic properties are introduced in this section.

Definition 1. *The $IVFN_{set}$ A on $\mathfrak{A}$ is of the form $A = \left\{\left\langle\left[\mathcal{T}\boldsymbol{r}_A^-(\hbar), \mathcal{T}\boldsymbol{r}_A^+(\hbar)\right], \left[\mathcal{I}\boldsymbol{m}_A^-(\hbar), \mathcal{I}\boldsymbol{m}_A^+(\hbar)\right], \left[\mathcal{F}\boldsymbol{a}_A^-(\hbar), \mathcal{F}\boldsymbol{a}_A^+(\hbar)\right]\right\rangle \middle| \hbar \in \mathfrak{A}\right\}$ where $\mathcal{T}\boldsymbol{r}_A(p) = \mathcal{T}\boldsymbol{r}_A^-(\hbar), \mathcal{T}\boldsymbol{r}_A^+(\hbar) : \mathfrak{A} \to [0,1]$ represents the least and greatest bounds of **truthmd**, $\mathcal{I}\boldsymbol{m}_A(\hbar) = \left[\mathcal{I}\boldsymbol{m}_A^-(\hbar), \mathcal{I}\boldsymbol{m}_A^+(\hbar)\right] : \mathfrak{A} \to [0,1]$ represents the least and greatest bounds of **indeterminacy md**, and $\mathcal{F}\boldsymbol{a}_A(\hbar) = \left[\mathcal{F}\boldsymbol{a}_A^-(\hbar), \mathcal{F}\boldsymbol{a}_A^+(\hbar)\right] : \mathfrak{A} \to [0,1]$ represents the least and greatest bounds of **falsity md**, $\forall\, \hbar \in \mathfrak{A}$ to the set A, respectively, with $0 \le (\mathcal{T}\boldsymbol{r}_A(\hbar))^3 + (\mathcal{F}\boldsymbol{a}_A(\hbar))^3 \le 1$ and $0 \le (\mathcal{I}\boldsymbol{m}_A(\hbar))^3 \le 1$, $0 \le (\mathcal{T}\boldsymbol{r}_A(\hbar))^3 + (\mathcal{F}\boldsymbol{a}_A(\hbar))^3 + (\mathcal{I}\boldsymbol{m}_A(\hbar))^3 \le 2$ means $0 \le (\mathcal{T}\boldsymbol{r}_A(\hbar))^3 + (\mathcal{F}\boldsymbol{a}_A(\hbar))^3 + (\mathcal{I}\boldsymbol{m}_A(\hbar))^3 \le 2 \forall\, \hbar \in \mathfrak{A}$.*

In the following, Figure 2 depicted the Geometric representation of the IVN_{set}, $IVPN_{set}$, and $IVFN_{set}$.

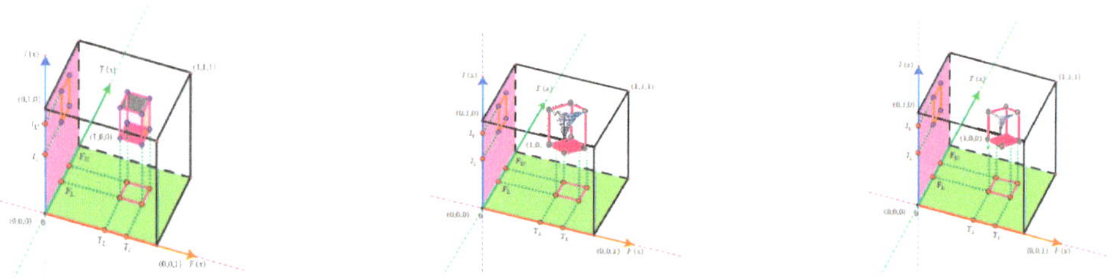

Geometric representation of the IVN_{set}   *Geometric representation of the $IVPN_{set}$*   *Geometric representation of the $IVFN_{set}$*

Figure 2. Geometric representation of the IVN_{set}, $IVPN_{set}$, and $IVFN_{set}$.

Definition 2. *For an $IVFN_{number}\alpha = \left(\left[\mathcal{T}\boldsymbol{r}_\alpha^{A-}, \mathcal{T}\boldsymbol{r}_\alpha^{A+}\right], \left[\mathcal{I}\boldsymbol{m}_\alpha^{A-}, \mathcal{I}\boldsymbol{m}_\alpha^{A+}\right], \left[\mathcal{F}\boldsymbol{a}_\alpha^{A-}, \mathcal{F}\boldsymbol{a}_\alpha^{A+}\right]\right)$, which satisfies $\left(\mathcal{T}\boldsymbol{r}_\alpha^{+A}\right)^3 + \left(\mathcal{I}\boldsymbol{m}_\alpha^{+A}\right)^3 + \left(\mathcal{F}\boldsymbol{a}_\alpha^{+A}\right)^3 \le 2$. Consider $\alpha = \left(\left[\mathcal{T}\boldsymbol{r}_\alpha^{A-}, \mathcal{T}\boldsymbol{r}_\alpha^{A+}\right], \left[\mathcal{I}\boldsymbol{m}_\alpha^{A-}, \mathcal{I}\boldsymbol{m}_\alpha^{A+}\right], \left[\mathcal{F}\boldsymbol{a}_\alpha^{A-}, \mathcal{F}\boldsymbol{a}_\alpha^{A+}\right]\right) = ([a,b],[c,d],[e,f])$ is a $IVFN_{number}$.*

Remark 1. *The $IVFN_{set}$ is an extension of the $IVFF_{set}$. The $IVFN_{number}$ occupies more space than the $IVFF_{number}$, $IVIF_{number}$, and $IVPF_{number}$. There is no doubt that the $IVFN_{set}$ is the more appropriate tool for finding the best alternative in complex MCDM uncertainty problems rather than the $IVFF_{set}$, $IVPF_{set}$, and $IVIF_{set}$.*

Definition 3. *Let $\mathfrak{K}$ and $\mathfrak{L}$ be two $IVFN_{set}$ on $\mathfrak{A}$, defined by:*

$$\mathfrak{K} = \left\{\left\langle \hbar, \mathcal{T}\mathbf{r}_{\mathfrak{K}}(\hbar), \mathcal{I}\mathbf{m}_{\mathfrak{K}}(\hbar), \mathcal{F}\mathbf{a}_{\mathfrak{K}}(\hbar)\right\rangle \middle| \hbar \in \mathfrak{A}\right\}$$
$$\mathfrak{L} = \left\{\left\langle \hbar, \mathcal{T}\mathbf{r}_{\mathfrak{L}}(\hbar), \mathcal{I}\mathbf{m}_{\mathfrak{L}}(\hbar), \mathcal{F}\mathbf{a}_{\mathfrak{L}}(\hbar)\right\rangle \middle| \hbar \in \mathfrak{A}\right\}$$

where $\mathcal{T}\mathbf{r}_{\mathfrak{K}}(\hbar) = \left[\mathcal{T}\mathbf{r}_{\mathfrak{K}}^-(\hbar), \mathcal{T}\mathbf{r}_{\mathfrak{K}}^+(\hbar)\right], \mathcal{I}\mathbf{m}_{\mathfrak{K}}(\hbar) = \left[\mathcal{I}\mathbf{m}_{\mathfrak{K}}^-(\hbar), \mathcal{I}\mathbf{m}_{\mathfrak{K}}^+(\hbar)\right], \mathcal{F}\mathbf{a}_{\mathfrak{K}}(\hbar) = \left[\mathcal{F}\mathbf{a}_{\mathfrak{K}}^-(\hbar), \mathcal{F}\mathbf{a}_{\mathfrak{K}}^+(\hbar)\right]$ and $\mathcal{T}\mathbf{r}_{\mathfrak{L}}(\hbar) = \left[\mathcal{T}\mathbf{r}_{\mathfrak{L}}^-(\hbar), \mathcal{T}\mathbf{r}_{\mathfrak{L}}^+(\hbar)\right], \mathcal{I}\mathbf{m}_{\mathfrak{L}}(\hbar) = \left[\mathcal{I}\mathbf{m}_{\mathfrak{L}}^-(\hbar), \mathcal{I}\mathbf{m}_{\mathfrak{L}}^+(\hbar)\right]$, $\mathcal{F}\mathbf{a}_{\mathfrak{L}}(\hbar) = \left[\mathcal{F}\mathbf{a}_{\mathfrak{L}}^-(\hbar), \mathcal{F}\mathbf{a}_{\mathfrak{L}}^+(\hbar)\right]$.

Then for all $\mathscr{k} \in \mathfrak{A}$

i. $\mathfrak{K}$ *is contained in* $\mathfrak{L}$ *if and only if* $\mathcal{T}\mathbf{r}_{\mathfrak{K}}^{-}(\mathscr{k}) \leq \mathcal{T}\mathbf{r}_{\mathfrak{L}}^{-}(\mathscr{k})$

$$\begin{gathered}\mathcal{T}\mathbf{r}_{\mathfrak{K}}^{-}(\mathscr{k}) \leq \mathcal{T}\mathbf{r}_{\mathfrak{L}}^{-}(\mathscr{k}), \mathcal{T}\mathbf{r}_{\mathfrak{K}}^{+}(\mathscr{k}) \leq \mathcal{T}\mathbf{r}_{\mathfrak{L}}^{+}(\mathscr{k}), \\ \mathcal{I}\mathbf{m}_{\mathfrak{K}}^{-}(\mathscr{k}) \geq \mathcal{I}\mathbf{m}_{\mathfrak{L}}^{-}(\mathscr{k}), \mathcal{I}\mathbf{m}_{\mathfrak{K}}^{+}(\mathscr{k}) \geq \mathcal{I}\mathbf{m}_{\mathfrak{L}}^{+}(\mathscr{k}), \\ \mathcal{F}\mathbf{a}_{\mathfrak{K}}^{-}(\mathscr{k}) \geq \mathcal{F}\mathbf{a}_{\mathfrak{L}}^{-}(\mathscr{k}), \mathcal{F}\mathbf{a}_{\mathfrak{K}}^{+}(\mathscr{k}) \geq \mathcal{F}\mathbf{a}_{\mathfrak{L}}^{+}(\mathscr{k})\end{gathered}$$

ii. *The union of* $\mathfrak{K}$ *and* $\mathfrak{L}$ *is the* $IVFN_{set}\mathfrak{D}$, *defined by*

$$\begin{gathered}\mathfrak{D} = \mathfrak{K} \cup \mathfrak{L} = \{\langle \mathscr{k}, \mathcal{T}\mathbf{r}_{\mathfrak{D}}(\mathscr{k}), \mathcal{I}\mathbf{m}_{\mathfrak{D}}(\mathscr{k}), \mathcal{F}\mathbf{a}_{\mathfrak{D}}(\mathscr{k})\rangle | \mathscr{k} \in \mathfrak{A}\}\text{where} \\ \mathcal{T}\mathbf{r}_{\mathfrak{D}}(\mathscr{k}) = \left[\mathcal{T}\mathbf{r}_{\mathfrak{D}}^{-}(\mathscr{k}), \mathcal{T}\mathbf{r}_{\mathfrak{D}}^{+}(\mathscr{k})\right], \mathcal{I}\mathbf{m}_{\mathfrak{D}}(\mathscr{k}) = \left[\mathcal{I}\mathbf{m}_{\mathfrak{D}}^{-}(\mathscr{k}), \mathcal{I}\mathbf{m}_{\mathfrak{D}}^{+}(\mathscr{k})\right], \mathcal{F}\mathbf{a}_{\mathfrak{D}}(\mathscr{k}) = \\ \left[\mathcal{F}\mathbf{a}_{\mathfrak{D}}^{-}(\mathscr{k}), \mathcal{F}\mathbf{a}_{\mathfrak{D}}^{+}(\mathscr{k})\right]\text{and} \\ \mathcal{I}\mathbf{m}_{\mathfrak{D}}^{-}(\mathscr{k}) = \max\left(\mathcal{I}\mathbf{m}_{\mathfrak{K}}^{-}(\mathscr{k}), \mathcal{I}\mathbf{m}_{\mathfrak{L}}^{-}(\mathscr{k})\right), \mathcal{I}\mathbf{m}_{\mathfrak{D}}^{+}(\mathscr{k}) = \max\left(\mathcal{I}\mathbf{m}_{\mathfrak{K}}^{+}(\mathscr{k}), \mathcal{I}\mathbf{m}_{\mathfrak{L}}^{+}(\mathscr{k})\right), \\ \mathcal{I}\mathbf{m}_{\mathfrak{D}}^{-}(\mathscr{k}) = \min\left(\mathcal{I}\mathbf{m}_{\mathfrak{K}}^{-}(\mathscr{k}), \mathcal{I}\mathbf{m}_{\mathfrak{L}}^{-}(\mathscr{k})\right), \mathcal{I}\mathbf{m}_{\mathfrak{D}}^{+}(\mathscr{k}) = \min\left(\mathcal{I}\mathbf{m}_{\mathfrak{K}}^{+}(\mathscr{k}), \mathcal{I}\mathbf{m}_{\mathfrak{L}}^{+}(\mathscr{k})\right), \\ \mathcal{F}\mathbf{a}_{\mathfrak{D}}^{-}(\mathscr{k}) = \min\left(\mathcal{F}\mathbf{a}_{\mathfrak{K}}^{-}(\mathscr{k}), \mathcal{F}\mathbf{a}_{\mathfrak{L}}^{-}(\mathscr{k})\right), \mathcal{F}\mathbf{a}_{\mathfrak{D}}^{+}(\mathscr{k}) = \min\left(\mathcal{F}\mathbf{a}_{\mathfrak{K}}^{+}(\mathscr{k}), \mathcal{F}\mathbf{a}_{\mathfrak{L}}^{+}(\mathscr{k})\right).\end{gathered}$$

or simply we can write,

$$\begin{gathered}\mathfrak{K} \cap \mathfrak{L} = \{\mathscr{k}, \left[\max\left(\mathcal{T}\mathbf{r}_{\mathfrak{K}}^{-}(\mathscr{k}), \mathcal{T}\mathbf{r}_{\mathfrak{L}}^{-}(\mathscr{k})\right), \max\left(\mathcal{T}\mathbf{r}_{\mathfrak{K}}^{+}(\mathscr{k}), \mathcal{T}\mathbf{r}_{\mathfrak{L}}^{+}(\mathscr{k})\right)\right], \\ \left[\min\left(\mathcal{I}\mathbf{m}_{\mathfrak{K}}^{-}(\mathscr{k}), \mathcal{I}\mathbf{m}_{\mathfrak{L}}^{-}(\mathscr{k})\right), \min\left(\mathcal{I}\mathbf{m}_{\mathfrak{K}}^{+}(\mathscr{k}), \mathcal{I}\mathbf{m}_{\mathfrak{L}}^{+}(\mathscr{k})\right)\right], \\ \left[\min\left(\mathcal{F}\mathbf{a}_{\mathfrak{K}}^{-}(\mathscr{k}), \mathcal{F}\mathbf{a}_{\mathfrak{L}}^{-}(\mathscr{k})\right), \min\left(\mathcal{F}\mathbf{a}_{\mathfrak{K}}^{+}(\mathscr{k}), \mathcal{F}\mathbf{a}_{\mathfrak{L}}^{+}(\mathscr{k})\right)\right]|, \mathscr{k} \in \mathfrak{A}\}\end{gathered}$$

iii. *The intersection of* $\mathfrak{K}$ *and* $\mathfrak{L}$ *is the* $IVFN_{set}\mathfrak{D}$, *defined by*

$$\begin{gathered}\mathfrak{D} = \mathfrak{K} \cap \mathfrak{L} = \{\langle \mathscr{k}, \mathcal{T}\mathbf{r}_{\mathfrak{D}}(\mathscr{k}), \mathcal{I}\mathbf{m}_{\mathfrak{D}}(\mathscr{k}), \mathcal{F}\mathbf{a}_{\mathfrak{D}}(\mathscr{k})\rangle | \mathscr{k} \in \mathfrak{A}\} \\ \mathcal{T}\mathbf{r}_{\mathfrak{D}}(\mathscr{k}) = \left[\mathcal{T}\mathbf{r}_{\mathfrak{D}}^{-}(\mathscr{k}), \mathcal{T}\mathbf{r}_{\mathfrak{D}}^{+}(\mathscr{k})\right], \mathcal{I}\mathbf{m}_{\mathfrak{D}}(\mathscr{k}) = \left[\mathcal{I}\mathbf{m}_{\mathfrak{D}}^{-}(\mathscr{k}), \mathcal{I}\mathbf{m}_{\mathfrak{D}}^{+}(\mathscr{k})\right], \\ \mathcal{F}\mathbf{a}_{\mathfrak{D}}(\mathscr{k}) = \left[\mathcal{F}\mathbf{a}_{\mathfrak{D}}^{-}(\mathscr{k}), \mathcal{F}\mathbf{a}_{\mathfrak{D}}^{+}(\mathscr{k})\right] \text{ and} \\ \mathcal{T}\mathbf{r}_{\mathfrak{D}}^{-}(\mathscr{k}) = \min\left(\mathcal{T}\mathbf{r}_{\mathfrak{K}}^{-}(\mathscr{k}), \mathcal{T}\mathbf{r}_{\mathfrak{L}}^{-}(\mathscr{k})\right), \mathcal{T}\mathbf{r}_{\mathfrak{D}}^{+}(\mathscr{k}) = \min\left(\mathcal{T}\mathbf{r}_{\mathfrak{K}}^{+}(\mathscr{k}), \mathcal{T}\mathbf{r}_{\mathfrak{L}}^{+}(\mathscr{k})\right), \\ \mathcal{I}\mathbf{m}_{\mathfrak{D}}^{-}(\mathscr{k}) = \max\left(\mathcal{I}\mathbf{m}_{\mathfrak{K}}^{-}(\mathscr{k}), \mathcal{I}\mathbf{m}_{\mathfrak{L}}^{-}(\mathscr{k})\right), \mathcal{I}\mathbf{m}_{\mathfrak{D}}^{+}(\mathscr{k}) = \max\left(\mathcal{I}\mathbf{m}_{\mathfrak{K}}^{+}(\mathscr{k}), \mathcal{I}\mathbf{m}_{\mathfrak{L}}^{+}(\mathscr{k})\right), \\ \mathcal{F}\mathbf{a}_{\mathfrak{D}}^{-}(\mathscr{k}) = \max\left(\mathcal{F}\mathbf{a}_{\mathfrak{K}}^{-}(\mathscr{k}), \mathcal{F}\mathbf{a}_{\mathfrak{L}}^{-}(\mathscr{k})\right), \mathcal{F}\mathbf{a}_{\mathfrak{D}}^{+}(\mathscr{k}) = \max\left(\mathcal{F}\mathbf{a}_{\mathfrak{K}}^{+}(\mathscr{k}), \mathcal{F}\mathbf{a}_{\mathfrak{L}}^{+}(\mathscr{k})\right).\end{gathered}$$

or simply we can write.

$$\begin{gathered}\mathfrak{K} \cap \mathfrak{L} = \{\mathscr{k}, \left[\min\left(\mathcal{T}\mathbf{r}_{\mathfrak{K}}^{-}(\mathscr{k}), \mathcal{T}\mathbf{r}_{\mathfrak{L}}^{-}(\mathscr{k})\right), \min\left(\mathcal{T}\mathbf{r}_{\mathfrak{K}}^{+}(\mathscr{k}), \mathcal{T}\mathbf{r}_{\mathfrak{L}}^{+}(\mathscr{k})\right)\right], \\ \left[\max\left(\mathcal{I}\mathbf{m}_{\mathfrak{K}}^{-}(\mathscr{k}), \mathcal{I}\mathbf{m}_{\mathfrak{L}}^{-}(\mathscr{k})\right), \max\left(\mathcal{I}\mathbf{m}_{\mathfrak{K}}^{+}(\mathscr{k}), \mathcal{I}\mathbf{m}_{\mathfrak{L}}^{+}(\mathscr{k})\right)\right], \\ \left[\max\left(\mathcal{F}\mathbf{a}_{\mathfrak{K}}^{-}(\mathscr{k}), \mathcal{F}\mathbf{a}_{\mathfrak{L}}^{-}(\mathscr{k})\right), \max\left(\mathcal{F}\mathbf{a}_{\mathfrak{K}}^{+}(\mathscr{k}), \mathcal{F}\mathbf{a}_{\mathfrak{L}}^{+}(\mathscr{k})\right)\right]|, \mathscr{k} \in \mathfrak{A}\}\end{gathered}$$

iv. *The complement of* $\mathfrak{K}$ *is the* $IVFN_{set}\mathfrak{K}^{c}$, *defined by*

$$\begin{gathered}\mathfrak{K}^{c} = \{\langle \mathscr{k}, \mathcal{T}\mathbf{r}_{\mathfrak{K}^{c}}(\mathscr{k}), \mathcal{I}\mathbf{m}_{\mathfrak{K}^{c}}(\mathscr{k}), \mathcal{F}\mathbf{a}_{\mathfrak{K}^{c}}(\mathscr{k})\rangle | \mathscr{k} \in \mathfrak{A}\}\text{where} \\ \mathcal{T}\mathbf{r}_{\mathfrak{K}^{c}}(\mathscr{k}) = \mathcal{F}\mathbf{a}_{\mathfrak{K}}(\mathscr{k}) = \left[\mathcal{F}\mathbf{a}_{\mathfrak{K}}^{-}(\mathscr{k}), \mathcal{F}\mathbf{a}_{\mathfrak{K}}^{+}(\mathscr{k})\right] \\ \mathcal{I}\mathbf{m}_{\mathfrak{K}^{c}}^{-}(\mathscr{k}) = 1 - \mathcal{I}\mathbf{m}_{\mathfrak{K}}^{+}(\mathscr{k}), \mathcal{I}\mathbf{m}_{\mathfrak{K}^{c}}^{+}(\mathscr{k}) = 1 - \mathcal{I}\mathbf{m}_{\mathfrak{K}}^{-}(\mathscr{k}) \\ \mathcal{F}\mathbf{a}_{\mathfrak{K}^{c}}(\mathscr{k}) = \mathcal{T}\mathbf{r}_{\mathfrak{K}}(\mathscr{k}) = \left[\mathcal{T}\mathbf{r}_{\mathfrak{K}}^{-}(\mathscr{k}), \mathcal{T}\mathbf{r}_{\mathfrak{K}}^{+}(\mathscr{k})\right]\end{gathered}$$

or simply we can write.

$$\mathfrak{K}^{c} = \{\langle \mathscr{k}, \left[\mathcal{F}\mathbf{a}_{\mathfrak{K}}^{-}(\mathscr{k}), \mathcal{F}\mathbf{a}_{\mathfrak{K}}^{+}(\mathscr{k})\right], \left[1 - \mathcal{I}\mathbf{m}_{\mathfrak{K}}^{+}(\mathscr{k}), 1 - \mathcal{I}\mathbf{m}_{\mathfrak{K}}^{-}(\mathscr{k})\right], \left[\mathcal{T}\mathbf{r}_{\mathfrak{K}}^{-}(\mathscr{k}), \mathcal{T}\mathbf{r}_{\mathfrak{K}}^{+}(\mathscr{k})\right]\rangle | \mathscr{k} \in \mathfrak{A}\}.$$

Definition 4. *The* $IVFN_{set}$ *is known as an absolute* $IVFN_{set}$, *denoted by* $1_{\mathfrak{A}}$, $\Leftrightarrow$ *its membership values are defined as*

$$\begin{gathered}\left[\mathcal{T}\mathbf{r}_{\mathfrak{K}}^{-}(\mathscr{k}), \mathcal{T}\mathbf{r}_{\mathfrak{K}}^{+}(\mathscr{k})\right] = [1,\ 1]; \\ \left[\mathcal{I}\mathbf{m}_{\mathfrak{K}}^{-}(\mathscr{k}),\ \mathcal{I}\mathbf{m}_{\mathfrak{K}}^{+}(\mathscr{k})\right] = [0,\ 0] \\ \left[\mathcal{F}\mathbf{a}_{\mathfrak{K}}^{-}(\mathscr{k}), \mathcal{F}\mathbf{a}_{\mathfrak{K}}^{+}(\mathscr{k})\right] = [0,\ 0].\end{gathered}$$

Definition 5. *The empty* $IVFN_{set}$ *is denoted by* $0_{\mathfrak{A}}$, *if its membership values are defined as*

$$\begin{gathered}\left[\mathcal{T}\boldsymbol{r}_{\mathfrak{K}}^{-}(\mathscr{k}), \mathcal{T}\boldsymbol{r}_{\mathfrak{K}}^{+}(\mathscr{k})\right] = [0,0]; \\ \left[\mathcal{I}\boldsymbol{m}_{\mathfrak{K}}^{-}(\mathscr{k}),\ \mathcal{I}\boldsymbol{m}_{\mathfrak{K}}^{+}(\mathscr{k})\right] = [1,1]; \\ \left[\mathcal{F}\boldsymbol{a}_{\mathfrak{K}}^{-}(\mathscr{k}), \mathcal{F}\boldsymbol{a}_{\mathfrak{K}}^{+}(\mathscr{k})\right] = [0,0].\end{gathered}$$

Example 1. *Consider two* $IVFN_{set}$, *defined over* $\mathfrak{A}$ *as*

$$\mathfrak{K}=\left\{\begin{array}{c}\langle p_1,[0.85,0.90],[0.80,0.85],[0.80,0.90]\rangle,\langle p_2,[0.85,0.85],[0.80,0.80],[0.80,0.90]\rangle,\\ \langle p_3,[0.90,0.95],[0.83,0.86],[0.82,0.81]\rangle\end{array}\right\}$$
$$\mathfrak{L}=\left\{\begin{array}{c}\langle p_1,[0.80,0.90],[0.80,0.80],[0.80,0.90]\rangle,\langle p_2,[0.81,0.85],[0.82,0.82],[0.84,0.91]\rangle,\\ \langle p_3,[0.92,0.95],[0.85,0.87],[0.83,0.85]\rangle\end{array}\right\}$$

then

$$\mathfrak{K}\cap\mathfrak{L}=\left\{\begin{array}{c}\langle p_1,[0.80,0.90],[0.80,0.85],[0.80,0.90]\rangle,\langle p_2,[0.81,0.85],[0.82,0.82],[0.84,0.91]\rangle,\\ \langle p_3,[0.90,0.95],[0.85,0.87],[0.83,0.85]\rangle\end{array}\right\}$$
$$\mathfrak{K}\cup\mathfrak{L}=\left\{\begin{array}{c}\langle p_1,[0.85,0.90],[0.80,0.80],[0.80,0.90]\rangle,\langle p_2,[0.85,0.85],[0.80,0.80],[0.80,0.90]\rangle,\\ \langle p_3,[0.92,0.95],[0.83,0.86],[0.82,0.81]\rangle\end{array}\right\}$$
$$\mathfrak{K}^c=\left\{\begin{array}{c}\langle p_1,[0.80,0.90],[0.15,0.20],[0.85,0.90]\rangle,\langle p_2,[0.80,0.90],[0.20,0.20],[0.85,0.85]\rangle,\\ \langle p_3,[0.82,0.81],[0.14,0.17],[0.83,0.86]\rangle\end{array}\right\}$$

Theorem 1. *For any $IVFN_{set}$, $\mathfrak{K}$ is defined on the absolute $IVFN_{set}\mathfrak{A}$.*

i. $\left.\begin{array}{c}\mathfrak{K}\cup 0_{\mathfrak{A}}=\mathfrak{K}\\ \mathfrak{K}\cap 1_{\mathfrak{A}}=\mathfrak{K}\end{array}\right\}$*(Identity Law)*

ii. $\left.\begin{array}{c}\mathfrak{K}\cap 0_{\mathfrak{A}}=0_{\mathfrak{A}}\\ \mathfrak{K}\cup 1_{\mathfrak{A}}=1_{\mathfrak{A}}\end{array}\right\}$*(Domination Law)*

Proof.

(i) Let $\mathfrak{K}$ and $0_{\mathfrak{A}}$ be two $IVFN_{set}$ on $\mathfrak{A}$, defined by

$$\mathfrak{K}=\left\{\left\langle k,\left[\mathcal{T}\mathbf{r}_{\mathfrak{K}}^{-}(k),\mathcal{T}\mathbf{r}_{\mathfrak{K}}^{+}(k)\right],\left[\mathcal{I}\mathbf{m}_{\mathfrak{K}}^{-}(k),\mathcal{I}\mathbf{m}_{\mathfrak{K}}^{+}(k)\right],\left[\mathcal{F}\mathbf{a}_{\mathfrak{K}}^{-}(k),\mathcal{F}\mathbf{a}_{\mathfrak{K}}^{+}(k)\right]\right\rangle\middle|k\in\mathfrak{A}\right\}$$

$0_{\mathfrak{A}}$, is defined as follows: $0_{\mathfrak{A}}=\{\langle k,[0,\ 0],[1,\ 1],[1,\ 1]\rangle|k\in\mathfrak{A}\}$
So, $\mathfrak{K}\cup 0_{\mathfrak{A}}=\left\{k,\left[\max\left(\mathcal{T}\mathbf{r}_{\mathfrak{K}}^{-}(k),0\right),\max\left(\mathcal{T}\mathbf{r}_{\mathfrak{K}}^{+}(k),0\right)\right],\right.$

$$\left[\min\left(\mathcal{I}\mathbf{m}_{\mathfrak{K}}^{-}(k),1\right),\min\left(\mathcal{I}\mathbf{m}_{\mathfrak{K}}^{+}(k),1\right)\right],\left[\min\left(\mathcal{F}\mathbf{a}_{\mathfrak{K}}^{-}(k),1\right),\min\left(\mathcal{F}\mathbf{a}_{\mathfrak{K}}^{+}(k),1\right)\right]\left|k\in\mathfrak{A}\right\}$$

Therefore, $\mathfrak{K}\cup 0_{\mathfrak{A}}=\left\{\left\langle k,\left[\mathcal{T}\mathbf{r}_{\mathfrak{K}}^{-}(k),\mathcal{T}\mathbf{r}_{\mathfrak{K}}^{+}(k)\right],\left[\mathcal{I}\mathbf{m}_{\mathfrak{K}}^{-}(k),\mathcal{I}\mathbf{m}_{\mathfrak{K}}^{+}(k)\right],\left[\mathcal{F}\mathbf{a}_{\mathfrak{K}}^{-}(k),\mathcal{F}\mathbf{a}_{\mathfrak{K}}^{+}(k)\right]\right\rangle\right|$ $k\in\mathfrak{A}\}$

$$\mathfrak{K}\cup 0_{\mathfrak{A}}=\mathfrak{K}$$

In a similar way, we can prove $\mathfrak{K}\cap 1_{\mathfrak{A}}=\mathfrak{K}$

(ii) Let $\mathfrak{K}$ and $0_{\mathfrak{A}}$ be two $IVFN_{set}$ on $\mathfrak{A}$, defined by

$$\mathfrak{K}=\left\{\left\langle k,\left[\mathcal{T}\mathbf{r}_{\mathfrak{K}}^{-}(k),\mathcal{T}\mathbf{r}_{\mathfrak{K}}^{+}(k)\right],\left[\mathcal{I}\mathbf{m}_{\mathfrak{K}}^{-}(k),\ \mathcal{I}\mathbf{m}_{\mathfrak{K}}^{+}(k)\right],\left[\left[\mathcal{F}\mathbf{a}_{\mathfrak{K}}^{-}(k),\mathcal{F}\mathbf{a}_{\mathfrak{K}}^{+}(k)\right\rangle\right|k\in\mathfrak{A}\right\}$$

$0_{\mathfrak{A}}$, is defined as follows: $0_{\mathfrak{A}}=\{\langle k,[0,\ 0],[1,\ 1],[1,\ 1]\rangle|k\in\mathfrak{A}\}$
So, $\mathfrak{K}\cap 0_{\mathfrak{A}}=\left\{k,\left[\min\left(\mathcal{T}\mathbf{r}_{\mathfrak{K}}^{-}(k),0\right),\min\left(\mathcal{T}\mathbf{r}_{\mathfrak{K}}^{+}(k),0\right)\right],\right.$

$$\left[\max\left(\mathcal{I}\mathbf{m}_{\mathfrak{K}}^{-}(k),1\right),\max\left(\mathcal{I}\mathbf{m}_{\mathfrak{K}}^{+}(k),1\right)\right],\left[\max\left(\mathcal{F}\mathbf{a}_{\mathfrak{K}}^{-}(k),1\right),\max\left(\mathcal{F}\mathbf{a}_{\mathfrak{K}}^{+}(k),1\right)\right]\left|k\in\mathfrak{A}\right\}$$

Therefore, $\mathfrak{K}\cap 0_{\mathfrak{A}}=\{\langle k,[0,\ 0],[1,\ 1],[1,\ 1]\rangle|k\in\mathfrak{A}\}$

$$\mathfrak{K}\cap 0_{\mathfrak{A}}=0_{\mathfrak{A}}$$

In the similar way, we can prove $\mathfrak{K}\cup 1_{\mathfrak{A}}=1_{\mathfrak{A}}$

□

Definition 6. *Suppose*

$$\mathfrak{K} = \left\{ \left\langle \left[\mathcal{T}\mathbf{r}_{\mathfrak{K}}^{-}(\mathcal{k}), \mathcal{T}\mathbf{r}_{\mathfrak{K}}^{+}(\mathcal{k})\right], \left[\mathcal{I}\mathbf{m}_{\mathfrak{K}}^{-}(\mathcal{k}), \mathcal{I}\mathbf{m}_{\mathfrak{K}}^{+}(\mathcal{k})\right], \left[\left[\mathcal{F}\mathbf{a}_{\mathfrak{K}}^{-}(\mathcal{k}), \mathcal{F}\mathbf{a}_{\mathfrak{K}}^{+}(\mathcal{k})\right]\right\rangle : \mathcal{k} \in \mathfrak{A} \right\}$$

and

$$\mathfrak{L} = \left\{ \left\langle \left[\mathcal{T}\mathbf{r}_{\mathfrak{L}}^{-}(\mathcal{k}), \mathcal{T}\mathbf{r}_{\mathfrak{L}}^{+}(\mathcal{k})\right], \left[\mathcal{I}\mathbf{m}_{\mathfrak{L}}^{-}(\mathcal{k}), \mathcal{I}\mathbf{m}_{\mathfrak{L}}^{+}(\mathcal{k})\right], \left[\mathcal{F}\mathbf{a}_{\mathfrak{L}}^{-}(\mathcal{k}), \mathcal{F}\mathbf{a}_{\mathfrak{L}}^{+}(\mathcal{k})\right]\right\rangle : \mathcal{k} \in \mathfrak{A} \right\}$$

be two $IVFN_{set}$ *, then*

$$A_{\mathrm{IVFN_{set}}} + B_{\mathrm{IVFN_{set}}} = \left\{ \left\langle \begin{matrix} \mathcal{k}_1 + \mathcal{k}_2, \left[\mathcal{T}\mathbf{r}_{\mathfrak{K}}^{-}(\mathcal{k}) + \mathcal{T}\mathbf{r}_{\mathfrak{L}}^{-}(\mathcal{k}) - \mathcal{T}\mathbf{r}_{\mathfrak{K}}^{-}(\mathcal{k})\mathcal{T}\mathbf{r}_{\mathfrak{L}}^{-}(\mathcal{k}), \mathcal{T}\mathbf{r}_{\mathfrak{K}}^{+}(\mathcal{k}) + \mathcal{T}\mathbf{r}_{\mathfrak{L}}^{-}(\mathcal{k}) - \mathcal{T}\mathbf{r}_{\mathfrak{K}}^{+}(\mathcal{k})\mathcal{T}\mathbf{r}_{\mathfrak{L}}^{+}(\mathcal{k})\right], \\ \left[\mathcal{I}\mathbf{m}_{\mathfrak{K}}^{-}(\mathcal{k})\mathcal{I}\mathbf{m}_{\mathfrak{L}}^{-}(\mathcal{k}), \mathcal{I}\mathbf{m}_{\mathfrak{K}}^{+}(\mathcal{k})\mathcal{I}\mathbf{m}_{\mathfrak{L}}^{+}(\mathcal{k})\right], \\ \left[\mathcal{F}\mathbf{a}_{\mathfrak{K}}^{-}(\mathcal{k})\mathcal{F}\mathbf{a}_{\mathfrak{L}}^{-}(\mathcal{k}), \mathcal{F}\mathbf{a}_{\mathfrak{K}}^{+}(\mathcal{k})\mathcal{F}\mathbf{a}_{\mathfrak{L}}^{+}(\mathcal{k})\right] \end{matrix} \right\rangle \right\}, \mathcal{k} \in \mathfrak{A}$$

$$A_{\mathrm{IVFN_{set}}} \cdot B_{\mathrm{IVFN_{set}}} = \left\{ \left\langle \begin{matrix} \mathcal{k}_1\mathcal{k}_2, \left[\mathcal{T}\mathbf{r}_{\mathfrak{K}}^{-}(\mathcal{k})\mathcal{T}\mathbf{r}_{\mathfrak{L}}^{-}(\mathcal{k}), \mathcal{T}\mathbf{r}_{\mathfrak{K}}^{+}(\mathcal{k})\mathcal{T}\mathbf{r}_{\mathfrak{L}}^{+}(\mathcal{k})\right], \\ \left[\mathcal{I}\mathbf{m}_{\mathfrak{K}}^{-}(\mathcal{k}) + \mathcal{I}\mathbf{m}_{\mathfrak{L}}^{-}(\mathcal{k}) - \mathcal{I}\mathbf{m}_{\mathfrak{K}}^{-}(\mathcal{k})\mathcal{I}\mathbf{m}_{\mathfrak{L}}^{-}(\mathcal{k}), \mathcal{I}\mathbf{m}_{\mathfrak{K}}^{+}(\mathcal{k}) + \mathcal{I}\mathbf{m}_{\mathfrak{L}}^{+}(\mathcal{k}) - \mathcal{I}\mathbf{m}_{\mathfrak{K}}^{+}(\mathcal{k})\mathcal{I}\mathbf{m}_{\mathfrak{L}}^{+}(\mathcal{k})\right], \\ \left[\mathcal{F}\mathbf{a}_{\mathfrak{K}}^{-}(\mathcal{k}) + \mathcal{F}\mathbf{a}_{\mathfrak{L}}^{-}(\mathcal{k}) - \mathcal{F}\mathbf{a}_{\mathfrak{K}}^{-}(\mathcal{k})\mathcal{F}\mathbf{a}_{\mathfrak{L}}^{-}(\mathcal{k}), \mathcal{F}\mathbf{a}_{\mathfrak{K}}^{+}(\mathcal{k}) + \mathcal{F}\mathbf{a}_{\mathfrak{L}}^{+}(\mathcal{k}) - \mathcal{F}\mathbf{a}_{\mathfrak{K}}^{+}(\mathcal{k})\mathcal{F}\mathbf{a}_{\mathfrak{L}}^{+}(\mathcal{k})\right] \end{matrix} \right\rangle \right\}, \mathcal{k} \in \mathfrak{A}$$

Definition 7. *Let* $\alpha = \left(\left[\mathcal{T}r_{\alpha}^{A-}, \mathcal{T}r_{\alpha}^{A+}\right], \left[\mathcal{I}m_{\alpha}^{A-}, \mathcal{I}m_{\alpha}^{A+}\right], \left[\mathcal{F}a_{\alpha}^{A-}, \mathcal{F}a_{\alpha}^{A+}\right]\right)$, $\alpha_1 = \left(\left[\mathcal{T}r_{\alpha_1}^{A-}, \mathcal{T}_{\alpha_1}^{A+}\right], \left[\mathcal{I}m_{\alpha_1}^{A-}, \mathcal{I}_{\alpha_1}^{A+}\right], \left[\mathcal{F}a_{\alpha_1}^{A-}, \mathcal{F}a_{\alpha_1}^{A+}\right]\right)$ *and* $\alpha_2 = \left(\left[\mathcal{T}r_{\alpha_2}^{A-}, \mathcal{T}r_{\alpha_2}^{A+}\right], \left[\mathcal{I}m_{\alpha_2}^{A-}, \mathcal{I}m_{\alpha_2}^{A+}\right], \left[\mathcal{F}a_{\alpha_2}^{A-}, \mathcal{F}a_{\alpha_2}^{A+}\right]\right)$ *be three* $IVFN_{number}$. *Then*

(i) $\alpha_1 = \alpha_2$ *if and only if* $\mathcal{T}\mathbf{r}_{\alpha_1}^{A-} = \mathcal{T}\mathbf{r}_{\alpha_2}^{A-}, \mathcal{I}\mathbf{m}_{\alpha_1}^{A-} = \mathcal{I}\mathbf{m}_{\alpha_2}^{A-}, \mathcal{F}\mathbf{a}_{\alpha_1}^{A-} = \mathcal{F}\mathbf{a}_{\alpha_2}^{A-}$

(ii) $\alpha_1 \prec \alpha_2$ *if and only if*

(iii) $\mathcal{T}\mathbf{r}_{\alpha_1}^{A-} \le \mathcal{T}\mathbf{r}_{\alpha_2}^{A-}, \mathcal{T}\mathbf{r}_{\alpha_1}^{A+} \le \mathcal{T}\mathbf{r}_{\alpha_2}^{A+}; \mathcal{I}\mathbf{m}_{\alpha_1}^{A-} \ge \mathcal{I}\mathbf{m}_{\alpha_2}^{A-}, \mathcal{I}\mathbf{m}_{\alpha_1}^{A-} \ge \mathcal{I}\mathbf{m}_{\alpha_2}^{A-}; \mathcal{F}\mathbf{a}_{\alpha_1}^{A-} \ge \mathcal{F}\mathbf{a}_{\alpha_2}^{A-}; \mathcal{F}\mathbf{a}_{\alpha_2}^{A+} \ge \mathcal{F}\mathbf{a}_{\alpha_2}^{A+}$

(iv) $\alpha_1 \bigoplus \alpha_2 =$

$$\left[\begin{matrix} \sqrt[3]{\left(\mathcal{T}\mathbf{r}_{\alpha_1}^{A-}\right)^3 + \left(\mathcal{T}\mathbf{r}_{\alpha_2}^{A-}\right)^3 - \left(\mathcal{T}\mathbf{r}_{\alpha_1}^{A-}\right)^3 . \left(\mathcal{T}\mathbf{r}_{\alpha_2}^{A-}\right)^3}, \sqrt[3]{\left(\mathcal{T}\mathbf{r}_{\alpha_1}^{A+}\right)^3 + \left(\mathcal{T}\mathbf{r}_{\alpha_2}^{A+}\right)^3 - \left(\mathcal{T}\mathbf{r}_{\alpha_1}^{A+}\right)^3 . \left(\mathcal{T}\mathbf{r}_{\alpha_2}^{A+}\right)^3}, \\ \left[\mathcal{I}\mathbf{m}_{\alpha_1}^{A-}\mathcal{I}\mathbf{m}_{\alpha_2}^{A-}, \mathcal{I}\mathbf{m}_{\alpha_1}^{A+}\mathcal{I}\mathbf{m}_{\alpha_2}^{A+}\right], \left[\mathcal{F}\mathbf{a}_{\alpha_1}^{A-}\mathcal{F}\mathbf{a}_{\alpha_2}^{A-}, \mathcal{F}\mathbf{a}_{\alpha_1}^{A+}\mathcal{F}\mathbf{a}_{\alpha_2}^{A+}\right] \end{matrix}\right]$$

(v) $\alpha_1 \bigotimes \alpha_2 =$

$$\left[\begin{matrix} \left[\mathcal{T}\mathbf{r}_{\alpha_1}^{A-} . \mathcal{T}\mathbf{r}_{\alpha_2}^{A-}, \mathcal{T}\mathbf{r}_{\alpha_1}^{A+} . \mathcal{T}\mathbf{r}_{\alpha_2}^{A+}\right] \\ \left[\sqrt[3]{\left(\mathcal{I}\mathbf{m}_{\alpha_1}^{A-}\right)^3 + \left(\mathcal{I}\mathbf{m}_{\alpha_2}^{A-}\right)^3 - \left(\mathcal{I}\mathbf{m}_{\alpha_1}^{A-}\right)^3 . \left(\mathcal{I}\mathbf{m}_{\alpha_2}^{A-}\right)^3}, \sqrt[3]{\left(\mathcal{I}\mathbf{m}_{\alpha_1}^{A+}\right)^3 + \left(\mathcal{I}\mathbf{m}_{\alpha_2}^{A+}\right)^3 - \left(\mathcal{I}\mathbf{m}_{\alpha_1}^{A+}\right)^3 . \left(\mathcal{I}\mathbf{m}_{\alpha_2}^{A+}\right)^3}\right] \\ \left[\sqrt[3]{\left(\mathcal{F}\mathbf{a}_{\alpha_1}^{A-}\right)^3 + \left(\mathcal{F}\mathbf{a}_{\alpha_2}^{A-}\right)^3 - \left(\mathcal{F}\mathbf{a}_{\alpha_1}^{A-}\right)^3 . \left(\mathcal{F}\mathbf{a}_{\alpha_2}^{A-}\right)^3}, \sqrt[3]{\left(\mathcal{F}\mathbf{a}_{\alpha_1}^{A+}\right)^3 + \left(\mathcal{F}\mathbf{a}_{\alpha_2}^{A+}\right)^3 - \left(\mathcal{F}\mathbf{a}_{\alpha_1}^{A+}\right)^3 . \left(\mathcal{F}\mathbf{a}_{\alpha_2}^{A+}\right)^3}\right] \end{matrix}\right]$$

(vi) $k\alpha =$

$$\left(\left[\sqrt[3]{1 - \left(1 - \left(\left(\mathcal{T}\mathbf{r}_{\alpha}^{A-}\right)^3\right)^k\right)}, \sqrt[3]{1 - \left(1 - \left(\left(\mathcal{T}\mathbf{r}_{\alpha}^{A+}\right)^3\right)^k\right)}\right], \left[\left(\mathcal{I}\mathbf{m}_{\alpha}^{A-}\right)^k, \left(\mathcal{I}\mathbf{m}_{\alpha}^{A+}\right)^k\right], \left[\left(\mathcal{F}\mathbf{a}_{\alpha}^{A-}\right)^k, \left(\mathcal{F}\mathbf{a}_{\alpha}^{A+}\right)^k\right]\right)$$

(vii) $\alpha^k =$

$$\left(\left[\left(\mathcal{T}\mathbf{r}_{\alpha}^{A-}\right)^k, \left(\mathcal{T}\mathbf{r}_{\alpha}^{A+}\right)^k\right], \left[\sqrt[3]{1 - \left(1 - \left(\left(\mathcal{I}\mathbf{m}_{\alpha}^{A-}\right)^3\right)^k\right)}, \sqrt[3]{1 - \left(1 - \left(\left(\mathcal{I}\mathbf{m}_{\alpha}^{A+}\right)^3\right)^k\right)}\right], \left[\sqrt[3]{1 - \left(1 - \left(\left(\mathcal{F}\mathbf{a}_{\alpha_1}^{A-}\right)^3\right)^k\right)}, \sqrt[3]{1 - \left(1 - \left(\left(\mathcal{F}\mathbf{a}_{\alpha_2}^{A-}\right)^3\right)^k\right)}\right]\right).$$

Remark 2.

i. *If* $\alpha = ([a,b],[c,d],[e,f]) = ([1,1],[0,0],[0,0])$ *and* $k > 0$ *then,*

$$k\alpha = \left(\left[\sqrt[3]{1 - \left(1 - (a^3)^k\right)}, \sqrt[3]{1 - \left(1 - (b^3)^k\right)}\right], \left[(c)^k, (d)^k\right], \left[(e)^k, (f)^k\right]\right) = ([1,1],[0,0],[0,0])\alpha^k$$
$$= \left(\left[(a)^k, (b)^k\right], \left[\sqrt[3]{1 - \left(1 - (c)^3\right)^k}, \sqrt[3]{1 - \left(1 - (d)^3\right)^k}\right], \left[\sqrt[3]{1 - \left(1 - \left((e)^3\right)^k\right)}, \sqrt[3]{1 - \left(1 - \left((f)^3\right)^k\right)}\right]\right)$$
$$= ([1,1],[0,0],[0,0])$$

ii. *If* $\alpha = ([a,b],[c,d],[e,f]) = ([0,0],[1,1],[1,1])$ *and* $k > 0$ *then,*

$$k\alpha = \left(\left[\sqrt[3]{1-\left(1-(a^3)^k\right)}, \sqrt[3]{1-\left(1-(b^3)^k\right)}\right], \left[(c)^k, (d)^k\right], \left[(e)^k, (f)^k\right]\right) = ([0,0],[1,1],[1,1])\alpha^k$$
$$= \left(\left[(a)^k, (b)^k\right], \left[\sqrt[3]{1-\left(1-\left(c\right)^3\right)^k}, \sqrt[3]{1-\left(1-\left(d\right)^3\right)^k}\right], \left[\sqrt[3]{1-\left(1-\left((e)^3\right)^k\right)}, \sqrt[3]{1-\left(1-\left((f)^3\right)^k\right)}\right]\right)$$
$$= ([0,0],[1,1],[1,1])$$

iii. *If* $k = 1$ *then* $k\alpha = \alpha; \alpha^k = \alpha$

Definition 8. *Consider* $\alpha_j = \left(\left[\mathcal{T}r^{A-}_{\alpha_j}, \mathcal{T}r^{A+}_{\alpha_j}\right], \left[\mathcal{I}m^{A-}_{\alpha_j}, \mathcal{I}m^{A+}_{\alpha_j}\right], \left[\mathcal{F}a^{A-}_{\alpha_j}, \mathcal{F}a^{A+}_{\alpha_j}\right]\right)$ *is a set of the* $IVFN_{number}$ *where* $j = 1,2,\ldots,r$. *Then, the* $IVFNW_{average}$ *operator is as follows:*

$IVFNWA(\alpha_1, \alpha_2, ..\alpha_r) = \ominus_{j=1}^{r} w_j\alpha_j$ where w_j is weight value with $w_j \in [0,1]$ and $\sum_{j=1}^{r} w_j = 1$

$$IVFNWA(\alpha_1,\alpha_2,..\alpha_r) = \left[\left(1-\prod_{j=1}^{r}\left(1-\left(\mathcal{T}\mathbf{r}^{A-}_{\alpha_j}\right)^3\right)^{w_j}\right)^{\frac{1}{3}}, \left(1-\prod_{j=1}^{r}\left(1-\left(\mathcal{T}\mathbf{r}^{A+}_{\alpha_j}\right)^3\right)^{w_j}\right)^{\frac{1}{3}}\right],$$
$$\left[\prod_{j=1}^{r}\left(\mathcal{I}\mathbf{m}^{A-}_{\alpha_j}\right)^{w_j}, \prod_{j=1}^{r}\left(\mathcal{I}\mathbf{m}^{A+}_{\alpha_j}\right)^{w_j}\right], \left[\prod_{j=1}^{r}\left(\mathcal{F}\mathbf{a}^{A-}_{\alpha_j}\right)^{w_j}, \prod_{j=1}^{r}\left(\mathcal{F}\mathbf{a}^{A+}_{\alpha_j}\right)^{w_j}\right]$$

Definition 9. *Consider* $\alpha_j = \left(\left[\mathcal{T}r^{A-}_{\alpha_j}, \mathcal{T}r^{A+}_{\alpha_j}\right], \left[\mathcal{I}m^{A-}_{\alpha_j}, \mathcal{I}m^{A+}_{\alpha_j}\right], \left[\mathcal{F}a^{A-}_{\alpha_j}, \mathcal{F}a^{A+}_{\alpha_j}\right]\right)$ *is a set of the* $IVFN_{number}$ *where* $j = 1,2,\ldots,r$. *Then, the* $IVFNW_{graph}$ *operator is as follows:* $IVFNWG(\alpha_1, \alpha_2, ..\alpha_r) = \ominus_{j=1}^{r}\alpha_j^{w_j}$ *where* w_j *is weight value with* $w_j \in [0,1]$ *and* $\sum_{j=1}^{r} w_j = 1$

$$IVFNW_{graph}(\alpha_1,\alpha_2,..\alpha_r)$$
$$= \left(\left[\prod_{j=1}^{r}\left(\mathcal{T}\mathbf{r}^{A-}_{\alpha_j}\right)^{w_j}, \prod_{j=1}^{r}\left(\mathcal{T}\mathbf{r}^{A+}_{\alpha_j}\right)^{w_j}\right], \left[\left(1-\prod_{j=1}^{r}\left(1-\left(\mathcal{I}\mathbf{m}^{A-}_{\alpha_j}\right)^3\right)^{w_j}\right)^{\frac{1}{3}}, \left(1-\prod_{j=1}^{r}\left(1-\left(\mathcal{I}\mathbf{m}^{A+}_{\alpha_j}\right)^3\right)^{w_j}\right)^{\frac{1}{3}}\right],\right.$$
$$\left.\left[\left(1-\prod_{j=1}^{r}\left(1-\left(\mathcal{F}\mathbf{a}^{A-}_{\alpha_j}\right)^3\right)^{w_j}\right)^{\frac{1}{3}}, \left(1-\prod_{j=1}^{r}\left(1-\left(\mathcal{F}\mathbf{a}^{A+}_{\alpha_j}\right)^3\right)^{w_j}\right)^{\frac{1}{3}}\right]\right)$$

4. Score and Accuracy Function for the $IVFN_{number}$

Finding the solutions to Multi-Criteria Decision-Making (MCDM) problems in an uncertainty situation is a challenging task in today's world. In real-time situations, the membership values of $\mathcal{T}r$, $\mathcal{F}a$ and $\mathcal{I}n$ for a certain problem cannot be an exact value but are defined by possible interval values. So, researchers introduced the IVF_{set}, $IVIF_{set}$ and IVN_{set}. There are many studies available in the literature about grouping operators and determination methods in Table 2. In the Decision-Making (DM) process, one can find the best alternative among a set of feasible ones by using MCDM techniques. HWang and Yoon [26] introduced TOPSIS, which is another well-known MCDM approach to finding the best alternative. To date, the IF_{set}, $IVIF_{set}$, and IVN_{set} are widely used in DM problems. Additionally, the SN_{set} and IVN_{set} are extensions of the N_{set}.

Singh et al. [24] defined score and accuracy functions using N_{set} to solve problems in MCDM for ranking the SVN_{set} and IVN_{set}.

Table 2. Literature Survey.

Authors	Topic	Year
Nayagam et al. [27,28]	Ranking method on the $IVIF_{set}$.	2007 and 2008
Xu, Liu, and Xie [29,30]	Weighted SF and AF to rank the $IVIF_{set}$.	2007 and 2009
Ye [31]	Novel AF for ranking the different alternatives under the IF_{set} and $IVIF_{set}$.	2009
Yager [6]	Aggregation operators in the Pythagorean environment.	2013
Ye [32]	Correlation coefficient under SVN_{set}.	2013
Yager [7]	PF_{set}.	2014
Garg [9]	AF for the $IVPF_{set}$.	2016
Garg [25]	$IPFW_{average}$ and $IPFW_{graph}$ operators in the DM problem in the $IVPF_{set}$ environment.	2016
Garg [25]	Correlation coefficient between the PF_{set}.	2016

Definition 10. *Score functions of the* $SVN_{set.}$ *Let* $A = \{\langle \hbar, [\mathcal{T}r_A^-(\hbar), \mathcal{T}r_A^+(\hbar)], [\mathcal{I}m_A^-(\hbar), \mathcal{I}m_A^+(\hbar)], [\mathcal{F}a_A^-(\hbar), \mathcal{F}a_A^+(\hbar)]\rangle | \hbar \in \mathfrak{A}\}$. *That is,* $\tilde{A} = ([a, b], [c, d], [e, f])$ *be an* IN_{number}. *The Score function (SF) of the* SVN_{set} *is interpreted as* $S(\alpha) = \frac{2+a+b-2c-2d-e-f}{4}$, *where* $S(\alpha) \in [0,1]$ *(Şahin and Nancy [33–35])*

$$S(\alpha) = \frac{4 + (a + b - 2c - 2d - e - f)(4 - a - b - e - f)}{8}$$

where $S(\alpha) \in [0,1]$ *(Singh et al. [2])*

$$S(\alpha) = (2 + a + b - 2c - 2d - e - f)(2(4 - a - b - c - d)),$$

where $S(\alpha) \in [0,1]$ *and* $a + b + c + d \neq 4$ *as* $0 \leq a \leq b \leq 1, 0 \leq c \leq d \leq 1$.

$$H(\alpha) = \frac{(a + b - d(1 - b) - c(1 - a) - f(1 - c) - e(1 - d)}{2},$$

$H(\alpha) \in [0,1]$ *(Sahin [34]).*

Definition 11. *An Accuracy functions of the* $SVN_{set.}$ *Let* $A = \{\langle \hbar, \mathcal{T}r_A(\hbar), \mathcal{I}m_A(\hbar), \mathcal{F}a_A(\hbar)\rangle | \hbar \in \mathfrak{A}\}$ *be the* SVN_{set}. *For convenience, the* $N_{set}A = \langle a, b, c \rangle$, *(ahin and Nancy* [34,35] is defined as $S(\alpha) = \frac{1+a-2b-c}{2}$, $S(\alpha) \in [0,1]$

$$S(\alpha) = \frac{1 + (a - 2b - c)(2 - a - c)}{2}, \; S(\alpha) \in [0,1]$$

The Accuracy function (AF) of $SVN_{set}f$ *(Nancy and Şahin [34,35]) is interpreted as*

$$H(\alpha) = a - b(1 - a) - c(1 - b), H(\alpha) \in [0,1]$$
$$H(\alpha) = a - 2b - c, \; H(\alpha) \in [0,1].$$

Definition 12. *Score and accuracy functions of the* $IVPF_{set}$ *and* $IVPF_{number}$. *Score function of the* $\boldsymbol{PF_{set}}$ *A on S is given by Zhang et al. [21], who introduced the (SF) as* $S(\alpha) = (\mathcal{T}r_A)^2 - \mathcal{F}a_A$, *where* $\alpha = (\mathcal{T}r_A, \mathcal{F}a_A)$ *and* $S(\alpha) \in [-1, 1]$. *The AF is* $(\alpha) = (\mathcal{T}r_A)^2 + (\mathcal{F}a_A)^2$, *where* $H(\alpha) \in [0,1]$.

Score and Accuracy functions of the $IVPF_{set}$

$$S(\alpha) = \langle [a, b], [c, d] \rangle \text{ where} [a, b] \subseteq [0, 1], [c, d] \subseteq [0,1] \text{ and } b^2 + d^2 \leq 1.$$

The score function of the $IVPF_{number}$ is $S(\alpha) = \frac{a^2+b^2-c^2-d^2}{2}$, *where* $S(\alpha) \in [-1, 1]$

The accuracy function for the $IVPF_{number}$ is $(\alpha) = \frac{a^2+b^2+c^2+d^2}{2}$, where $H(\alpha) \in [0, 1]$. Garg [31] observed that the above SF and AF for the $IVPF_{number}$ are suitable for certain cases; for example, $\alpha_1 = \langle [0, 0.5], [0.1, 0.7] \rangle$ and $\alpha_2 = \langle [0.3, 0.4], [0.5, 0.5] \rangle$ are the two $IVPF_{set}$, then we obtain, $S(\alpha_1) = S(\alpha_2) = -0.1250$ and $H(\alpha_1)) = H(\alpha_2) = 0.3750$. Hence, he proposed an improved score function as follows:

$$L(\alpha) = \frac{(a^2 - c^2)\left(1 + \left(\sqrt{(1 - a^2 - c^2)}\right)\right) + (b^2 - d^2)\left(1 + \left(\sqrt{(1 - b^2 - d^2)}\right)\right)}{2},$$

where $L(\alpha) \in [-1, 1]$

Based on the improved score function, he gave the following comparison law for the DM process by the $IVPF_{number}$

if $L(\alpha) < L(\beta)$, then $\alpha < \beta$, $L(\alpha) > L(\beta)$, then $\alpha > \beta$, $L(\alpha) = L(\beta)$, then $\alpha = \beta$. He also verified this with the above two examples,

$$L(\alpha_1) = -0.1912 \text{ and } L(\alpha_2) = -0.2246, \text{ the alternative } \alpha_1 \text{ is better than } \alpha_2 \text{ and}$$
$$L(\alpha_1) = -0.3368 and L(\alpha_2) = -0.3233, \; the\ alternative\ \alpha_2\ is\ better\ than\ \alpha_1.$$

Definition 13. *Score and accuracy functions of the FF_{set} and $IVFF_{number}$. Senapati and Yager [10] proposed the FF_{set} in 2019. They have also compared it to other kinds of F_{set}. Complement operator and set of operations for the FF_{set} were found. They defined SF and AF for the FF_{set} ranking and applied it to the DM problem. Score function of the FF_{set} is $S(\alpha) = (\mathcal{T}r_A)^3 - (\mathcal{F}a_A)^3$ where $\alpha = (\mathcal{T}r_A, \mathcal{F}a_A)$ and $S(\alpha) \in [-1, 1]$. The accuracy function of the FF_{set} is $H(\alpha) = (\mathcal{T}r_A)^3 + (\mathcal{F}a_A)^3$ where $H(\alpha) \in [0, 1]$. Senapati and Yager [10] explained the SF and values lie between [−1,1]. Later, Laxminarayan Sahoo [36] observed that $SF(F) \in [-1, 1]$ and the function are positive when $SF(F) \in [0, 1]$ and negative when $SF(F) \in [-1, 0)$. To score functions when score values lie in the interval between 0 and 1, he has also introduced the following formulae.*

$$(\text{Type 1})\ S_{1F}(\widetilde{F}) = \frac{1 + \mathcal{T}r_A^3 - \mathcal{F}a_A^3}{2}$$
$$(\text{Type 2})\ S_{2F}(\widetilde{F}) = \frac{1 + 2\mathcal{T}r_A^3 - \mathcal{F}a_A^3}{3}$$
$$(\text{Type 3})\ S_{3F}(\widetilde{F}) = \frac{(1 + \mathcal{T}r_A^3 - \mathcal{F}a_A^3)(|\mathcal{T}r_A - \mathcal{F}a_A|)}{2}$$

Rani et al. [15] introduced the following:

The score function of the $IVFF_{number}$ $\lambda = \langle [a, b], [c, d] \rangle$ where $[a, b] \subseteq [0, 1]$, $[c, d] \subseteq [0, 1]$ and $b^3 + d^3 \leq 1$. $S(\alpha) = \frac{a^3+b^3-c^3-d^3}{2}$ where $S(\alpha) \in [-1, 1]$

The accuracy function for the $IVFF_{number}$ is $H(\alpha) = \frac{a^3+b^3+c^3+d^3}{2}$ where $H(\alpha) \in [0, 1]$

Jeevaraj [16] introduced a new score function for comparing such types of $IVFF_{number}$, as follows:

$$S(\alpha) = \frac{-a^3 + b^3 + c^3 - d^3}{2} \text{ where } S(\alpha) \in [-0.5, 0.5]$$

The accuracy function for the $IVFF_{number}$ is $H(\alpha) = \frac{-a^3+b^3-c^3+d^3}{2}$ where $H(\alpha) \in [-0.5, 0.5]$

Rani et al. [15] introduced a new score function for comparing such types of $IVFF_{number}$, as follows:

$$S(\alpha) = \frac{(a^3 - c^3)\left(1 + \sqrt{(1 - a^3 - c^3)}\right) + (b^3 - d^3)\left(1 + \sqrt{(1 - b^3 - d^3)}\right)}{2}, where\ S(\alpha) \in [-1, 1].$$

Definition 14. *Proposed Score Functions of the IVFN$_{set}$(IVFN$_{set}$)}* $\langle[\mathcal{Tr}_A^-(\hbar), \mathcal{Tr}_A^+(\hbar)], [\mathcal{Im}_A^-(\hbar), \mathcal{Im}_A^+(\hbar)], [\mathcal{Fa}_A^-(\hbar), \mathcal{Fa}_A^+(\hbar)]\rangle = \alpha = \langle[a,b], [c,d], [e, f]\rangle$ *where* $[a,b] \subseteq [0, 1], [c,d] \subseteq [0, 1], [e,f] \subseteq [0, 1]$ *and* $b^3 + d^3 + f^3 \leq 1.$

The score functions of the $IVFN_{set}$

$$S_1(\alpha) = \frac{(a^3+b^3-c^3-d^3-e^3-f^3)}{2} \text{ where } S_1(\alpha) \in [-1, 1]$$

$$S_2(\alpha) = \frac{(a^3+b^3+c^3+d^3+e^3+f^3)}{2} \text{ where } S_2(\alpha) \in [0, 1]$$

$$S_3(\alpha) = \frac{4+(a^3+b^3-2c^3-2d^3-e^3-f^3)(4-a^3-b^3-c^3-d^3-e^3-f^3)}{8} \text{ where } S_3(\alpha) \in [0, 1]$$

For maximum property, $\langle[0,0], [0,0], [1, 1]\rangle$ *and minimum property,* $\langle[1, 1], [0, 0], [0, 0.]\rangle$

See in Table 3.

Table 3. Values of score functions for different membership values.

a	b	c	d	e	f	S_1	S_2	S_3
0.8	0.85	0.85	0.8	0.9	0.92	−0.753833	0.46999225	0.420965198
0.8	0.85	0.85	0.85	0.9	0.91	−0.792348	0.47961825	0.442667238
0.8	0.8	0.85	0.85	0.9	0.95	−0.8953125	0.479828125	0.439103631
0.8	0.85	0.82	0.85	0.9	0.91	−0.7609695	0.471773625	0.4243537
0.8	0.85	0.85	0.85	0.85	0.91	−0.7349105	0.465258875	0.406265978
0.85	0.9	0.8	0.8	0.8	0.85	−0.4545625	0.449421875	0.397060871

5. Applications of Interval-Valued Fermatean Neutrosophic Numbers

MCDM techniques are used to solve real-world problems in the context of uncertainty. There are two famous methods that help determine the solution to MCDM problems. The Analytical Hierarchy Process (AHP) is one of these two methods that can be used to analyze such problems by branching techniques to identify the best solution through the weight of the criterion. TOPSIS is another of the most popular MCDM models that helps select the best solutions. But in the AHP model, the number of criteria does not give clear information, whereas TOPSIS determines the ranking based on several criteria. In this technique, ideal values are either positive or negative based on the shortest and farthest distances.

In this section, we study the lecturer evaluation along with the $IVFN_{set}$. This study presents a ranking of the six different lecturers who work at one of the leading institutions in Tamil Nadu based on weighted performance evaluation criteria.

Anh Duc Do et al. [37] divided the criteria for evaluating the efficiency and talent of lecturers in an educational institution into four main groups: self-evaluation, manager valuation, peer evaluation, and student-based evaluation (Wu et al. [38]), as shown in the below Figure 3.

It is noted that the above-listed criteria may differ with respect to the infrastructure, level of students, salary given to the faculty, and workload of each institution. So, we have modified the above list of criteria and sub-criteria. We follow the following criteria structure for the lecturer evaluation in Figure 4 and Table 4:

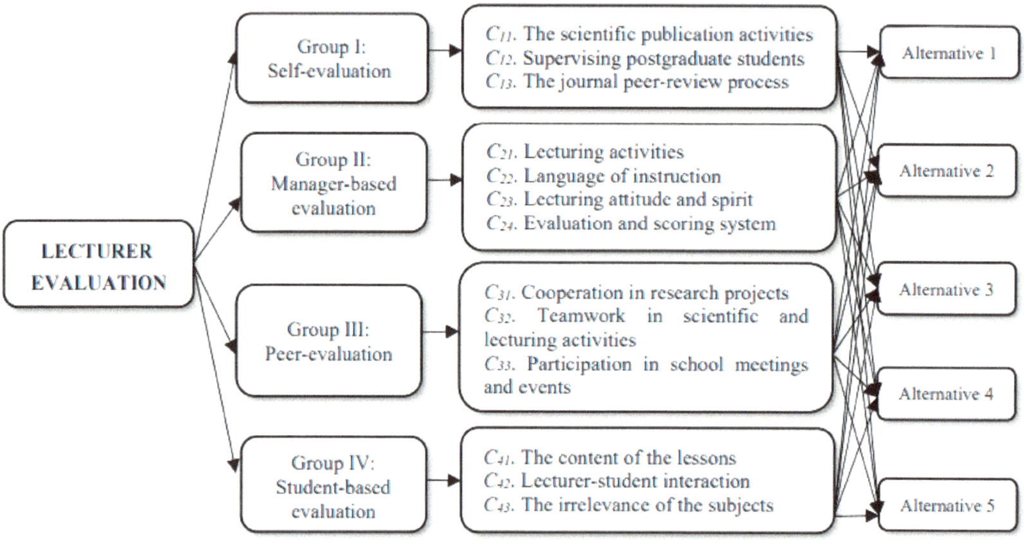

Figure 3. Lecturer evaluation—criteria.

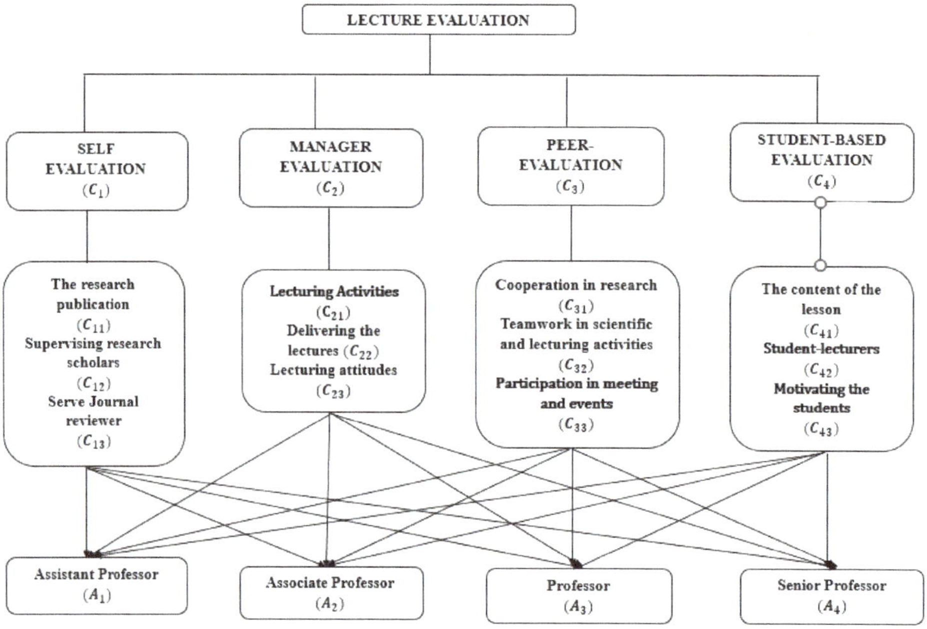

Figure 4. Modified criteria used in lecturer evaluation.

Table 4. Criteria and sub-criteria—Lecturer evaluation framework.

Name and Number Criteria	Description
Scientific publication (C_{11})	Faculty research publication in reputed journals is an important factor in the academic community in developing countries. The proportionality of the number of published articles in the last two years with the total in a year is measured by this criterion.
Supervising research scholars (C_{12})	Guiding the scholar is an essential criterion for the evaluation of a lecturer in any academic institution. Scholars expect their supervisors to be more efficient people and should have updated knowledge to perform their research activities. The number of scholars under a lecturer is also one of the key factors for this criterion. If the supervisor needs the minimum time to publish an article with their scholars, this reflects the capability of the lecturer.
Serve Journal reviewer (C_{13})	Becoming a peer reviewer in an indexed journal is one of the most important steps to reaching academic success as a lecturer. This will happen only when a lecturer has more knowledge in their research field. Lecturers' feedback about the submitted articles, suggestions to improve the article, and recommendations to the editors of the journal about the status of the articles.
Lecturing activities (C_{21})	It represents the number of hours a lecturer has spent teaching the subject to their students according to the allotted slot. In general, at the institutions, the duration of each lecture is about 50 mins to 1h. The number of publications can be considered with lecture time.
Language of instruction (C_{22})	This criterion measures the use of the lecturer's non-native language.
Lecturing attitude (C_{23})	Lecturing attitude includes coming to class late, canceling classes without a reason, etc.
Cooperation in research (internally funded) projects (C_{31})	Under this criterion, the lecturer gives importance to maintaining research records and involvement to reduce the time spent complementing the projects while also exchanging their knowledge.
Teamwork in scientific and teaching activities(C_{32})	This criterion includes the lecturer's contribution in various fields and the number of resources to increase the count of research publications as a team. Inter-department research publications contribute more to the institutional ranking system.
Participation in institutional meetings and events (C_{33})	Organizing institutional events like convocation, college day, scholarship day, and sports day will be successful only when lecturers build good relationships with their co-workers and students.
The content of the lessons (C_{41})	The teaching and learning process involves the quality of the teaching materials given, and lecturers should elaborate on real-world problems during their lectures.
Student–Lecturer (C_{42})	A healthy relationship between Lecturer–student includes the expectation that the lecturer should share their experience and knowledge among all the students without any special treatment or discrimination. Lecturers should maintain a decent relationship with their students and respect the decorum of their institution.
Motivating the students (C_{43})	Each lecturer acts as a mentor for at least a small group of students. Lecturers should advise the students regarding internal problems like the interactions of each student with their classmates, family issues, and disciplinary actions.

Using the TOPSIS method, the solution of the MCDM problem concludes the relationship between the shortest distance from the positive ideal solution and the farthest distance from the negative ideal solution. The ideal classical TOPSIS method can be presented using the following five levels:

Level 1: Construct the DM matrix $\left(C = [c_{ij}]_{m \times n}\right)$.

Level 2: Find the Normalized DM $\left(R = [r_{ij}]_{m \times n}\right)$.

Level 3: Find the $+ve$ and $-ve$ ideal solutions (PIS and NIS).

Level 4: Calculate the separation measures for both ideal solutions.

Level 5: Finalize the best alternative.

Any educational institution needs to evaluate the quality of the faculty members in the four different positions $A = (A_1, A_2, A_3, A_4)$ according to four criteria: self-evaluation (C_1), managerevaluation (C_2), peer evaluation (C_3), and student-based evaluation (C_4). In every appraisal of the institution, we must measure the quality and quantity of the work performed by different designations of the faculty members. This is mandatory for the gradual growth of the institution. Based on the past five years of data in an educational institution, we construct a decision matrix in terms of the Interval-valued Fermatean Neutrosophic values. Since measuring the faculty's strength is not based on an exact single value and these values fail under the uncertainty environment, we use $IVFF_{set}$. The past five years data was obtained through a questionnaire prepared and circulated among all faculty members at a leading education institute in south India.

Level 1: For a multiple attribute decision-making problem, let $C = (C_1, C_2, C_3, C_4)$ be a discrete set of alternatives. $A = (A_1, A_2, A_3, A_4)$ be the set of attributes. $W = (w_1, w_2, w_3, w_4)^T$ be the weighting vector of the attributes, and $\sum_{j=1}^{4} w_{j=1}$ where $\omega = (0.30, 0.30, 0.20)^T$ be unknown.

In ***Level 1***, the construct decision matrix, $C = [c_{ij}]_{m \times n}$ is the decision matrix, where $\langle [\mathcal{T}\mathbf{r}_A^-(\hbar), \mathcal{T}\mathbf{r}_A^+(\hbar)], [\mathcal{I}\mathbf{m}_A^-(\hbar), \mathcal{I}\mathbf{m}_A^+(\hbar)], [\mathcal{F}\mathbf{a}_A^-(\hbar), \mathcal{F}\mathbf{a}_A^+(\hbar)] \rangle$ and is in the form of the $IVFF_{set}$.

See in Table 5.

Table 5. Criteria and alternatives with interval-valued Fermatean Neutrosophic values.

Alternatives\ Criteria	A_1	A_2	A_3	A_4
C_1	([0.85, 0.90], [0.85, 0.85], [0.80, 0.80])	([0.85, 0.85], [0.85, 0.87], [0.83, 0.85])	([0.81, 0.91], [0.86, 0.89], [0.82, 0.86])	([0.87, 0.92], [0.85, 0.85], [0.80, 0.80])
C_2	([0.85, 0.91], [0.85, 0.86], [0.80, 0.84])	([0.82, 0.90], [0.80, 0.85], [0.80, 0.80])	([0.85, 0.92], [0.85, 0.85], [0.80, 0.83])	([0.85, 0.91], [0.80, 0.85], [0.81, 0.85])
C_3	([0.85, 0.93], [0.85, 0.87], [0.80, 0.81])	([0.85, 0.91], [0.81, 0.85], [0.80, 0.80])	([0.85, 0.91], [0.85, 0.87], [0.80, 0.82])	([0.80, 0.90], [0.85, 0.85], [0.80, 0.80])
C_4	([0.85, 0.94], [0.85, 0.88], [0.80, 0.82])	([0.85, 0.92], [0.82, 0.85], [0.80, 0.80])	([0.82, 0.92], [0.85, 0.85], [0.82, 0.82])	([0.80, 0.94], [0.83, 0.85], [0.80, 0.80])

That is, the DM matrix

$$C = \begin{pmatrix} ([0.85,0.90],[0.85,0.85],[0.80,0.80]) & ([0.85,0.85],[0.85,0.87],[0.83,0.85]) & ([0.81,0.91],[0.86,0.89],[0.82,0.86]) & ([0.87,0.92],[0.85,0.85],[0.80,0.80]) \\ ([0.85,0.91],[0.85,0.86],[0.80,0.84]) & ([0.82,0.90],[0.80,0.85],[0.80,0.80]) & ([0.85,0.92],[0.85,0.85],[0.80,0.83]) & ([0.85,0.91],[0.80,0.85],[0.81,0.85]) \\ ([0.85,0.93],[0.85,0.87],[0.80,0.81]) & ([0.85,0.91],[0.81,0.85],[0.80,0.80]) & ([0.85,0.91],[0.85,0.87],[0.80,0.82]) & ([0.80,0.90],[0.85,0.85],[0.80,0.80]) \\ ([0.85,0.94],[0.85,0.88],[0.80,0.82]) & ([0.85,0.92],[0.82,0.85],[0.80,0.80]) & ([0.82,0.92],[0.85,0.85],[0.82,0.82]) & ([0.80,0.94],[0.83,0.85],[0.80,0.80]) \end{pmatrix}$$

The numbers $([0.85,\ 0.90],\ [0.85,\ 0.85],\ [0.80,\ 0.80])$, corresponding to A_1 and C_1, represent that the degree of A_1 supports C_1, which lies in [0.85, 0.90], but the degree of A_1 does not support C_1, which lies in $[0.85,\ 0.85]$. Also, the degree of A_1 neutral to C_1, which lies in $[0.80,\ 0.80]$. All other degrees of alternativehave the same meaning.

In general, benefit and cost fall into these two categories. Normalize these values into a dimensionless matrix through which criteria can be compared easily. The construction of a Normalized Decision Matrix (NDM) is obtained at the next level by using the rule below:

$$R = [r_{ij}]_{m \times n} \text{ is the NDM, where } R = \begin{cases} d_{ij}, & if\ criterion\ C_{ij}\ is\ of\ the\ benefit\ type \\ \overline{d_{ij}}, & if\ criterion\ C_{ij}\ is\ of\ the\ cost\ type \end{cases}$$

$$\overline{d_{ij}} = \langle [\mathcal{F}_A^-(p), \mathcal{F}_A^+(p)], [1 - \mathcal{I}_A^-(p), 1 - \mathcal{I}_A^+(p)], [\mathcal{T}_A^-(p), \mathcal{T}_A^+(p)] \rangle$$

Level 2: As the criteria of C_2 and C_4 are the cost criteria and C_1 and C_3 are the benefit criteria, the NFM-DM of R is given by

$$R = \begin{pmatrix} ([0.85,0.90],[0.85,0.85],[0.80,0.80]) & ([0.83,0.85],[0.15,0.13],[0.85,0.85]) & ([0.81,0.91],[0.86,0.89],[0.82,0.86]) & ([0.80,0.80],[0.15,0.15],[0.87,0.92]) \\ ([0.85,0.91],[0.85,0.86],[0.80,0.84]) & ([0.80,0.80],[0.20,0.15],[0.82,0.90]) & ([0.85,0.92],[0.85,0.85],[0.80,0.83]) & ([0.81,0.85],[0.20,0.15],[0.85,0.91]) \\ ([0.85,0.93],[0.85,0.87],[0.80,0.81]) & ([0.80,0.80],[0.19,0.15],[0.85,0.91]) & ([0.85,0.91],[0.85,0.87],[0.80,0.82]) & ([0.80,0.80],[0.15,0.15],[0.80,0.90]) \\ ([0.85,0.94],[0.85,0.88],[0.80,0.82]) & ([0.80,0.90],[0.18,0.15],[0.85,0.92]) & ([0.82,0.92],[0.85,0.85],[0.82,0.82]) & ([0.80,0.80],[0.17,0.15],[0.80,0.94]) \end{pmatrix}$$

Level 3: Converting R into their collective score matrix—using $S_3(\alpha)$

$$M = \begin{pmatrix} 0.3919 & 0.4892 & 0.4397 & 0.4183 \\ 0.4224 & 0.4412 & 0.4208 & 0.4548 \\ 0.4280 & 0.4273 & 0.4170 & 0.4505 \\ 0.4458 & 0.4665 & 0.4056 & 0.4319 \end{pmatrix}$$

Level 4: In this level, ideal solutions consist of selecting the best values for each attribute from all alternatives.

Generally, the values of l^+ are complements of l^- and vice versa. The degree of l^+ to 1 and 0 is fixed, but the decision-maker may vary it. Hence, we consider $IVFNPI_{set}l^+$ and $IVFNNI_{set}l^-$ as follows:

$$l^+ = \langle [\max(a_{ij}), \max(b_{ij})]; [\min(c_{ij}), \min(d_{ij})]; [\min(e_{ij}), \min(f_{ij})] \rangle$$
$$l^- = \langle [\min(a_{ij}), \min(b_{ij})]; [\max(c_{ij}), \max(d_{ij})]; [\max(e_{ij}), \max(f_{ij})] \rangle \text{among all attributes.}$$

The PIS and NIS of two alternatives are found as

$$\begin{aligned} l^+ &= \{\langle [0.85,0.94]; [0.82,0.85]; [0.80,0.80] \rangle, \langle [0.85,0.92]; [0.80,0.85]; [0.80,0.80] \rangle, \\ &\quad \langle [0.85,0.92]; [0.85,0.85]; [0.80,0.82] \rangle, \langle [0.87,0.94]; [0.80,0.85]; [0.80,0.80] \rangle\} \\ l^- &= \{\langle [0.85,0.90]; [0.85,0.88]; [0.80,0.84] \rangle, \langle [0.82,0.85]; [0.85,0.87]; [0.83,0.85] \rangle, \\ &\quad \langle [0.81,0.91]; [0.86,0.89]; [0.83,0.86] \rangle, \langle [0.80,0.90]; [0.85,0.85]; [0.81,0.85] \rangle \\ S_3(l^+) &= (0.4127 \quad 0.3537 \quad 0.4161 \quad 0.4194) \\ S_3(l^-) &= (0.4245 \quad 0.3593 \quad 0.4459 \quad 0.3863) \end{aligned}$$

The distance between A_i and the ideal solution is calculated in ***level 5***

$$M_i^+ = \sum_{j=1}^{n} d\left(A_{ij}, A_j^+\right) = \sqrt{\sum_{j=1}^{n} \left[w_j (S_3(l^+) - S_3(r_{ij}))^2\right]^2}^2$$
$$M_i^- = \sum_{j=1}^{n} d\left(A_{ij}, A_j^-\right) = \sqrt{\sum_{j=1}^{n} \left[w_j (S_3(r_{ij}) - S_3(l^-))^2\right]^2}^2$$

Level 5: To compute the closeness coefficient (CC):

$$CC_K = \frac{M_K^-}{M_K^- + M_K^+}, K = 1,2,3,4$$

See in Table 6.

Table 6. Closeness coefficient for each alternative.

B_i	M_i^+	M_i^-	CC_i
A_1	0.0055	0.0051	0.4793
A_2	0.0023	0.0022	0.4902
A_3	0.0016	0.0071	0.8134
A_4	0.0038	0.0597	0.9396

Level 6: Based on the values of C_i, we rank the alternatives and select the best alternative(s). Therefore, the final and optimized ranking of the four major alternatives is $A_4 \succ A_3 \succ A_2 \succ A_1$, and thus, the best alternative is A_4.

6. Results and Discussion

In this approach, we describe a combination of quantitative assessment and multi-criteria decision-making models to evaluate lecturers' performances from various perspectives: self-assessment, peer assessment, managerial assessment, and student-based evaluation. This approach aims to overcome the challenge of differentiating between lecturers' potential capacities and their actual teaching effectiveness. In our article, we have introduced a new variant of the $\boldsymbol{N_{set}}$ called Interval-Valued Fermatean Neutrosophic Set ($\boldsymbol{IVFN_{set}}$). This new variant specifically deals with situations where there is partial ignorance, leading to uncertainty about whether something is true, false, or exists in an uncertain region. This concept is applied independently to a multi-decision process. This study expands upon the concept of Fermatean Neutrosophic Set ($\boldsymbol{FN_{set}}$), presenting an extension in the form of the $\boldsymbol{IVFN_{set}}$. The article highlights the algebraic properties and set theoretical aspects of the $\boldsymbol{IVFN_{set}}$, likely discussing how this new variant handles and represents partial ignorance in more detail. This research appears to be addressing a crucial challenge in education by proposing an innovative approach that considers various assessment perspectives and handles uncertainty effectively through the $\boldsymbol{IVFN_{set}}$. The presented results highlight the practical application and effectiveness of our methodology in making informed decisions about lecturers' performances.

Faculty evaluation is a crucial component of higher education institutions and plays a significant role in shaping educational goals and national development strategies. Evaluating faculty performance is essential for maintaining teaching competency, promoting scientific research, and creating a conducive learning environment. The importance of evaluating faculty performance in terms of teaching competency as a tool for decision-making, including employment and dismissal in this assessment, is seen as a means to ensure the quality of education and contribute to the overall development of the country's education system. Higher educational institutions should function as scientific research centers and encourage faculty to engage in research activities. This dual role of teaching and research contributes to the institution's credibility and the advancement of knowledge. Faculty evaluation is seen as a way to create an equal environment that fosters cooperative strategies among faculty members and nurtures the learning spirit of each student. This suggests that a well-structured evaluation system can positively impact the overall educational atmosphere. Assessing faculty performance provides a comprehensive perspective on the institution's achievements, including improving learning outcomes, identifying and nurturing young talents, and indirectly contributing to the country's wealth. Such assessments also establish the institution's reputation at both global and local levels. The evaluation process involves various complex factors such as personal interests, development strategies, and fairness in assessment. It is acknowledged that fair and accurate assessment is challenging and requires a multi-dimensional approach, including input from principals/managers, students, and peer reviews. The absence of appropriate standards and tools can lead to inaccuracies and subjectivity in evaluating faculty competence. We suggest that a well-rounded, multi-dimensional assessment process can enhance faculty knowledge, teaching capabilities, and professional development. As a whole, the multi-faceted nature of faculty evaluation, its significance in the educational landscape, and the challenges associated with implementing a fair and effective assessment system place an emphasis on considering local context, fostering research, and promoting a cooperative learning environment. This underscores the holistic approach required to evaluate and enhance faculty performance in higher education institutions.

The criteria and methods used in a Multi-Criteria Decision-Making (MCDM) process assess the performance and relative importance of lecturers. We have mentioned two popular MCDM models—the Analytical Hierarchy Process (AHP) and the Technique for Order Preference by Similarity to Ideal Solution (TOPSIS)—that are commonly used to handle such assessments. The assessment process involves evaluating lecturers based on standards related to research capacity, teaching capacity, and service activities. These criteria are likely important aspects in determining the overall performance of lecturers.

MCDM involves making decisions based on multiple criteria that might be conflicting or competing. It is a way to handle complex decision scenarios that cannot be addressed using single criteria. AHP is a widely used MCDM method that breaks down complex problems into a hierarchical structure of criteria and sub-criteria. It allows assigning weights to these criteria based on their relative importance and then comparing alternatives based on these weighted criteria. AHP is particularly useful for dealing with structured problems and hierarchical decision contexts. The application of Neutrosophic Sets and related concepts in the context of lecturer evaluation uses Multi-Criteria Decision-Making (MCDM) techniques. Smarandache [2] introduced the concept of a Neutrosophic Set, which is characterized by three membership degrees: truth membership (T), indeterminacy membership (I), and falsity membership (F). These membership degrees are defined within the real standard or nonstandard unit interval. This concept allows for dealing with uncertainty and imprecision in various domains, including education. Neutrosophic Sets can be applied to educational problems when dealing with ranges that fall within the defined interval. This approach can help address issues related to imprecision and uncertainty in educational contexts. Wang et al. [3] introduced the concepts of a single-valued Neutrosophic Set and an interval-valued Neutrosophic Set. The interval-valued Neutrosophic Set extends the concept of the Neutrosophic Set by incorporating interval values for the membership degrees. This approach has been used in various fields, including decision-making sciences, social sciences, and the humanities, to handle problems involving vague, indeterminate, and inconsistent information. Ye [31] introduced the interval Neutrosophic Linguistic Set, which involves new aggregation operators for interval Neutrosophic linguistic information. This concept contributes to handling uncertain linguistic information. Broumi et al. [39] extended the TOPSIS (Technique for Order Preference by Similarity to Ideal Solution) method to accommodate uncertain linguistic information within interval Neutrosophic Sets. This extension allows for decision-making when dealing with complex and uncertain data. The passage highlights that there is a lack of research integrating hierarchical TOPSIS with interval Fermatean Neutrosophic Sets, especially in the context of lecturer evaluation. This integration could address the limitations of traditional approaches to evaluating lecturers, which often face complexity and uncertainty. The study presented in the passage focuses on evaluating lecturers using MCDM models. The goal is to combine the hierarchical Neutrosophic TOPSIS technique, and the interval-valued complex set in a Neutrosophic environment to improve lecturer evaluation. The application of Neutrosophic Sets and related concepts to address the challenges of uncertainty and imprecision in lecturer evaluation uses MCDM techniques. By combining these innovative approaches, this study aims to provide a more effective and robust framework for assessing and ranking lecturers' performances.

Comparing with other models: The following table lists the results of the comparison. The proposed method and the classic TOPSIS method can solve problems in uncertain environments. However, the TOPSIS and AHP techniques have some disadvantages in terms of calculation methods and results. Moreover, the extent of the interval-valued Neutrosophic TOPSIS does not consider the capacity of each lecturer in the specific time period.

Method	Ranking
Interval neutrosophic TOPSIS (Chi and Liu [40]). Chi, P., and Liu, P. (2013). An extended TOPSIS method for the multiple attribute decision making problems based on interval neutrosophic set. Neutrosophic Sets and Systems, 1, 1–8.	$A_2 > A_3 > A_5 > A_1 > A_4$
AHP (Saaty [41]) Saaty, T. L. (1980). The analytic hierarchy process. New York, NY: McGraw-Hill Inc, 17–34.	$A_3 > A_2 > A_5 > A_4 > A_1$

Method	Ranking
TOPSIS (Hwang and Yoon [26]) Hwang, C.-L., and Yoon, K. (1981). Multiple Attribute Decision Making: Methods and Applications A State-of-the-Art Survey. Berlin Heidelberg: Springer-Verlag.	$A_3 > A_2 > A_5 > A_4 > A_1$
Interval complex Neutrosophic set (Anh Duc Doet al. [36]) Anh Duc Doa, Minh Tam Pham, Thi Hang Dinh, The Chi Ngo, Quoc Dat Luue, Ngoc Thach Phamf, Dieu Linh Hag, and Hong Nhat Vuong, Evaluation of lecturers' performance using a novel hierarchical multi-criteria model based on an interval complex Neutrosophic set, Decision Science Letters 9 (2020) 119–14.	$A_1 > A_3 > A_2 > A_5 > A_4$
The present work evaluates the quality of the faculty members in the four different positions $\boldsymbol{A} = (\boldsymbol{A}_1, \boldsymbol{A}_2, \boldsymbol{A}_3, \boldsymbol{A}_4)$ according to four criteria, namely self-evaluation $(\boldsymbol{C}_1)$, managerevaluation $(\boldsymbol{C}_2)$, peer evaluation $(\boldsymbol{C}_3)$, and student-based evaluation $(\boldsymbol{C}_4)$.	$A_4 \succ A_3 \succ A_2 \succ A_1$

7. Conclusions

In this article, our study developed a comprehensive assessment methodology using a hierarchical structure and a hierarchical TOPSIS (Technique for Order of Preference by Similarity to Ideal Solution) approach, incorporating interval-valued complex Neutrosophic Sets for evaluating lecturer capability. The goals of this study seem to include addressing the potential competition between lecturers that can arise from such evaluations and ensuring fairness and transparency in the process. This study's methodology is designed to handle the complexity of assessment and decision-making in education and management systems. The hierarchical approach is then compared with other related methods to highlight its advantages and practicality. The results indicate that the proposed approach is effective and not limited to just lecturer evaluation; it can potentially be applied to other decision-making problems as well. However, as mentioned, there are certain limitations to this study. Unfortunately, you have not specified what those limitations are. Nonetheless, you also mentioned that future work is proposed to enhance the accuracy of lecturer evaluation. This improvement could be valuable for supporting real-world, dynamic decision-making in educational contexts. In summary, this study appears to contribute a novel approach to lecturer evaluation using a hierarchical structure and TOPSIS methodology, with an emphasis on fairness and transparency. The results suggest its efficiency and broader applicability, though there are acknowledged limitations that may guide future research.

This paper introduces the concept of the $\boldsymbol{IVFN_{set}}$ and its algebraic properties with an example. Also, we introduce a new set of score functions for the $\boldsymbol{IVFN_{set}}$ and use these functions to evaluate the lectures' performances that were studied.

8. Further Study

1. To define interval-valued Fermatean Neutrosophic Numbers.
2. To study the interval-valued Triangular Fermatean Neutrosophic Linear Programming Problem.
3. To study the interval-valued Fermatean trapezoidal and Fermatean triangular Neutrosophic numbers.

Author Contributions: Conceptualization, R.S. and M.S.; methodology, R.S.; validation, R.S., M.S., and S.B.; formal analysis, S.B. and M.T.; investigation, S.B. and M.V.; writing—original draft preparation, R.S.; writing—review and editing, S.B. and M.V; visualization, P.K.S. All authors have read and agreed to the published version of the manuscript.

Funding: There is no funding for this paper.

Data Availability Statement: Not applicable.

Acknowledgments: The authors thank the anonymous reviewers for their valuable comments and suggestions.

Conflicts of Interest: The authors declare no conflict of interest.

References

1. Zadeh, L.A. Fuzzy sets. *Inf. Control* **1965**, *8*, 338–353. [CrossRef]
2. Smarandache, F. Neutrosophic set—A generalization of the intuitionistic fuzzy set. *Int. J. Pure Appl. Math.* **2005**, *24*, 287–297. [CrossRef]
3. Wang, H.; Smarandache, F.; Sunderraman, R.; Zhang, Y.Q. Single valued neutrosophic sets. *Multispace Multistruct.* **2010**, *4*, 410–413.
4. Wang, H.; Smarandache, F.; Sunderraman, R.; Zhang, Y.Q. Interval neutrosophic sets and logic: Theory and applications in computing: Theory and applications in computing. *Infin. Study* **2005**, *5*, 21–38.
5. Yager, R.R. Pythagorean fuzzy subsets. In Proceedings of the Joint IFSA World Congress and NAFIPS Annual Meeting, Edmonton, AB, Canada, 24–28 June 2013.
6. Yager, R.R.; Abbasov, A.M. Pythagorean membership grades, complex numbers, and decision-making. *Int. J. Intell. Syst.* **2013**, *28*, 436–452. [CrossRef]
7. Yager, R.R. Pythagorean membership grades in multi-criteria decision-making. *IEEE Trans. Fuzzy Syst.* **2014**, *22*, 958–965. [CrossRef]
8. Jansi, R.; Mohana, K.; Smarandache, F. Correlation Measure for Pythagorean Neutrosophic Sets with T and F as Dependent Neutrosophic Components. *Neutrosophic Sets Syst.* **2019**, *30*, 16.
9. Garg, H. A novel accuracy function under interval-valued Pythagorean fuzzy environment for solving multicriteria decision making problem. *J. Intell. Fuzzy Syst.* **2016**, *31*, 529–540. [CrossRef]
10. Senapati, T.; Yager, R. Fermatean Fuzzy Sets. *J. Ambient Intell. Humaniz. Comput.* **2019**, *11*, 663–674. [CrossRef]
11. Sweety, C.A.C.; Jansi, R. Fermatean Neutrosophic Sets. *Int. J. Adv. Res. Comput. Commun. Eng.* **2021**, *10*, 24–27.
12. Peng, X.; Yang, Y. Fundamental Properties of Interval-Valued Pythagorean Fuzzy Aggregation Operators. *Int. J. Intell. Syst.* **2016**, *31*, 444–487. [CrossRef]
13. Stephen, S.; Helen, M. Interval-valued Neutrosophic Pythagorean Sets and their Application in decision-making using IVNP-TOPSIS. *Int. J. Innov. Res. Sci. Eng. Technol. (IJIRSET)* **2021**, *10*, 114571–114578.
14. Thamizhendhi, G.; Kiruthica, C.; Suresh, S. Fematean fuzzy hypergraph. *J. Hunan Univ. Nat. Sci.* **2021**, *48*, 2333–2340.
15. Rani, P.; Mishra, A.R. Interval-valued fermatean fuzzy sets with multi-criteria weighted aggregated sum product assessment-based decision analysis framework. *Neural Comput. Appl.* **2022**, *34*, 8051–8067. [CrossRef] [PubMed]
16. Jeevaraj, S. Ordering of interval-valued Fermatean fuzzy sets and its applications. *Expert Syst. Appl.* **2021**, *185*, 115613. [CrossRef]
17. Palanikumar, M.; Iampan, A. Spherical Fermatean Interval Valued Fuzzy Soft Set Based on Multi Criteria Group decision-making. *ICIC Int.* **2022**, *18*, 607–619.
18. Liu, D.; Liu, Y.; Chen, X. Fermatean fuzzy linguistic set and its application in multicriteria decision making. *Int. J. Intell. Syst.* **2018**, *34*, 878–894. [CrossRef]
19. Broumi, S.; Sundareswaran, R.; Shanmugapriya, M.; Nordo, G.; Talea, M.; Bakali, A.; Smarandache, F. *Interval-Valued Fermatean Neutrosophic Graphs, Decision-Making: Applications in Management and Engineering*; SCImago Journal Rank: Belgrade, Serbia, 2022.
20. Gorzałczany, M.B. A method of inference in approximate reasoning based on interval-valued fuzzy sets. *Fuzzy Sets Syst.* **1987**, *21*, 1–17. [CrossRef]
21. Zhang, H.Y.; Wang, J.Q.; Chen, X.H. Interval neutrosophic sets and their application in multicriteria decision-making problems. *Sci. World J.* **2014**, *15*, 645953. [CrossRef]
22. Wang, T. The Projection Model with Unknown Weight Information under Interval Neutrosophic Environment and Its Application to Software Quality-in-Use Evaluation. *Math. Probl. Eng.* **2020**, *2020*, 7279420. [CrossRef]
23. Broumi, S.; Sundareswaran, R.; Shanmugapriya, M.; Bakali, A.; Talea, M. Theory and Applications of Fermatean Neutrosophic Graphs. *Neutrosophic Sets Syst.* **2022**, *50*, 248–286.
24. Singh, A.; Bhat, S.A. A novel score and accuracy function for neutrosophic sets and their real-world applications to multi-criteria decision-making process. *Neutrosophic Sets Syst.* **2021**, *41*, 168–197.
25. Garg, H. A novel correlation coefficient between pythagorean fuzzy sets and its applications to decision-making processes. *Int. J. Intell. Syst.* **2016**, *31*, 1234–1253. [CrossRef]
26. Hwang, C.L.; Yoon, K. *Multiple Attribute Decision-Making*; Springer: Berlin, Germany, 1981.
27. Nayagam, V.L.G.; Jeevaraj, S.; Sivaraman, G. Complete Ranking of Intuitionistic Fuzzy Numbers. *Fuzzy Inf. Eng.* **2008**, *8*, 1971–1974. [CrossRef]
28. Nayagam, V.L.G.; Jeevaraj, S.; Dhanasekaran, P. An intuitionistic fuzzy multi-criteria decision-making method based on non-hesitance score for interval-valued intuitionistic fuzzy sets. *Soft Comput.* **2018**, *21*, 7077–7082. [CrossRef]
29. Xu, Z.S. Method for aggregating interval-valued intuitionistic fuzzy information and their application to decision-making. *Control. Decis.* **2007**, *22*, 1179–1187.

30. Liu, Y.; Xie, N. Amelioration operators of fuzzy number intuitionistic fuzzy geometric and their application to Multi-criteria decision making. In Proceedings of the 2009 Chinese Control and Decision Conference, Guilin, China, 17–19 June 2009; pp. 6172–6176. [CrossRef]
31. Ye, J. A multicriteria decision-making method using aggregation operators for simplified neutrosophic sets. *J. Intell. Fuzzy Syst.* **2014**, *26*, 2459–2466. [CrossRef]
32. Ye, J. Multicriteria decision-making method using the correlation coefficient under single-value neutrosophic environment. *Int. J. Gen. Syst.* **2013**, *42*, 386–439. [CrossRef]
33. Garg, H. Generalized intuitionistic fuzzy multiplicative interactive geometric operators and their application to multiple criteria decision-making. *Int. J. Machine Learn. Cybern.* **2016**, *7*, 1075–1092. [CrossRef]
34. Sahin, R. Multi-criteria neutrosophic decision-making method based on score and accuracy functions under neutrosophic environment. *arXiv* **2014**, arXiv:1412.5202.
35. Garg, H. An Improved Score Function for Ranking Neutrosophic Sets and Its Application to Decision-Making Process. *Int. J. Uncertain. Quantif.* **2016**, *6*, 377–385. [CrossRef]
36. Sahoo, L. Similarity measures for Fermatean fuzzy sets and its applications in group decision-making. *Decis. Sci. Lett.* **2022**, *11*, 167–180.
37. Do, A.D.; Pham, M.T.; Dinh, T.H.; Ngo, T.C.; Luu, Q.D.; Pham, N.T.; Ha, D.L.; Vuong, H.N. Evaluation of lecturers' performance using a novel hierarchical multi-criteria model based on an interval complex Neutrosophic set. *Decis. Sci. Lett.* **2020**, 119–144. [CrossRef]
38. Wu, H.-Y.; Chen, J.-K.; Chen, I.-S.; Zhuo, H.-H. Ranking universities based on performance evaluation by a hybrid MCDM model. *Measurement* **2012**, *45*, 856–880. [CrossRef]
39. Broumi, S.; Ye, J.; Smarandache, F. An Extended TOPSIS Method for Multiple Attribute Decision Making based on Interval Neutrosophic Uncertain Linguistic Variables. *Neutrosophic Sets Syst.* **2015**, *8*, 22–31.
40. Chi, P.; Liu, P. An Extended TOPSIS Method for the Multiple Attribute Decision Making Problems Based on Interval Neutrosophic Set. *Neutrosophic Sets Syst.* **2013**, *1*, 63–70.
41. Saaty, T.L. *The Analytic Hierarchy Process*; McGraw-Hill: New York, NY, USA, 1980.

mathematics

Article

Modeling and Verification of Uncertain Cyber-Physical System Based on Decision Processes †

Na Chen [1], Shengling Geng [1,2,3,*] and Yongming Li [1,4]

1 The College of Computer, Qinghai Normal University, Xining 810008, China; chenna@snnu.edu.cn (N.C.); liyongm@snnu.edu.cn (Y.L.)
2 Academy of Plateau Science and Sustainability, People's Government of Qinghai Province & Beijing Normal University, Xining 810004, China
3 The State Key Laboratory of Tibetan Intelligent Information Processing and Application, Qinghai Normal University, Xining 810008, China
4 School of Mathematics and Computer Science, Shanxi Normal University, Xi'an 710062, China
* Correspondence: geng_sl@126.com

† This paper is an extension version of the conference paper: Chen, N.; Geng, S.; Li, L. Modeling and verification of CPS based on uncertain hybrid timed automaton. In Proceedings of the 6th IEEE Cyber Science and Technology Congress (CyberSciTech 2021), Special Session on Intelligent Computing in Cyber-Physical Social Systems (CyberIC), Calgary, AB, Canada, 25–28 October 2021.

Abstract: Currently, there is uncertainty in the modeling techniques of cyber-physical systems (CPS) when faced with the multiple possibilities and distributions of complex system behavior. This uncertainty leads to the system's inability to handle uncertain data correctly, resulting in lower reliability of the system model. Additionally, existing technologies struggle to verify the activity and safety of CPS after modeling, lacking a dynamic verification and analysis approach for uncertain CPS properties.This paper introduces a generalized possibility decision process as a system model. Firstly, the syntax and semantics of generalized possibility temporal logic with decision processes are defined. Uncertain CPS is extended by modeling it based on time-based differential equations and uncertainty hybrid time automaton. After that, model checking is performed on the properties of activity and safety using fuzzy linear time properties. Finally, a cold–hot hybrid constant-temperature system model is used for simulation experiments. By combining theory and experiments, this paper provides a new approach to the verification of uncertain CPS, effectively addressing the state explosion problem. It plays a crucial role in the design of uncertain CPS and offers a key solution for model checking in the presence of uncertainty.

Keywords: cyber-physical system; uncertain hybrid timed automaton; generalized possibilistic decision processes; scheduler; activity; safety; Ptolemy II; modeling; simulation

MSC: 68Q10

Citation: Chen, N.; Geng, S.; Li, Y. Modeling and Verification of Uncertain Cyber-Physical System Based on Decision Processes. *Mathematics* **2023**, *11*, 4122. https://doi.org/10.3390/math11194122

Academic Editor: Michael Voskoglou

Received: 21 August 2023
Revised: 24 September 2023
Accepted: 26 September 2023
Published: 29 September 2023

1. Introduction

The cyber-physical system (CPS) is a cutting-edge technology that combines computing, communication, and remote control functions [1,2]. It represents the latest advancement in complex embedded information and physical network systems [3]. The CPS comprises three main components: the physical entity, computing entity, and interactive entity [4], as illustrated in Figure 1. By incorporating artificial intelligence (AI) into its hardware, the CPS enables automatic control, decision-making, and judgment capabilities, thereby influencing both the computing entities and physical entities through a feedback mechanism. Furthermore, the CPS facilitates human–computer interaction [5] to achieve optimal outcomes.

Model checking [6,7], as a formal and automatic verification technique, has found extensive applications in diverse domains such as computer software and hardware systems, communication protocols, control systems, and security authentication protocols. During the verification process of complex concurrent systems, it is common to encounter uncertain and inconsistent information. For instance, complex computing tasks generated by autonomous vehicles in intelligent autonomous transport systems [8], among others. Classic model checking, which is based on the probability measure, may face challenges when dealing with uncertain verification problems in practical systems [7]. While it has been widely used for analyzing and verifying stochastic systems [9], there are situations where non-additivity problems arise, and these cannot be adequately addressed or measured by traditional probability-based models.

To overcome these limitations, Li et al. [10,11] proposed a possibility measure-based model-checking approach. The possibility measure is a branch of fuzzy set theory and a generalization of the probability measure. Unlike the probability measure, the possibility measure does not adhere to the principle of additivity. In their approach, Li et al. apply fuzzy mathematics, which is rooted in the possibility measure, to model checking [12]. By doing so, they provide a framework for analyzing and verifying uncertain systems that cannot be effectively measured or verified using traditional probability models. The possibility measure-based model-checking approach allows for a more flexible handling of uncertainty by considering the degree of membership or likelihood of events occurring. This approach expands the range of problems that can be addressed and provides an alternative method for analyzing and verifying stochastic systems in practical scenarios where non-additivity problems arise.

A lot of quantitative model-checking techniques have been proposed in the modeling of a system with uncertain information [13], but there are still some important unsolved issues. The problem lies in the uncertainty of system behavior when confronted with multiple possibilistic distributions of complex systems. For example, multi-agent systems possess complex dynamic structures and behavioral characteristics, necessitating the incorporation of additional quantifiable information to depict their dynamic behavioral features [14,15]. Moreover, these possibilistic distributions are not always measurable. The purpose of modeling is to interface with the environment by uncertain actions to satisfy the properties of the system. Thus, it is necessary to consider the uncertain information of those actions. In order to permit both possibilistic and uncertain choices, we introduce the notion of generalized possibilistic decision processes (GPDP) and schedulers selecting actions that will be performed [16]. The GPDP serves as a theoretical foundation for the uncertainty verification of complex systems by enabling transitions between states to satisfy multiple possibilistic distributions.

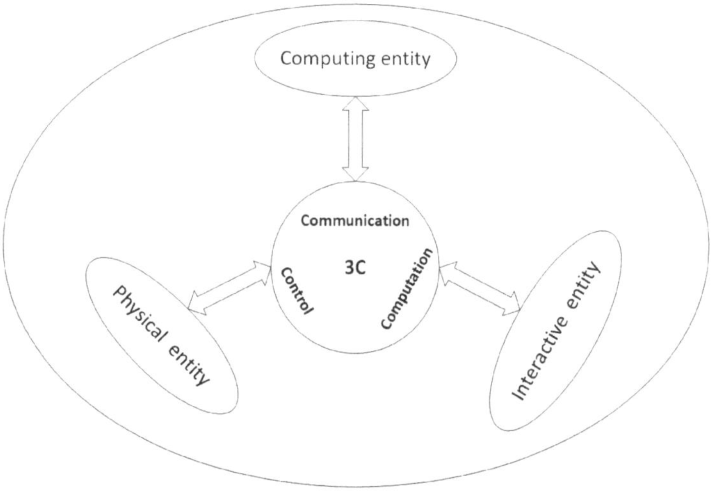

Figure 1. CPS structure.

Ptolemy II is an open-source simulation modeling tool that has gained popularity for its ability to address challenges related to uncertainty modeling, management, and optimal decision control in CPS [3]. While other tools like Simulink/Stateflow and UML are widely used, their close integration and lack of specialized features make it difficult to effectively handle uncertainty in CPS. Ptolemy II [17], developed by researchers at UC Berkeley, offers a comprehensive solution for system design, modeling, and simulation in hierarchical and heterogeneous systems. It provides powerful functionalities and a design environment that supports the entire development phase. This integrated approach allows for a smooth transition from a conceptual model to a real system design, resulting in a shorter design process and improved component reuse. By leveraging Ptolemy II, designers and researchers can enhance the consistency between the authenticity of the system and its simulation results [18]. This capability is crucial for validating the performance and behavior of complex CPS, where uncertainty and dynamic interactions play a significant role.

The main contributions of this paper include the following aspects:

(1) Construct a CPS system model based on the generalized possibility decision process, and define the CPS syntax and semantics of the generalized possibility linear temporal logic in the CPS system model;
(2) By introducing clock invariants, the extended modeling of CPS system model is carried out based on differential equations of time and uncertainty hybrid time automaton, and the uncertain CPS extended model is obtained;
(3) Based on the possibility measure theory and the CPS syntax and semantics of generalized possibility linear temporal logic, the activity and security of the uncertain CPS extended model are verified dynamically, and the execution path of the uncertain CPS extended model is optimized according to the dynamic verification results;
(4) Used preset modeling tools to model and simulate the uncertain CPS extended model, analyze the CPS dynamic execution process of the uncertain CPS extended model, and refine the dynamic behavior output of the uncertain CPS extended model based on the analysis results of the CPS dynamic execution process.

This article includes the following sections, excluding the present introduction. In Section 2, the necessary basic concepts and definitions are provided. In Section 3, the semantics of the generalized possibility decision process are presented. In Section 4, the CPS syntax and semantics of generalized possibility linear temporal logic are defined. Section 5 introduces clock invariants to extend the uncertainty CPS. In Section 6, a dynamic verification analysis is carried out on the attributes of uncertain CPS. Section 7 uses preset modeling tools to model and simulate the extended model of uncertain CPS. Finally, our overall conclusions are presented in Section 8.

2. Preliminaries

In this section, we give some basic knowledge about the hybrid system and the generalized possibility theory introduced in [10,12].

2.1. Hybrid System

A hybrid system is a type of system that combines continuous dynamics and discrete events. It represents a system where both continuous processes, such as physical processes governed by differential equations, and discrete events, such as state changes or mode switches, are present. This combination allows for the modeling and analysis of complex systems that exhibit both continuous and discrete behaviors. A hybrid automaton is commonly used to describe the system's behavior. A hybrid automaton is a mathematical model that captures the dynamics of a hybrid system. In the context of CPS, a hybrid system typically refers to a system that integrates physical processes with computational and communication elements. It can be defined as follows.

Definition 1 (see [19]). *A hybrid automaton can be represented by a six-element tuple, denoted as* $H = (I, O, T, Init, M, E)$, *where:*

(1) *I: The set of input ports represents external signals or inputs that can influence the behavior of the automaton. These inputs can trigger state transitions or affect the continuous dynamics of the system.*
(2) *O: The set of output ports represents the signals or information that the automaton produces as a result of its internal dynamics and interactions with the environment. These outputs could be measurements, control signals, or any relevant information about the system.*
(3) *T: The set of state variables represents the internal variables or parameters that define the state of the system, which capture the internal state of the system and can change continuously over time. The state set* Q_T *is a mathematical representation of all possible values that these variables can take.*
(4) *Init: This component is responsible for initializing the distribution operation within the hybrid automaton. It sets the initial conditions or constraints on the state variables.*
(5) *M: The set of control modes represents different operational modes or behaviors that the automaton can exhibit. Each control mode specifies a set of continuous dynamics and discrete transitions that govern the system's behavior in that mode.*
(6) *E: The set of internal actions represents the transformational relations between between different control modes or states in the hybrid automaton. They describe the instantaneous transitions or jumps between modes that can occur based on certain conditions or events.*

Remark 1. *The port mentioned in the definition facilitates communication between the system and its external environment. The communication port operates in two modes: read and write, which are denoted by "?" and "!", respectively. For example, "port?" indicates input data received by the port, while "port!" represents output data transmitted by the port.*

Our hybrid process model is built upon extensive research on the hybrid automaton, which is considered as an encapsulated intelligent agent [20,21]. This research focuses on developing a formal model for hybrid systems by combining discrete transition systems with differential equations. By incorporating continuous evolution and discrete updating, CPS are capable of representing real-world scenarios and describing the system's state transition relationships [22]. As a result, the hybrid automaton assumes a crucial role in establishing a strong foundation for CPS studies.

2.2. Generalized Possibility Theory

Possibility measure theory [23] deals with the incomplete information and uncertain information of the system. Unlike probability measure theory, possibility measure theory contains possibility measure and necessity measure, which can deal with fine information better. In addition, the possibility measure is non-additive, to deal with the practical application system makes more sense.

Definition 2 (see [16]). *Let us assume that* U *is a nonempty set with measurable subsets. In this context, a possibility measure is defined as a function* Π *from the power set* 2^U *to the interval* $[0, 1]$ *with the following properties.*

(1) $\Pi(\varnothing) = 0$;
(2) $\Pi(U) = 1$;
(3) $\Pi(\bigcup E_i) = \bigvee \Pi(E_i)$.

For any subset family $\{E_i\}$ *of the universe set* U, *we can denote the supremum or least upper bound of the real number family* $\{a_i\}_{i\in I}$ *as* $\bigvee_{i\in I} a_i$. *Similarly, the infimum or largest lower bound of the real number family* $\{a_i\}_{i\in I}$ *can be represented as* $\bigwedge_{i\in I} a_i$.

If Π *satisfies only conditions (1) and (3), it is referred to as a generalized possibility measure.*

2.3. Generalized Possibilistic Kripke Structure

A generalized possibilistic Kripke structure refers to an extension of the traditional Kripke structure that incorporates possibilistic reasoning. It combines the principles of Kripke semantics with possibilistic logic to capture uncertainty and possibility in a more flexible and nuanced manner. In a generalized possibilistic Kripke structure, the set of possible worlds represents different states or scenarios of a system, similar to a traditional Kripke structure. However, instead of assigning a binary truth value (true or false) to propositions in each world, a generalized possibilistic Kripke structure assigns a degree of possibility or belief to each proposition in each world. A generalized possibilistic Kripke structure is defined as follows.

Definition 3. *A generalized possibilistic Kripke structure (GPKS, in short) is a tuple* $M = (S, P, I, AP, L)$*, where*

(1) *S is a countable, nonempty set of states;*
(2) *P: $S \times S \to [0,1]$ is a function, called a possibilistic transition distribution function;*
(3) *I: $S \to [0,1]$ is a function, called a possibilistic initial distribution function;*
(4) *AP is a set of atomic propositions;*
(5) *L: $S \times AP \to [0,1]$ is a possibilistic labeling function, which can be viewed as function mapping a state s to the fuzzy set of atomic propositions, which are possible in the state s, i.e., $L(s,a)$ denotes the possibility or truth value of atomic proposition a that is supposed to hold in s.*

Furthermore, if the set S and AP are finite sets, then $M = (S, P, I, AP, L)$ is called a finite GPKS.

Remark 2. *If we require the transition possibility distribution and initial distribution to be normal, i.e., $\bigvee_{s' \in S} P(s,s') = 1$ and $\bigvee_{s \in S} I(s) = 1$, and the labeling function L is also crisp, i.e., $L : S \times AP \to \{0,1\}$, then we obtain the notion of possibilistic Kripke structure [16]. In this case, we also say that M is normal. This is one of the reasons why we call the structure a defined generalized possibilistic Kripke structure.*

3. Generalized Possibility Decision Processes

The differences between GPDP and the Markov decision processes [24,25] are as follows: (1) the transfer weight of the Markov decision process reflects the frequency of events, while the transfer weight of GPDP feeds back the possibility of reaching the target state; (2) In the Markov decision processes, the sum of transfer weights starting from the same state is 1, but GPDP does not have this constraint; (3) The label function in the Markov decision process is clear, while the label function in GPDP is fuzzy. Therefore, in this paper, a GPDP similar to Markov decision processes is proposed as a model of uncertainty systems, which is specifically defined as follows.

Definition 4 (see [16]). *A GPDP is a tuple with six elements* $M' = (S, Act, P, I', AP, L)$ *where*

(1) *S is a countable, nonempty set of states;*
(2) *Act is a set of actions;*
(3) *P: $S \times Act \times S \to [0,1]$ is a transition possibility function such that for all states $s \in S$ and actions $\alpha \in Act$, there is a state $t \in S$, such that $P(s, \alpha, t) > 0$;*
(4) *I': $S \to [0,1]$ is a possibilistic initial distribution function, with an existing state s such that $I'(s) > 0$;*
(5) *AP is a set of the atomic propositions;*
(6) *L: $S \times AP \to [0,1]$ is a possibilistic labeling function, where $L(s,a)$ denotes the possibility or truth value of atomic proposition a that is supposed to hold in s.*

An action α is considered *enabled* in state s if and only if $\bigvee_{t \in S} P(s, \alpha, t) > 0$. We define the set $Act(s) = \{\alpha \in Act \mid \bigvee_{t \in S} P(s, \alpha, t) > 0\}$. It is a requirement that for any state $s \in S$, the set $Act(s) \neq \varnothing$. We refer to each state t for which $P(s, \alpha, t) > 0$ as an *α-successor* of s.

Remark 3.

(1) *The possibilistic transition function P, which maps from $S \times Act \times S$ to the interval $[0, 1]$, can be conveniently represented by a fuzzy matrix, also denoted as P, i.e.,*

$$P_\alpha(s, t) = (P(s, \alpha, t))_{s,t \in S}. \tag{1}$$

P_α is also called the fuzzy possibility α- transition matrix of M'.

(2) *The direct successors and predecessors of a state can be defined as follows. For a given state s from the set S, an action α from the set Act, and a subset T of states from S, the possibility of transitioning from state s to a state in T via action α is denoted as $P(s, \alpha, T)$, i.e.,*

$$P(s, \alpha, T) = \bigvee_{t \in T} P(s, \alpha, t). \tag{2}$$

The set of α-successors of a state s, denoted as $Post(s, \alpha)$, can be defined as follows. $Post(s, \alpha)$ represents the collection of states that can be reached from state s by taking action α, i.e.,

$$Post(s, \alpha) = \{t \in S \mid P(s, \alpha, t) > 0\}. \tag{3}$$

It should be noted that the set of α-successors of state s, denoted as $Post(s, \alpha) = \varnothing$ if and only if action α is not a member of the enabled action set $Act(s)$. On the other hand, the set $Pre(t)$, which represents the pairs (s, α) where state s belongs to S and action α belongs to $Act(s)$ such that $t \in Post(s, \alpha)$, can be expressed as follows.

$$Pre(t) = \{(s, \alpha) \in S \times Act \mid P(s, \alpha, t) > 0\}. \tag{4}$$

Example 1. *Figure 2 depicts a 3-state GPDP M', where the circle represents the state, the symbol outside the circle represents the state name, the symbol inside the circle represents the true value of the atomic proposition in the state, the labeled arc represents the transition, and the circle with the input arrow represents the initial state.*

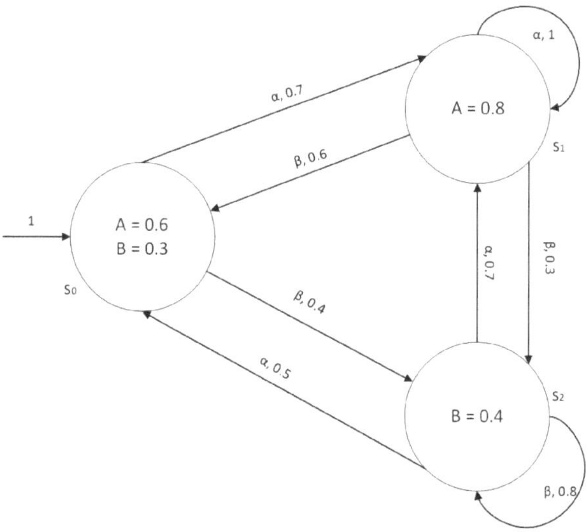

Figure 2. A GPDP M'.

Then, the state space of M' is $S = \{s_0, s_1, s_2, s_3\}$;

State s is the only initial state, i.e., $I(s_0) = 1$ and $I(s_1) = I(s_2) = 0$;

The set of atomic propositions is $AP = \{A, B\}$;

The sets of enabled actions are $Act(s_0) = \{\alpha, \beta\}$ with $P(s_0, \alpha, s_1) = 0.7$, $P(s_0, \beta, s_2) = 0.4$; $Act(s_1) = \{\alpha, \beta\}$ with $P(s_1, \alpha, s_1) = 1, P(s_1, \beta, s_0) = 0.6, P(s_1, \beta, s_2) = 0.3$; $Act(s_2) = \{\alpha, \beta\}$ with $P(s_2, \beta, s_2) = 0.8, P(s_2, \alpha, s_0) = 0.5, P(s_2, \alpha, s_1) = 0.7$;

The labeling functions are $L(s_0, A) = 0.6, L(s_0, B) = 0.3, L(s_1, A) = 0.8, L(s_2, B) = 0.4$;

For state s_0, $Post(s_0, \alpha) = \{s_1\}, Post(s_0, \beta) = \{s_2\}, Pref(s_0) = \{(s_1, \beta), (s_2, \alpha)\}$.

By using the state order $s_0 < s_1 < s_2$, the matrix P and the vector I is given by:

$$P_\alpha = \begin{pmatrix} 0 & 0.7 & 0 \\ 0 & 1 & 0 \\ 0.5 & 0.7 & 0 \end{pmatrix}, P_\beta = \begin{pmatrix} 0 & 0 & 0.4 \\ 0.6 & 0 & 0.3 \\ 0 & 0 & 0.8 \end{pmatrix}, I = \begin{pmatrix} 1 \\ 0 \\ 0 \end{pmatrix}.$$

Definition 5. *(Path in a GPDP). In GPDP $M = (S, Act, P, I, AP, L)$, an infinite path fragment is an infinite sequence $s_0\alpha_1 s_1\alpha_2 s_2\alpha_3 \cdots \in (S \times Act)^\omega$, satisfying the condition that $P(s_i, \alpha_{i+1}, s_{i+1}) > 0$ for all $i \geqslant 0$. A finite path fragment is any finite prefix of π that ends in a state. The set $Paths(s)$ represents the collection of infinite path fragments that start in state s, while $Paths_{fin}(s)$ denotes the set of finite path fragments that start in s. Let $Paths(M) = \bigcup_{s \in S} Paths(s)$ and $Paths_{fin}(M) = \bigcup_{s \in S} Paths_{fin}(s)$.*

Reasoning about the possibilities of path sets in a GPDP relies on the resolution of uncertainty. This resolution is performed by a scheduler. Once α has been chosen, there are no constraints imposed on the possibilistic choice that is resolved.

Definition 6. *(Scheduler). In a GPDP $M = (S, Act, P, I, AP, L)$, a scheduler for M is a function $\mathfrak{S} : S^+ \to Act$, where $\mathfrak{S}(s_0 s_1 \cdots s_n)$ belongs to $Act(s_n)$ for $s_0 s_1 \cdots s_n \in S^+$. A path (fragment)*

$$\pi = s_0 \xrightarrow{\alpha_1} s_1 \xrightarrow{\alpha_2} s_2 \xrightarrow{\alpha_3} \cdots$$

is referred to as an $\mathfrak{S}$- path (fragment) if $\alpha_i = \mathfrak{S}(s_0 \cdots s_{i-1})$ for all $i > 0$.

Definition 7. *Let M' be a GPDP with state space S. Scheduler $\mathfrak{S}$ on M' is memoryless if and only if for each sequence $s_0 s_1 \cdots s_n \in S^+$ and $t_0 t_1 \cdots t_m \in S^+$ with $s_n = t_m$, such that*

$$\mathfrak{S}(s_0 s_1 \cdots s_n) = \mathfrak{S}(t_0 t_1 \cdots t_m).$$

In this case, $\mathfrak{S}$ can be viewed as a function $\mathfrak{S} : S \to Act$. Stated in words, scheduler $\mathfrak{S}$ is memoryless if it always simply selects one alternative (i.e., action) per state while ignoring all others.

Example 2. *For instance, the scheduler $\mathfrak{S}_\alpha$ always selects the action α in state s. Scheduler $\mathfrak{S}_\beta$ always selects the action β in state s, as shown in Figure 3.*

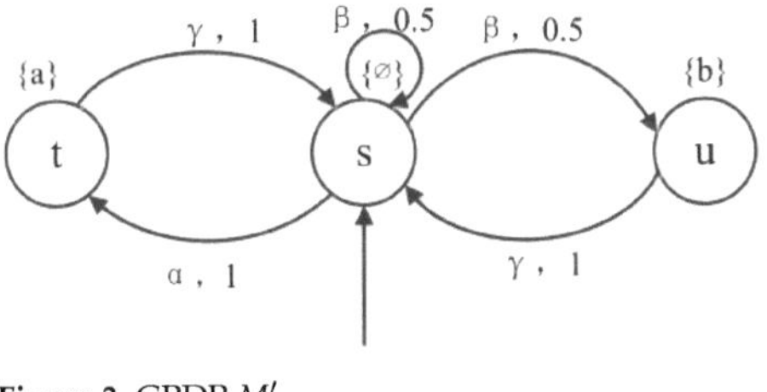

Figure 3. GPDP M'.

The only $\mathfrak{S}_\alpha$-*path* in M' is $s \xrightarrow{\alpha} t \xrightarrow{\gamma} s \xrightarrow{\alpha} \cdots$. The path $s \xrightarrow{\beta} s \xrightarrow{\beta} s \xrightarrow{\beta} u \xrightarrow{\gamma} s \xrightarrow{\beta} u \cdots$ is a $\mathfrak{S}_\beta$-*path*. Let $\mathfrak{S}$ be a scheduler that selects action α when returning from state u, and action β otherwise. Thus, $\mathfrak{S}(s_0 \cdots s_n s) = \alpha$ if $s_n = u$, and $\mathfrak{S}(s_0 \cdots s_n s) = \beta$ otherwise. Additionally, let $\mathfrak{S}(s) = \alpha$. It is important to note that this scheduler makes decisions based on the one-but-last visited state. In states u and t, the only enabled action γ is chosen. The GPDP $M'_{\mathfrak{S}_\beta}$ can be represented as an infinite chain: $s \xrightarrow{\beta} u \xrightarrow{\gamma} s \xrightarrow{\beta} u \cdots$.

Definition 8. *Given a GPDP M', the cylinder set of $\hat{\pi} = s_0\alpha_1 s_1\alpha_2 \cdots s_n\alpha_{n+1} \in \mathfrak{S}\text{-}Paths_{fin}(M)$ is defined as:*

$$Cyl(\hat{\pi}) = \{\pi \in \mathfrak{S}\text{-}Paths(M) \mid \hat{\pi} \in Pref(\pi)\}, \tag{5}$$

where $Pref(\pi) = \{\pi' \mid \pi' \text{ is a finite prefix of } \pi\}$. Then, as shown in [10], $\Omega = 2^{\mathfrak{S}\text{-}Paths(M)}$ is an algebra generated by $\{Cyl(\hat{\pi}) \mid \hat{\pi} \in \mathfrak{S}\text{-}Paths_{fin}(M)\}$ on $\mathfrak{S}\text{-}Paths(M)$. That is to say, $\Omega = 2^{\mathfrak{S}\text{-}Paths(M)}$ is the unique subalgebra of $2^{\mathfrak{S}\text{-}Paths(M)}$, which is closed under arbitrary unions and arbitrary intersections containing $\{Cyl(\hat{\pi}) \mid \hat{\pi} \in Pref(\pi)\}$.

Definition 9. *For a GPDP M', a function $Po^{M'} : \mathfrak{S}\text{-}Paths(M') \to [0,1]$ is defined as follows:*

$$Po^{M'}(\pi) = I(s_0) \wedge \bigwedge_{i=0}^{\infty} P(s_i, \mathfrak{S}(\hat{\pi}_i), s_{i+1}) \tag{6}$$

for any $\pi = s_0\alpha_1 s_1\alpha_2 \cdots \in \mathfrak{S}\text{-}Paths(M)$. $\hat{\pi}_n = s_0 s_1 \cdots s_n$, such that $P(s_{n-1}, \mathfrak{S}(\hat{\pi}_{n-1}), s_n) > 0$. Hence, the execution sequence is

$$s_0 \xrightarrow{\mathfrak{S}(\hat{\pi}_0)} s_1 \xrightarrow{\mathfrak{S}(\hat{\pi}_1)} s_2 \xrightarrow{\mathfrak{S}(\hat{\pi}_2)} \cdots.$$

We often identify $\pi = s_0\mathfrak{S}(\hat{\pi}_0)s_1\mathfrak{S}(\hat{\pi}_1)s_2\mathfrak{S}(\hat{\pi}_2)\cdots$ Furthermore, for any $E \subseteq \mathfrak{S}\text{-}Paths(M')$, we define

$$Po^{M'}(E) = \bigvee\{Po^{M'}(\pi) \mid \pi \in E\}. \tag{7}$$

Then, we have a well-defined function.

$$Po^{M'} : 2^{\mathfrak{S}\text{-}Paths(M)} \to [0,1],$$

$Po^{M'}$ is called the generalized possibility measure over $\Omega = 2^{\mathfrak{S}\text{-}Paths(M')}$.

4. Generalized Possibilistic Linear-Temporal Logic with Schedulers

Definition 10 (see [26]). *Given the atomic proposition AP, the generalized possibilistic linear-temporal logic (GPoLTL) syntax of an uncertain CPS is defined as follows:*

$$\mathfrak{S}\lfloor\varphi\rfloor ::= r \mid a \mid \mathfrak{S}\lfloor\varphi_1 \wedge \varphi_2\rfloor \mid \mathfrak{S}\lfloor\neg\varphi\rfloor \mid \mathfrak{S}\lfloor\bigcirc\varphi\rfloor \mid \mathfrak{S}\lfloor\varphi_1 \sqcup \varphi_2\rfloor,$$

where $r \in [0,1]$ and $a \in AP$.

Under GPDP, the semantics of the GPoLTL formula are related to schedulers, possibility information, and fuzzy logic on the set of atomic propositions AP. We give the semantics of GPoLTL in two aspects in the following.

Definition 11. *Let φ be a GPoLTL formula. The language semantics of φ over the alphabet $\Sigma=[0,1]^{AP}$ (or $\Sigma=l^{AP}$ for some finite subset $l \in [0,1]$) is a fuzzy ω-language; i.e., $\|\mathfrak{S}\lfloor\varphi\rfloor\|: \Sigma^\omega \to [0,1]$, which is defined iteratively as follows, for $\sigma = A_0A_1\cdots \in \Sigma^\omega$, write $\sigma_j = A_jA_{j+1}\cdots$.*

Then, the GPoLTL language semantics of an uncertain CPS is defined as follows.

$$\|r\|(\sigma) = r; \tag{8}$$

$$\|a\|(\sigma) = A_0(a); \tag{9}$$

$$\|\mathfrak{S}\lfloor\varphi_1 \wedge \varphi_2\rfloor\|(\sigma) = \|\mathfrak{S}\lfloor\varphi_1\rfloor\|(\sigma) \wedge \|\mathfrak{S}\lfloor\varphi_2\rfloor\|(\sigma); \tag{10}$$

$$\|\mathfrak{S}\lfloor\neg\varphi\rfloor\|(\sigma) = 1 - \|\mathfrak{S}\lfloor\varphi\rfloor\|(\sigma); \tag{11}$$

$$\|\mathfrak{S}\lfloor\bigcirc\varphi\rfloor\|(\sigma) = \|\mathfrak{S}\lfloor\varphi\rfloor\|(\sigma_1); \tag{12}$$

$$\|\mathfrak{S}\lfloor\varphi_1 \sqcup \varphi_2\rfloor\|(\sigma) = \bigvee_{j \geqslant 0}(\|\mathfrak{S}\lfloor\varphi_2\rfloor\|(\sigma_j) \wedge \bigwedge_{i<j}\|\mathfrak{S}\lfloor\varphi_1\rfloor\|(\sigma_i)); \tag{13}$$

$$\|\mathfrak{S}\lfloor\Diamond\varphi\rfloor\|(\sigma) = \bigvee_{j \geqslant 0}\|\mathfrak{S}\lfloor\varphi\rfloor\|(\sigma_j); \tag{14}$$

$$\|\mathfrak{S}\lfloor\Box\varphi\rfloor\|(\sigma) = \bigwedge_{j \geqslant 0}\|\mathfrak{S}\lfloor\varphi\rfloor\|(\sigma_j). \tag{15}$$

Definition 12. *Let $M' = (S, Act, P, I, AP, L)$ be a GPDP, $a \in AP$, and $\mathfrak{S}$ be the scheduler defined in M'. For atomic propositions r, a, regardless of resolution of the uncertainty, its path semantics over M' are fuzzy sets on Paths(M'); i.e., $\|\varphi\|$:Paths$(M) \to [0,1]$.*

For any path, the path semantics of GPoLTL with schedulers are interpreted as

$$\|r\|(\pi) = r; \tag{16}$$

$$\|a\|(\pi) = L(s_0, a). \tag{17}$$

For a path formula φ, its semantics depend on the schedulers, and its path semantics over M are $\|\mathfrak{S}\lfloor\varphi\rfloor\| : \mathfrak{S}\text{-}Paths(M) \to [0,1]$, which is defined recursively for $\pi = s_0\mathfrak{S}(\hat{\pi}_0)s_1\mathfrak{S}(\hat{\pi}_1)s_2\cdots$ as follows.

$$\|\mathfrak{S}\lfloor\varphi_1 \wedge \varphi_2\rfloor\|(\pi) = \|\varphi_1\|_{\mathfrak{S}}(\pi) \wedge \|\varphi_2\|_{\mathfrak{S}}(\pi); \tag{18}$$

$$\|\mathfrak{S}\lfloor\varphi_1 \sqcup \varphi_2\rfloor\|(\pi) = \bigvee_{j \geqslant 0}(\|\varphi_2\|_{\mathfrak{S}}(\pi_j) \wedge \bigwedge_{i<j}\|\varphi_1\|_{\mathfrak{S}}(\pi_i)); \tag{19}$$

$$\|\mathfrak{S}\lfloor\neg\varphi\rfloor\|(\pi) = 1 - \|\varphi\|_{\mathfrak{S}}(\pi); \tag{20}$$

$$\|\mathfrak{S}\lfloor\bigcirc\varphi\rfloor\|(\pi) = \|\bigcirc\varphi\|_{\mathfrak{S}}(\pi); \tag{21}$$

The until operator allows derivation of the temporal modalities $\Diamond$ ("eventually", sometimes in the future) and $\Box$ ("always", from now on forever) as usual.

$\Diamond\varphi = true \sqcup \varphi$, $\Box\varphi = \neg\Diamond\neg\varphi$, here, true = 1.

Let Q be an uncertain CPS model operating under a specific scheduler. π represents an execution trace of Q, while φ denotes an attribute description formula. The notation $||\varphi||(\pi)$ represents the execution trace of Q that satisfies the attribute φ. In other words, $||\varphi||Q : Paths(Q) \to [0,1]$ quantifies the possibility of $Paths(Q)$ satisfying the attribute φ. Here, π refers to an infinite path, $\pi \in Paths(Q)$, which can be expressed as $\pi = s_0s_1s_2\cdots$. π_j denotes the suffix of the trace starting from step j, i.e., $\pi = s_js_{j+1}\cdots$. The value of the variable y in step j of x is denoted as $V = (\pi, j, y)$.

In the uncertain CPS system Q, an infinite path is expressed as $\pi = s_0s_1s_2\cdots \in S^\omega$, and a finite path is denoted as $\pi = s_0s_1\cdots s_n (n \in N)$. The notation $Paths(Q)$ denotes the set of infinite paths in the uncertain CPS system Q, while $Paths_{fin}Q$ represents the set of finite paths.

Definition 13. *For a GPDP without terminal states, i.e., for any state s, there exists a state t such that $P(s,t) > 0$. The trace of the infinite path fragment $\pi = s_0\alpha_0s_1\alpha_1\cdots$ is defined as $trace(\pi) = L(s_0)L(s_1)\cdots$.*

To simplify notation, we use $L(\pi)$ to represent the trace of the infinite path π. Similarly, for a finite path fragment $\hat{\pi} = s_0\alpha_0s_1\alpha_1\cdots s_n$, the trace is defined as $L(\hat{\pi}) = L(s_0)L(s_1)\cdots L(s_n)$.

The execution of a system model starts from an initial state and serves as a means to validate the model. During each step of execution, the model selects a single enabled action from the current state, and the actions are executed in an uncertain order.

The dynamic execution trace π of an uncertain CPS can be represented as either a finite or an infinite sequence:

$s_0 \xrightarrow{l_1} s_1 \xrightarrow{l_2} s_2 \cdots s_{k-1} \xrightarrow{l_k} \cdots$

Here, each state s_i is connected to the next state s_{i+1} by an action label l_i. The sequence can continue indefinitely if it is an infinite trace, capturing the ongoing behavior of the system. In this representation, $s_k =< p_k, v_k >$ represents the state of the system, where p_k is the control mode of the system and v_k is the current variable value. Additionally, l_k indicates the duration of time that the system stays at state s_i. This trace captures the sequence of states, control modes, variable values, and durations of the system's behavior over time.

Definition 14. *Let P be a fuzzy linear-time property over AP and $M = (S, Act, P, I, AP, L)$ be a finite GPDP without terminal states. Then, the possibility of $M' = (S, Act, P, I, AP, L)$ satisfies P at state s, denoted by $Po_{\mathfrak{S}}(s \models P)$, and is defined as*

$$Po_{\mathfrak{S}}(s \models P) = \bigvee_{\pi \in \mathfrak{S}\text{-}Paths(s)} Po(\pi) \wedge P(L(\pi)). \tag{22}$$

5. Extended of an Uncertain CPS Model

The Uncertain CPS Extended Model describes a CPS as a complex embedded network system that integrates physical, computing, and interactive entities. The motion process in the physical world is represented using dynamic time continuity. Meanwhile, the system behavior is modeled using a finite state machine to capture event-driven discrete processes in the computational world [4]. This paper aims to perform CPS modeling and simulation by employing the uncertain hybrid time automaton. In this way, not only the informatization and discretization can be effectively achieved, but also the physicalization and continuation of the discrete event model can be realized.

5.1. Differential Equation Modeling Based on Time

In an uncertain CPS, the state of a physical entity exhibits a clear and continuous dynamic continuity, with its state transformation relying on continuous time [17].

For instance, let us consider the thermostat state model (as depicted in Figure 4) as an example. By utilizing time-based differential equations, the dynamic behavior of an uncertain CPS can be modeled in the following manner.

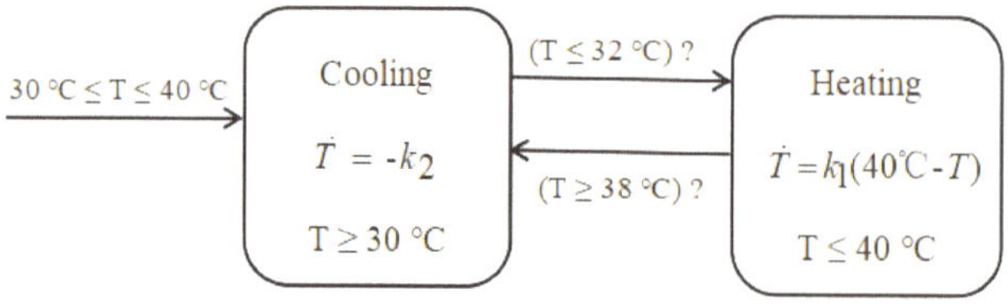

Figure 4. Thermostat model of uncertain hybrid timed automaton.

$$\dot{T} = k_1(40\ ^\circ\text{C} - T) \tag{23}$$

$$\dot{T} = -k_2 \tag{24}$$

In Equation (23) , the temperature variable T represents a continuous-time variable, with the constraint ($T \leqslant 40\ ^\circ$C). It is important to note that the dynamic behavior follows a linear pattern, with k_1 representing a constant quantity. In Equation (24) describes the dynamics of temperature change, with k_2 also being a constant quantity.

5.2. Hybrid Timed Automaton Modeling Based on Uncertainty

Uncertainty is crucial in the operation of a CPS [19]. CPS components are interconnected rather than isolated. Modeling a CPS solely using the embedded control approach is inadequate due to the close integration of software and hardware [18]. To address this challenge, introducing a clock invariant and incorporating the notion of possibility into the classic hybrid automaton becomes necessary. This approach helps resolve the issue of closeness and enables the definition of an uncertain hybrid timed automaton system model.

Definition 15. *The uncertain hybrid timed automaton H_P is defined by a tuple consisting of nine elements, as shown below.*

$$H_p = (I, O, T, Init, M, A_x|x \in I, A_y|y \in O, A, CI).$$

- *I represents a set that includes the values of the input ports. For example, an input set $x?v$ contains input values v, where $x \in I$.*
- *O represents a set that includes the values of the output ports. For instance, an output set $y!v$ contains output values v, where $y \in O$.*
- *T represents the set of state variables, and Q_T represents the defined state set.*
- *$Init$ represents the possibility initialization distribution operation, which determines the possibility of the initial state set, denoted as $[Init] \leq Q_T$.*
- *M corresponds to the set of control modes.*
- *$\{A_x| \in I\}$ signifies that, for each input port x, the input task set A_x describes the input actions using a guard condition on T. The update of the input action set is defined as $t \xrightarrow{x?v} t'$, transitioning from the read set $T \cup \{x\}$ to the write set T. In other words, it follows the pattern $Guard \xrightarrow{x?v} Update$.*
- *$\{A_y|y \in O\}$ indicates that, for each output port y, each output task in the output task set A_y defines the update description of the output action set as $t \xrightarrow{y!v} t'$, transitioning from the read set $T \cup \{y\}$ to the write set T based on the guard condition on T. In other words, it follows the pattern $Guard \xrightarrow{y!v} Update$.*
- *A represents the set of internal actions, where each action is determined by a guard condition on T and is updated from the read set T to the write set T. These internal actions may also include an output action in the form of $t \xrightarrow{\varepsilon} t'$.*
- *CI represents a clock invariant, which is a Boolean expression on the state variable T. Given a state t and a positive real value of time $\delta > 0$, if the state $t + \delta$ satisfies the expression CI for all values of t' within the range $0 \leq t' \leq \delta$, then the transition $t \xrightarrow{\delta} t + \delta$ is considered a time action.*

6. Uncertain CPS Dynamic Verification and Analysis

A reactive CPS can be impacted by factors like fairness issues, input/output handling, and system execution correctness. These problems could be solved by temporal logic, which is a very effective formal method. Fuzzy temporal logic is capable of extending propositional and predicate logic for it takes the infinite behavior of feedback in uncertain CPS into consideration. A fuzzy (or possibilistic) temporal logic, say, the fuzzy linertime property (LT property), provides an intuitive and accurate annotation system for establishing relationships and execution as well.

6.1. Activity

Activity indicates that something good will happen eventually in the operation of an uncertain CPS. Checking whether an attribute satisfies the activity involves evaluating whether a model fulfills the properties specified by temporal logic. GPoLTL is used here in this paper to describe the activity. The definition of GPoLTL suggests that there are four types of activity, namely, eventually reachability, always reachability, repeated reachability, and persistence reachability.

Remark 4.

(1) *Eventually reachability can be represented by the "eventually" operator, which is symbolized as* $\Diamond$. *The "eventually" operator can be nested to enforce a sequence of events in a specific order. When an assignment on a path satisfies a formula* φ, *it means that the path conforms to the GPoLTL formula* $\Diamond\varphi$. *For example, if an assignment in the path* $\pi = (x_1, y_1)(x_2, y_2)\cdots$ *satisfies the expression* $(x = y)$, *indicating that for some* j, $x_j = y_j$, *the path* π *satisfies the GPoLTL formula* $\Diamond(x = y)$. *Thus, the formula* $\Diamond(x = y)$ *represents the requirement that eventually, at a certain step, the values of variables* x *and* y *are equal.*

(2) *Always reachability is represented by the "always" operator, which is symbolized as* $\Box$. *When all assignments on the path meet the requirement of* φ, *the path satisfies the GPoLTL formula* $\Box\varphi$. *For instance, if all assignment on path* $\pi = (x_1, y_1)(x_2, y_2)\cdots$ *satisfy the expression* $(x = y)$, *meaning that* $x_j = y_j$ *for each* j, *then the path satisfies the GPoLTL formula* $\Box(x = y)$. *That is to say that the formula* $\Box(x = y)$ *represents the requirement that variables* x *and* y *should always be equal.*

(3) *Repeated reachability is represented by the "always-eventually" operator , which is symbolized as* $\Box\Diamond\varphi$. *If every position* i *on the path satisfies the formula* $\Diamond\varphi$, *it implies that for each position* i, *there exists a future position* $j \geq i$, *where* φ *is satisfied. Moreover, there exists an infinite sequence of positions* $j_1 < j_2 < j_3\cdots$, *where* φ *is satisfied at each position. In simpler terms, if* φ *is satisfied recursively or repeatedly, then the formula* $\Box\Diamond$ *is satisfied. For instance, the path* $\pi = (x_1, y_1)(x_2, y_2)\cdots$ *satisfies the recursive formula* $\Box\Diamond(x = 0)$. *For an infinite number of positions* j, *when* $x_j = 0$, x *needs to be repeatedly assigned 0.*

(4) *Persistence reachability is represented by "eventually always", which is expressed as* $\Diamond\Box\varphi$. *If there exists a position* j *that satisfies the always formula* $\Box\varphi$, *meaning that every position after* j *satisfies* φ, *then* $\Diamond\Box\varphi$ *is satisfied. In other words, the formula* $\Diamond\Box\varphi$ *must be continuously satisfied and held. For example, if for a specific position* j, *every* $k \geq j$ *satisfies* $x_k = 0$ *(or if it is not equal to 0, for a finite number of positions), then the path* $\pi = (x_1, y_1)(x_2, y_2)\cdots$ *has the persistence formula* $\Diamond\Box\varphi(x = 0)$.

An uncertain CPS is a system that incorporates a perception and control feedback loop to achieve repeated environmental perception for controlling physical equipment. In an uncertain CPS, each program within the system will repeatedly enter its key part. The key part represents the state of the system, denoted as s_i, forming an execution trace π, which can be a finite or infinite sequence: $< s_0, t_0 >\mapsto< s_1, t_1 >\mapsto \cdots \mapsto< s_n, t_n >\mapsto \cdots$ The system needs to run continuously to maintain its activity. The primary challenge lies in calculating the measure of the system satisfying the desired path to a specific state set B.

Definition 16. *Suppose that* Q *is an uncertain CPS model that satisfies the property* φ, *where* φ *is a GPoLTL formula. The possibility measure of* Q *is denoted as* $Po(Q \models \varphi)$, *which is defined as* $Po(Q \models \varphi) = Po_s\{\pi \in Paths(s) | \pi \models \varphi\}$. *Here,* $B \subseteq S$ *represents a state set within the uncertain CPS model.*

The reachability analysis using GPDP Q as the system model calculates the possibility of reaching state set B. The state set B refers to the possibility of rarely accessing to the bad state set or the possibility of repeatedly accessing to the good state set. It is expressed by the mapping function as $B : S \to [0, 1]$.

Then, $\Diamond B, \Box B, \Box\Diamond B, \Diamond\Box B$ can be regarded as a fuzzy linear property on the set of state s. The definition is as follows: $\Diamond B(\pi) = \bigvee_{j\geq 0} B(s_j), \Box B(\pi) = \bigwedge_{j\geq 0} B(s_j)$,

$\Box\Diamond B(\pi) = \bigwedge_{i\geq 0}\bigvee_{j\geq i} B(s_j)$, $\Diamond\Box B(\pi) = \bigvee_{j\geq i}\bigwedge_{i\geq 0} B(s_j)$.

With a given GPDP and fuzzy linear property P, calculate the probability that the path with scheduler $\mathfrak{S}$ satisfies P. We consider four properties, namely, eventually reachability, always reachability, repeated reachability, and persistence reachability.

(1) The possibility measure for eventually reachability in an uncertain system model Q, satisfying the property $\Diamond B$, is expressed as follows.

$$\begin{aligned} Po_{\mathfrak{S}}(\Diamond B) &= Po_{\mathfrak{S}}(s \models \Diamond B)_{s \in S} \\ &= \bigvee_{\pi \in \mathfrak{S}\text{-}Paths(s)} Po_{\mathfrak{S}}(\pi) \wedge \Diamond B(\pi) \\ &= \bigvee_{\pi = s_0 s_1 \cdots \in \mathfrak{S}\text{-}Paths(s)} \wedge \bigvee_{j=0}^{\infty} P(s_j, \mathfrak{S}(\hat{\pi}_j), s_{j+1}) \wedge \bigvee_{j=0}^{\infty} B(s_j); \end{aligned}$$

(2) The possibility measure for always reachability in an uncertain system model Q, satisfying the property $\Box B$, is expressed as follows.

$$\begin{aligned} Po_{\mathfrak{S}}(\Box B) &= Po_{\mathfrak{S}}(s \models \Box B)_{s \in S} \\ &= \bigvee_{\pi \in \mathfrak{S}\text{-}Paths(s)} Po_{\mathfrak{S}}^{M_s}(\pi) \wedge \Box B(\pi) \\ &= \bigvee_{\pi = s_0 s_1 \cdots \in \mathfrak{S}\text{-}Paths(s)} Po_{\mathfrak{S}}^{M_s}(\pi) \wedge \bigwedge_{j=0}^{\infty} P(s_j, \mathfrak{S}(\hat{\pi}_j), s_{j+1}) \wedge \bigwedge_{j=0}^{\infty} B(s_j); \end{aligned}$$

(3) The possibility measure of repeated reachability in an uncertain system model Q, satisfying the property $\Box\Diamond B$, is expressed as follows.

$$\begin{aligned} Po_{\mathfrak{S}}(\Box\Diamond B) &= Po_{\mathfrak{S}}(s \models \Box\Diamond B)_{s \in S} \\ &= \bigvee_{\pi \in \mathfrak{S}\text{-}Paths(s)} Po_{\mathfrak{S}}(\pi) \wedge \Box\Diamond B(\pi) \\ &= \bigvee_{\pi = s_0 s_1 \cdots \in \mathfrak{S}\text{-}Paths(s)} Po_{\mathfrak{S}}(\pi) \wedge \bigwedge_{i \geq 0} \bigvee_{j \geq i} B(s_j); \end{aligned}$$

(4) The possibility measure for persistence reachability in an uncertain system model Q, satisfying the property $\Diamond\Box B$, is expressed as follows.

$$\begin{aligned} Po_{\mathfrak{S}}(\Diamond\Box B) &= Po_{\mathfrak{S}}(s \models \Diamond\Box B)_{s \in S} \\ &= \bigvee_{\pi \in \mathfrak{S}\text{-}Paths(s)} Po_{\mathfrak{S}}(\pi) \wedge \Diamond\Box B(\pi) \\ &= \bigvee_{\pi = s_0 s_1 \cdots \in \mathfrak{S}\text{-}Paths(s)} Po_{\mathfrak{S}}(\pi) \wedge \bigvee_{i \geq 0} \bigwedge_{j \geq i} B(s_j). \end{aligned}$$

Property 1. *In an uncertain CPS model Q with the PoLTL formula φ, if a state is reachable along any path starting from the initial state q_0, then the following condition applies:*

(1) $\Box\varphi \leftrightarrow \varphi \wedge \bigcirc\Box\varphi$
(2) $\Box\Diamond\varphi \leftrightarrow \bigcirc\Box\Diamond\varphi \leftrightarrow \Diamond\Box\Diamond\varphi$

The first equivalent expression of the property can be summarized by the following three points. (i) If a path satisfies the formula $\Box\varphi$, it implies that the path satisfies φ at all positions, regardless of the specific choice of φ. (ii) The formula $\Box\varphi$ is more expressive than φ, meaning it captures a broader range of possible behaviors. (iii) If both the current position satisfies φ and the next position satisfies $\Box\varphi$, then $\Box\varphi$ is considered satisfied, indicating a persistent satisfaction of the property.

The second equivalent of the property can be summarized as follows. (i) Irrespective of the position, if a path satisfies the recursive formula $\Box\Diamond\varphi$ at a specific position (e.g., the first position), then the subsequent position along the path also satisfies the same recursive formula $\Box\Diamond\varphi$, and vice versa. (ii) In fact, for any given path π and any positions i and j

along that path, the satisfaction of $\Box\Diamond\varphi$ at position (π, i) is equivalent to the satisfaction of $\Box\Diamond\varphi$ at position (π, j).

Please note that these equivalences have been provided in a more concise form. For a detailed explanation and proof, please refer to the specific reference [27] mentioned.

6.2. Safety of the Fuzzy Regular Language

The safety possibility measure of a fuzzy regular language is determined by assessing whether the language satisfies the defined safety requirements. It involves analyzing the behaviors exhibited during limited execution and verifying if they violate the specified requirements. The aim is to ensure that no harmful or unwanted outcomes occur. This analysis helps in evaluating the degree of possibility for the fuzzy regular language to be considered safe, based on the absence of bad prefixes in infinite strings that satisfy the *LT* property P_{safe} [10].

This study analyzes nonconforming behaviors using limited execution to verify if they violate safety requirements. Safety requirements aim to prevent any undesirable outcomes. In classic examples, the security property is defined such that if any infinite string σ in the *LT* property P_{safe} does not contain a bad prefix, then this *LT* property is considered safe (i.e., $\sigma \in P_{safe}$). In general, we can express this property as follows.

Let P_{safe} be a fuzzy *LT* property. If, for every $\sigma \in P_{safe}$, there exists a finite prefix $\hat{\sigma_i}$ (where $i \in N$) such that every infinite string σ' in the form $\sigma' = \theta_1\theta_2\cdots\theta_i\cdots$, where θ_i belongs to the set $\hat{\sigma_i}$, is contained in P_{safe}, then the fuzzy language $\Sigma^* \longrightarrow [0,1]$ satisfying P_{safe} is considered safe. Here, each finite string $\hat{\sigma_i}$ is referred to as a good prefix of P_{safe}. In other words, if every string σ in P_{safe} can be extended indefinitely by appending symbols from its corresponding good prefix $\hat{\sigma_i}$, and all resulting infinite strings are also contained within P_{safe}, then the fuzzy language $\Sigma^* \longrightarrow [0,1]$ satisfying P_{safe} is deemed safe.

Definition 17. *Let $H_P = (I, O, T, Init, M, \{A_x|x \in I\}, \{A_y|y \in O\}, A, CI)$ represent an uncertain hybrid timed automaton, and $N = (Q, \Sigma, \delta, J, F)$ denote a fuzzy finite automaton. The tensor product of these two automata is defined as $H_P \otimes N = (M \times Q, I', O', T', Init', \{A'_x|x \in I'\}, \{A'_y|y \in O'\}, A', CI')$. Here, for any $(m,q) \in M \times Q, A'(m,q) = (m,q), I'(m,q) = I(m) \wedge \bigvee_{q_0 \in Q} J(q_0) \wedge \delta(q_0, A(m), q)$. The transfer possibility distribution of $H_p \otimes N$ is given by $P'_{safe}((m,q),(m',q')) = P_{safe}(m,m') \wedge \delta(q, A(m'), q')$.*

Theorem 1. *Suppose that P_{safe} is a fuzzy regular safety attribute that ensures the acceptance of $Pref(P_{safe})$ by a deterministic fuzzy finite automaton N. H_P represents an uncertain hybrid timed automaton, where m is a state within H_P. Then, $Po^{H_P}(m \models P_{safe}) = Po^{H_P \otimes N}(m, q_m) \models \Box B$, which $q_m = \delta(q_0, A(m)), B = M \times F = \sum_{m \in M, q \in Q} F(q)/(m,q)$.*

In this context, we are considering a scenario in which P_{safe} guarantees that the requirements specified by $Pref(P_{safe})$ are fulfilled by the deterministic fuzzy finite automaton N. In simpler terms, for any state (m,q) in the combined automaton $H_P \otimes N$, the value $B(m,q)$ is equal to $F(q)$. This means that the possibilisty of satisfying P_{safe} in H_P is determined by the possibilistic of satisfying the corresponding property $\Box B$ in the tensor product, where B is calculated based on the states and accepting states of N. For a more detailed understanding and comprehensive analysis, it is recommended to refer to the specific literature [10] mentioned.

Theorem 2. *Suppose P_{safe} is a fuzzy ω regular property, guaranteeing that it is accepted by the fuzzy Buchi finite automaton N, denoted as $A_\omega(N) = P_{safe}$. In this case, we can define $Po^{H_P}(m \models P_{safe} = P^{H_{P_m} \otimes N}(I' \models \Box\Diamond B))$, where $B = M \times F = \sum_{m \in M, q \in Q} F(q)/(m,q)$.*

Proof. $Po(m \models P_{safe}) = \bigvee_{\pi \in Paths(M)} Po^{H_{P_m}(\pi)} \wedge P_{safe}(A(\pi))$
$= \bigvee_{\pi \in Paths(M)} Po^{H_{P_m}}(\pi) \wedge A(N)(A(\pi))$
$= \bigvee_{\pi = m_0 m_1 \cdots \in Paths(M)} Po^{H_{P_m}}(\pi) \wedge \bigvee \{J(q_0) \wedge \bigwedge_{i \geq 0} \delta(q_i, \sigma_{i+1}, q_{i+1}) \wedge \bigwedge_{i \geq 0} \bigvee_{j \geq i} F(q_j) \backslash q_i \in Q(\forall i \geq 0)\}$
$= \bigvee_{\pi \in m_0 m_1 \cdots \in Paths(M)} \bigvee_{q_0 \in Q} \bigvee_{q_1 q_2 \cdots \in \delta^{\omega}(q_0, A(\pi))} J(q_0) \wedge \delta(q_0, A(m_0), q_1) \wedge \bigwedge_{i \geq 0} P_{safe}(m_i, m_{i+1})$
$\wedge \delta(q_i, A(m_i), q_{i+1}) \bigwedge_{i \geq 0} \bigvee_{j \geq i} F(q_j)$
$= \bigvee_{q_1 \in Q} \bigvee_{\pi' = (m_0, q_1)(m_1, q_2) \cdots \in Paths(H_{P_m} \otimes N(m, q_1))} I'(m_0, q_1) \wedge \bigwedge_{i \geq 0} P'_{safe}((m_i, q_{i+1}, (m_{i+1}, q_{i+2})) \wedge$
$\bigwedge_{i \geq 0} \bigvee_{j \geq i} B(m_j, q_{j+1})$
$= Po^{H_{P_m} \otimes N}(I' \models \Box \Diamond B)$
Hence, $Po^{H_P}(m \models P_{safe} = P^{H_{P_m} \otimes N}(I' \models \Box \Diamond B))$. □

In simpler terms, this indicates that in the uncertain hybrid timed automaton, we can calculate the possibility $Po(m \models P_{safe})$ by considering the possibilistic of event $\Box \Diamond B$ in the $H_{P_m} \otimes N$ structure, where B is defined as the Cartesian product of M and F.

6.3. Model Checking Algorithm

For the properties of reachability, f=$Po(\Diamond B)$, f=$Po(\Box B)$, f=$Po(\Box \Diamond B)$, f=$Po(\Diamond \Box B)$, we could use the fixpoint techniques to calculate the value, see Algorithm 1.

Algorithm 1 The Fixpoint.
Input: A function f from the set of possibility distributions over the state set S into itself.
Output: The fixpoint f.

```
procedure FIXPOINT(B,f)
    B := False      *the Least Fixpoint*
    B := True       *the Greatest Fixpoint*
    B' := f(B)
    while B ≠ B' do
        B ← B'
        B' ← f(B)
    end while
    return B
end procedure
```

What is the time complexity of possibilities-based model checking? Different properties bear different time complexity. For the fixpoint techniques of $Po(\Diamond B)$, $Po(\Box B)$, $Po(\Box \Diamond B)$, $Po(\Diamond \Box B)$, each fixpoint requires $O(|S|^3)$, see [12].

7. Case-Study

In this section, we use the example of uncertainty thermostats in CPS to illustrate the application of model checking techniques in generalized possibility decision processes. We can describe the thermostat model by an uncertain hybrid time automaton, and use Ptolemy II for modeling and simulation. A dynamic execution sequence of the uncertain CPS thermostat system is analyzed using a simulation diagram to ensure their consistency and effectiveness.

7.1. Hybrid Timed Automaton Model Based on Uncertain

The thermostatic control system is a feedback control system in CPS that regulates heating and ventilation automatically. It can be represented by an uncertain hybrid timed automaton, as depicted in Figure 4. The output of the thermostat model process is the temperature. The formal model of the system can be expressed as follows.

- The system does not have any input variables.
- The system includes an output variable, T, of continuous type (*cont* type, in short) that undergoes continuous changes over time.
- The system has a discrete state variable, M, which can take values from the set $\{cooling, heating\}$.
- There is an initial possibility value assigned to the variable M, which is set to $cooling$. The initial possibility value for T can be any value within the range of 30 °C to 40 °C.
- There is no discrete action involved in transmitting the temperature value as an output task.
- Two internal tasks are present for two-mode switching. The first task guards the condition ($M = cooling \wedge T \leqslant 32$ °C) and updates M to $heating$. The second task guards the condition ($M = heating \wedge T \geqslant 38$ °C) and updates M to $cooling$.
- The output variable T is identical to the state variable T.
- The derivative of T is defined as $-k_2$ if assigning the value $cooling$ to M, otherwise it is defined as $k_1(40\ °C - T)$.
- The continuous time invariant CI is defined as $M = cooling$ implies $T \geqslant 30$ °C and $M = heating$ implies $T \leqslant 40$ °C.

The thermostat operates in two modes: (1) when M is set to $heating$, the heater is activated, and (2) when M is set to $cooling$, the heater is turned off. In the heating mode, the initial temperature value generates a unique response signal, reflecting how the temperature changes over time based on the continuous temperature variation described by the differential equation $\dot{T} = k_1(40\ °C - T)$. It is important to note that the system can only remain in the heating mode if the constraint ($T \leqslant 40$ °C) is satisfied. If the constraint is violated, the mode must be switched to the $cooling$ mode. The condition ($T \geqslant 38$ °C) ensures the mode switching, meaning that whenever the temperature exceeds 38 °C, the mode will immediately switch to $cooling$.

When the thermostat is in $cooling$ mode, the temperature follows the differential equation $\dot{T} = -k_2$, resulting in a linear decrease over time. If the temperature falls below 30 °C, the system must switch to the $heating$ mode to meet the constraint ($T \geqslant 30$ °C). The mode switching from $cooling$ to $heating$ occurs whenever the temperature drops below 32 °C, as indicated by the guard condition ($T \leqslant 32$ °C). It is important to note that the system temperature ranges between 30 °C and 40 °C, which is influenced not only by the temperature itself but also by the system's state. When the temperature is around the desired set value, there may be small fluctuations or jitter caused by the switching on or off of the heater. This jitter occurs because the system is trying to maintain the temperature within a narrow range. As the temperature approaches the set value, the heater may turn on to raise the temperature or turn off to prevent overheating. However, the overall strategy of switching between $cooling$ and $heating$ modes effectively manages these fluctuations .

In this thermostat model, mode switching takes place at unpredictable times. This means that, even with a fixed initial temperature, there are multiple possible operational scenarios. The presence of uncertain transitions is particularly valuable for modeling malfunctions in CPS where fault information may be unavailable.

7.2. Simulation Based on Ptolemy II

Ptolemy II, as an open-source modeling and simulation tool, stands out from other modeling tools by offering support for hierarchical modeling of heterogeneous systems. As a result, Ptolemy II serves as a suitable modeling environment for designing uncertain CPS. In this study, Ptolemy II is utilized to model a CPS thermostat with uncertainty and failure, as depicted in Figure 5. In the heating state of the Finite State Machine (FSM), both outgoing transitions become feasible when their execution conditions (i.e., both being true) are satisfied. The two uncertain transitions are highlighted in red.

The results of executing the uncertain thermostat model are presented in Figures 6 and 7. It is important to note that the heater can only be activated for a brief period, maintaining the temperature around the threshold of 30 °C. The initial temperature of the system (T_0) is set within the range of 30 °C to 40 °C, and the system mode is initially set to *cooling*. Taking $T_0 = 40$ °C, $k_1 = 0.1$, and $k_2 = -0.05$ as constants, the execution of the thermostat process can be divided into two stages: *cooling* and *heating*. The system mode remains unchanged within each stage, while the temperature varies continuously over time according to the differential equation corresponding to the current mode. Any mode switch results in a discontinuous change in the system's state.

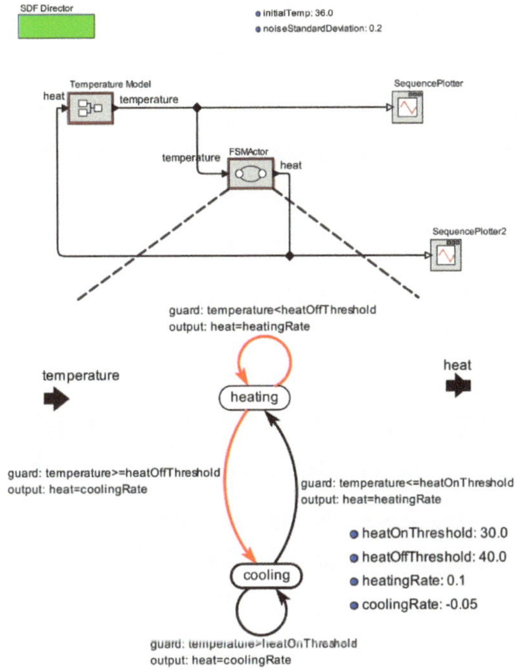

Figure 5. Uncertain CPS thermostat model.

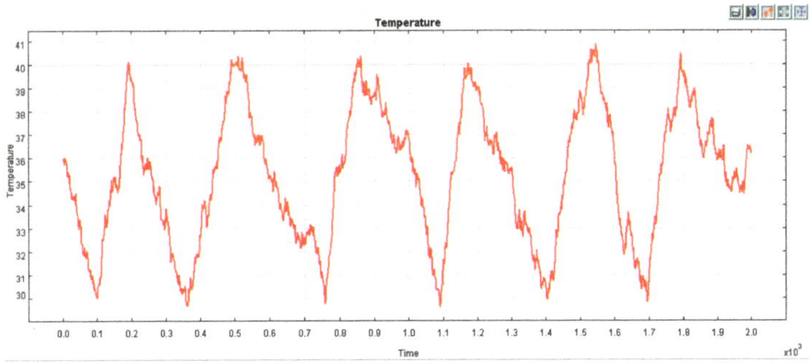

Figure 6. Temperature variation of the uncertain CPS thermostat model.

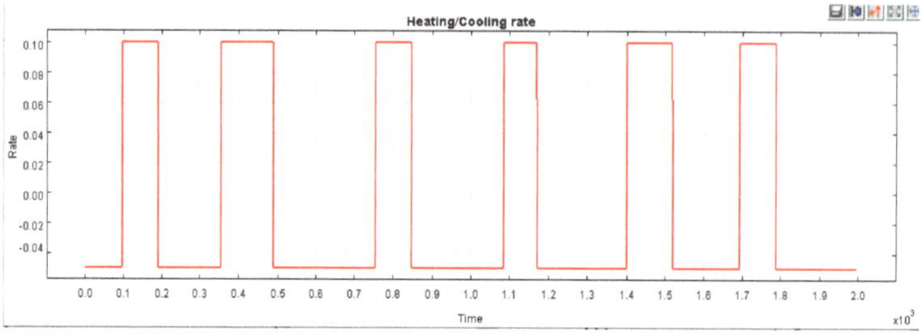

Figure 7. Rate variation of the uncertain CPS thermostat model.

If the system switches to *cooling* mode at time t^*, with the temperature at that time denoted as T^*, the temperature remains at $T^* - k_2(t - t^*)$ until the next mode switch. Assuming T^* is at least 32 °C, the process remains active in *cooling* mode for a duration ranging from $(T^* - 32)/k_2$ seconds to $(T^* - 30)/k_2$ seconds.

On the other hand, if the system switches to *heating* mode at time t^* with the temperature at that time as t^*, the temperature at time t remains at $40 - (40 - T^*)e^{-k_1(t-t*)}$ until the next mode switch occurs. Assuming T^* is at least 38 °C, the process remains active for a minimum duration of $ln(2/(40 - T^*))/k_1$ seconds in the *heating* mode. If the temperature remains below 40 °C, the system may stay in this mode indefinitely.

7.3. Uncertain CPS Dynamic Execution Based on the Hybrid Timed Automaton

The results of the uncertain CPS thermostat model depicted in Figures 6 and 7 demonstrate the initiation of CPS possibility execution within the hybrid timed automaton, starting from the initial state. At each step, the execution requires the performance of an input action, an output action, an internal action, or a time action. A dynamic execution sequence of the model corresponding to the alternating time and internal actions is shown as follows:

$$(cooling, 36) \xrightarrow{0.14} (cooling, 30) \xrightarrow{\varepsilon} (heating, 30) \xrightarrow{0.1} (heating, 40) \xrightarrow{\varepsilon} (cooling, 40) \xrightarrow{0.3} (cooling, 30) \xrightarrow{\varepsilon} (heating, 30) \xrightarrow{0.1} (heating, 40).$$

During each time action, the hybrid process consistently generates the temperature value as output. For example, in the first time action lasting 0.14 units of time, the temperature signal is determined by $\bar{T}(t) = 36 - (-0.05)t$. Similarly, in the second time action with a duration of 0.1 units of time, the temperature signal is defined by $40 - 9e^{-0.1t}$.

A CPS combines the event-driven, discrete behavior model of a state machine with a dynamic continuous model based on time. This integration involves refining the current state of an uncertain hybrid timed automaton by considering the dynamic behavior of the output in relation to the dynamic behavior of the next input [4]. In most CPS applications, a clock variable is used to measure the system's dynamic changes at specific times. The transition state of this clock variable is linear, enabling the timed automaton to construct both simple and complex systems based on the clock.

In conclusion, the behavior of the system is contingent upon the mode it operates in, whether it is *cooling* or *heating*. It is important to acknowledge that the precise mechanism and algorithm for mode switching may vary depending on the system's complexity. Real-world implementations might incorporate additional factors such as hysteresis, which helps prevent frequent mode toggling, and feedback control loops to ensure stable and efficient temperature regulation. These details offer a deeper comprehension of the *cooling* and *heating* modes, their respective temperature dynamics, and the conditions that determine their activation and duration.

This paper integrates the uncertainty of intelligent thermostats in typical feedback control systems in CPS based on the framework of generalized possibility measures. It demonstrates the application of model checking techniques in the decision-making process under generalized possibility and analyzes how uncertain CPS can integrate physical systems with digital intelligence, real-time data analysis, and autonomous decision-making to enhance efficiency, reliability, and performance in various environments. However, there are certain limitations. In the next steps, we will combine possibility model checking techniques and their related attributes, along with specific real-world examples, to investigate the uncertainty of CPS in complex uncertain environments.

8. Conclusions

This paper presents the modeling and verification of uncertain CPS based on decision processes, building upon a previous international conference paper [27]. Considering the complexity and uncertainty factors in real-life scenarios, along with the uncertainty and dynamic characteristics of CPS, this paper proposes new methods for handling uncertain data using possibility processing. We first introduce the concept of GPDP to describe uncertain CPS behavior. Furthermore, we define the syntax and semantics of CPS using GPoLTL with decision processes. The theoretical validation of the system's liveness and safety properties is performed, and a model checking algorithm is presented. Finally, an intelligent thermostatic system is modeled, and simulation experiments are conducted. The dynamic continuous properties of the system are described using time-based differential equations, and the modeling of uncertain hybrid systems is represented using time-based state machines, allowing for the refinement of each state using time-based state refinement [28]. This paper ensures the consistency between theory and experiments by combining both approaches.

The uncertainty in CPS is effectively addressed by utilizing the uncertain hybrid timed automaton as a formal modeling tool. The establishment of a formal modeling language using GPoLTL for uncertain CPS attributes is a significant contribution. This language enables precise specification and reasoning about uncertain CPS properties, facilitating a thorough analysis of system behavior. The syntax and semantics of GPoLTL are precisely defined, providing a solid foundation for reasoning about uncertain CPS. The utilization of possibility measure calculation in the proposed model serves as a means of verification. This approach quantitatively measures the likelihood of different system behaviors, considering the uncertainties present in the CPS. By incorporating possibility measures, the model enhances the verification process, providing a more comprehensive understanding of system reliability, liveness, and safety properties.

This study effectively utilizes decision processes to address the problem of handling possibility information in uncertain CPS. It not only mitigates the issue of state space explosion but also provides a solution for dealing with possibility information in CPS. This provides a significant opportunity for advancing the design of uncertain CPS and holds great importance in the study of uncertainty in CPS within complex systems. While this research has shed light on several important aspects, it has also raised numerous questions that warrant further investigation. Future studies should delve into exploring uncertainty in CPS within the context of fuzzy mathematics, while considering the relevant properties of its algorithm and computation tree logic.

Author Contributions: Conceptualization, N.C. and Y.L.; methodology, N.C. and Y.L.; software, N.C. and S.G.; validation, N.C. and S.G.; formal analysis, N.C.; investigation, N.C.; data curation, N.C.; writing—original draft preparation, N.C.; writing—review and editing, N.C.; visualization, N.C.; supervision, N.C.; project administration, S.G.; funding acquisition, S.G. All authors have read and agreed to the published version of the manuscript.

Funding: This work was supported by National Key R&D plan (Grant No: 2020YFC1523305), the National Natural Science Foundation (Grant No: 12071271, Grant No: 11671244) and Key R&D and transformation plan of Qinghai Province (No. 2022-QY-203).

Data Availability Statement: Data available on request from the authors.

Conflicts of Interest: The authors declare that they have no conflicts of interest to report regarding the present study.

References

1. Lee, E.A. Cyber Physical Systems: Design Challenges. In Proceedings of the International Symposium on Object/Component/Service-Oriented Real-Time Distributed Computing (ISORC), Orlando, FL, USA, 5–7 May 2008.
2. He, J. Cyber-physical systems. *Commun. Chin. Comput. Soc.* **2010**, *6*, 25–29.
3. Chen, N.; Geng, S. *Modeling and Attribute Verification of Uncertain CPS*; Qinghai Normal University: Qinghai, China, 2016.
4. Liu, X.; Wang, Y.Z.X.A. Research and design for the modeling simulation of CPS. *Comput. Sci.* **2012**, *39*, 32–35.
5. Chen, N.; Geng, S.L.Y.A. Property verification of CPS based on possibility hybrid automaton. *J. Shaanxi Norm. Univ. Natural Sci. Ed.* **2016**, *44*, 26–32.
6. Clarke, E.; Grumberg, O.P.D. *Model Checking*; The MIT Press: London, UK, 1999.
7. Dovier, A.; Quintarelli, E. Applying model-checking to solve queries on semistructured data—ScienceDirect. *Comput. Lang. Syst. Struct.* **2009**, *35*, 143–172.
8. Gao, H.; Huang, W.; Liu, T.; Yin, Y.; Li, Y. PPO2: Location Privacy-Oriented Task Offloading to Edge Computing Using Reinforcement Learning for Intelligent Autonomous Transport Systems. *IEEE Trans. Intell. Transp. Syst.* **2023**, *24*, 7599–7612. [CrossRef]
9. Baier, C.; Katoen, J. *Principles of Model Checking*; The MIT Press: London, UK, 2008.
10. Li, Y.; Li, L. Model Checking of Linear-Time Properties Based on Possibility Measure. *IEEE Trans. Fuzzy Syst.* **2013**, *21*, 842–854. [CrossRef]
11. Yongming, L.I. Two methods for possibilistic linear temporal logic model checking. *J. Shaanxi Norm. Univ.* **2014**, *42*, 21–25.
12. Li, Y.; Li, Y.; Ma, Z. Computation Tree Logic Model Checking Based on Possibility Measures. *Fuzzy Sets Syst.* **2015**, *262*, 44–59. [CrossRef]
13. Liang, C.J.; Li, Y.M. The Model Checking Problem of Computing Tree Logic Based on Generalized Possibility Measures. *Tien Tzu Hsueh Pao/Acta Electron. Sin.* **2017**, *45*, 2641–2648.
14. Zheng, Y.; Ma, J.; Wang, L. Consensus of Hybrid Multi-Agent Systems. *IEEE Trans. Neural Netw. Learn. Syst.* **2018**, *29*, 1359–1365. [CrossRef] [PubMed]
15. Li, T.; Zhang, J.F. Consensus Conditions of Multi-Agent Systems with Time-Varying Topologies and Stochastic Communication Noises. *IEEE Trans. Autom. Control.* **2010**, *55*, 2043–2057. [CrossRef]
16. Zhanyou, M.A.; Yongming, L.I. Model checking generalized possibilistic computation tree logic based on decision processes. *Sci. Sin. Inf.* **2016**, *46*, 1591–1607.
17. Eker, J.; Janneck, J.W.; Lee, E.A.; Liu, J.; Liu, X.; Ludvig, J.; Neuendorffer, S.; Sachs, S.; Xiong, Y. Taming heterogeneity-the Ptolemy approach. *Proc. IEEE* **2003**, *91*, 127–144. [CrossRef]
18. Xu, H.Z.; Li, R.F.; Zeng, L.N. Modeling and simulation of cyber-physical system based on Ptolemy. *J. Syst. Simul.* **2014**, *26*, 1633–1638.
19. Chen, M.C.; Zhang, G. *Research on Verification of Trustworthiness for CPS Software Based on Statistical Model Checking*; Suzhou University: Suzhou, China, 2014.
20. Henzinger, T. The theory of hybrid automata. In Proceedings of the 11th Annual IEEE Symposium on Logic in Computer Science, New Brunswick, NJ, USA, 27–30 July 1996; pp. 278–292. [CrossRef]
21. Zhao, W.M.; Zhang, M. Modeling and verification services of Internet of things based on spatial I/O hybrid automata. *Sci. Technol. Bull.* **2014**, *30*, 95–100.
22. Chen, N.; Geng, S.L.Y.A. Modeling method of CPS based on possibility hybrid automata. *J. Xi'An Univ. Posts Telecommun.* **2016**, *1*, 101–105.
23. Zadeh, L. Fuzzy sets. *Inf. Control.* **1965**, *8*, 338–353. [CrossRef]
24. Ding, X.; Smith, S.L.; Belta, C.; Rus, D. Optimal Control of Markov Decision Processes With Linear Temporal Logic Constraints. *IEEE Trans. Autom. Control.* **2014**, *59*, 1244–1257. [CrossRef]
25. Hahn, E.M.; Han, T.; Zhang, L. Synthesis for PCTL in Parametric Markov Decision Processes. In Proceedings of the NASA Formal Methods, Berlin/Heidelberg, Germany, 18–20 April 2011; pp. 146–161.
26. Li, Y. Quantitative model checking of linear-time properties based on generalized possibility measures. *Fuzzy Sets Syst.* **2017**, *320*, 17–39. [CrossRef]
27. Chen, N.; Geng, S.; Li, L. Modeling and verification of CPS based on uncertain hybrid timed automaton. In Proceedings of the 2021 IEEE International Conference on Dependable, Autonomic and Secure Computing, International Conference on Pervasive Intelligence and Computing, International Conference on Cloud and Big Data Computing, International Conference on Cyber Science and Technology Congress (DASC/PiCom/CBDCom/CyberSciTech), Online, 25–28 October 2021; pp. 971–978. . [CrossRef]
28. Li, X.Y.; Wang, Y.Z.X.E.A. Approach for Cyber-Physical System Simulation Modeling. *J. Syst. Simul.* **2014**, *3*, 631–637.

mathematics MDPI

Article

Utilizing m-Polar Fuzzy Saturation Graphs for Optimized Allocation Problem Solutions

Abdulaziz M. Alanazi [1], Ghulam Muhiuddin [1,*], Bashair M. Alenazi [1], Tanmoy Mahapatra [2] and Madhumangal Pal [2]

1 Department of Mathematics, Faculty of Science, University of Tabuk, P.O. Box 741, Tabuk 71491, Saudi Arabia; am.alenezi@ut.edu.sa (A.M.A.); 391000093@stu.ut.edu.sa (B.M.A.)
2 Department of Applied Mathematics with Oceanology and Computer Programming, Vidyasagar University, Midnapore 721 102, India; tmahapatrapmath@gmail.com (T.M.); mmpalvu@gmail.com (M.P.)
* Correspondence: chishtygm@gmail.com

Abstract: It is well known that crisp graph theory is saturated. However, saturation in a fuzzy environment has only lately been created and extensively researched. It is necessary to consider m components for each node and edge in an m-polar fuzzy graph. Since there is only one component for this idea, we are unable to manage this kind of circumstance using the fuzzy model since we take into account m components for each node as well as edges. Again, since each edge or node only has two components, we are unable to apply a bipolar or intuitionistic fuzzy graph model. In contrast to other fuzzy models, mPFG models produce outcomes of fuzziness that are more effective. Additionally, we develop and analyze these kinds of mPFGs using examples and related theorems. Considering all those things together, we define saturation for a m-polar fuzzy graph (mPFG) with multiple membership values for both vertices and edges; thus, a novel approach is required. In this context, we present a novel method for defining saturation in mPFG involving m saturations for each element in the membership value array of a vertex. This explains α-saturation and β-saturation. We investigate intriguing properties such as α-vertex count and β-vertex count and establish upper bounds for particular instances of mPFGs. Using the concept of α-saturation and α-saturation, block and bridge of mPFG are characterized. To identify the α-saturation and β-saturation mPFGs, two algorithms are designed and, using these algorithms, the saturated mPFG is determined. The time complexity of these algorithms is $O(|V|^3)$, where $|V|$ is the number of vertices of the given graph. In addition, we demonstrate a practical application where the concept of saturation in mPFG is applicable. In this application, an appropriate location is determined for the allocation of a facility point.

Keywords: m-polar fuzzy graph; saturated fuzzy graph, α-saturation; β-saturation; saturation in m-polar fuzzy graph.

MSC: 05C72; 03E72

Citation: Alanazi, A.M.; Muhiuddin, G.; Alenazi, B.M.; Mahapatra, T.; Pal, M. Utilizing m-Polar Fuzzy Saturation Graphs for Optimized Allocation Problem Solutions. *Mathematics* **2023**, *11*, 4136. https://doi.org/10.3390/math11194136

Academic Editor: Michael Voskoglou

Received: 31 August 2023
Revised: 25 September 2023
Accepted: 28 September 2023
Published: 30 September 2023

1. Introduction

Graph theory is a powerful mathematical framework used to model relationships and connections among objects. In many real-world applications, it is essential to understand the strength or degree of association between various elements within a graph. Saturation is a concept that plays a crucial role in quantifying this degree of connection and is particularly significant in both traditional graphs and fuzzy graphs.

In traditional graph theory, saturation refers to the level of connectivity or completeness within a graph. More formally, the saturation of a vertex in a graph is a measure of how many edges are incident upon that vertex concerning the total possible number of edges it could have. In simpler terms, it tells us how closely a particular vertex is connected to others in the graph.

1.1. Research Background and Related Work

Fuzzy graph theory extends the traditional graph theory to capture uncertainty and imprecision in relationships. In fuzzy graphs, saturation takes on a more nuanced meaning. Instead of sharp connectivity values (0 or 1), vertices in fuzzy graphs are associated with degrees of membership that represent the strength of connections.

Saturation in fuzzy graphs involves quantifying the degree to which a vertex is related to other vertices in a fuzzy and uncertain context. It allows us to express the level of association between vertices as fuzzy values, which can be continuous and gradual. This approach is particularly valuable in situations where the connections between elements are not binary but exhibit varying degrees of affinity.

Applications of saturation in fuzzy graphs can be found in fields such as decision-making, pattern recognition, image processing, and artificial intelligence, where imprecise information needs to be modelled and analyzed.

In both traditional and fuzzy graphs, the concept of saturation offers valuable insights into the structure and dynamics of networks and relationships. Whether dealing with crisp, well-defined connections in traditional graphs or handling uncertainty and fuzziness in fuzzy graphs, saturation provides a quantitative measure for characterizing the strength and extent of associations, enabling more informed decision-making and analysis in various domains.

Zadeh [1], in 1965, discovered the ambiguity of the real-life situation and the phenomenon of uncertainty and introduced a fuzzy set that changed how science and technology were portrayed. Zhang [2] explained the bipolar fuzzy set idea as well as presented the possibility of bipolar fuzzy sets in different environmental analyses [3]. First, Kaufman [4] studied the fuzzy graph concept. After that, Rosenfeld [5] supplied the possibility of nodes and edges along with several theoretical ideas such as paths, connectedness, cycle, etc., in fuzziness. Different concepts are presented after that on fuzzy graphs [6]. Several definitions and real-life applications have been studied in [7]. Some new concepts of the fuzzy graph and their generalization are also discussed by Mordeson and Mathew [8]. Nair and Cheng [9] provided fuzzy graphs with fuzzy cliques. Saturation on the fuzzy graph is presented first by Mathew et al. [10]. Chen et al. [11] first presented mPFG. Later on, Ghorai and Pal [12] first introduced density on mPFG. Akram et al. [13,14] studied on a few edge properties of mPFG. Next, Mahapatra et al. [15] studied fuzzy fractional colouring on fuzzy graphs. They also discussed the threshold graph on mPF environment [16]. They also initiated the mPF tolerance graph [17]. Mandal et al. [18] studied the application of strong arcs on mPFG. They also worked on different types of arcs on mPFG [19]. Subrahmanyam [20] also introduced different types of products on mPFG. Several works on fuzzy graphs and their generalization were developed by Nagoorgani et al. [21–24]. For more terminology on fuzzy graphs and its generalized concept, one can see [25–30].

1.2. Framework of This Study

This paper is structured as follows: Section 2 describes some useful definitions in these manuscripts. In Section 3, we have discussed the definitions of the strong node as well as strong edge (SE) count, α-node as well as α-edge count, β-node as well as β-edge count of mPFG and give the lower and upper bound of them in an mPFG. In Section 3.1, we investigate node and edge counts of some well-known mPFG. In Section 4, we introduced saturation in mPFG with the help of α-saturation and β-saturation. Section 5 describes algorithms used to find α-saturated and β-saturated mPFG. Here, we also developed saturation in mPFG. Saturation in mPFG has been used to resolve an application in real life based on an allocation problem, which has been given in Section 6. Finally, a conclusion has been made in Section 7.

1.3. Motivation of the Work

Many issues in daily life have been resolved utilising data from various sources or origins. The multi-polarity of this data collection is represented. We might not be well structured in this sort of polarity by the concepts of fuzzy models or bipolar fuzzy models. For example, we consider a graph model on social groups to explain whether the group is active or not with respect to attributes of cooperation, team spirit, awareness, controlling power, good behaviour, creativeness, etc. We need to express this situation using the 3-polar fuzzy model because these terms are inherently uncertain. A fuzzy model, an intuitionistic fuzzy model, or a bipolar fuzzy model cannot be used to deal with this problem. Thus, the m-polar fuzzy model is more suitable than any fuzzy model. The development and analysis of these kinds of mPFGs with relevant instances and theorems is also quite fascinating. The previous theories about the saturation of mPFGs are unquestionably improved by these definitions and theorems, and they are more trustworthy when it comes to resolving any challenging real-world issue. If anyone considers an example to model a location problem such that there are three components of each node and edge, where the edges MV are given depending on the following criteria: {Condition of roads, traffic jams on the roads, and the communication system between two cities}. This real-life problem can be solved with the help of saturation in mPFG.

1.4. Notations and Symbols

In this section, we revise some of the significant and practical notations that are utilised throughout the whole work to establish the theories. Table 1 provides the abbreviated forms and their meanings.

Table 1. Abbreviation form of some terms.

Full Name	Abbreviation Form
Fuzzy graph	FG
m-polar fuzzy graph	mPFG
Underlying crisp graph	UGC
Membership value	MV
m-polar fuzzy set	mPFS
Strength of connectedness	SC
Strong edge	SE
Maximal spanning tree	MST

2. Preliminaries

In this section, we quickly review several terminologies related to mPFG, such as complete mPFG, strong mPFG, path in mPFG etc.

This article's current $p_s : [0,1]^m \to [0,1]$ denotes s^{th} projection mapping material and $s = 1, 2, \ldots, m$ stands for $s = 1(1)m$.

Definition 1 ([12]). *An mPFG is denoted as $H = (\tilde{V}, \sigma, \gamma)$ over a crisp graph $H^* = (\tilde{V}, \tilde{E})$, where $\tilde{V}$ and $\tilde{E}$ respectively denote the set of vertices and edges of H^*. The functions $\sigma : \tilde{V} \to [0,1]^m$ and $\gamma : \tilde{V} \times \tilde{V} \to [0,1]^m$ represent the membership value of vertices and edges, respectively. Also, $p_i \circ \gamma(x,t) \le p_i \circ \sigma(x) \wedge p_i \circ \sigma(t)$ for every $i = 1(1)m$ and $(x,t) \in \tilde{V} \times \tilde{V}$, while $\gamma(x,t) = 0$ for every $(x,t) \in (\tilde{V} \times \tilde{V} - \tilde{E})$.*

Definition 2 ([12]). *An mPFG $H = (\tilde{V}, \sigma, \gamma)$ is called a complete mPFG if $p_s \circ \gamma(x,t) = \{p_s \circ \sigma(x) \wedge p_s \circ \sigma(t)\}$, for each $x, t \in \tilde{V}$ and $s = 1(1)m$.*

Definition 3 ([12]). *An mPFG $H = (\tilde{V}, \sigma, \gamma)$ is called an mPF strong graph if*

$$p_s \circ \gamma(x,t) = \{p_s \circ \sigma(x) \wedge p_s \circ \sigma(t)\},$$

for every $(x,t) \in \tilde{E}$ *and* $s = 1(1)m$.

Definition 4 **([13]).** *Let* $H = (\tilde{V},\sigma,\gamma)$ *be an mPFG and let* $P : x_1, x_2, \ldots, x_k$ *be a path in* H. $S(P)$ *denotes the strength of* P*, which is defined as* $S(P) = (\gamma_1^k(x_t,x_j), \gamma_2^k(x_t,x_j), \ldots, \gamma_m^k(x_t,x_j))$*, where* $\gamma_s^k(x_t,x_j) = \min_{1 \le t < j \le k} p_s \circ \gamma(x_t,x_j)$.

The strength of connectedness of the path between x_1 *and* x_k *is given as follows:* $CONN_G(x_1,x_k) = (p_1 \circ \gamma(x_t,x_j)^{\infty}, p_2 \circ \gamma(x_t,x_j)^{\infty}, \ldots, p_m \circ \gamma(x_t,x_j)^{\infty})$*, where* $(p_s \circ \gamma(x_t,x_j)^{\infty}) = \max_{n \in N}\{p_s \circ \gamma^n(x_t,x_j)\}$.

Definition 5 **([19]).** *Suppose* $H = (V,\alpha,\mu)$ *is an mPFG and let* (x,z) *be an edge in* G*. If* $\forall$ $s = 1(1)m$, $p_s \circ \mu(x,z) > p_s \circ CONN_{H-(x,z)}(x,z)$ *holds, then* (x,z) *is called* α*-strong.*
$\forall\, s = 1(1)m$*, if*

$$p_s \circ \mu(x,z) = p_s \circ CONN_{H-(x,z)}(x,z) \text{ holds},$$

then (x,z) *is called* β*-strong.*

$\forall\, s = 1(1)m$*, if*

$$p_s \circ \mu(x,z) < p_s \circ CONN_{H-(x,z)}(x,z) \text{ holds},$$

then (x,z) *is called* δ*-strong, respectively.*

Definition 6 **([18]).** *An mPFG* $H = (V,\sigma,\mu)$ *is said to be mPF tree if there exists a spanning mPF subgraph* $H' = (V,\sigma',\mu')$*, which is an mPF tree and* $p_s \circ \mu'(a,c) = 0$ *means* $p_s \circ CONN_{H'}(a,c) > p_s \circ \mu'(a,c)$*, for* $s = 1(1)m$.

Definition 7 **([18]).** *Suppose* $H = (V,\alpha,\mu)$ *is an mPFG. An arc* (a,c) *is said to be an mPF bridge if deletion of it decreases the SC between some other pair of nodes of* H.

Definition 8 **([12]).** *Suppose* $H = (V,\sigma,\mu)$ *as well as* $H' = (V',\sigma',\mu')$ *are two mPFGs. If there exists a mapping* $\phi : H \to H'$ *such that* $s = 1(1)m$

(i) $\quad p_s \circ \sigma(a) = p_s \circ \sigma'(\phi(a)), \forall\, a \in V.$

(ii) $\quad p_s \circ \mu(a,c) = p_s \circ \mu'(\phi(a),\phi(c)), \forall\, (a,c) \in \widetilde{V \times V}.$

Then H*, as well as* H'*, are called isomorphic. We write it as* $H \cong H'$.

3. Node as Well as Edge Saturation Counts of *m*PFG

The node and edge saturation counts in *m*PFG are defined here and characterized also. An *m*PFG's node saturation count and edge saturation count both show the proportion of SEs in the *m*PFG and the *m*PFG's mean strong degree, respectively. Here, we consider $\sigma(u) = \mathbf{1} = (1,1,\ldots,1), \forall u \in V$.

Definition 9. *Suppose* H *is an mPFG. Then the strong node count of* H *is indicated by* $S_V(H)$ *and given as*

$$p_s \circ S_V(H) = \frac{Sum\ of\ s^{th}\ components\ of\ MV\ of\ all\ SE\ of\ H}{|V|}$$
$$= \frac{Sum\ of\ s^{th}\ components\ of\ MV\ of\ all\ \alpha - strong\ edge\ or\ \beta - strong\ edge\ of\ H}{|V|}$$

$\forall s = 1(1)m.$

The SE count of H is indicated by $S_E(H)$ as well as given by

$$p_s \circ S_V(H) = \frac{Sum\ of\ s^{th}\ components\ of\ MV\ of\ all\ SE\ of\ H}{|E|}$$
$$= \frac{Sum\ of\ s^{th}\ components\ of\ MV\ of\ all\ \alpha strong\ edge\ or\ \beta - strong\ edge\ of\ H}{|E|}$$

$\forall s = 1(1)m.$

Definition 10. *Let H be an mPFG having UCG H^*. Then the α-node count $\alpha_V(H)$ of H is defined as*

$$p_s \circ \alpha_V(H) = \frac{Sum\ of\ s^{th}\ components\ of\ MV\ of\ all\ \alpha - SE\ of\ H}{|V|}$$

$\forall s = 1(1)m.$

The α-SE count $\alpha_E(H)$ of H is given by

$$p_s \circ \alpha_E(H) = \frac{Sum\ of\ s^{th}\ components\ of\ MV\ of\ all\ \alpha - SE\ of\ H}{|E|}$$

$\forall s = 1(1)m.$

Definition 11. *Let H be an mPFG having UCG H^*. Then the β-node count $\beta_V(H)$ of H is defined as*

$$p_s \circ \beta_V(H) = \frac{Sum\ of\ s^{th}\ components\ of\ MV\ of\ all\ \beta - SE\ of\ H}{|V|}$$

$\forall s = 1(1)m.$

The β-SE count $\beta_E(H)$ of H is given by

$$p_s \circ \beta_E(H) = \frac{Sum\ of\ s^{th}\ components\ of\ MV\ of\ all\ \beta - SE\ of\ H}{|E|}$$

$\forall s = 1(1)m.$

Example 1. *Here, we take a 3PFG, shown in Figure 1, to depict the above definitions. Here, we take into account all crisp nodes.*

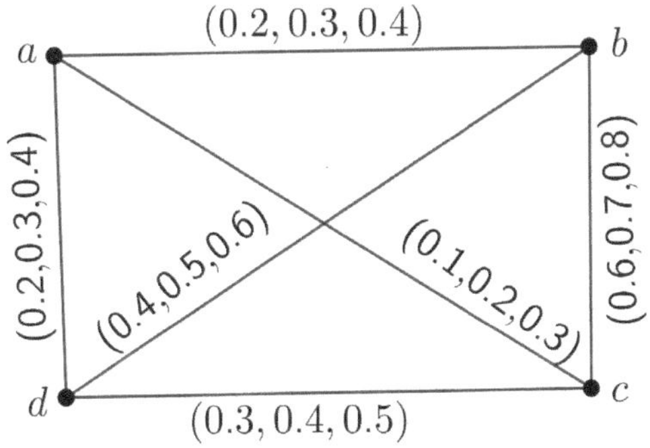

Figure 1. A 3PFG H for illustration of Example 1.

Here, the classified edges are given in Table 2.

Table 2. Classification of edges of Figure 1.

Edge	Classification
(a,b)	β-strong
(b,c)	α-strong
(a,d)	β-strong
(b,d)	α-strong
(a,c)	δ-strong
(d,c)	δ-strong

α-node count of H is

$$\alpha_V(H) = (\frac{0.6+0.4}{4}, \frac{0.7+0.5}{4}, \frac{0.8+0.6}{4}) = (0.25, 0.3, 0.35)$$

and α-edge count of H is

$$\alpha_E(H) = (\frac{0.6+0.4}{6}, \frac{0.7+0.5}{6}, \frac{0.8+0.6}{6}) = (0.16, 0.2, 0.23)$$

β-node count of H is

$$\beta_V(H) = (\frac{0.2+0.2}{4}, \frac{0.3+0.3}{4}, \frac{0.4+0.4}{4}) = (0.1, 0.15, 0.2)$$

and β-edge count of H is

$$\beta_E(H) = (\frac{0.2+0.2}{6}, \frac{0.3+0.3}{6}, \frac{0.4+0.4}{6}) = (0.067, 0.1, 0.13)$$

Strong-node count of H is

$$S_V(H) = (\frac{1.4}{4}, \frac{1.8}{4}, \frac{2.2}{4}) = (0.35, 0.45, 0.55)$$

and Strong-edge count of H is

$$S_E(H) = (\frac{1.4}{6}, \frac{1.8}{6}, \frac{2.2}{6}) = (0.23, 0.3, 0.36)$$

Every edge in a mPF tree is α-strong, according to Theorem 3.18 of [19]. Therefore, $p_s \circ \alpha_V(G) = \frac{n-1}{n}$ and $p_s \circ \alpha_E(G) = \frac{n-1}{n-1} = 1$, where $n =$ no. of nodes in a mPF tree G as a whole.

The number of α-strong nodes never surpasses the number of nodes for any other mPFG than the mPF tree. For a complete mPFG, all possible edges can be made β-strong by allotting the same MV to the nodes. Then $p_s \circ \beta_V(G) = \frac{\binom{n}{2}}{2}$ and $p_s \circ \beta_E(G) = \frac{\binom{n}{2}}{\binom{n}{2}} = 1$, $s = 1(1)m$.

Depending on the above observation, we can say the following:

Proposition 1. *Suppose H is an mPFG where $|V| = n$. Then*

(i) $0 \le p_s \circ \alpha_V(H) \le \frac{n-1}{n}$.
(ii) $0 \le p_s \circ \alpha_E(H) \le 1$.
(iii) $0 \le p_s \circ \beta_V(H) \le \frac{\binom{n}{2}}{2}$.
(iv) $0 \le p_s \circ \beta_E(H) \le 1$.
(v) $0 \le p_s \circ S_V(H) \le \frac{\binom{n}{2}}{2}$.
(vi) $0 \le p_s \circ S_E(H) \le 1$.

$s = 1(1)m$.

Proposition 2. *Suppose H is an mPF tree. Then* $0 \leq p_s \circ \alpha_V(H) \leq p_s \circ \alpha_E(H), s = 1(1)m$.

Proof. As H is an mPF tree, therefore $p_s \circ \alpha_V(H) = \frac{n-1}{n}, s = 1(1)m$ and $p_s \circ \alpha_E(H) = \frac{n-1}{n-1} = 1, s = 1(1)m$. Hence, $0 \leq p_s \circ \alpha_V(H) \leq p_s \circ \alpha_E(H), s = 1(1)m$. □

3.1. Vertex and Edge Counts of Some Well-Known mPFG

In this portion, we talk over saturation counts of mPFG structures such as mPF cycles, trees as well as blocks in mPFG. Some necessary parts for these structures are also obtained.

Theorem 1. *Suppose H is an mPFG where* $|V| = w$. *Then, the following condition is identical:*

(i) *H be an mPF tree.*
(ii) $p_s \circ \alpha_V(H) = \frac{w-1}{w}$ *as well as* $p_s \circ \alpha_E(H) = 1, s = 1(1)m$.
(iii) $w \times p_s \circ \alpha_V(H) = (w-1) \times p_s \circ \alpha_E(H), s = 1(1)m$.

Proof. $(i) \Rightarrow (ii)$ is completed previously. $(ii) \Rightarrow (iii)$ Suppose that $p_s \circ \alpha_V(H) = \frac{w-1}{w}$ and $p_s \circ \alpha_E(H) = 1, s = 1(1)m$.

$$\begin{aligned} p_s \circ \alpha_V(H) &= \frac{w-1}{w} \\ \Rightarrow w \times p_s \circ \alpha_V(H) &= (w-1) \\ \Rightarrow w \times p_s \circ \alpha_V(H) &= (w-1) \times 1 \\ \Rightarrow w \times p_s \circ \alpha_V(H) &= (w-1) \times p_s \circ \alpha_E(H) \qquad [\text{As } p_s \circ \alpha_E(H) = 1] \end{aligned}$$

Hence, $n \times p_s \circ \alpha_V(H) = (w-1) \times p_s \circ \alpha_E(H), s = 1(1)m$. $(iii) \Rightarrow (i)$ Suppose that $w \times p_s \circ \alpha_V(H) = (w-1) \times p_s \circ \alpha_E(H), s = 1(1)m$.

Since,

$$\begin{aligned} w \times p_s \circ \alpha_V(H) &= (w-1) \times p_s \circ \alpha_E(H) \\ \Rightarrow \frac{p_s \circ \alpha_V(H)}{p_s \circ \alpha_E(H)} &= \frac{(w-1)}{w} \\ \Rightarrow \frac{p_s \circ \alpha_V(H)}{p_s \circ \alpha_E(H)} &= \frac{(w-1)}{w} = p_s \circ \alpha_V(H), \end{aligned}$$

this shows that $p_s \circ \alpha_E(H) = 1, s = 1(1)m$.

Hence, H is connected and acyclic only when every edge is α-strong; therefore, H is a tree. □

Theorem 2. *Suppose H is a connected mPFG. H is an mPF tree iff* $p_s \circ \alpha_V(H) = p_s \circ S_V(H)$ *as well as* $p_s \circ \alpha_E(H) = p_s \circ S_E(H), s = 1(1)m$.

Proof. Suppose H is a connected mPFG as well as an mPF tree. Now, from Theorem 3.19 of [18], we know that H is free from β-SEs. Therefore,

$$p_s \circ \beta_V(H) = \frac{0}{|V|} = 0, \ s = 1(1)m$$

and

$$p_s \circ \beta_E(H) = \frac{0}{|E|} = 0, \ s = 1(1)m.$$

Therefore,

$$p_s \circ \alpha_V(H) = p_i \circ S_V(H), \ s = 1(1)m$$

and

$$p_s \circ \alpha_E(H) = p_s \circ S_E(H), \ s = 1(1)m.$$

Conversely, let $p_s \circ \alpha_V(H) = p_s \circ S_V(H)$ and $p_s \circ \alpha_E(H) = p_s \circ S_E(H)$, for $s = 1, 2, \ldots, m$. Whenever H defines a cycle, then H is an mPF tree. Take C to represent a cycle in H. Hence, C must have only α-strong and δ-SEs only. Again, consider that H does not have all α-SEs. Therefore, H contains at least one δ-SE. Suppose e is an δ-SE. Then, we remove it from C. If a unique MST is found, then the condition is complete. Otherwise, we remove each δ-SE individually from C until we get a specific MST of H. □

Theorem 3. *Let a connected mPFG H be an mPF tree iff* $p_s \circ \alpha_V(H) = p_s \circ \alpha_V(F), s = 1(1)m$ *, where F is MST of G.*

Proof. Let H be an mPF tree. So, H and F are isomorphic. Therefore,

$$\begin{aligned} p_s \circ \alpha_V(H) &= \frac{count\ of\ \alpha - SE\ of\ H}{no.\ of\ nodes} \\ &= \frac{count\ of\ \alpha - SE\ of\ F}{no.\ of\ nodes} \\ &= p_s \circ \alpha_V(F) \end{aligned}$$

$s = 1(1)m$. □

Now, we consider another case. Let H contain a cycle C. Then, it is not free from δ-SE. Let q be a δ-SE . If $H - q$ is a tree, then $H - q$ and F are isomorphic. Therefore,

$$p_s \circ \alpha_V(H) = p_s \circ \alpha_V(F),\ s = 1(1)m.$$

If $H - q$ is not a tree, then we delete the δ-SEs in $H - e$ in a similar way to obtain an MST F of H, such that $p_s \circ \alpha_V(H) = p_s \circ \alpha_V(F), s = 1(1)m$.

Conversely, let $p_s \circ \alpha_V(H) = p_s \circ \alpha_V(F), s = 1(1)m$, in which F corresponds to H's MST. We have to show that H is an mPF tree. Supposing H is not an mPF tree, it must have one β-SE, say (a, b). Let $c - d$ be another path P in H for which $p_s \circ \mu(c, d) \geq p_s \circ \mu(a, b)$, $s = 1(1)m$ and $\forall\ (c, d) \in P$. Now, the joining of P and (a, b) creates a cycle in H. Let k be the count of α-SEs, which are incident at a. To find F, take (a, b) out of H since it has the least weight in C. Then the count of α-SEs connected to c in F is $k + 1$. Suppose the remaining counts of α-SEs are k_1. Hence, $p_s \circ \alpha_V(H) = \frac{k+1}{|V|}$ as well as $p_s \circ \alpha_V(F) = \frac{k+k_1+1}{|V|}$, $s = 1(1)m$, which is a contrast. This contradiction leads to the theorem.

4. Saturation in m-Polar Fuzzy Graph

Here, saturation in terms of the node and edge counts is presented. In this section, we also studied some of its interesting facts. We also studied saturated blocks in mPFG.

Definition 12. *Suppose H is an mPFG. Then H is called α-saturate (α − S) if it must have one α-SEs incident with each node of H. H is said to be β-strong saturate if it must have one β-SE incident with each node of H.*

Definition 13. *Suppose H is an mPFG. H is called a saturate graph if it has at least one α-SE as well as β-SEs incident with every node of H. Otherwise, H is called an unsaturated mPFG.*

Example 2. *To illustrate the above definition, we consider a 3PFG H displayed in Figure 2 whose nodes all have MV* $(1, 1, 1)$.

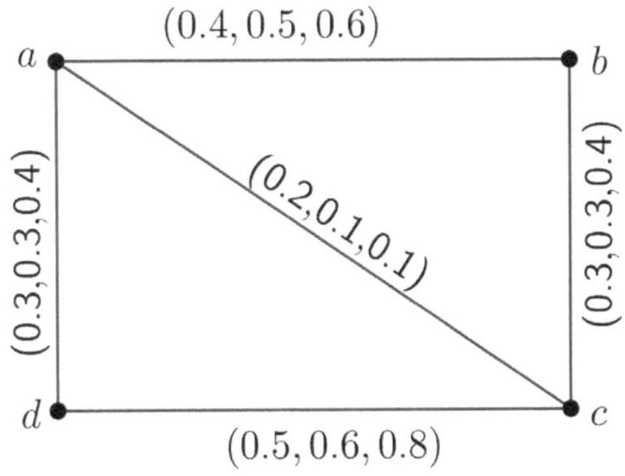

Figure 2. 3PFG H having four nodes.

Here, we see that the edges $(a, b), (c, d)$ are α-SEs and $(c, b), (a, d)$ are β-SEs. The edges (a, c) are δ-SE. Each node is connected with α-SE and β-SE. Therefore, H is a saturated 3PFG.

Theorem 4. *Suppose H as well as $H' = (V', \sigma', \mu')$ are two isomorphic mPFGs. If H is saturated, H' is also saturated.*

Proof. Let $\phi : H \to H'$ be the isomorphism between two mPFGs. To show H' is saturated, we have to show that each node is connected with at least one α-SE as well as β-SEs. Let $w' \in V'$. Then there must be a node, say w, in H for which $\phi(w) = w'$. Since H is saturated, therefore w is incident with at least one α-SE and one β-SE. Since, H and H' are isomorphic with each other, therefore, w' is also incident with at least one α-SE and one β-SE. Hence, H' is also saturated.

Let H be an mPFG having UCG H^* where $|V| = k$. We define a finite collection $\alpha_S(H) = (n_1, n_2, \ldots, n_k)$ called α-strong sequence where, $n_j =$ is the count of α-SEs connected to node v_j. We define a finite collection $\beta_S(H) = (n_1, n_2, \ldots, n_k)$ called β-strong sequence where, $n_j =$ count of β-SEs connect at node v_j. Since the count of SEs of $H =$ (the count of α-SEs of H + the count of β-SEs of H), therefore,

$$\sum_{n_j \in \alpha_S(H)} n_j + \sum_{n_j \in \beta_S(H)} n_j = \sum_{n_j \in S_S(H)} n_j$$

□

Theorem 5. *Suppose H is an mPFG having UGC H^* where $|V| = k$. Then H is α-saturated iff $\sum_{n_j \in \alpha_S(H)} n_j \geq k$.*

Proof. Suppose H is an α-saturated mPFG. Therefore, at least one α-SE is incident with each node of H. Thus,

$$\sum_{n_j \in \alpha_S(H)} n_j \geq 1 + 1 + \ldots + 1$$

$$\Rightarrow \sum_{n_j \in \alpha_S(H)} n_j \geq k$$

Conversely, let $\sum_{n_j \in \alpha_S(H)} n_j \geq k$. Then, all k nodes of H are connected with at least one α-SE. Therefore, H is α-saturated mPFG. □

Theorem 6. *Suppose H is an mPFG where $|V| = k$. Then H is β-saturated iff* $\sum_{n_j \in \beta_S(H)} n_j \geq k$.

Proof. Similar to the above theorem. □

Theorem 7. *Suppose H is an mPFG where $|V| = k$. If H is β-saturated, then* $\sum_{n_j \in S_S(H)} n_j \geq 2k$.

Proof. Let H be saturated. Therefore, each node of H is connected with at least one α-SE and one β-SE. Thus, $\sum_{n_j \in S_S(H)} n_j \geq 2k$. □

Theorem 8. *Suppose H is an mPFG with UGC H^* where $|V| = w$. If*

(i) $p_s \circ \alpha_V(H) \geq 0.5$ *if α-saturated.*
(ii) $p_s \circ \beta_V(H) \geq 0.5$ *if β-saturated.*
(iii) $p_s \circ S_V(H) \geq 1$ *if saturated.*

$s = 1(1)m$.

Proof. (i) Let H be α-S. Then every node of H is incident with at least one α-SE. Therefore, H must have $\frac{w}{2}$, α-SEs. Therefore, $p_s \circ \alpha_V(H) \geq \frac{\frac{w}{2}}{w} = 0.5$. (ii) Similar to the above. (iii) Let H be saturated. Therefore, every node of H is connected, having a minimum of α-SEs and β-SEs. Therefore, the count of SEs of $H =$ (the count of α-SEs of H + the count of β-SEs of $H) \geq \frac{w}{2} + \frac{w}{2} = n$. Hence, $p_s \circ S_V(H) \geq \frac{w}{w} = 1$. □

In Figure 3, all the nodes have MV $(1,1,1)$, that is $\sigma(a_j) = (1,1,1),\ for\ j = 1,2,\ldots,12$. The edges MV are $\mu(a_j, a_k) = (0.6, 0.6, 0.6)$, where $1 \leq j < k \leq 12$ and j is odd and k is even. The edges MV is $\mu(a_j, a_k) = (0.4, 0.4, 0.4)$, where $1 < j < k < 12$ and j is even and k is odd. The edge MV between a_1 and a_{12} is $(0.4, 0.4, 0.4)$.

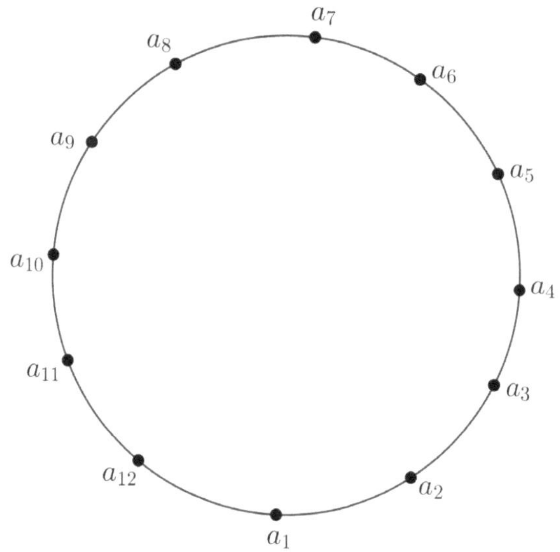

Figure 3. 3PFG H having an even number of nodes.

In Figure 3, we see that all the edges having MV $(0.6, 0.6, 0.6)$ are α-strong and the edges having MV $(0.4, 0.4, 0.4)$ are β-strong. Therefore, Figure 3 is saturated.

In Figure 4, all the nodes have MV $(1,1,1)$, that is $\sigma(a_j) = (1,1,1),\ for\ j = 1,2,\ldots,9$. The edges MV is $\mu(a_j, a_k) = (0.5, 0.5, 0.5)$, where $1 \leq j < k \leq 9$ and j is odd and k is even.

The edges MV are $\mu(a_j, a_k) = (0.7, 0.7, 0.7)$, where $1 < j < k < 9$ and j is even and k is odd. The edge MV between a_1 and a_9 is $(0.5, 0.5, 0.5)$.

In Figure 4, we see that all the edges having MV $(0.7, 0.7, 0.7)$ are α-strong and the edges having MV $(0.5, 0.5, 0.5)$ are β-strong. Therefore, Figure 4 is unsaturated as the node a_1 connected with both the β-SEs.

One simple observation of the above discussion is that Figure 3 has an even number of nodes while Figure 4 has an odd number of nodes. Thus, the next hypothesis applies.

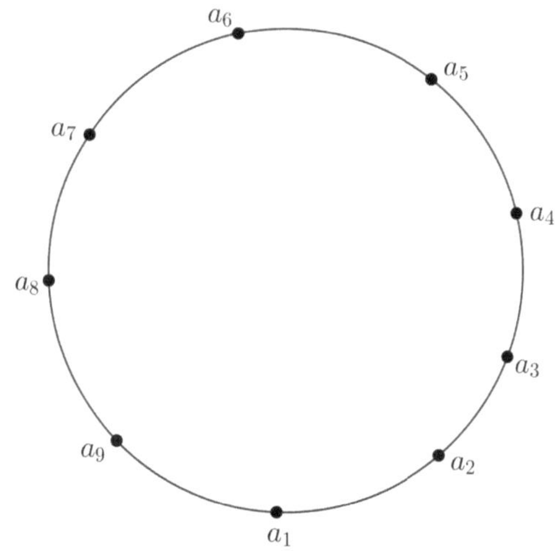

Figure 4. 3PFG G having odd number of nodes.

Theorem 9. *Suppose C_n is an mPF cycle. If the next two hold, it is saturated:*

(i) $n = 2t$, *t is a positive integer.*
(ii) *α-SE as well as β-SEs occur as an alternate C_n.*

Proof. Let C_n be an mPF cycle. Therefore, it is free from δ-SEs. All arcs occurring on C_n are α-SE or β-SE. Let us assume that C_n is saturated. Therefore, each node is connected with at least one α-SE and one β-SEs. Hence, the count of α-SEs $= t =$ the count of β-SEs. Therefore, $n = 2t$. Again, every node connected with both α-SEs as well as β-SEs happen if they occur as an alternate C_n. □

Conversely, let C_n be a fuzzy cycle with an even number of nodes in which each node is connected with both α-SEs and β-SEs alternatively. Therefore, each node is connected with precisely one α-SE and β-SEs. Hence, C_n is a saturated fuzzy cycle.

Theorem 10. *Suppose G is an mPF cycle. If H is saturated, it must be a block.*

Proof. Since H is saturated, each node is connected with at least one α-SE as well as one β-SE. Again, since H is an mPF cycle, every node is connected with just two nodes. Therefore, each node contains precisely one alpha-SE and one beta-SE. Hence, removing any node from H may not decrease SC between other nodes. This shows that H is free from mPF cut node; therefore, H is a block. □

Theorem 11. *Let H be an mPF cycle. If H is an mPF block, then either it is β-saturated or it is saturated.*

Proof. Let a block be H. We demand that H is free from δ-SEs. If possible, let e be a δ-SE. Then the remaining edges must be α-SE; therefore, G contains $n - 2$ fuzzy cut nodes, which is an irrelevance. So, H has no δ-SEs. Thus, H is free from δ-SEs. □

If H has only α-SEs as well as β-SEs, they appear alternatively; otherwise, the block shape will not be found. If the count of α-SEs = the count of β-SEs $=\frac{n}{2}$, then H is α-saturated as well as β-saturated; therefore, it is saturated. If the count of α-SEs is less than the count of β-SEs, then H must be only β-S. For another case, when the count of α-SEs is greater than the count of β-SEs, this will not be true as it does not form a block. If every of arc is β-strong of H, then it must be β-saturated. Therefore, the theorem is proved.

Theorem 12. *A complete mPFG has no δ-arcs.*

Proof. Suppose G is a complete mPFG. Let G have a δ-arc. Let (p,q) be the δ-arcs. Then we have,

$$p_s \circ \mu(p,q) < p_s \circ CONN_{G-(p,q)}\mu(p,q),\ s = 1(1)m.$$

□

In G, a stronger path P that excludes the arc (p,q) must exist. Suppose $p_s \circ \mu(p,q) = t_i$, $s = 1(1)m$ and the strength of P are $(u_1, u_2, \ldots, u_m)$. Therefore, we have $t_i < u_i$, $s = 1(1)m$. Suppose r is the first node after u in the path P. Then, we have

$$p_s \circ \mu(p,r) > t_i,\ \forall\, s = 1(1)m \tag{1}$$

In a similar way, let s be the last node before q in the path P. Again, we also have

$$p_s \circ \mu(s,q) > t_i,\ \forall\, s = 1(1)m \tag{2}$$

Since G is a complete mPFG, we therefore have $p_s \circ \mu(p,t) = min\{p_s \circ \sigma(p), p_s \circ \sigma(t)\}$, $s = 1(1)m$ as well as $\forall\ (p,t) \in E$. Therefore, at least one of $p_s \circ \sigma(p)$ or $p_s \circ \sigma(t)$ is t_i, $s = 1(1)m$.

Therefore, (1) will contradict if $p_s \circ \sigma(p) = t_i$, $s = 1(1)m$ and (2) will contradict if $p_s \circ \sigma(t) = t_i$, for $s = 1(1)m$.

Hence, we conclude the theorem.

Theorem 13. *Suppose H is an mPFG. An arc (a,c) is a bridge if it is α-strong.*

Proof. Suppose (a,c) is an mPF bridge. Then we have from the definition of mPF bridge,

$$p_s \circ CONN_{H-(a,c)}(a,c) < p_s \circ CONN_H(a,c), for\ s = 1(1)m \tag{3}$$

Again, from Theorem 3.11 of [19], we have

$$p_s \circ \mu(a,c) = p_s \circ CONN_H(a,c), s = 1(1)m \tag{4}$$

From Equations (3) and (4), we get $p_s \circ \mu(a,c) > p_s \circ CONN_{H-(a,c)}(a,c)$, $s = 1(1)m$. Hence, (a,c) be α-SE.

Conversely, suppose (a,c) is an α-SE. Then, we have (a,c) as the one and only strongest path in between a and c, and the removal of (a,c) will decrease the SC of a and c. Therefore, (a,c) is a bridge. □

Theorem 14. *A complete mPFG has at most one α-SE.*

Proof. We know that complete mPFG have at most one mPF bridge. Again, from Theorem 13, we have an arc (a,b) that is an mPF bridge iff it is α-SE. Hence, a complete mPFG has at most one α-SE. □

Proposition 3. *Every complete mPFG has at most $\binom{w}{2}$ or $\binom{w}{2}$-1 β-SEs.*

Theorem 15. *If H is a complete mPFG having w nodes, then few disparities hold.*

(i) $0 \leq p_s \circ \alpha_V(H) \leq \frac{1}{w}$.
(ii) $\frac{w^2-w-2}{2w} \leq p_s \circ \beta_V(H) \leq \frac{w-1}{2}$.
$s = 1(1)m$.

Proof. With the help of Theorem 14, we conclude that H can have at most one α-SE. Hence, we have $p_s \circ \alpha_V(H) \leq \frac{1}{w}, s = 1(1)m$. Again, clearly $p_s \circ \alpha_V(H) \geq 0, s = 1(1)m$. Therefore, $0 \leq p_s \circ \alpha_V(H) \leq \frac{1}{w}, s = 1(1)m$.

Again, from Proposition 3, we are aware that the minimal number of β-SEs is $\binom{w}{2}-1$. Therefore,

$$p_s \circ \beta_V(H) \geq \frac{w(\frac{w-1}{2}) - 1}{w}$$
$$\geq \frac{w^2 - w - 2}{2w}$$

Thus, $\frac{w^2-w-2}{2w} \leq p_s \circ \beta_V(H) \leq \frac{w-1}{2}, s = 1(1)m$.

Next, we will try to find out the upper limit of the α-node count for a block in mPFG. □

Theorem 16. *If H is an mPF block, we have $p_s \circ \alpha_V(G) \leq 0.5, s = 1(1)m$.*

Proof. To prove this, we first try to determine the maximum count of α-SEs of H. Let $|V| = n$. We know that if more than one α-SEs are connected with a common node, then the node is a mPF cut node. Since H is an mPF block, it therefore has no mPF cut node. Therefore, the maximum count of α-SEs of H is $\frac{w}{2}$. Thus, $p_s \circ \alpha_V(H) \leq \frac{\frac{w}{2}}{w} = 0.5$, $s = 1(1)m$. □

Theorem 17. *An mPF block H is α-saturated then $p_s \circ \alpha_V(H) = 0.5, s = 1(1)m$.*

Proof. Let H be α-saturated. Since H is an mPF block, it therefore has no mPF cut node. Hence, every node is incident with exactly unique α-SE. Therefore, H contains exactly $\frac{w}{2}$ the count of α-SEs. Thus, $p_s \circ \alpha_V(H) = \frac{\frac{w}{2}}{w} = 0.5$, for $s = 1(1)m$. □

5. Algorithms

In this section, three algorithms are designed to find α-saturated mPFG, β-saturated mPFG and saturated mPFG.

Let $H^* = (V, E)$ be the crisp graph for the given mPFG.

Step 1 assigns the membership values to all nodes, and Step 2 does the same for all edges. So, the time complexities for these steps are $O(|V|)$ and $O(|E|)$, respectively. Finding connectedness between a pair of vertices is equivalent to finding all pairs' shortest paths. Many algorithms are available to find all pairs of shortest paths, and their time complexity depends on the specific algorithm, data structure and type of graphs. Let such time complexity be $O(\chi(G))$. So, the time complexity of Step 3 is $O(\chi(G))$. Step 4 and Step 5 take $O(|E|)$ and $O(|V|)$, respectively. Step 6 takes only $O(|V|)$ time. Hence, the total time complexity of Algorithm 1 is $O(|V| + |E|) + O(\chi(G)) = O(|E| + \chi(G))$. In the worst case, $O(\chi(G)) = O(|V|^3)$. So, the worst case time complexity of Algorithm 1 is $O(|V|^3)$, as the maximum value of $|E|$ is $|V|^2$.

The time complexities of Algorithms 2 and 3 are the same as in Algorithm 1.

Algorithm 1 An algorithm to find α-saturation in mPFG

Input: A mPFG $H = (V, \sigma, \mu)$.
Output: Finding α-saturated mPFG.
Step 1: Put the MV of nodes a_j, $j = 1(1)w$.
Step 2: Put the MV of edges that satisfied $p_s \circ \mu(a_j, a_k) \leq \inf\{p_s \circ \sigma(a_j), p_s \circ \sigma(a_k)\}$, $s = 1(1)m$.
Step 3: Calculate $p_s \circ CONN_{H-((a_j,a_k))}(a_j, a_k), for\ s = 1(1)m,\ \forall(a_j, a_k) \in E$.
Step 4: Verify $p_s \circ \mu(a_j, a_k) > p_s \circ CONN_{H-(a_j,a_k)}(a_j, a_k), \forall(a_j, a_k) \in E$.
Step 5: Select all α-SEs in H.
Step 6: Check whether every node is connected with at least one α-SE or not.

Algorithm 2 An algorithm to find β-saturation in mPFG

Input: A mPFG $H = (V, \sigma, \mu)$.
Output: Finding β-saturated mPFG.
Step 1: Put the MV of nodes a_j, $j = 1(1)w$.
Step 2: Put the MV of edges that satisfied $p_s \circ \mu(a_j, a_k) \leq \inf\{p_s \circ \sigma(a_j), p_s \circ \sigma(a_k)\}$, $s = 1(1)m$.
Step 3: Find $p_s \circ CONN_{H-((a_j,a_k))}(a_j, a_k), for\ s = 1(1)m,\ \forall(a_j, a_k) \in E$.
Step 4: Verify $p_s \circ \mu(a_j, a_k) = p_s \circ CONN_{H-(a_j,a_k)}(a_j, a_k), \forall(a_j, a_k) \in E$.
Step 5: Select all β-SEs in H.
Step 6: Check whether every node is connected with at least one β-SE or not.

Algorithm 3 An algorithm to find saturation in mPFG

Input: A mPFG $H = (V, \sigma, \mu)$.
Output: Finding saturated mPFG.
Step 1: Put the MV of nodes a_j, $j = 1(1)w$.
Step 2: Put the MV of edges that satisfied $p_s \circ \mu(a_j, a_k) \leq \inf\{p_s \circ \sigma(a_j), p_s \circ \sigma(a_k)\}$, $s = 1(1)m$.
Step 3: Using Algorithms 1 and 2 identified all α-strong as well as β-SEs in G.
Step 4: Check whether every node is connected with at least one α-SE as well as β-SEs or not.

6. Application

Decision-making in allocation problems is a multifaceted process that requires a systematic approach, consideration of various factors, and a balance between optimizing objectives and meeting constraints. Effective decision-making in allocation can lead to improved resource utilization, cost savings, and overall better outcomes for organizations and society. The mPFG is a fundamental mathematical framework that depicts facts from real life that are related by graphical systems, where nodes and edges are made up of m-polar fuzzy information. In this section, we attempt to resolve a specific allocation problem using saturation in mPFG.

6.1. Model Construction

Education is a crucial concern for everyone in the current world. Everyone gets the chance to read and write thanks to the 2005 Right to Education (RTE) law. IIT (Indian Institute of Technology) is one of the most significant universities in India's educational system. Therefore, it is not a simple undertaking for any Government to construct an IIT in a town among other towns.

In this case, nine towns $(a_1, a_2, \ldots, a_9)$ are regarded as nodes. If there is a road link between two nodes, then there will be an edge. Here, we use saturation in 3PFG G to solve the allocation problem. Since the town is fixed in nature, we can therefore assign the MV of each node $(1, 1, 1)$, that is, $\sigma(a_i) = (1, 1, 1)$, for $i = 1, 2, \ldots, 9$. The edge MVs are calculated depending on three criteria. Those criteria are as follows: {Condition of roads, traffic jams on the roads, communication system between two cities}. All the indicators of an edge between two towns are uncertain in nature. We can calculate the edge MVs by remembering the relation $p_s \circ \mu(a,c) \leq inf\{p_s \circ \sigma(a), p_s \circ \sigma(c)\}$, $s = 1(1)m$. The model 3PFG is shown in Figure 5.

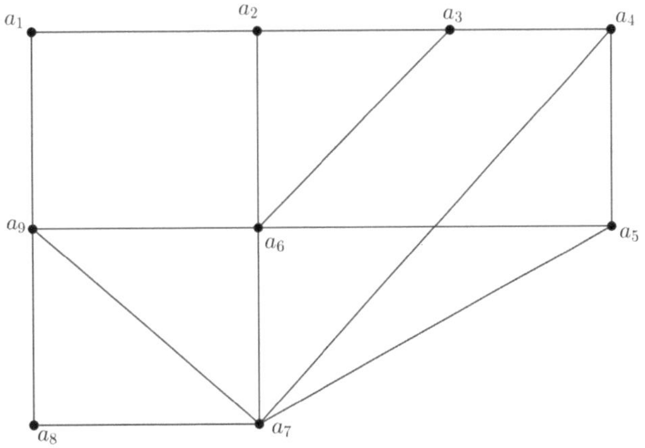

Figure 5. Model 3PFG G.

Here, the edges MV are given in Table 3.

Table 3. The edge membership value of Figure 5.

Edge	Membership Value
(a_1, a_2)	$(0.5, 0.4, 0.3)$
(a_2, a_3)	$(0.5, 0.4, 0.3)$
(a_3, a_4)	$(0.3, 0.2, 0.1)$
(a_4, a_5)	$(0.3, 0.2, 0.1)$
(a_5, a_7)	$(0.6, 0.5, 0.4)$
(a_7, a_8)	$(0.5, 0.4, 0.3)$
(a_8, a_9)	$(0.3, 0.2, 0.1)$
(a_1, a_9)	$(0.7, 0.6, 0.5)$
(a_7, a_9)	$(0.6, 0.5, 0.4)$
(a_6, a_9)	$(1, 0.9, 0.8)$
(a_6, a_7)	$(0.6, 0.5, 0.4)$
(a_5, a_6)	$(0.6, 0.5, 0.4)$
(a_2, a_6)	$(0.8, 0.7, 0.6)$
(a_3, a_6)	$(0.5, 0.4, 0.3)$
(a_4, a_7)	$(0.7, 0.6, 0.5)$

6.2. Illustration of Membership Values

Here, the model network system contains nine nodes and fifteen edges. It can be seen from the given 3PFG that every town is connected to others through some paths. So, first, we want to check whether the connections between towns are α, β or δ-strong. Next, we find out the saturation node in Figure 5. After calculating $CONN_{G-(a,b)}$, for all $(a,b) \in E$, we find out which edges are α, β or δ-strong. Then, by the routine computations, we get the classification of edges. Here, the classified edges are given in Table 4.

Table 4. Classification of edges of Figure 5.

Edge	Classification
(a_1, a_2)	δ-strong
(a_2, a_3)	δ-strong
(a_3, a_4)	δ-strong
(a_4, a_5)	δ-strong
(a_5, a_7)	δ-strong
(a_7, a_8)	α-strong
(a_8, a_9)	δ-strong
(a_1, a_9)	α-strong
(a_7, a_9)	δ-strong
(a_6, a_9)	α-strong
(a_6, a_7)	δ-strong
(a_5, a_6)	δ-strong
(a_2, a_6)	α-strong
(a_3, a_6)	β-strong
(a_4, a_7)	α-strong

We can observe that the model 3PFG G only has one β-SE. The node a_6, which is incident with at least one α-SE and one β-SE, is the sole saturation node in the model 3PFG G.

6.3. Decision Making

The town a_6 is the most favourable location to set up the IIT (Indian Institute of Technology) among all the towns taken into consideration in our suggested model since it is the sole saturation node in the model 3PFG G. Decision-making in allocation problems is critical to operations management and resource allocation across various domains, including business, logistics, healthcare, and government. Allocation problems involve distributing limited resources among competing demands or tasks in an optimal or efficient manner. These decisions play a significant role in determining the overall performance, cost-effectiveness, and fairness of an allocation process.

We know that saturation in mPFG plays an important role in this allocation problem through the above discussion. Moreover, we also recognize that saturation in mPFG is more applicable than saturation in FG in the allocation problem.

Comparative study

First, Mathew et al. [10] introduced a saturation graph in the light of fuzziness. Later on, Mathew et al. [6,7] also worked on different properties of saturated FGs. So, none of the results discussed earlier are applicable when the model is considered in another environment, such as in m-polar fuzzy sets. This is why the proposed model in this paper plays a significant role in such situations to give better results.

Advantages and limitations of the proposed Work

Some of the advantages of the proposed work are as follows:

(i) This work mainly depends on m-polar fuzzy logic network system.
(ii) Many important definitions and theorems are presented in this study, which are very useful.
(iii) A real application of a m-polar fuzzy saturation graph is presented in the allocation problem system.

Some of the limitations of this study are given as follows:

(i) This work mainly focuses on the m-polar fuzzy graph.
(ii) If the membership value of the character is given in a different interval-valued m-polar fuzzy environment, then the m-polar fuzzy threshold graph cannot be used.
(iii) This type of work is mainly used in allocation problems.

7. Conclusions

In this paper, α-saturation and β-saturation in mPFG, along with its several properties, are initiated. Node, as well as edge saturation count in mPFG and a few of its facts on some well-known mPFGs, are also introduced. The upper and lower bound of a node and edge saturation count in mPFG are also investigated. Saturation in mPFG by using α-saturation and β-saturation are also discussed here, along with some of its intersecting properties. Using saturation in mPFG, an application is also given in the last part of this paper. Depending on the mPFG, our research will be expanded to uncover other traits and potential uses. To the best of our knowledge, no work has been conducted on α-saturation and β-saturation before this present work on mPFG. Several results have been presented in this paper. The connection between α-saturation and β-saturation is not established here. This should be conducted in later work. Until now, the saturation on interval-valued m-polar fuzzy soft graphs, saturation on balanced IVmPF graphs, and saturation on self-centered IVmPF graphs were not investigated by any researchers.

Author Contributions: Conceptualization, G.M. and M.P.; methodology, A.M.A. and T.M.; software, B.M.A.; validation, T.M.; investigation, A.M.A. and G.M.; data curation, T.M., A.M.A. and B.M.A.; visualization, M.P. All authors have read and agreed to the published version of the manuscript.

Funding: The authors extend their appreciation to the Deanship of Scientific Research at University of Tabuk for funding this work through research group no. S-0140-1443.

Data Availability Statement: Not applicable.

Acknowledgments: The authors are highly grateful to the learned reviewers for their constructive comments, which led to an improvement in the quality of the paper. The authors extend their appreciation to the Deanship of Scientific Research at University of Tabuk for funding this work through research group no. S-0140-1443.

Conflicts of Interest: There is no conflict of interest between the authors and the institute where the work has been carried out. We have not used any type of external data.

References

1. Zadeh, L.A. Fuzzy sets. *Inf. Control.* **1965**, *8*, 338–353. [CrossRef]
2. Zhang, R.W. Bipolar fuzzy sets and relations: A computational framework for cognitive modeling and multiagent decision analysis. *Proc. IEEE Conf.* **1994**, 305–309. [CrossRef]
3. Zhang, R.W. Bipolar fuzzy sets. *Proc. IEEE Conf.* **1998**, *1*, 835–840.
4. Kauffman, A. *Introduction a la Theorie des Sous-Emsembles Flous;* Masson: Paris, France, 1973.
5. Rosenfeld, A. *Fuzzy Graphs, Fuzzy Sets and Their Application;* Academic Press: New York, NY, USA, 1975; pp. 77–95.
6. Mathew, S.; Sunitha, M.S. *Fuzzy Graphs: Basics, Concepts and Applications;* Lap Lambert Academic Publishing GmbH KG: Saarbrücken, Germany, 2012; ISBN 10: 3659212342/13: 9783659212345.
7. Sunitha, S.M.; Mathew, S. Fuzzy graph theory: A survey. *Ann. Pure Appl. Math.* **2013**, *4*, 92–110.
8. Mordeson, J.N.; Nair, P.S. *Fuzzy Graph and Fuzzy Hypergraphs;* Physica-Verlag: Heidelberg, Germany, 2000.

9. Nair, P.S.; Cheng, S.C. Cliques and fuzzy cliques in fuzzy graphs. In Proceedings of the Joint 9th IFSA World Congress and 20th NAFIPS International Conference, Vancouver, BC, Canada, 25–28 July 2001; Volume 4, pp. 2277–2280.
10. Mathew, S.; Yang, L.H.; Mathew, K.J. Saturation in Fuzzy Graphs. *New Math. Nat. Comput.* **2018**, *14*, 113–128. [CrossRef]
11. Chen, J.; Li, S.; Ma, S.; Wang, X. *m*-polar fuzzy sets: An extension of bipolar fuzzy sets. *Hindawi Publ. Corp. Sci. World J.* **2014**, *2014*, 1–8. [CrossRef] [PubMed]
12. Ghorai, G.; Pal, M. On some operations and density of *m*-polar fuzzy graphs. *Pac. Sci. Rev. Nat. Sci. Eng.* **2015**, *17*, 14–22. [CrossRef]
13. Akram, M.; Adeel, A. *m*-polar fuzzy graphs and *m*-polar fuzzy line graphs. *J. Discret. Math. Sci. Cryptogr.* **2017**, *20*, 1597–1617. [CrossRef]
14. Akram, M.; Wassem, N.; Dudek, W.A. Certain types of edge *m*-polar fuzzy graph. *Iran. J. Fuzzy Syst.* **2016**, *14*, 27–50.
15. Mahapatra, T.; Ghorai, G.; Pal, M. Fuzzy fractional colouring on a fuzzy graph with its application. *J. Ambient. Intell. Humaniz. Comput.* **2020**, *11*, 5771–5784. [CrossRef]
16. Mahapatra, T.; Pal, M. An investigation on *m*-polar fuzzy threshold graph and its application on resource power controlling system. *J. Ambient. Intell. Humaniz. Comput.* **2022**, *13*, 501–514. [CrossRef]
17. Mahapatra, T.; Pal, M. An investigation on *m*-polar fuzzy tolerance graph and its application. *Neural Comput. Appl.* **2022**, *34*, 3007–3017.
18. Mandal, S.; Sahoo, S.; Ghorai, G.; Pal, M. Application of strong arcs in *m*-polar fuzzy graphs. *Neural Process. Lett.* **2019**, *50*, 771–784. [CrossRef]
19. Mandal, S.; Sahoo, S.; Ghorai, G.; Pal, M. Different Types of Arcs in *m*-polar fuzzy graphs with the application. *J. Mult. Valued Log. Soft Comput.* **2018**, *34*, 263–282.
20. Subrahmanyam, B.A. Products of *m*-polar fuzzy graphs. *Int. J. Res. Electron. Comput. Eng.* **2018**, *6*, 1358–1362.
21. Nagoorgani, A.; Malarvizhi, J. Isomorphism properties on strong fuzzy graphs. *Int. J. Algorithms Comput. Math.* **2009**, *2*, 39–47.
22. Nagoorgani, A.; Malarvizhi, J. Isomorphism on fuzzy graphs. *Int. J. Math. Comput. Phys. Electr. Comput. Eng.* **2012**, *6*, 517–523.
23. Nagoorgani, A.; Latha, S. Isomorphism on irregular fuzzy graphs. *Int. J. Mathmatical Sci. Eng. Appl.* **2012**, *6*, 193–208.
24. Nagoorgani, A.; Latha, S. Isomorphic properties of highly irregular fuzzy graph and its complement. *Theor. Math. Appl.* **2013**, *3*, 161–181.
25. Akram, M.; Li, S.G.; Shum, K.P. Antipodal bipolar fuzzy graphs. *Ital. J. Pure Appl. Math.* **2013**, *31*, 97–110.
26. Anjali, N.; Mathew, S. On blocks and stars in fuzzy graphs. *J. Intell. Fuzzy Syst.* **2015**, *28*, 1659–1665. [CrossRef]
27. Bhutani, K.R. On automorphism of fuzzy graphs. *Pattern Recognit. Lett.* **1989**, *9*, 159–162. [CrossRef]
28. Hayat, K.; Raja, M.S.; Lughofer, E.; Yaqoob, N. New group-based generalized interval-valued q-rung orthopair fuzzy soft aggregation operators and their applications in sports decision-making problems. *Comput. Appl. Math.* **2023**, *42*, 4. [CrossRef]
29. Krishnaveni, P.; Balasundaram, S.R. Generating fuzzy graph based multi-document summary of text based learning materials. *Expert Syst. Appl.* **2023**, *214*, 119–165. [CrossRef]
30. Muhiuddin, G.; Takallo, M.M.; Jun Y.B; Borzooei, R.A. Cubic graphs and their application to a traffic flow problem. *Int. J. Comput. Intell. Syst.* **2020**, *13*, 1265–1280. [CrossRef]

mathematics MDPI

Article

Some Classes of Soft Functions Defined by Soft Open Sets Modulo Soft Sets of the First Category

Zanyar A. Ameen [1,*] and Mesfer H. Alqahtani [2]

1 Department of Mathematics, College of Science, University of Duhok, Duhok 42001, Iraq
2 Department of Mathematics, University College of Umluj, University of Tabuk, Tabuk 48322, Saudi Arabia; m_halqahtani@ut.edu.sa
* Correspondence: zanyar@uod.ac

Abstract: Soft continuity can contribute to the development of digital images and computational topological applications other than the field of soft topology. In this work, we study a new class of generalized soft continuous functions defined on the class of soft open sets modulo soft sets of the first category, which is called soft functions with the Baire property. This class includes all soft continuous functions. More precisely, it contains various classes of weak soft continuous functions. The essential properties and operations of the soft functions with the Baire property are established. It is shown that a soft continuous with values in a soft second countable space is identical to a soft function with the Baire property, apart from a topologically negligible soft set. Then we introduce two more subclasses of soft functions with the Baire property and examine their basic properties. Furthermore, we characterize these subclasses in terms of soft continuous functions. At last, we present a diagram that shows the relationships between the classes of soft functions defined in this work and those that exist in the literature.

Keywords: soft set of the first category; soft set of the second category; soft set with the Baire property; soft function with the Baire property

MSC: 54A99; 54E52; 54F65; 03E99

Citation: Ameen, Z.A.; Alqahtani, M.H. Some Classes of Soft Functions Defined by Soft Open Sets Modulo Soft Sets of the First Category. *Mathematics* **2023**, *11*, 4368. https://doi.org/10.3390/math11204368

Academic Editor: Michael Voskoglou

Received: 23 September 2023
Revised: 16 October 2023
Accepted: 17 October 2023
Published: 20 October 2023

1. Introduction

The reduction in uncertainty is one of the most crucial features that must be addressed in order to improve the robustness of the results acquired from data analysis. However, breaking down the existing uncertainty in order to remove it is frequently a difficult task. For this reason, numerous mathematical techniques created for data analysis ended up short of fulfilling these objectives. Fuzzy sets [1], rough sets [2], and probability are a few of the key mathematical techniques that try to remove uncertainty from data analysis. Divergences from classical mathematics with the goal of removing uncertainty have been made as a result of getting better results with various set types. The decision-making procedures have experienced certain issues as a result of their inability to effectively represent uncertainty. Considering that the lack of a parameterization tool is the primary cause of these challenges, the authors of [3] proposed soft sets. Soft sets represent a particularly effective mathematical model for processing decision-making procedures that focus on the selection of the best alternative since objects supplying parameters can be described in this way. This prompts the fast development of the theory of soft sets and its related field in a short measure of time and gives different applications of soft sets in real-world applications (see, [4–9]).

Then, various mathematical branches have been studied in soft set environments. Soft topology is one of the branches introduced in [10,11] as a fresh generality of classical topology. The aforementioned work was crucial to the development of soft topology.

After that, in soft set contexts, many traditional topological properties have been generalized, for instance, soft separation axioms [12], soft second countable spaces [13], soft separable spaces [12], soft connected spaces [14], soft compact spaces [15], soft extremally disconnected spaces [16], soft submaximal spaces [17], and soft paracompact spaces [14].

It is understood that soft open sets are the building blocks of soft topology, but other classes of soft sets can contribute to the growth of soft topology. Namely, soft dense [18], soft codense [19], soft somewhat open [20], soft nowhere dense [18], soft meager (first category soft set) [18], soft semiopen [21], soft α-open [22], and soft sets with the Baire property [23].

In addition to soft topology, soft continuity is useful in the development of computational topological applications and digital images [24]. Soft continuity of functions was defined by Zorlutuna et al. [25] in 2012. Afterwards, multiple generalized forms of soft continuous functions started to appear in the literature. Namely: soft $\mathcal{U}$-continuous functions [26], soft C-continuous functions [27], soft ω-continuous functions [28], soft somewhat continuous functions [20], soft α-continuous functions [22], soft semicontinuous functions [29], etc.

The concept of functions with the Baire property was studied by many mathematicians as a tool for developing several fields of mathematics, such as (descriptive) set theory, general topology, and measure theory (see [30–32]). In an analogous manner, studying functions with the Baire property in soft settings will have an interchangeable role in soft topology and soft measure theory. The latter statement and the rich literature on the generalized classes of soft continuous functions with their applications motivate us to investigate the so-called "soft functions with the Baire property"with two more subclasses of such soft functions.

The primary contributions of this paper are follows:

- We introduce a wide class of soft functions, named soft functions with the Baire property, via a mix of topological and algebraic structures, which includes various classes of generalized soft continuous functions.
- We find some conditions under which the class (or a subclass) of soft functions with the Baire property is identical to soft continuity.
- We characterize a subclass of soft functions with the Baire property in terms of the set of soft points of soft discontinuity.

We arrange the content of the paper as follows: Section 2 recalls some properties and operations of soft set theory and some soft topology. Section 3 collects and studies some classes of soft sets with the Baire property in soft topological spaces. In Section 4, we introduce the concept of soft functions with the Baire property and characterize them in terms of soft continuity. In Section 5, we define two subclasses of soft functions with the Baire property and study them. After that, we find their connections to some known classes of generalized soft continuous functions. In Section 6, we finish this work with a brief conclusion.

2. Preliminaries

We start with an overview of soft sets along with some operations.

Definition 1 ([3]). *Let F be a set-valued mapping from a subset A of a set of parameters E into the power set 2^X of an initial universe X. An ordered pair $(F, A) = \{(a, F(a)) : a \in A\}$ is called the soft set over X.*

The class of all soft subsets of X along with A is denoted by $SS(X, A)$.

Definition 2 ([7]). *The soft complement $(F, A)^c$ of a soft set (F, A) is a soft set (F^c, A), whereas $F^c : A \to 2^X$ is a mapping for which $F^c(a) = X - F(a)$ for each $a \in A$.*

Remark 1. *One can easily extend a soft set (F, A) to the soft set (F, E) by assuming $F(a) = \emptyset$ for all $a \in E - A$.*

Definition 3 **([33]).** *A null soft set with respect to A, (Φ, A), is soft set (F, A) over X if $F(a) = \emptyset$ for each $a \in A$. An absolute soft set with respect to A, (X, A), is a soft set (F, A) such that $F(a) = X$ for each $a \in A$. The null and absolute soft sets are denoted by (Φ, E) and (X, E), respectively.*

Notice that $((F, A)^c)^c = (F, A)$, $(\Phi, A)^c = (X, A)$, and $(X, A)^c = (\Phi, A)$.

Definition 4 **([13]).** *A finite (resp. countable) soft set (F, A) is such a soft set that $F(a)$ is finite (resp. countable) for each $a \in A$. Otherwise, it is called infinite (resp. uncountable).*

Definition 5 **([34]).** *A soft set (F, A) over X is said to be a soft point, referred to x_a, if $F(a) = \{x\}$ and $F(a') = \emptyset$ for each $a' \in A$ such that $a \neq a'$, $a \in A$. The collection of all soft points in X associate with A is denoted by $SP(X, A)$.*

Definition 6 **([7,35]).** *Let (F, A), (G, B) be soft sets, where $A, B \subseteq E$. Then (F, A) is a soft subset of (G, B), denoted by $(F, A)\tilde{\subseteq}(G, B)$, if $A \subseteq B$ and $F(a) \subseteq G(a)$ for all $a \in A$. The two soft sets are said to be equal, denoted by $(F, A) = (G, B)$, if $(F, A)\tilde{\subseteq}(G, B)$ and $(G, B)\tilde{\subseteq}(F, A)$.*

Definition 7 **([33]).** *Let $\{(F_i, A) : i \in I\}$ be a family of soft sets over X, where I is any index set.*

1. *The soft union of (F_i, A) is defined to be the soft set $(F, A) = \tilde{\bigcup}_{i \in I}(F_i, A)$ such that $F(a) = \bigcup_{i \in I} F_i(a)$ for each $a \in A$.*
2. *The soft intersection of (F_i, A) is defined to be the soft set $(F, A) = \tilde{\bigcap}_{i \in I}(F_i, A)$ such that $F(a) = \bigcap_{i \in I} F_i(a)$ for each $a \in A$.*

Definition 8 **([33,36]).** *Let $(F, A), (G, A) \in SS(X, A)$. Then*

1. *The soft set difference (F, A) and (G, A) is defined to be the soft set $(H, A) = (F, A) - (G, A)$, where $H(a) = F(a) - G(a)$ for all $a \in A$.*
2. *The soft symmetric difference of (F, A) and (G, A) is defined by $(F, A)\tilde{\Delta}(G, A) = [(F, A) - (G, A)]\tilde{\cup}[(G, A) - (F, A)]$.*

   One can easily check that $(F, A) - (G, A) = (F, A)\tilde{\cap}(G, A)^c$.

In what follows, by two distinct soft points $x_a, y_{a'}$ we mean either $x \neq y$ or $a \neq a'$ and by two disjoint soft sets $(F, A), (G, A)$ over X, we mean $(F, A)\tilde{\cap}(G, A) = (\Phi, A)$.

Definition 9 **([11]).** *A family $\theta\tilde{\subseteq}SS(X, A)$ is called a soft topology over X if*

1. *$(\Phi, A), (X, A) \in \theta$,*
2. *$(F, A), (G, A) \in \theta$ implies $(F, A)\tilde{\cap}(G, A) \in \theta$, and*
3. *$\{(F_i, A) : i \in I\}\tilde{\subseteq}\theta$ implies $\tilde{\bigcup}_{i \in I}(F_n, A) \in \theta$.*

The triple (X, θ, A) is called a soft topological space. The elements of θ are called soft open sets, and their complements are called soft closed sets. The set of all soft closed sets is denoted by θ^c.

Definition 10 **([11]).** *Let $(Y, A) \neq (\Phi, A)$ be a soft subset of (X, θ, A). Then $\theta_{(Y,A)} = \{(G, A)\tilde{\cap}\,(Y, A) : (G, A) \in \theta\}$ is called a relative soft topology over Y and $(Y, \theta_{(Y,A)}, A)$ is a soft subspace of (Y, θ, A).*

Lemma 1 **([11]).** *Let $(Y, \theta_{(Y,A)}, A)$ be a soft subspace of (Y, θ, A) and let $(F, A)\tilde{\subseteq}(Y, A) \in \theta$. Then $(F, A) \in \theta_{(Y,A)}$ iff $(F, A) \in \theta$.*

Definition 11 **([10]).** *A (countable) soft base for a soft topology θ is a (countable) family $\mathcal{B}\tilde{\subseteq}\theta$ such that elements of θ are soft unions of elements of $\mathcal{B}$.*

Lemma 2 ([11]). *Let (X, θ, A) be a soft topological space, then for each $a \in A$, the collection $\theta(a) = \{F(a) : (F, A) \in \theta\}$ is a (crisp) topology on X.*

Definition 12 ([37]). *A soft topology generated by a collection $\mathcal{C}\tilde{\subseteq}SS(X, A)$ is the intersection of all soft topologies over X including $\mathcal{C}$.*

Definition 13 ([38]). *Let $(G, A)\tilde{\subseteq}(X, \theta, A)$. Then (G, A) is a soft neighborhood of $x_a \in SP(X, A)$ if there exists $(U, A) \in \theta(x_a)$ such that $x_a \in (U, A)\tilde{\subseteq}(G, A)$, where $\theta(x_a)$ is the family of all soft open sets containing x_a.*

Definition 14 ([11]). *Let $(W, A)\tilde{\subseteq}(X, \theta, A)$. Then*

1. $cl(W, A) = \tilde{\cap}\{(F, A) : (W, A)\tilde{\subseteq}(F, A), (F, A) \in \theta^c\}$ *is called the soft closure of* (W, A).
2. $int(W, A) = \tilde{\cup}\{(F, A) : (F, A)\tilde{\subseteq}(W, A), (F, A) \in \theta\}$ *is called the soft interior of* (W, A).

Lemma 3 ([39]). *Let $(F, A), (G, A)\tilde{\subseteq}(X, \theta, A)$. Then*

1. $int((F, A)\tilde{\cap}(G, A)) = int(F, A)\tilde{\cap}int(G, A)$.
2. $cl((F, A)\tilde{\cap}(G, A))\tilde{\subseteq}cl(F, A)\tilde{\cap}cl(G, A)$.

Lemma 4 ([39]). *Let $(F, A)\tilde{\subseteq}(X, \theta, A)$. Then*

$$int((F, A)^c) = (cl((F, A)))^c \text{ and } cl((F, A)^c) = (int((F, A)))^c.$$

Definition 15 ([39,40]). *Let $(F, A)\tilde{\subseteq}(X, \theta, A)$. The soft boundary of (F, A) is given by $b(F, A) = cl(F, A) - int(F, A)$.*

Definition 16. *Let $(F, A), (G, A)\tilde{\subseteq}(X, \theta, A)$. Then (F, A) is called*

1. *soft clopen [41] if (F, A) is both soft open and soft closed.*
2. *soft regular open [42] if $int(cl(F, A)) = (F, A)$.*
3. *soft G_δ [19] if $(F, A) = \tilde{\cap}_{n=1}^{\infty}(G_n, A)$, where $(G_n, A) \in \theta$.*
4. *soft F_σ [19] if $(F, A) = \tilde{\cup}_{n=1}^{\infty}(F_n, A)$, where $(F_n, A) \in \theta^c$.*
5. *soft dense in (G, A) [18,19] if $(G, A)\tilde{\subseteq}cl(F, A)$.*
6. *soft nowhere dense [18] if $int(cl(F, A)) = (\Phi, A)$.*
7. *soft semiopen set [21] if $(F, A)\tilde{\subseteq}cl(int(F, A))$.*
8. *soft α-open set [22] if $(F, A)\tilde{\subseteq}int(cl(int(F, A)))$.*
9. *soft meager [18,43] (or a soft set of the first category) if $(F, A) = \tilde{\cup}_{n=1}^{\infty}(F_n, A)$, where each (F_n, A) is soft nowhere dense, otherwise (F, A) is of the second category.*

The collection of all soft sets of the first category (resp. soft sets of the second category, soft nowhere dense sets) over X is denoted by $\mathcal{M}(X, A)$ (resp. $\mathcal{S}(X, A), \mathcal{N}(X, A)$). Examples on the aforementioned classes of soft sets can be found in [43], Example 1.

Definition 17 ([18,19]). *A soft topological space (X, θ, A) is called soft Baire if the soft intersection of each countable collection of soft open dense sets in (X, θ, A) is soft dense. Equivalently, each non-null soft open set in (X, θ, A) is of the second category.*

Definition 18 ([44]). *A non-null class $\tilde{I}\tilde{\subseteq}SS(X, A)$ is called a soft ideal over X if $\tilde{I}$ satisfies the following conditions:*

1. *If $(F, A), (G, A) \in \tilde{I}$, then $(F, A)\tilde{\cup}(G, A) \in \tilde{I}$.*
2. *If $(G, A) \in \tilde{I}$ and $(F, A)\tilde{\subseteq}(G, A)$, then $(F, A) \in \tilde{I}$.*

$\tilde{I}$ is called a soft σ-ideal if (1) holds for many (countable) soft sets. We denote the family of soft ideals over X by $\mathcal{I}(X, A)$.

Remark 2 ([43]). *For any soft topological space (X, θ, A), $\mathcal{M}(X, A)$ forms a soft σ-ideal and $\mathcal{N}(X, A)$ forms a soft ideal.*

Definition 19 ([45]). *A collection $\Sigma \widetilde{\subseteq} SS(X, A)$ is a soft algebra over X if:*

1. $(\Phi, A) \in \Sigma$,
2. $(F, A) \in \Sigma$ *implies* $(F, A)^c \in \Sigma$, *and*
3. $(F_n, A) \in \Sigma$, *for all* $n = 1, 2, \ldots, k$, *implies* $\widetilde{\bigcup}_{n=1}^{k} (F_n, A) \in \Sigma$.

If (3) holds true for many (countable) members of Σ, Σ is said to be a soft σ-algebra on X (see [46]).

Definition 20 ([47]). *Let $\mathcal{F} \widetilde{\subseteq} SS(X, A)$. The soft intersection of all soft σ-algebras over X containing $\mathcal{F}$ is a soft σ-algebra and it is called the soft σ-algebra generated by $\mathcal{F}$ and is referred to as $\sigma(\mathcal{F})$.*

Definition 21 ([15]). *A soft topological space (X, θ, A) is called soft compact if every cover of (X, A) by soft open sets has a finite subcover.*

Definition 22 ([11]). *A soft topological space (X, θ, A) is called soft regular if each $x_a \in SP(X, A)$ and each $(G, A) \in \theta$, there exists $(H, A) \in \theta$ such that $x_a \in (H, A) \widetilde{\subseteq} cl(H, A) \widetilde{\subseteq} (G, A)$.*

Definition 23 ([13]). *A soft topological space (X, θ, A) is called soft second countable if it has a countable soft base.*

Definition 24 ([25,48]). *Let $SS(X, A), SS(Y, B)$ be collections of soft sets, and let $p : X \to Y, q : A \to B$ be mappings. The image of a soft set $(F, A) \widetilde{\subseteq} (X, A)$ under $g : SS(X, A) \to SS(Y, B)$ is a soft subset $g(F, A) = (g(F), q(A))$ of (Y, B) which is given by*

$$g(F)(b) = \begin{cases} \bigcup_{a \in q^{-1}(b) \cap A} p(F(a)), & q^{-1}(b) \cap A \neq \varnothing \\ \varnothing, & \text{otherwise,} \end{cases}$$

for each $b \in B$.

The inverse image of a soft set $(G, B) \widetilde{\subseteq} (Y, B)$ under g is a soft subset $g^{-1}(G, B) = (g^{-1}(G), q^{-1}(B))$ such that

$$(g^{-1}(G)(a) = \begin{cases} p^{-1}(G(q(a))), & q(a) \in B \\ \varnothing, & \text{otherwise,} \end{cases}$$

for each $a \in A$.

The soft mapping g is injective (resp. surjective, bijective) if both p and q are injective (resp. surjective, bijective).

Lemma 5 ([25]). *Let $g : SS(X, A) \to SS(Y, B)$ be a soft function and $(W, B) \in SS(Y, B)$. Then*

$$g^{-1}((W, B)^c) = (g^{-1}(W, B))^c.$$

Definition 25. *A soft function $g : (X, \theta, A) \to (Y, \vartheta, B)$ is said to be*

1. *soft continuous [25] if $g^{-1}(G, B) \in \theta$ for each $(G, B) \in \vartheta$.*
2. *soft semicontinuous [29] if $g^{-1}(G, B)$ is soft semiopen for each $(G, B) \in \vartheta$.*
3. *soft α-continuous [22] if $g^{-1}(G, B)$ is soft α-open for each $(G, B) \in \vartheta$.*

3. Classes of Soft Sets with the Baire Property

We recall and study some properties of certain classes of soft sets that have the Baire property.

Definition 26 ([23,36]). *Let $(F,A)\tilde{\subseteq}(X,\theta,A)$. It is said that (F,A) is soft open modulo $\mathcal{M}(X,A)$ if there exists $(G,A)\in\theta$ such that $(F,A)\tilde{\Delta}(G,A)\in\mathcal{M}(X,A)$. Soft open sets modulo $\mathcal{M}(X,A)$ are named soft sets with the Baire property. The family of all soft sets over X with the Baire property is denoted by $\mathcal{B}(X,\theta,A)$.*

One can easily check that (F,A) has the Baire property iffit is of the form $(F,A)=(G,A)\tilde{\Delta}(P,A)$, where $(G,A)\in\theta$ and $(P,A)\in\mathcal{M}(X,A)$.

Lemma 6 ([23]). *Let $(F,A)\tilde{\subseteq}(X,\theta,A)$. The following properties are equivalent:*

1. $(F,A)\in\mathcal{B}(X,\theta,A)$.
2. *if* $(F,A)=(H,A)\tilde{\Delta}(P,A)$, *where* (H,A) *is soft regular open and* $(P,A)\in\mathcal{M}(X,A)$.
3. *if* $(F,A)=(K,A)\tilde{\Delta}(Q,A)$, *where* $(K,A)\in\theta^c$ *and* $(Q,A)\in\mathcal{M}(X,A)$.
4. *if* $(F,A)=[(D,A)-(R,A)]\tilde{\cup}(S,A)$, *where* $(D,A)\in\theta^c$ *and* $(R,A),(S,A)\in\mathcal{M}(X,A)$.
5. *if* $(F,A)=[(G,A)-(M,A)]\tilde{\cup}(N,A)$, *where* $(G,A)\in\theta$ *and* $(M,A),(N,A)\in\mathcal{M}(X,A)$.
6. *if* $(F,A)=(U,A)\tilde{\cup}(L,A)$, *where* (U,A) *is a soft* G_δ *set and* $(L,A)\in\mathcal{M}(X,A)$.
7. *if* $(F,A)=(W,A)-(T,A)$, *where* (W,A) *is a soft* F_σ *set and* $(T,A)\in\mathcal{M}(X,A)$.
8. *if there exists* $(V,A)\in\mathcal{M}(X,A)$ *such that* $(F,A)-(V,A)$ *is soft clopen in* $(V,A)^c$.

Lemma 7 ([23]). *Let $(F,A)\tilde{\subseteq}(X,\theta,A)$. If $(F,A)\in\mathcal{B}(X,\theta,A)$, then $(F,A)^c\in\mathcal{B}(X,\theta,A)$.*

Lemma 8 ([23]). *Let $(F,A),(Y,A)\tilde{\subseteq}(X,\theta,A)$. If $(F,A)\in\mathcal{B}(X,\theta,A)$, then $(F,A)\tilde{\cap}(Y,A)\in\mathcal{B}(X,\theta_{(Y,A)},A)$.*

Lemma 9 ([23]). *Let $(F,A),(Y,A)\tilde{\subseteq}(X,\theta,A)$. If $(F,A)\in\mathcal{B}(X,\theta_{(Y,A)},A)$, $(Y,A)\in\mathcal{B}(X,\theta,A)$, then $(F,A)\in\mathcal{B}(X,\theta,A)$.*

We are now in a position to define two subclasses of soft sets of the Baire property. We have seen that $(F,A)\in\mathcal{B}(X,\theta,A)$ iff $(F,A)=(G,A)-(P,A)\tilde{\cup}(Q,A)$, where (G,A) or $(G,A)^c\in\theta$ and $(Q,A)\in\mathcal{M}(X,A)$. From this representation, we introduce the following soft sets:

Definition 27. *Let $(F,A)\tilde{\subseteq}(X,\theta,A)$. Then (F,A) is said to be of the first type if $(F,A)=(G,A)-(P,A)$, where (G,A) or $(G,A)^c\in\theta$ and $(P,A)\in\mathcal{M}(X,A)$. And it is of the second type if $(F,A)=(H,A)\tilde{\cup}(Q,A)$, where (H,A) or $(H,A)^c\in\theta$ and $(Q,A)\in\mathcal{M}(X,A)$. We will hereafter refer to soft sets of the first and second types as ST_1-sets and ST_2-sets, respectively.*

Lemma 10. *Let $(F,A)\tilde{\subseteq}(X,\theta,A)$. Then (F,A) is an ST_1-set iff $(F,A)^c$ is an ST_2-set.*

Proof. Let (F,A) be an ST_1-set. Then $(F,A)=(G,A)-(P,A)$ for some (G,A) or $(G,A)^c\in\theta$ and $(P,A)\in\mathcal{M}(X,A)$. Now, $(F,A)^c=\left((G,A)-(P,A)\right)^c=(G,A)^c\tilde{\cup}(P,A)$, where $(G,A)^c$ or $(G,A)\in\theta$ and $(P,A)\in\mathcal{M}(X,A)$. Thus, $(F,A)^c$ is an ST_2-set.

The converse is similar. □

Lemma 11. *Let $(F,A),(G,A)\tilde{\subseteq}(X,\theta,A)$ such that $(G,A)\in\theta$ or $(G,A)\in\theta^c$. If (F,A) is an ST_i-set, then $(F,A)\tilde{\cap}(G,A)$ is an ST_i-set, for $i=1,2$.*

Proof. Straightforward. □

Lemma 12. *Let* $(D,A)\tilde{\subseteq}(X,\theta,A)$. *If* (D,A) *is soft dense in* (X,A), *then* $cl[(G,A)\tilde{\cap}(D,A)] = cl(G,A)$ *for each* $(G,A)\in\theta$.

Proof. Let $(G,A)\in\theta$. Since $(G,A)\tilde{\cap}(D,A)\tilde{\subseteq}(G,A)$, so $cl[(G,A)\tilde{\cap}(D,A)]\tilde{\subseteq}cl(G,A)$. On the other hand, we need to show $cl(G,A)\tilde{\subseteq}cl[(G,A)\tilde{\cap}(D,A)]$. Consider the following with applying Lemma 3:

$$\begin{aligned}(G,A)-cl[(G,A)\tilde{\cap}(D,A)] &= (G,A)\tilde{\cap}(cl[(G,A)\tilde{\cap}(D,A)])^c\\ &= int(G,A)\tilde{\cap}int([(G,A)\tilde{\cap}(D,A)]^c)\\ &= int(G,A)\tilde{\cap}int[(G,A)^c\tilde{\cup}(D,A)^c])\\ &= int([(G,A)\tilde{\cap}(D,A)^c]\tilde{\cup}[(G,A)\tilde{\cap}(G,A)^c])\\ &= int[(G,A)\tilde{\cap}(D,A)^c]\\ &= (G,A)\tilde{\cap}int[(D,A)^c]\\ &= (G,A)-cl(G,A)\\ &= (G,A)-(X,A)\\ &= (\Phi,A).\end{aligned}$$

This proves that $(G,A)\tilde{\subseteq}cl[(G,A)\tilde{\cap}(D,A)]$ implies $cl(G,A)\tilde{\subseteq}cl[(G,A)\tilde{\cap}(D,A)]$. Thus, $cl(G,A) = cl[(G,A)\tilde{\cap}(D,A)]$. □

Lemma 13. *Let* $(F,A)\tilde{\subseteq}(X,\theta,A)$. *Then* (F,A) *is a soft* α*-open set iffthen* $(F,A) = (G,A)-(N,A)$, *where* $(G,A)\in\theta$ *and* $(N,A)\in\mathcal{N}(X,A)$.

Proof. Suppose (F,A) is a soft α-open set. Consider the identity

$$(F,A) = int(cl(int(F,A))) - [int(cl(int(F,A))) - (F,A)].$$

Since $(F,A)\tilde{\subseteq}int(cl(int(F,A)))$, then $int(F,A)\tilde{\subseteq}int(cl(int(F,A)))$. Therefore, we have $int(cl(int(F,A))) \quad -(F,A)\tilde{\subseteq}int(cl(int(F,A))) - int(F,A)$, which implies $int(cl(int(F,A))) -(F,A)\in\mathcal{N}(X,A)$ since $int(cl(int(F,A))) - int(F,A)\in\mathcal{N}(X,A)$. If we set $(G,A) = int(cl(int(F,A)))$ and $(N,A) = int(cl(int(F,A))) - (F,A)$, then we conclude that $(F,A) = (G,A)-(N,A)$ for some $(G,A)\in\theta$ and $(N,A)\in\mathcal{N}(X,A)$.

Conversely, if $(F,A) = (G,A)-(N,A)$, where $(G,A)\in\theta$ and $(N,A)\in\mathcal{N}(X,A)$. Now, $(F,A) = (G,A)\tilde{\cap}(N,A)^c$. Therefore, applying Lemma 3 , we have $int(F,A) = int(G,A)\tilde{\cap}\, int((N,A)^c) = (G,A)\tilde{\cap}int((N,A)^c)$. Since $int((N,A)^c)$ is soft dense, it follows from Lemma 12, $cl(int(F,A)) = cl(G,A)\tilde{\supseteq}(G,A)$ and thus $(G,A)\tilde{\subseteq}int(cl(int(F,A)))$. But, clearly, $(F,A)\tilde{\subseteq}(G,A)$. Hence, (F,A) is soft α-open. □

Proposition 1. *Let* $(F,A)\tilde{\subseteq}(X,\theta,A)$. *If* (F,A) *is a soft* α*-open set, then* (F,A) *is an* ST_1*-set.*

Proof. It follows from the fact that $\mathcal{N}(X,A)\tilde{\subseteq}\mathcal{M}(X,A)$. □

Proposition 2. *Let* $(F,A)\tilde{\subseteq}(X,\theta,A)$. *If* (F,A) *is a soft semiopen set, then* (F,A) *is an* ST_2*-set.*

Proof. Suppose (F,A) is a soft semiopen set in (X,θ,A). From Theorem 3.1 in [29], one can find $(G,A)\in\theta$ such that $(G,A)\tilde{\subseteq}(F,A)\tilde{\subseteq}cl(G,A)$. Consider, the identity $(F,A) = (G,A)\tilde{\cup}((F,A)-(G,A))$. Since (G,A) is soft open, then $cl(F,A)-(G,A)\in\mathcal{N}(X,A)$ and so $cl(F,A)-(G,A)\in\mathcal{M}(X,A)$. But $(F,A)-(G,A)\tilde{\subseteq}cl(F,A)-(G,A)$, therefore $(F,A)-(G,A)\in\mathcal{M}(X,A)$. Set $(N,A) = (F,A)-(G,A)$. Therefore, $(F,A) = (G,A)\tilde{\cup}(N,A)$. Hence, (F,A) is an ST_2-set. □

This is a suitable place to illustrate the connections between the previously stated soft sets.

Generally, none of the above arrows are reversible, as is shown in the following example:

Example 1. *Let $\mathbb{R}$ be the set of real number and A be a set of parameters. Let θ be the soft topology on $\mathbb{R}$ generated by $\{(a, F(a)) : F(a) = (t,s); t,s \in \mathbb{R}; t < s, a \in A\}$. The soft set $(F, A) = \{(a, [(-1,0) - \mathbb{Q}] \cup [(0,1) \cap \mathbb{Q}]) : a \in A\}$ has the Baire property but is neither an ST_1-set nor an ST_2-set, where $\mathbb{Q}$ is the set of rationals. The soft set $(G, A) = \{(a, \mathbb{R} - \mathbb{Q}) : a \in A\}$ is an ST_1-set but not soft α-open. The soft set $(H, A) = \{(a, (-1,0) \cup (0,1) \cup \{2\}) : a \in A\}$ is an ST_2-set but not soft semiopen. The soft set $(D, A) = \{(a, C) : a \in A\}$ is an ST_2-set but not an ST_1-set, where C is the ternary Cantor set. While (G, A) is an ST_1-set but not an ST_2-set.*

The counterexample for other cases are available in the literature.

4. Soft Functions with the Baire Property

Definition 28. *A soft function $g : (X, \theta, A) \to (Y, \vartheta, B)$ is said to have the Baire property if $g^{-1}(H, B) \in \mathcal{B}(X, \theta, A)$ for each $(H, B) \in \vartheta$.*

The Baire property is evidently present in all soft continuous functions. There are, on the other hand, soft functions that have the Baire property but are not soft continuous.

Example 2. *Consider the soft topological space (X, θ, A) given in Example 1. Define a soft function $g : (X, \theta, A) \to (X, \theta, A)$ by*

$$g(x_a) = \begin{cases} x_a, & \text{if } x_a \notin \{0_a, 1_a\}; \\ 0_a, & \text{if } x_a = 1_a; \\ 1_a, & \text{if } x_a = 0_a. \end{cases}$$

One can easily show g has the Baire property because the inverse image of any soft open set is either a soft open set or a soft open sets union a soft set containing one of the soft points and both though are soft sets the Baire property. On the other hand g cannot be soft continuous. Take the soft open set $(G, A) = \{(a, (-\varepsilon, \varepsilon)) : a \in A\}$, where $\varepsilon < 1$. Then

$$g^{-1}(G, A) = \{(a, (-\varepsilon, 0) \cup (0, \varepsilon) \cup \{1\}) : a \in A\}.$$

not a soft open set and hence g is not a soft continuous function.

Theorem 1. *A soft function $g : (X, \theta, A) \to (Y, \vartheta, B)$ has the Baire property iff $g^{-1}(R, B) \in \mathcal{B}(X, \theta, A)$ for each $(R, B) \in \vartheta^c$.*

Proof. It follows from Lemma 7. □

Proposition 3. *Let $g : (X, \theta, A) \to (Y, \vartheta, B)$ have the Baire property and $(F, A) \widetilde{\subseteq} (X, \theta, A)$. Then $g|_{(F,A)}$ has the Baire property.*

Proof. Let $(H, A) \in \vartheta$. Then $g^{-1}|_{(F,A)}(H, A) = g^{-1}(H, A) \widetilde{\cap} (F, A)$. By hypothesis, we have $g^{-1}(H, A) \in \mathcal{B}(X, \theta, A)$ and, by Lemma 8, $g^{-1}|_{(F,A)}(H, A) \in \mathcal{B}(X, \theta_{(F,A)}, A)$ □

Theorem 2. *Let $g : (X, \theta, A) \to (Y, \vartheta, B)$ be a soft function and let (X, θ, A) be soft compact. If $g|_{(H,A)}$ has the Baire property for each $(H, A) \in \theta$, then g has the Baire property.*

Proof. Let $\{(H_i, A) : i \in I\}$ be a soft open cover of (X, A). Let $(V, B) \in \vartheta$. By assumption, $(g|_{(H_i,A)})^{-1}(V, B)$ has the Baire property in (H_i, A) for each i. Since each soft open set has the Baire property, by Lemma 9, $(g|_{(H_i,A)})^{-1}(V, B) = g^{-1}(V, B) \widetilde{\cap} (H_i, A) \in \mathcal{B}(X, \theta, A)$.

And, by soft compactness of (X, θ, A), one can find a finite subset $I_0 \subseteq I$ such that $(X, A) = \widetilde{\bigcup}_{i \in I_0}(H_i, A)$. Now,

$$\begin{aligned} g^{-1}(V,B) &= g^{-1}(V,B)\widetilde{\cap}\left(\widetilde{\bigcup}_{i\in I_0}(H_i,A)\right) \\ &= \widetilde{\bigcup}_{i\in I_0}\left(g^{-1}(V,B)\widetilde{\cap}(H_i,A)\right) \\ &= \widetilde{\bigcup}_{i\in I_0}\left[\left(g|_{(H_i,A)}\right)^{-1}(V,B)\right]. \end{aligned}$$

Therefore, since $\mathcal{B}(X, \theta, A)$ is closed under finite soft unions, $g^{-1}(V, B) \in \mathcal{B}(X, \theta, A)$ and thus, g has the Baire property. □

Proposition 4. *Let $g : (X, \theta, A) \to (Y, \vartheta, B)$, $h : (Y, \vartheta, B) \to (Z, \eta, C)$ be soft functions. If g has the Baire property and h is soft continuous, then $h \circ g$ has the Baire property.*

Proof. Let $(V, C) \in \eta$. By soft continuity of h, $h^{-1}(V, C) \in \vartheta$. Since g has the Baire property, so $g^{-1}(h^{-1}(V, C)) \in \theta$. But $(h \circ g)^{-1} = g^{-1}(h^{-1}(V, C))$. Hence, $h \circ g$ has the Baire property. □

Proposition 5. *Let $(F, A)\widetilde{\subseteq}(X, \theta, A)$. Then $(F, A) \in \mathcal{B}(X, \theta, A)$ iff the characteristic soft function $\chi_{(F,A)}$ of (F, A) has the Baire property.*

Proof. The characteristic soft function $\chi_{(F,A)}$ of (F, A) is a soft function $\chi_{(F,A)} : (X, \theta, A) \to (\{0, 1\}, \vartheta_{discrete}, B)$, which is defined by

$$\chi_{(F,A)}(x_a) = \begin{cases} 1_b & \text{if } x_a \in (F,A); \\ \\ 0_{b'} & \text{if } x_a \notin (F,A), \end{cases}$$

where $\vartheta_{discrete}$ is the soft discrete topology on $\{0, 1\}$. Suppose $(F, A) \in \mathcal{B}(X, \theta, A)$. Let $(V, B) \in \vartheta_{discrete}$. Then

$$\chi^{-1}_{(F,A)}(V,B) = \begin{cases} (X,A), & \text{if } 1_b, 0_{b'} \in (V,B) \\ (F,A), & \text{if } 1_b \in (V,B), 0_{b'} \notin (V,B) \\ (F,A)^c, & \text{if } 1_b \notin (V,B), 0_{b'} \in (V,B) \\ (\Phi,A), & \text{if } 1_b, 0_{b'} \notin (V,B). \end{cases}$$

All those soft sets are in $\mathcal{B}(X, \theta, A)$ since $\mathcal{B}(X, \theta, A)$ is a soft σ-algebra. Thus, $\chi_{(F,A)}$ has the Baire property.

Conversely, since $\{1_b\} \in \vartheta$ and it contains 1_b, by assumption, $\chi^{-1}_{(F,A)}(\{1_b\}) = (F, A) \in \mathcal{B}(X, \theta, A)$. The proof is finished. □

Theorem 3. *Let $g : (X, \theta, A) \to (Y, \vartheta, B)$ be a soft function such that (Y, ϑ, B) is soft second countable. Then g has the Baire property iffthere exists $(P, A) \in \mathcal{M}(X, A)$ such that $g|_{(P,A)^c}$ is soft continuous.*

Proof. Assume g has the Baire property. We need to construct $(P, A) \in \mathcal{M}(X, A)$ for which $h = g|_{(P,A)^c}$ is soft continuous. Let $(H, B) \in \vartheta$ and let $\mathfrak{B} = \{(G_n, B) : n = 1, 2, \cdots\}$ be a countable soft base of (Y, ϑ, B). Then $(H, B) = \widetilde{\bigcup}_{i=1}^{\infty}(G_i, B)$ for some (G_i, B) in $\mathfrak{B}$. Since g has the Baire property, so $g^{-1}(G_n, B) \in \mathcal{B}(X, \theta, A)$ for each n. By Lemma 6,

$$g^{-1}(G_n, B) = (U_n, A) - (P_n, A)\widetilde{\cup}(Q_n, A),$$

where $(U_n, A) \in \theta$, $(P_n, A), (Q_n, A) \in \mathcal{M}(X, A)$. Set $(P, A) = \tilde{\bigcup}_{n=1}^{\infty}(P_n, A)\tilde{\cup}(Q_n, A)$. Then $(P, A) \in \mathcal{M}(X, A)$ since $\mathcal{M}(X, A)$ is a soft σ-ideal. It remains to show that h is soft continuous. Since

$$h^{-1}(H, B) = g^{-1}(H, B)\tilde{\cap}(P, A)^c,$$

then

$$\begin{aligned} h^{-1}(H, B) &= g^{-1}\Big(\widetilde{\bigcup}_{i=1}^{\infty}(G_i, B)\Big)\tilde{\cap}(P, A)^c \\ &= \widetilde{\bigcup}_{i=1}^{\infty} g^{-1}(G_i, B)\tilde{\cap}(P, A)^c \\ &= \widetilde{\bigcup}_{i=1}^{\infty}((U_i, A) - (P_i, A)\tilde{\cup}(Q_i, A))\tilde{\cap}(P, A)^c. \end{aligned}$$

Since $(P_i, A)\tilde{\cup}(Q_i, A)\tilde{\subseteq}(P, A)$, therefore,

$$\Big((U_i, A) - (P_i, A)\tilde{\cup}(Q_i, A)\Big)\tilde{\cap}(P, A)^c = (U_i, A)\tilde{\cap}(P, A)^c.$$

This implies that $h^{-1}(H, B) = (\tilde{\bigcup}_{i=1}^{\infty}(U_i, A))\tilde{\cap}(P, A)^c$. Since $\tilde{\bigcup}_{i=1}^{\infty}(U_i, A)$ is soft open in (X, A), so $h^{-1}(H, B)$ is a soft open set in $(P, A)^c$. Thus, h is soft continuous.

Conversely, suppose there exists $(P, A) \in \mathcal{M}(X, A)$ such that $g|_{(P,A)^c}$ is soft continuous. Let $(V, B) \in \vartheta$. By assumption, $h^{-1}(V, B) = g^{-1}(V, B)\tilde{\cap}(P, A)^c$. That is, $g^{-1}(V, B)\tilde{\cap}(P, A)^c = (U, A)\tilde{\cap}(P, A)^c$, where $(U, A) \in \theta$. Now,

$$\begin{aligned} g^{-1}(V, B) &= [g^{-1}(V, B)\tilde{\cap}(P, A)^c]\widetilde{\bigcup}[g^{-1}(V, B)\tilde{\cap}(P, A)] \\ &= [(U, A)\tilde{\cap}(P, A)^c]\widetilde{\bigcup}[g^{-1}(V, B)\tilde{\cap}(P, A)]. \end{aligned}$$

Since $(P, A) \in \mathcal{M}(X, A)$, $(Q, A) = g^{-1}(V, B)\tilde{\cap}(P, A)\tilde{\subseteq}(P, A)$ implies $(Q, A) \in \mathcal{M}(X, A)$. Therefore, $g^{-1}(V, B) = (U, A) - (P, A)\tilde{\cup}(Q, A)$. By Lemma 6, $g^{-1}(V, B) \in \mathcal{B}(X, \theta, A)$ and hence, g has the Baire property. □

5. Subclasses of Soft Functions with the Baire Property

We introduce two subclasses of soft functions with the Baire property in this section and discuss their fundamental properties.

Definition 29. *A soft function $g : (X, \theta, A) \to (Y, \vartheta, B)$ is said to be the Baire soft function of the first type (or shortly, BST_1) if $g^{-1}(H, B)$ is an ST_1-set for each $(H, B) \in \vartheta$. It is the Baire soft function of the second type (or shortly, BST_2) if $g^{-1}(H, B)$ is an ST_2-set for each $(H, B) \in \vartheta$.*

By the use of Proposition 5, one can construct the following:

Example 3. *Consider the soft topological space $(\mathbb{R}, \theta, A)$ given in Example 1 and let $\vartheta_{discrete}$ be the soft discrete topology on $\{0, 1\}$. Assume the soft function $g : (X, \theta, A) \to (\{0, 1\}, \vartheta_{discrete}, B)$ is defined by*

$$g(x_a) = \begin{cases} 1_b & \text{if } x_a \in (G, A); \\ \\ 0_{b'} & \text{if } x_a \notin (G, A), \end{cases}$$

where $(G, A) = \{(a, \mathbb{R} - \mathbb{Q}) : a \in A\}$ such that $\mathbb{Q}$ is the set of rationals. Then, g is a BST_1-function but not BST_2 since $g^{-1}(\{1_b\}) = (G, A)$ is an ST_1-set but not an ST_2-set, see Example 1. If we replace (G, A) by the soft set $(D, A) = \{(a, C) : a \in A\}$, where C is the ternary Cantor set, we obtain a BST_2-function but not BST_1. On the other hand, if we replace (G, A) by the soft set $(F, A) = \{(a, [(-1, 0) - \mathbb{Q}] \cup [(0, 1) \cap \mathbb{Q}]) : a \in A\}$, we obtain a soft function with the Baire property but neither BST_1 nor BST_2.

Proposition 6. *A soft function* $g:(X,\theta,A)\to(Y,\vartheta,B)$ *is* BST_i *iff* $g^{-1}(H,B)$ *is an* ST_j*-set for each* $(H,B)\in\vartheta^c$, $i,j=1,2$ *and* $i\neq j$.

Proof. We only prove when $i=1$ and $j=2$, the other case is the same. Suppose g is BST_1. Let $(H,B)\in\vartheta^c$. Then $(H,B)^c\in\vartheta$. By assumption, $g^{-1}((H,B)^c)$ is an ST_1-set. But, by Lemma 5, $g^{-1}((H,B)^c)=\left(g^{-1}(H,B)\right)^c$. By Lemma 10, $g^{-1}(H,B)$ is an ST_2-set.

The converse is clear. □

Proposition 7. *A soft function* $g:(X,\theta,A)\to(Y,\vartheta,B)$ *is* BST_1 *if it is soft* α*-continuous.*

Proof. Apply Proposition 1. □

Proposition 8. *A soft function* $g:(X,\theta,A)\to(Y,\vartheta,B)$ *is* BST_2 *if it is soft semicontinuous.*

Proof. Apply Proposition 2. □

The earlier two propositions and Figure 1 imply

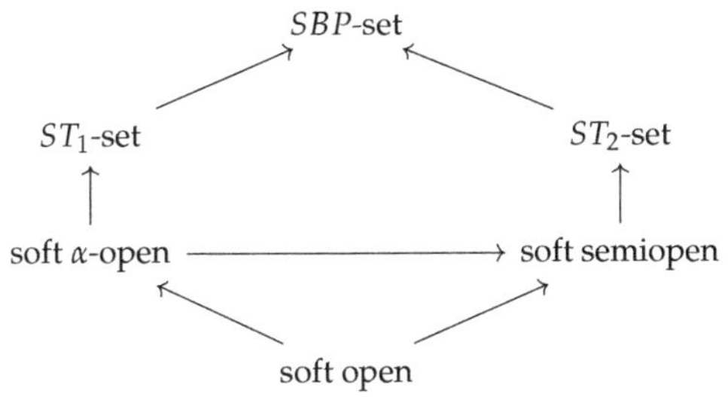

Figure 1. Generalized soft open sets.

Where an SBP-set means a soft set with the Baire property.

Corollary 1. *If* $g:(X,\theta,A)\to(Y,\vartheta,B)$ *is a soft continuous function, then it is* BST_i, *for* $i=1,2$.

Theorem 4. *Let* $g:(X,\theta,A)\to(Y,\vartheta,B)$ *be a soft function such that* $(X,\theta A)$ *is soft Baire and* (Y,ϑ,B) *is soft regular. Then* g *is* BST_1 *iff* g *is soft continuous.*

Proof. Suppose g is BST_1 and $x_a\in SP(X,A)$. Let $(H,B)\in\vartheta$ that contains $g(x_a)$. By soft regularity of (Y,ϑ,B), there exists $(V,B)\in\vartheta$ such that $g(x_a)\in(V,B)\widetilde{\subseteq}cl(V,B)\widetilde{\subseteq}(H,B)$. Since g is BST_1, so $g^{-1}(V,B)=(G,A)-(P,A)$ for some $(G,A)\in\theta$ and $(P,A)\in\mathcal{M}(X,A)$. Evidently, $x_a\in(G,A)$. To show the soft continuity of g, it suffices to show that $g(G,A)\widetilde{\subseteq}cl(V,B)$. Suppose otherwise that $g(x'_{a'})\notin cl(V,B)$ for some $x'_{a'}\in(G,A)$. This means that there exists $(W,B)\in\vartheta$ containing $g(x'_{a'})$ such that $(V,B)\widetilde{\cap}(W,B)=(\Phi,B)$ and $g^{-1}(W,B)=(U,A)-(Q,A)$, where $(U,A)\in\theta$ and $(Q,A)\in\mathcal{M}(X,A)$. Since $x'_{a'}\in(G,A)\widetilde{\cap}(U,A)$, so $(\Phi,A)\neq(G,A)\widetilde{\cap}(U,A)\in\theta$. Now, we have

$$\begin{aligned}(\Phi,A)&=g^{-1}(V,B)\widetilde{\cap}g^{-1}(W,B)\\&=(G,A)-(P,A)\widetilde{\cap}(U,A)-(Q,A)\\&=[(G,A)\widetilde{\cap}(U,A)]-[(P,A)\widetilde{\cap}(Q,A)].\end{aligned}$$

This means that $(G,A)\widetilde{\cap}(U,A)\widetilde{\subseteq}(P,A)\widetilde{\cap}(Q,A)$, which is not possible since $(X,\theta A)$ is a soft Baire space. Hence, we must have $g(G,A)\widetilde{\subseteq}cl(V,B)\widetilde{\subseteq}(H,B)$ which implies g is soft continuous.

Conversely, if g is soft continuous, then for each $(V,B) \in \vartheta$, $g^{-1}(V,B) \in \theta$. Clearly $g^{-1}(V,B)$ can be written as $g^{-1}(V,B)(G,A) - (\Phi,A)$ and thus $g^{-1}(V,B)$ is an ST_1-set. Hence, g is BST_1. □

Lemma 14. *Let $g : (X,\theta,A) \to (Y,\vartheta,B)$ be a soft function and let $\{(G_i,B) : i \in I\}$ be a soft base of ϑ. The set $\mathcal{D}(g)$ of all soft points of soft discontinuity of g is of the form*

$$\mathcal{D}(g) = \widetilde{\bigcup}_{i\in I}\Big(g^{-1}(G_i,B) - int(g^{-1}(G_i,B))\Big) \tag{1}$$

Proof. Let $x_a \in SP(X,A)$. If x_a is a soft point of soft discontinuity of g, then there exists $(H_{y_b},B) \in \vartheta$ containing $y_b = g(x_a)$ such that x_a is not a soft interior point of $g^{-1}(H_{y_b},B)$. That is, $x_a \in \big[g^{-1}(H_{y_b},B) - int(g^{-1}(H_{y_b},B))\big]$. Since $\{(G_i,B) : i \in I\}$ is a soft base of ϑ, one can find some (G_i,B) such that $(G_i,B)\widetilde{\subseteq}(H_{y_b},B)$. Therefore, $x_a \in \widetilde{\bigcup}_{i\in I}\big[g^{-1}(G_i,B) - int(g^{-1}(G_i,B))\big]$.

Conversely, if for a soft point $x_a \in SP(X,A)$, there exists $i \in I$ such that $x_a \in \big[g^{-1}(G_i,B) - int(g^{-1}(G_i,B))\big]$. This implies that $(G_i,B) \in \vartheta$ containing $g(x_a)$ for which $g^{-1}(G_i,B)$ is not a soft open set over X, and thus g is not soft continuous at x_a. □

Proposition 9. *Let $g : (X,\theta,A) \to (Y,\vartheta,B)$ be a soft function. If the set $\mathcal{D}(g)$ of all soft points of soft discontinuity of g is in $\mathcal{M}(X,A)$, then g is BST_2.*

Proof. Suppose $\mathcal{D}(g) \in \mathcal{M}(X,A)$. Let $(H,B) \in \vartheta$. Since the soft set $(F,A) = g^{-1}(H,B) - int(g^{-1}(H,B))\widetilde{\subseteq}\mathcal{D}(g)$, then $(F,A) \in \mathcal{M}(X,A)$. Therefore, $g^{-1}(H,B) = int(g^{-1}(H,B))\widetilde{\cup}\,(F,A)$ implies $g^{-1}(H,B)$ is ST_2. Hence, g is BST_2. □

Proposition 10. *Let $g : (X,\theta,A) \to (Y,\vartheta,B)$ be a soft function. If g is BST_2 and (Y,ϑ,B) is soft second countable, then the set $\mathcal{D}(g)$ of all soft points of soft discontinuity of g is in $\mathcal{M}(X,A)$.*

Proof. Let $\{(G_n,B) : n = 1,2,\cdots\}$ be a countable soft base of ϑ. By (1) in Lemma 14,

$$\mathcal{D}(g) = \widetilde{\bigcup}_{n=1}^{\infty}\Big(g^{-1}(G_n,B) - int(g^{-1}(G_n,B))\Big).$$

Since g is BST_2, so $g^{-1}(G_n,B) - int(g^{-1}(G_n,B)) \in \mathcal{M}(X,A)$, and thus $\mathcal{D}(g) \in \mathcal{M}(X,A)$ as $\mathcal{M}(X,A)$ is closed under countable soft unions. □

From Propositions 9 and 10, we have the following result:

Theorem 5. *Let $g : (X,\theta,A) \to (Y,\vartheta,B)$ be a soft function such that (Y,ϑ,B) is soft second countable. Then g is BST_2 iff $\mathcal{D}(g)$ is in $\mathcal{M}(X,A)$.*

We conclude this work by presenting the Figure 2 below:

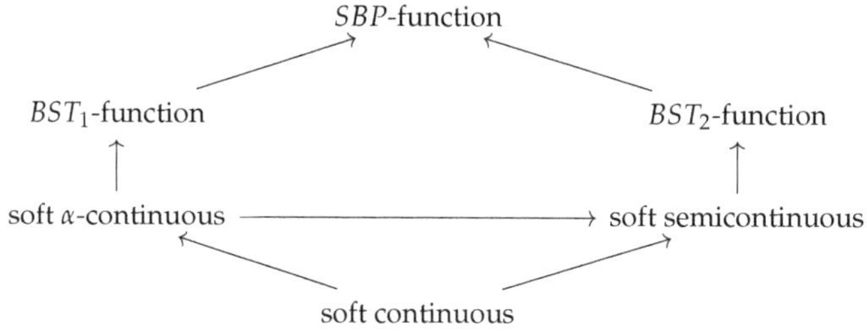

Figure 2. Generalized soft continuous functions.

Where SBP-function means a soft function with the Baire property.

One can derive from Proposition 5 and Examples 1 and 3 that the remaining examples demonstrating the opposites of the aforementioned arrows are untrue.

6. Conclusions and Future Work

Soft continuity is one of the most natural topics in the field of soft topology, which is a combination of topology and soft set theory. Soft continuity between soft topological spaces has a rich literature. After recalling and studying certain classes of soft sets with the Baire property, we have first started by defining the concept of soft functions having the Baire property. A soft function with the Baire property sends soft open sets back to soft sets with the Baire property. Basic operations on soft functions with the Baire property are discussed, along with some basic properties. We have seen that each soft continuous function is a soft function with the Baire property. The converse is generally false. We have shown that a soft function from a soft topological space into a soft second countable space has the Baire property if and only if there exists a soft set of the first category such that the restriction of the soft function to its complement is soft continuous. Secondly, we have introduced two subfamilies of soft functions with the Baire property called soft functions with the first and second types. We have studied these types of soft functions and established some of their characterizations. In particular, we have proved that a soft function from a soft Baire space into a soft regular space is of the first type if and only if it is soft continuous. And a soft function is of the second type if and only if the set of its discontinuous soft points is a soft set of the first category, provided that the range of the soft function is soft second countable. Moreover, we have shown that soft functions with the first type or second type are weaker than certain natural classes of generalized soft continuous functions, like soft α-continuous and soft semicontinuous functions. Lastly, we have built the relationships between the classes of soft functions mentioned above and have offered some counterexamples that disprove the reverse of the relationships.

The conclusions in this article are preliminary, and more study will be necessary. These findings can also be seen as the foundation for researching new topics in soft topology and soft measure theory. Since the soft σ-algebra of soft set of the Baire property [43], a soft function with the Baire property can be considered a soft measurable function within the context of soft measure theory. As a result, soft functions can contribute to the growth of soft measure theory. Furthermore, by virtue of Proposition 5, one can study the determinacy of the Banach-Mazur game on a certain soft topological space when the characteristic soft function of each soft subset has the Baire property.

Author Contributions: Conceptualization, Z.A.A. and M.H.A.; Methodology, Z.A.A.; Formal Analysis, Z.A.A. and M.H.A.; Investigation, Z.A.A. and M.H.A.; Writing Original Draft Preparation, Z.A.A.; Writing Review & Editing, Z.A.A. and M.H.A.; Funding Acquisition, M.H.A. All authors have read and agreed to the published version of the manuscript.

Funding: This research received no external funding.

Data Availability Statement: Not applicable.

Conflicts of Interest: The authors declare no conflict of interest.

References

1. Zadeh, L. Fuzzy sets. *Inf. Control* **1965**, *8*, 338–353. [CrossRef]
2. Pawlak, Z. Rough sets. *Int. J. Comput. Inf. Sci.* **1982**, *11*, 341–356. [CrossRef]
3. Molodtsov, D. Soft set theory—First results. *Comput. Math. Appl.* **1999**, *37*, 19–31. [CrossRef]
4. Dalkılıç, O.; Demirtaş, N. Algorithms for Covid-19 outbreak using soft set theory: Estimation and application. *Soft Comput.* **2022**, *27*, 3203–3211. [CrossRef] [PubMed]
5. Ergül, Z.G.; Demirtaş, N.; Dalkılıç, O. Analysis of parameter relationships influencing prostate cancer using the soft set model. In Proceedings of the International Conference on Applied Engineering and Natural Sciences, New York, NY, USA, 9–10 September 2023; Volume 1; pp. 682–687.

6. Maji, P.; Roy, A.R.; Biswas, R. An application of soft sets in a decision making problem. *Comput. Math. Appl.* **2002**, *44*, 1077–1083. [CrossRef]
7. Pei, D.; Miao, D. From soft sets to information systems. In Proceedings of the 2005 IEEE International Conference on Granular Computing, Beijing, China, 25–27 July 2005; IEEE: New York, NY, USA, 2005; Volume 2, pp. 617–621.
8. Voskoglou, M.G. Fuzziness, indeterminacy and soft sets: Frontiers and perspectives. *Mathematics* **2022**, *10*, 3909. [CrossRef]
9. Voskoglou, M.G. A Combined use of soft sets and grey numbers in decision making. *J. Comput. Cogn. Eng.* **2023**, *2*, 1. [CrossRef]
10. Çağman, N.; Karataş, S.; Enginoglu, S. Soft topology. *Comput. Math. Appl.* **2011**, *62*, 351–358. [CrossRef]
11. Shabir, M.; Naz, M. On soft topological spaces. *Comput. Math. Appl.* **2011**, *61*, 1786–1799. [CrossRef]
12. Bayramov, S.; Gunduz, C. A new approach to separability and compactness in soft topological spaces. *TWMS J. Pure Appl. Math.* **2018**, *9*, 82–93.
13. Das, S.; Samanta, S. Soft metric. *Ann. Fuzzy Math. Inf.* **2013**, *6*, 77–94.
14. Lin, F. Soft connected spaces and soft paracompact spaces. *Int. J. Math. Comput.* **2013**, *7*, 277–283.
15. Aygünoğlu, A.; Aygün, H. Some notes on soft topological spaces. *Neural Comput. Appl.* **2012**, *21*, 113–119. [CrossRef]
16. Asaad, B.A. Results on soft extremally disconnectedness of soft topological spaces. *J. Math. Comput. Sci.* **2017**, *17*, 448–464. [CrossRef]
17. Al Ghour, S.; Ameen, Z.A. On soft submaximal spaces. *Heliyon* **2022**, *8*, e10574. [CrossRef]
18. Riaz, M.; Fatima, Z. Certain properties of soft metric spaces. *J. Fuzzy Math.* **2017**, *25*, 543–560.
19. Ameen, Z.A.; Khalaf, A.B. The invariance of soft Baire spaces under soft weak functions. *J. Interdiscip. Math.* **2022**, *25*, 1295–1306. [CrossRef]
20. Ameen, Z.A.; Asaad, B.A.; Al-shami, T.M. Soft somewhat continuous and soft somewhat open functions. *TWMS J. Pure Appl. Math.* **2023**, *13*, 92–806.
21. Chen, B. Soft semi-open sets and related properties in soft topological spaces. *Appl. Math. Inf. Sci.* **2013**, *7*, 287–294. [CrossRef]
22. Akdag, M.; Ozkan, A. Soft α-open sets and soft α-continuous functions. *Abstr. Appl. Anal.* **2014**, *2014*, 891341. [CrossRef]
23. Ameen, Z.A.; Alqahtani, M.H. Congruence representations via soft ideals in soft topological spaces. *Axioms (Communicated)*, **2023**.
24. Öztunç, S.; Ihtiyar, S. Soft isomorphism for digital images and computational topological applications. *J. Intell. Fuzzy Syst.* **2023**, *44*, 3011–3021. [CrossRef]
25. Zorlutuna, İ.; Akdag, M.; Min, W.; Atmaca, S. Remarks on soft topological spaces. *Ann. Fuzzy Math. Inform.* **2012**, *3*, 171–185.
26. Ameen, Z.A. A non-continuous soft mapping that preserves some structural soft sets. *J. Intell. Fuzzy Syst.* **2022**, *42*, 5839–5845. [CrossRef]
27. Al Ghour, S. Soft C-continuity and soft almost C-continuity between soft topological spaces. *Heliyon* **2023**, *9*, e16363. [CrossRef]
28. Al Ghour, S.; Al-Saadi, H. Soft slight omega-continuity and soft ultra-separation axioms. *Mathematics* **2023**, *11*, 3334. [CrossRef]
29. Mahanta, J.; Das, P.K. On soft topological space via semiopen and semiclosed soft sets. *Kyungpook Math. J.* **2014**, *54*, 221–236. [CrossRef]
30. Kuratowski, K. *Topology: Volume I*; Elsevier: Amsterdam, The Netherlands, 2014; Volume 1.
31. Oxtoby, J.C. *Measure and Category: A Survey of the Analogies between Topological and Measure Spaces*; Springer Science & Business Media: Berlin/Heidelberg, Germany, 2013; Volume 2.
32. Szymanski, A. Proper functions with the Baire property. *Ann. New York Acad. Sci.* **1992**, *659*, 176–181. [CrossRef]
33. Ali, M.I.; Feng, F.; Liu, X.; Min, W.K.; Shabir, M. On some new operations in soft set theory. *Comput. Math. Appl.* **2009**, *57*, 1547–1553. [CrossRef]
34. Xie, N. Soft points and the structure of soft topological spaces. *Ann. Fuzzy Math. Inf.* **2015**, *10*, 309–322.
35. Maji, P.K.; Biswas, R.; Roy, A.R. Soft set theory. *Comput. Math. Appl.* **2003**, *45*, 555–562. [CrossRef]
36. Ameen, Z.A.; Al-shami, T.M.; Asaad, B.A. Further properties of soft somewhere dense continuous functions and soft Baire spaces. *J. Math. Comput. Sci.* **2024**, *32*, 54–63. [CrossRef]
37. Al Ghour, S.; Ameen, Z.A. Maximal soft compact and maximal soft connected topologies. *Appl. Comput. Intell. Soft Comput.* **2022**, *2022*, 9860015. [CrossRef]
38. Nazmul, S.; Samanta, S. Neighbourhood properties of soft topological spaces. *Ann. Fuzzy Math. Inf.* **2013**, *6*, 1–15.
39. Hussain, S.; Ahmad, B. Some properties of soft topological spaces. *Comput. Math. Appl.* **2011**, *62*, 4058–4067. [CrossRef]
40. Azzam, A.; Ameen, Z.A.; Al-shami, T.M.; El-Shafei, M.E. Generating soft topologies via soft set operators. *Symmetry* **2022**, *14*, 914. [CrossRef]
41. Al Ghour, S. Boolean algebra of soft Q-Sets in soft topological spaces. *Appl. Comput. Intell. Soft Comput.* **2022**, *2022*, 5200590. [CrossRef]
42. Yüksel, S.; Tozlu, N.; Ergül, Z.G. Soft regular generalized closed sets in soft topological spaces. *Int. J. Math. Anal.* **2014**, *8*, 355–367. [CrossRef]
43. Ameen, Z.A.; Alqahtani, M.H. Baire category soft sets and thier symmetric local properties. *Symmetry* **2023**, *15*, 1810. [CrossRef]
44. Kandil, A.; AE Tantawy, O.; A El-Sheikh, S.; M Abd El-latif, A. Soft ideal theory soft local function and generated soft topological spaces. *Appl. Math. Inf. Sci.* **2014**, *8*, 1595–1603. [CrossRef]
45. Riaz, M.; Naeem, K.; Ahmad, M.O. Novel concepts of soft sets with applications. *Ann. Fuzzy Math. Inform.* **2017**, *13*, 239–251. [CrossRef]
46. Khameneh, A.Z.; Kilicman, A. On Soft σ-Algebras. *Malays. J. Math. Sci.* **2013**, *7*, 17–29.

47. Ameen, Z.A.; Al-shami, T.M.; Abu-Gdairi, R.; Mhemdi, A. The relationship between ordinary and soft algebras with an application. *Mathematics* **2023**, *11*, 2035. [CrossRef]
48. Kharal, A.; Ahmad, B. Mappings on soft classes. *New Math. Nat. Comput.* **2011**, *7*, 471–481. [CrossRef]

mathematics

MDPI

Article

Hyperconnectedness and Resolvability of Soft Ideal Topological Spaces

Ahmad Al-Omari [1,*,†] and Wafa Alqurashi [2,†]

[1] Department of Mathematics, Faculty of Sciences, Al-al-Bayt University, P.O. Box 130095, Mafraq 25113, Jordan
[2] Department of Mathematic, Faculty of Sciences, Umm Al-Qura University, P.O. Box 11155, Makkah 21955, Saudi Arabia; wkqurashi@uqu.edu.sa
* Correspondence: omarimath@aabu.edu.jo or omarimutah1@yahoo.com
† These authors contributed equally to this work.

Abstract: This paper introduces and explores the concept of soft ideal dense sets, utilizing soft open sets and soft local functions, to examine their fundamental characteristics under some conditions for the following notions: soft ideal hyperconnectedness, soft ideal resolvability, soft ideal irresolvability, and soft ideal semi-irresolvability in soft ideal topological spaces. Moreover, it explores the relationship between these notions if $\tau \sqcap \mathcal{I} = \phi_E$ is obtained in the soft set environment.

Keywords: soft open set; soft dense; soft ideal; soft ideal hyperconnected; soft ideal resolvable; soft ideal irresolvable; soft ideal semi-irresolvable

MSC: 54A05; 54A10; 54A40

1. Introduction

In 1999, Molodtsov [1] initially suggested the idea of soft sets as a broad mathematical tool for handling uncertain situations. Molodtsov effectively utilized soft theory in some areas, including probability, theory of measurement, smoothness of functions, Perron integration, operations research, Riemann integration, and so on, in [2].

Shabir and Naz [3] started researching soft topological spaces in 2011. They defined the topology on the collection τ of soft sets over X. Thus, they developed many features of soft regular spaces, soft normal spaces, soft separation axioms, soft open and soft closed sets, soft subspace, soft closure, and soft nbd of a point. They also defined the fundamental concepts of soft topological spaces.

Kandil and colleagues introduced the concept of the soft ideal for the first time [4]. Additionally, they presented the idea of soft local functions. These ideas are presented with the goal of identifying new soft topologies, termed soft topological spaces with soft ideal $(X_E, \tau, \overline{\mathcal{I}})$, from the original one. Numerous mathematical structures, such as soft group theory [5], soft ring theory [6], soft primals [7], soft algebras [8,9], soft category theory [10], ideal spaces [11], ideal resolvability [12], and so on, have been addressed by soft set theory. Similarly, the notion of soft topology through soft grills was introduced in [13]. Additionally, a large number of academics and researchers developed gentle versions of the traditional topological ideas, such as soft resolvable spaces [14], soft hyperconnected spaces [15], suitable soft spaces [7], soft ideal spaces [4,16,17], soft extremally disconnected spaces [18], soft Menger spaces [19], soft countable chain condition, and soft caliber [20]. From here on, we shall refer to a soft ideal topological space $(X_E, \tau, \overline{\mathcal{I}})$, a soft ideal space. The way this work is set out is as follows: Following the introduction, we discuss the definitions and findings that are necessary to understand the data in Section 2. Next, we recall the notion of soft local functions in Section 3. We study the fundamental operations on soft local functions. The definitions of soft hyperconnected and soft hyperconnected modulo ideal spaces, as well as a soft ideal topological space, are provided in Section 4.

Citation: Al-Omari, A.; Alqurashi, W. Hyperconnectedness and Resolvability of Soft Ideal Topological Spaces. *Mathematics* **2023**, *11*, 4697. https://doi.org/10.3390/math11224697

Academic Editor: Michael Voskoglou

Received: 31 October 2023
Revised: 16 November 2023
Accepted: 17 November 2023
Published: 19 November 2023

We look at the basic characteristics and connections between soft hyperconnected and soft hyperconnected modulo ideals. A soft ideal resolvable space is defined in Section 5 and it is demonstrated that soft ideal resolvable topologies over soft ideal resolvable subspace are also soft ideal resolvable. The concept of soft ideal semi-irresolvable space and an overview of its properties are provided in Section 6. In Section 7, we finish off by providing an overview of the major contributions and some recommendations for the future.

2. Preliminary

Here, we provide the fundamental concepts and the outcomes of soft set theory that are required for the follow-up.

Definition 1 ([1]). *Let X be an initial universe and E be a set of parameters. Let $P(X)$ denote the power set of X and A be a non-null subset of parameters E. A pair (F, A) symbolized by F_A is a soft set over X_E, where F is a mapping given by $F : A \to P(X)$. Otherwise put, a soft set over X_E is a parameterized family of subsets of the universe X_E. For a particular $e \in E$, $F(e)$ might be regarded as the set of e-approximate elements of the soft set $(F, E) = F_E$ and, if $e \notin E$, then $F(e) = \phi$, i.e., $F_E = \{F(e) : e \in E, F : E \to P(X)\}$. The collection of all these soft sets is symbolized by $SS(X)_E$.*

Definition 2 ([21]). *Let $F_E, G_E \in SS(X)_E$. Then*

1. *F_E is called a soft subset of G_E, denoted by $F_E \sqsubseteq G_E$, if $F(e) \subseteq G(e)$, for all $e \in E$.*
2. *F_E is called absolute, symbolized by X_E, if $F(e) = X$ for all $e \in E$.*
3. *F_E is called null, symbolized by ϕ_E, if $F(e) = \phi$ for all $e \in E$.*

In this case F_E is said to be a soft subset of G_E and G_E is said to be a soft superset of F_E, $F_E \sqsubseteq G_E$.

Definition 3 ([22]). *1. A soft set $F_E \in SS(X)_E$ is called a soft point in X_E if there exist $x \in X$ and $e \in E$ such that $F(e) = \{x\}$ and $F(e^c) = \phi$ for each $e^c \in E - \{e\}$. This soft point F_E is denoted by x_e.*

2. *Let Δ be an arbitrary index set and $\Omega = \{(F_\alpha)_E : \alpha \in \Delta\}$ be a subfamily of $SS(X)_E$. Then:*
   (a) *The union of all $(F_\alpha)_E$ is the soft set H_E, where $H(e) = \cup_{\alpha\in\Delta}(F_\alpha)_E(e)$ for each $e \in E$. We write $\sqcup_{\alpha\in\Delta}(F_\alpha)_E = H_E$.*
   (b) *The intersection of all $(F_\alpha)_E$ is the soft set M_E, where $M(e) = \cap_{\alpha\in\Delta}(F_\alpha)_E(e)$ for each $e \in E$. We write $\sqcap_{\alpha\in\Delta}(F_\alpha)_E = M_E$.*
3. *A soft set G_E in a soft topological space (X_E, τ) is called a soft neighborhood of the soft point $x_e \in X_E$ if there exists a soft open set H_E such that $x_e \in H_E \sqsubseteq G_E$.*

Definition 4 ([3]). *Let (X_E, τ) be a soft topological space and $F_E \in SS(X)_E$.*

1. *The soft closure of F_E, symbolized by $cl(F_E)$, is the intersection of all soft closed supersets of F_E, i.e., $cl(F_E) = \sqcap\{H_E : H_E$ is soft closed and $F_E \sqsubseteq H_E\}$.*
2. *The soft interior of F_E is the set $Int(F_E) = \sqcup\{H_E : H_E$ is soft open and $H_E \sqsubseteq F_E\}$.*
3. *A difference of two soft sets F_E and G_E over the common universe X_E, symbolized by $F_E - G_E$, is the soft set H_E for all $e \in E$, $H(e) = F(e) - G(e)$.*
4. *A complement of a soft set F_E, symbolized by F_E^c, is defined as follows. $F^c : E \to P(X)$ is a mapping given by $F^c(e) = X_E(e) - F(e)$, for all $e \in E$, and F^c is called a soft complement function of F_E.*
5. *Let F_E be a soft set over X_E and $x_e \in X_E$. We say that $x_e \in F_E$ denotes that x_e belongs to the soft set F_E whenever $x_e(e) \in F(e)$, for all $e \in E$.*

For more details of soft set theory and its applications in a variety of mathematical structures, see [18,23–27].

3. Soft Local Functions

Definition 5 ([4]). *The non-null collection of soft subsets $\mathcal{I}$ of $SS(X)_E$ is called a soft ideal on X_E if*

(a) $F_E \in \overline{\mathcal{I}}$ and $G_E \sqsubseteq F_E$, then $G_E \in \overline{\mathcal{I}}$.
(b) $F_E \in \overline{\mathcal{I}}$ and $G_E \subset \overline{\mathcal{I}}$, then $F_E \sqcup G_E \in \overline{\mathcal{I}}$.

Definition 6 ([4]). *Let $(X_E, \tau, \overline{\mathcal{I}})$ be a $\mathcal{SITS}$. Then, $\overline{F_E}^*(\overline{\mathcal{I}}, \tau)$ (or $\overline{F}_E^*$) $= \sqcup\{x_e \in X_E : O_{x_e} \sqcap F_E \notin \overline{\mathcal{I}}$ for every soft open set $O_{x_e}\}$ is called a soft local function of F_E with respect to $\overline{\mathcal{I}}$ and soft topology τ, where O_{x_e} is a soft open set containing x_e.*

A soft subset A_E of a soft ideal topological space "symbolized $\mathcal{SITS}$" $(X_E, \tau, \overline{\mathcal{I}})$ is said to be soft ideal dense if every soft point of X_E is in $\overline{A}_E^*$, i.e., if $\overline{A}_E^* = X_E$.

Remark 1. *For a $\mathcal{SITS}$ $(X_E, \tau, \overline{\mathcal{I}})$, if $D_E \sqsubseteq X_E$ is soft ideal dense, then X_E is also soft ideal dense, i.e., $\overline{X_E}^* = X_E$.*

A soft set $S_E \in SS(X)_E$ is called soft co-dense [28] if $Int(S_E) = \phi_E$.

Theorem 1. *Let $(X_E, \tau, \overline{\mathcal{I}})$ be a $\mathcal{SITS}$. Then, the next characteristics are interchangeable:*
(a) $\tau \sqcap \overline{\mathcal{I}} = \phi_E$, *where ϕ_E is a null soft set;*
(b) *If $S_E \in \overline{\mathcal{I}}$, then $Int(S_E) = \phi_E$;*
(c) *For any soft open F_E, we have $F_E \sqsubseteq \overline{F}_E^*$;*
(d) $X_E = \overline{X}_E^*$.

Proof. (a) $\rightarrow$ (b): Assume that $\tau \sqcap \overline{\mathcal{I}} = \phi_E$ and $S_E \in \overline{\mathcal{I}}$. Suppose that $x_e \in Int(S_E)$. Then, there exists a soft open set U_E such that $x_e \in U_E \sqsubseteq S_E$. Since $S_E \in \overline{\mathcal{I}}$, $U_E \in \overline{\mathcal{I}}$. This is contrary to $\tau \sqcap \overline{\mathcal{I}} = \phi_E$. Therefore, $Int(S_E) = \phi_E$.
(b) $\rightarrow$ (c): Assume that $x_e \in F_E$. Let $x_e \notin \overline{F}_E^*$; then, there exists soft open set U_{x_e} containing x_e such that $F_E \sqcap U_{x_e} \in \overline{\mathcal{I}}$. Since F_E is a soft open set, by (b) $x_e \in F_E \sqcap U_{x_e} = Int[F_E \sqcap U_{x_e}] = \phi_E$. This is incoherent, and so $x_e \in \overline{F}_E^*$ and $F_E \sqsubseteq \overline{F}_E^*$.
(c) $\rightarrow$ (d): Since X_E is a soft open set, $X_E = \overline{X}_E^*$.
(d) $\rightarrow$ (a): $X_E = \overline{X}_E^* = \{x_e \in X_E : U_E \sqcap X_E = U_E \notin \overline{\mathcal{I}}$ for all soft open sets U_E and $x_e \in U_E\}$. Then, $\tau \sqcap \overline{\mathcal{I}} = \phi_E$. □

4. Soft Hyperconnected Spaces

Definition 7. *Let $(X_E, \tau, \overline{\mathcal{I}})$ be a $\mathcal{SITS}$. We say that this space is:*
1. *Soft hyperconnected "symbolized $\mathcal{HC}$" [17] if every pair of non-null soft open sets of X_E has non-null intersection.*
2. *Soft $\mathcal{HC}$ modulo $\overline{\mathcal{I}}$ if the intersection of every two non-null soft open sets is not in $\overline{\mathcal{I}}$.*
3. *Soft ideal $\mathcal{HC}$ if every non-null soft open set is soft ideal dense in X_E.*

Lemma 1. *A $\mathcal{SITS}$ $(X_E, \tau, \overline{\mathcal{I}})$ is soft $\mathcal{HC}$ modulo $\overline{\mathcal{I}}$ iff there are no proper soft closed sets G_E and H_E such that $X_E - (G_E \sqcup H_E) \in \overline{\mathcal{I}}$.*

Proof. If there are proper soft closed sets G_E and H_E such that $X_E - [G_E \sqcup H_E] \in \overline{\mathcal{I}}$. If $H_E = \phi_E$, then $X_E - G_E \in \overline{\mathcal{I}}$. $X_E - G_E$ and X_E are non-null soft open sets with $X_E \sqcap (X_E - G_E) = (X_E - G_E) \in \overline{\mathcal{I}}$. This is incoherent. Hence, $G_E \neq \phi_E$ and $H_E \neq \phi_E$ are both proper soft closed sets. Then, $X_E - G_E$ and $X_E - H_E$ are non-null soft open sets. So, $(X_E - G_E) \sqcap (X_E - H_E) = X_E - (G_E \sqcup H_E) \in \overline{\mathcal{I}}$, which contradicts.

Conversely, assume that $A_E \neq \phi_E$ and $B_E \neq \phi_E$ are soft open sets in X_E. So, $X_E - A_E$ and $X_E - B_E$ are proper soft closed sets in X_E and $X_E - [(X_E - A_E) \sqcup (X_E - B_E)] \notin \overline{\mathcal{I}}$. This implies that $X_E - [X_E - (A_E \sqcap B_E)] \notin \overline{\mathcal{I}}$. Thus, $(A_E \sqcap B_E) \notin \overline{\mathcal{I}}$. Hence, $(X_E, \tau, \overline{\mathcal{I}})$ is soft $\mathcal{HC}$ modulo $\overline{\mathcal{I}}$. □

Theorem 2. *Let $(X_E, \tau, \overline{\mathcal{I}})$ be a $\mathcal{SITS}$ and $\tau \sqcap \overline{\mathcal{I}} = \phi_E$. Then, $(X_E, \tau, \overline{\mathcal{I}})$ is soft $\mathcal{HC}$ modulo $\overline{\mathcal{I}}$ if and only if (X_E, τ) is soft $\mathcal{HC}$.*

Proof. Assume that $(X_E, \tau, \overline{\mathcal{I}})$ is a soft $\mathcal{HC}$ modulo $\overline{\mathcal{I}}$. So, since $\phi_E \in \overline{\mathcal{I}}$, (X_E, τ) is soft $\mathcal{HC}$.

Conversely, let (X_E, τ) be a soft $\mathcal{HC}$ and A_E, B_E be non-null soft open sets. Then, $A_E \sqcap B_E$ is a non-null soft open set in (X_E, τ). Since $\tau \sqcap \overline{\mathcal{I}} = \phi_E$, $A_E \sqcap B_E \notin \overline{\mathcal{I}}$. Thus, $(X_E, \tau, \overline{\mathcal{I}})$ is soft $\mathcal{HC}$ modulo $\overline{\mathcal{I}}$. □

The following example show that, if $\tau \sqcap \overline{\mathcal{I}} \neq \phi_E$, Theorem 2 is not true.

Example 1. *Let $(X_E, \tau, \overline{\mathcal{I}})$ be a $\mathcal{SITS}$, where $X = \{h_1, h_2\}$, $E = \{e_1, e_2\}$ $\tau = \{X_E, \phi_E, \{(e_1, \{h_1\}), (e_2, \{h_2\})\}, \{(e_1, X_E), (e_2, \{h_2\})\}, \{(e_1, \{h_1\}), (e_2, \{X_E\})\}\}$, and $\overline{\mathcal{I}} = \{\phi_E, \{(e_1, \{h_1\})\}, \{(e_2, \{h_2\})\}, \{(e_1, \{h_1\}), (e_2, \{h_2\})\}\}$. Then, $\tau \sqcap \overline{\mathcal{I}} \neq \phi_E$.*

Since every pair of non-null soft open sets of X_E has non-null soft intersection, $(X_E, \tau, \overline{\mathcal{I}})$ is soft $\mathcal{HC}$. But it is clear that it is not soft $\mathcal{HC}$ modulo $\overline{\mathcal{I}}$.

Theorem 3. *A soft topological space (X_E, τ) is soft $\mathcal{HC}$ iff the union of two not soft dense sets is a not soft dense set.*

Proof. Assume that (X_E, τ) is soft $\mathcal{HC}$ and G_E, F_E are two not soft dense sets in (X_E, τ). Then there exist two non-null soft open sets U_E and V_E such that $U_E \sqcap G_E = \phi_E$ and $V_E \sqcap F_E = \phi_E$. Since (X_E, τ) is soft $\mathcal{HC}$, $U_E \sqcap V_E \neq \phi_E$. But $(U_E \sqcap V_E) \sqcap (G_E \sqcup F_E) = \phi_E$ and, hence, $G_E \sqcup F_E$ is not soft dense in (X_E, τ).

Conversely, if the condition is true in (X_E, τ) but (X_E, τ) is not soft $\mathcal{HC}$, then there exist two non-null soft open sets U_E and V_E such that $U_E \sqcap V_E = \phi_E$. Hence, $U_E \sqsubseteq X_E - V_E$ and $V_E \sqsubseteq X_E - U_E$. Then, $X_E - U_E$ and $X_E - V_E$ are not soft dense in (X_E, τ). But $(X_E - U_E) \sqcup (X_E - V_E) = X_E$. This contradicts the assertion that a union of two non-soft dense sets is also not a soft dense set. The theorem is therefore now proven. □

Lemma 2. *Let $(X_E, \tau, \overline{\mathcal{I}})$ be a $\mathcal{SITS}$. Then, $(X_E, \tau, \overline{\mathcal{I}})$ is soft ideal $\mathcal{HC}$ if and only if (X_E, τ) is soft $\mathcal{HC}$ and $\tau \sqcap \overline{\mathcal{I}} = \phi_E$.*

Proof. Clearly, every soft ideal $\mathcal{HC}$ space is soft $\mathcal{HC}$. Let U_E be a non-null soft open set in the soft ideal. Then, $\overline{U}_E^* = X_E$. Conversely, yet, since $U_E \in \overline{\mathcal{I}}$, $\overline{U}_E^* = \phi_E$. Hence, $X_E = \phi_E$. There is inconsistency here. Consequently, $\tau \sqcap \overline{\mathcal{I}} = \phi_E$.

Conversely, let U_E be a non-null soft open set. Let $x_e \in X_E$. Due to the soft $\mathcal{HC}$ property of (X_E, τ), every soft open set V_E containing x_e meets U_E. Moreover, $U_E \sqcap V_E$ is a soft open set and $U_E \sqcap V_E \notin \overline{\mathcal{I}}$ because $\tau \sqcap \overline{\mathcal{I}} = \phi_E$. Thus, $x_e \in \overline{U}_E^*$. This shows that U_E is soft ideal dense. □

Theorem 4. *Let $(X_E, \tau, \overline{\mathcal{I}})$ be a $\mathcal{SITS}$, where $\tau \sqcap \overline{\mathcal{I}} = \phi_E$. Then, a set D_E is soft ideal dense if and only if $(U_E - A_E) \sqcap D_E \neq \phi_E$ whenever U_E is non-null soft open and $A_E \in \overline{\mathcal{I}}$.*

Proof. Let D_E be soft ideal dense. So, $U_E \sqcap D_E \notin \overline{\mathcal{I}}$ for all non-null soft open sets U_E. Hence, for all $A_E \in \overline{\mathcal{I}}$, $(U_E - A_E) \sqcap D_E \neq \phi_E$, for, otherwise, $(U_E - A_E) \sqcap D_E = \phi_E$ and, hence, $\phi_E = U_E \sqcap (X_E - A_E) \sqcap D_E = (U_E \sqcap D_E) \sqcap (X_E - A_E)$. Therefore, $U_E \sqcap D_E \sqsubseteq A_E$. Since $A_E \in \overline{\mathcal{I}}$, $U_E \sqcap D_E \in \overline{\mathcal{I}}$, which is contrary to $U_E \sqcap D_E \notin \overline{\mathcal{I}}$. Therefore, $(U_E - A_E) \sqcap D_E \neq \phi_E$.

Conversely, let $(U_E - A_E) \sqcap D_E \neq \phi_E$ whenever U_E is a non-null soft open set and $A_E \in \overline{\mathcal{I}}$. Next, we assert that D_E is soft ideal dense. Let D_E be not soft ideal dense. Then, there exists some non-null soft open set U_E such that $U_E \sqcap D_E \in \overline{\mathcal{I}}$. Let $U_E \sqcap D_E = A_E$. So, since $\tau \sqcap \overline{\mathcal{I}} = \phi_E$, $U_E - A_E$ is non-null but $(U_E - A_E) \sqcap D_E = \phi_E$. This defies everything we had assumed. □

Theorem 5. *Let $(X_E, \tau, \overline{\mathcal{I}})$ be a $\mathcal{SITS}$, where $\tau \sqcap \overline{\mathcal{I}} = \phi_E$. Then, $(X_E, \tau, \overline{\mathcal{I}})$ is soft $\mathcal{HC}$ modulo $\overline{\mathcal{I}}$ if and only if $(U_E - A_E) \sqcap D_E \neq \phi_E$ whenever U_E and D_E are non-null soft open sets and $A_E \in \overline{\mathcal{I}}$.*

Proof. From Lemma 2 and Theorem 4, the proof follows. □

5. Soft Ideal Resolvable Spaces

A soft space (X_E, τ) is soft resolvable [14], symbolized $(\mathcal{RS})$, if X_E is the union of two soft dense subsets which are disjoint.

A $\mathcal{SITS}$ $(X_E, \tau, \overline{\mathcal{I}})$ is soft ideal $\mathcal{RS}$ if it has two disjoint soft ideal dense sets; alternatively, it is claimed to be soft ideal irresolvable, symbolized $(\mathcal{IRS})$.

Lemma 3. *Let $(X_E, \tau, \overline{\mathcal{I}})$ be a $\mathcal{SITS}$.*

(1) *$(X_E, \tau, \overline{\mathcal{I}})$ is soft ideal $\mathcal{RS}$ iff X_E is the union of two disjoint soft ideal dense sets.*
(2) *If $(X_E, \tau, \overline{\mathcal{I}})$ is soft ideal $\mathcal{RS}$, then $\tau \sqcap \overline{\mathcal{I}} = \phi_E$.*

Proof. (1) Let A_E and B_E be disjoint soft ideal dense sets. Then, $\overline{A}^*_E = X_E$ and $X_E = \overline{B}^*_E \sqsubseteq \overline{(X_E - A_E)}^*_E$, and, hence, $X_E = \overline{(X_E - A_E)}^*_E$. Therefore, X_E is the union of soft ideal dense sets A_E and $X_E - A_E$. The opposite is evident.

(2) Let A_E and B_E be disjoint soft ideal dense sets. So, by Theorem 3.2 of [4], we have $X_E = \overline{A}^*_E \sqsubseteq X^*_E$. Therefore, X_E is soft ideal dense. Thus, by Theorem 1, $\tau \sqcap \overline{\mathcal{I}} = \phi_E$. □

Remark 2. *In citekandil it was obtained that $\overline{Cl}^*(A_E) = A_E \sqcup \overline{A}^*_E$ is a soft Kuratowski closure operator. We will denote by $(X_E, \tau^*, \overline{\mathcal{I}})$ the soft topology generated by $\overline{Cl}^*$, that is, $\tau^* = \{U_E \sqsubseteq X_E : \overline{Cl}^*(X_E - U_E) = X_E - U_E\}$.*

Theorem 6 ([29])**.** *Let $(X_E, \tau, \overline{\mathcal{I}})$ be a $\mathcal{SITS}$. Then $\beta(\tau^*, \overline{\mathcal{I}}) = \{V_E - I : V_E$ is soft open set of $(X_E, \tau), I \in \overline{\mathcal{I}}\}$ is a basis for (X_E, τ^*).*

Theorem 7. *A $\mathcal{SITS}$ $(X_E, \tau, \overline{\mathcal{I}})$ is soft ideal $\mathcal{RS}$ if and only if (X_E, τ^*) is soft $\mathcal{RS}$ and $\tau \sqcap \overline{\mathcal{I}} = \phi_E$.*

Proof. Let $(X_E, \tau, \overline{\mathcal{I}})$ be soft ideal $\mathcal{RS}$. So, by Lemma 3 (1), $X_E = A_E \sqcup B_E$, where A_E and B_E are disjoint soft ideal dense sets of X_E. Note that $\overline{Cl}^*(A_E) = A_E \sqcup \overline{A}^*_E = A_E \sqcup X_E = X_E$. Hence, A_E and B_E are soft dense in (X_E, τ^*). Thus, (X_E, τ^*) is soft $\mathcal{RS}$. By Lemma 3 (2), $\tau \sqcap \overline{\mathcal{I}} = \phi_E$.

Conversely, let (X_E, τ^*) be soft $\mathcal{RS}$ and $\tau \sqcap \overline{\mathcal{I}} = \phi_E$. Suppose that $X_E = A_E \sqcup B_E$, $A_E \sqcap B_E = \phi_E$, and both A_E and B_E are soft dense in (X_E, τ^*). Let $x_e \in X_E$ and $x_e \notin \overline{A}^*_E$; then, there exists a soft open set U_E containing x_e such that $V_E = U_E \sqcap A_E \in \overline{\mathcal{I}}$. Since B_E is soft dense in (X_E, τ^*) and $\tau \sqcap \overline{\mathcal{I}} = \phi_E$, V_E is non-null and also $U_E \not\sqsubseteq A_E$. Hence, by Theorem 6, $W_E = U_E - V_E \in (X_E, \tau^*)$ is a non-null set and $W_E \sqcap A_E = \phi_E$. This contradicts the fact that A_E is soft dense in (X_E, τ^*). Thus, $x_e \in \overline{A}^*_E$ and, hence, A_E is soft ideal dense. A related argument demonstrates that B_E is soft ideal dense. Thus, $(X_E, \tau, \overline{\mathcal{I}})$ is soft ideal $\mathcal{RS}$. □

Definition 8 ([3])**.** *Let $Y_E \neq \phi_E$ be a soft subset of (X_E, τ, E); then, $\tau_{Y_E} = \{G_E \sqcap Y_E : G_E \in \tau\}$ is called a relative soft topology over Y and (Y_E, τ_{Y_E}, E) is a soft subspace of (X_E, τ, E).*

Lemma 4. *Let $Y_E \sqsubseteq X_E$ and $\overline{\mathcal{I}}$ be soft ideal in X_E. Then, $\overline{\mathcal{I}}_{Y_E} = \{I \in \overline{\mathcal{I}} : I \subseteq Y_E\} = \{I \sqcap Y_E : I \in \overline{\mathcal{I}}\}$ is soft ideal in Y_E.*

Lemma 5. *Let $(X_E, \tau, \overline{\mathcal{I}})$ be a $\mathcal{SITS}$. The non-null soft τ^*-open subspace of a soft ideal $\mathcal{RS}$ space is a soft ideal $\mathcal{RS}$ space.*

Proof. First, we know that the intersection of a soft dense and a soft open set is soft dense, so the soft resolvability is a soft open hereditary. Also, for all $A_E \in \tau^*$ we have $\tau^*_{|A} = (\tau_{|A})^*$. Thus, by Theorem 7, if $(X_E, \tau, \overline{\mathcal{I}})$ is soft ideal $\mathcal{RS}$ and A is τ^*-open, then (X_E, τ^*) is soft $\mathcal{RS}$; hence, $(A_E, \tau^*_{|A}) = (A_E, (\tau_{|A})^*)$ is soft $\mathcal{RS}$ and, thus, $(A_E, \tau_{|A}, \overline{\mathcal{I}}_{A_E})$ is soft ideal $\mathcal{RS}$. □

Theorem 8. *Let $(X_E, \tau, \overline{\mathcal{I}})$ be a $\mathcal{SITS}$. Simple expansion of soft ideal $\mathcal{RS}$ topologies over soft ideal $\mathcal{RS}$ subspace are soft ideal $\mathcal{RS}$.*

Proof. Let $(X_E, \tau, \overline{\mathcal{I}})$ be soft ideal $\mathcal{RS}$ and $S_E \sqsubseteq X_E$ be a soft ideal $\mathcal{RS}$ subspace. Let (D_E, D'_E) be the soft ideal resolution of $(S_E, \tau_{|S}, \overline{\mathcal{I}}_{S_E})$. We examine the next two instances:

Case (1): S_E is soft τ^*-dense in $(X_E, \tau, \overline{\mathcal{I}})$; that is, $X_E = S_E \sqcup S_E^*$. We first establish that D_E is soft ideal dense in $(X_E, \tau, \overline{\mathcal{I}})$. Let $x_e \in X_E$. Suppose that for some soft open set U_E with $x_e \in U_E$ we have $U_E \sqcap D_E \in \overline{\mathcal{I}}$. The two subcases that follow are ours.

Subcase (a): $x_e \in S_E$. Then, $V_E = U_E \sqcap S_E \in \tau_{|S}$ is a soft open set of x_e in $(S_E, \tau_{|S}, \overline{\mathcal{I}}_{S_E})$ such that $V_E \sqcap D_E = U_E \sqcap S_E \sqcap D_E \in \overline{\mathcal{I}}$ due to the heredity of $\overline{\mathcal{I}}$. This defies the assertion that D_E is soft ideal dense in $(S_E, \tau_{|S}, \overline{\mathcal{I}}_{S_E})$. So, D_E is soft ideal dense in $(X_E, \tau, \overline{\mathcal{I}})$.

Subcase (b): $x_e \notin S_E$. Since $X_E = S_E \sqcup S_E^*$, $x_e \in S_E$. To demonstrate that $x_e \in D_E^*$, we believe the opposite, i.e., there exists a soft open set U_E with $x_e \in U_E$ such that $U_E \sqcap D_R \in \overline{\mathcal{I}}$. Note that $U_E \sqcap S_E \neq \phi_E$; otherwise, $x_e \notin S_E^*$. Pick $y_e \in U_E \sqcap S_E \in \tau_{|S}$. Since $U_E \sqcap D_E \in \overline{\mathcal{I}}$, then, by heredity of $\overline{\mathcal{I}}$, $U_E \sqcap S_E \sqcap D_E \in \overline{\mathcal{I}}$. So, D_E is not soft ideal dense in $(S_E, \tau_{|S}, \overline{\mathcal{I}}_{S_E})$. By contradiction $x_e \in D_E^*$, i.e., D_E is soft ideal dense in $(X_E, \tau, \overline{\mathcal{I}})$. So, we have demonstrated that $D_E^* = X_E$. Using a comparable defense, $D_E^{'*} = X_E$. Let $x_e \in X_E$ and let $U_E \sqcup (V_E \sqcap S_E)$ be a soft open set of x_e in $(X_E, \tau(S_E), \overline{\mathcal{I}})$, where $\tau(S_E)$ is the simple expansion of τ over S_E. If $(U_E \sqcup (V_E \sqcap S_E)) \sqcap D_E \in \overline{\mathcal{I}}$, then, by heredity of $\overline{\mathcal{I}}$, $(V_E \sqcap S_E) \sqcap D_E$ is a member of $\overline{\mathcal{I}}$ so that V_E is a null set. Of course, $(V_E \sqcap S_E) \sqcap D_E$ cannot be a member of $\overline{\mathcal{I}}$ if V_E is non-null since then V_E must contain an element of S_E. So, x_e belongs to $U_E \sqcap D_E$, which is also not eligible to join with $\overline{\mathcal{I}}$ since $D_E^* = X_E$. This contradiction shows that D_E is soft $\tau(S_E)$-dense. Using a comparable defense of $D_E^{'}$, we determine that $(X_E, \tau(S_E), \overline{\mathcal{I}})$ is soft ideal $\mathcal{RS}$.

Case (2): S_E is not soft τ^*-dense in $(X_E, \tau, \overline{\mathcal{I}})$. Then, $S_E^{'} = X_E \setminus Cl^*(S_E)$, so it is τ^*-open and non-null. By Lemma 5, $S^{'}$ is soft ideal $\mathcal{RS}$ (more precisely said soft ideal $\mathcal{RS}$ with respect to S_E). Let (A_E, B_E) be the soft ideal resolution of $S^{'}$. By using reasoning akin to that of *Case (1)*, we can prove that $(D_E \sqcup A_E, D_E \sqcup B_E)$ is a soft ideal resolution of $(X_E, \tau, \overline{\mathcal{I}})$. Additionally, employing the same method as at the conclusion of *Case (1)*, we find that $(X_E \tau(S_E); \overline{\mathcal{I}})$ is soft ideal $\mathcal{RS}$.

□

Theorem 9. *A $\mathcal{SITS}$ $(X_E, \tau, \overline{\mathcal{I}})$ is soft ideal $\mathcal{RS}$ iff there exists a soft ideal dense set D_E such that, for all non-null soft open sets U_E and all $A_E \in \overline{\mathcal{I}}$, $U_E - A_E \neq \phi_E$ implies $(U_E - A_E) \not\sqsubseteq D_E$.*

Proof. Let $(X, \tau, \mathcal{I})$ be soft ideal $\mathcal{RS}$. So, by Remark 1 and Theorem 1, $\tau \sqcap \overline{\mathcal{I}} = \phi_E$. Now, there exist two disjoint soft ideal dense sets, say $D_E^{'}$ and $D_E^{''}$. We demonstrate that $(U_E - A_E) \not\sqsubseteq D_E^{'}$ whenever $U_E - A_E \neq \phi_E$ for all non-null soft open sets U_E and $A_E \in \overline{\mathcal{I}}$. If possible, let $(U_E - A_E) \sqsubseteq D_E^{'}$ for some non-null soft open set U_E and $A_E \in \overline{\mathcal{I}}$. Then, $(U_E - A_E) \sqcap D_E^{''} = \phi_E$. Now, since $\tau \sqcap \overline{\mathcal{I}} = \phi_E$, by Theorem 4 $D_E^{''}$ is not soft ideal dense. This is contrary to $D_E^{''}$ being soft ideal dense. Hence, $(U_E - A_E) \not\sqsubseteq D_E^{'}$ whenever $U_E - A_E \neq \phi_E$ for all non-null soft open sets U_E and $A_E \in \overline{\mathcal{I}}$.

However, allow the condition to persist in $(X_E, \tau, \overline{\mathcal{I}})$. Then, there exists a soft ideal dense set D_E such that $(U_E - A_E) \not\sqsubseteq D_E$ if $U_E - A_E \neq \phi_E$ for all non-null soft open sets U_E and $A_E \in \overline{\mathcal{I}}$. We show that $X_E - D_E$ is soft ideal dense. Let $X_E - D_E$ be not soft ideal dense. Then there exists a non-null soft open set V_E such that $V_E \sqcap (X_E - D_E) \in \overline{\mathcal{I}}$. Clearly, $V_E \sqcap (X_E - D_E) \neq \phi_E$, for otherwise $V_E \sqsubseteq D_E$, which is contrary to our assumption. Let $A_E = V_E \sqcap (X_E - D_E)$. Then, $V_E - A_E \neq \phi_E$. For if $V_E - A_E = \phi_E$ then $V_E \sqsubseteq A_E$ and, hence, $V_E \in \overline{\mathcal{I}}$, which suggests $V_E \sqcap D_E \in \overline{\mathcal{I}}$. Contrary to that, this D_E is soft ideal dense. Therefore, $V_E - A_E \sqsubseteq D_E$. It goes against our presumption once more. Thus, $X_E - D_E$ is soft ideal dense and so $(X_E, \tau, \overline{\mathcal{I}})$ is soft ideal $\mathcal{RS}$. □

Corollary 1. *A $\mathcal{SITS}$ $(X_E, \tau, \overline{\mathcal{I}})$ is soft ideal $\mathcal{IRS}$ iff, for each soft ideal dense set D_E, there exist a soft open set U_E and $A \in \overline{\mathcal{I}}$ such that $\phi_E \neq (U_E - A_E) \sqsubseteq D_E$.*

Theorem 10. *If $(X_E, \tau, \overline{\mathcal{I}})$ is a $\mathcal{SITS}$ such that $\tau \sqcap \overline{\mathcal{I}} = \phi_E$ and if D_E is soft ideal dense in $(X_E, \tau, \overline{\mathcal{I}})$, then, for all $Y_E = U_E - A_E$, where U_E is non-null soft open and $A_E \in \overline{\mathcal{I}}$, $Y_E \sqcap D_E$ is soft ideal dense in $(Y_E, \tau_{Y_E}, \overline{\mathcal{I}}_{Y_E})$.*

Proof. Clearly, we suppose that $\tau \sqcap \overline{\mathcal{I}} = \phi_E$. Then, by Proposition 11 of [3], a soft open set in Y_E is of the form $Y_E \sqcap O_E = (U_E - A_E) \sqcap O_E = (U_E \sqcap O_E) - A_E$, where O_E is a soft open set in (X_E, τ). Let $\phi_E \neq U_E \sqcap O_E - A_E$. Consider $\phi_E \neq ((U_E \sqcap O_E) - A_E) - B_E$, $B_E \in \overline{\mathcal{I}}_{Y_E}$. Then, since D_E is soft ideal dense and $U_E \sqcap O_E$ is a soft open set in (X_E, τ), by Theorem 4, $(U_E \sqcap O_E - (A_E \sqcup B_E)) \sqcap D_E \neq \phi_E$. Hence, $(((U_E \sqcap O_E) - A_E) - B_E) \sqcap D_E \neq \phi_E$. Therefore, again by Theorem 4, $Y_E \sqcap D_E$ is soft ideal dense in $(Y_E, \tau_{Y_E}, \overline{\mathcal{I}}_{Y_E})$. □

Theorem 11. *Let $(X_E, \tau, \overline{\mathcal{I}})$ be a $\mathcal{SITS}$ such that $\tau \sqcap \overline{\mathcal{I}} = \phi_E$ and $P_E \sqsubseteq Y_E = U_E - A_E$, where U_E is a non-null soft open set, $A_E \in \overline{\mathcal{I}}$. Then, P_E is soft ideal dense in $(Y_E, \tau_{Y_E}, \overline{\mathcal{I}}_{Y_E})$ if and only if $P_E = Y_E \sqcap D_E$, where D_E is soft ideal dense in $(X_E, \tau, \overline{\mathcal{I}})$.*

Proof. Assume that P_E is soft ideal dense in $(Y_E, \tau_{Y_E}, \overline{\mathcal{I}}_{Y_E})$. Consider the set $P_E \sqcup (X_E - Y_E)$. Then, $(P_E \sqcup (X_E - Y_E)) \sqcap O_E = (P_E \sqcap O_E) \sqcup ((X_E - Y_E) \sqcap O_E)$, where O_E is a non-null soft open set. Now, if $O_E \sqsubseteq X_E - Y_E$, then $P_E \sqsubseteq Y_E$ and $P_E \sqcap O_E = \phi_E$, and we have $(P_E \sqcup (X_E - Y_E)) \sqcap O_E = O_E$ which is not in $\overline{\mathcal{I}}$ because $\tau \sqcap \overline{\mathcal{I}} = \phi_E$. Moreover, if $O_E \sqcap Y_E \neq \phi_E$, then, since P_E is soft ideal dense in $(Y_E, \tau_{Y_E}, \overline{\mathcal{I}}_{Y_E})$, $P_E \sqcap (O_E \sqcap Y_E) \notin \overline{\mathcal{I}}_{Y_E}$ and so $P_E \sqcap O_E \notin \overline{\mathcal{I}}$. Therefore, $(P_E \sqcup (X_E - Y_E)) \sqcap O_E \notin \overline{\mathcal{I}}$. Thus, $(P_E \sqcup (X_E - Y_E)) = D_E$, say, is soft ideal dense in $(X_E, \tau, \overline{\mathcal{I}})$ and, hence, $P_E = Y_E \sqcap D_E$. Next, let $P_E = Y_E \sqcap D_E$, where D_E is soft ideal dense in $(X_E, \tau, \overline{\mathcal{I}})$. Hence, by Theorem 10, P_E is soft ideal dense in $(Y_E, \tau_{Y_E}, \overline{\mathcal{I}}_{Y_E})$. This completes the proof of the theorem. □

Note that, as per the condition in Theorem 11, for D_E soft ideal dense is necessary because if D_E is not soft ideal dense then $P_E = \phi_E$ for some non-null soft open set U_E, $A_E \in \overline{\mathcal{I}}$ and, hence, P_E is not soft ideal dense in $(Y_E, \tau_{Y_E}, \overline{\mathcal{I}}_{Y_E})$.

6. Soft Ideal Semi-Irresolvable Spaces

Next, we will define and go over the characteristics of a soft ideal semi-$\mathcal{IRS}$ space.

Definition 9. *A $\mathcal{SITS}$ $(X_E, \tau, \overline{\mathcal{I}})$ is a said to be soft ideal semi- $\mathcal{IRS}$ if for each soft ideal dense set D_E and each non-null soft open set U_E and $A_E \in \overline{\mathcal{I}}$ such that $U_E - A_E$ is non-null set, there exists a non-null soft open set V_E and $B_E \in \overline{\mathcal{I}}$ such that $\phi_E \neq (V_E - B_E) \sqsubseteq (U_E - A_E) \sqcap D_E$.*

Theorem 12. *A $\mathcal{SITS}$ $(X_E, \tau, \overline{\mathcal{I}})$ is a soft ideal semi- $\mathcal{IRS}$, iff the intersection of soft ideal dense sets is a soft ideal dense set, where $\tau \sqcap \overline{\mathcal{I}} = \phi_E$.*

Proof. Assume that $(X_E, \tau, \overline{\mathcal{I}})$ is a soft ideal semi- $\mathcal{IRS}$ and $\tau \sqcap \overline{\mathcal{I}} = \phi_E$. Let D'_E and D''_E be two soft ideal dense sets in $(X_E, \tau, \overline{\mathcal{I}})$. We demonstrate that $D'_E \sqcap D''_E$ is soft ideal dense. Consider $U_E - A_E$, where U is a non-null soft open set and $A_E \in \overline{\mathcal{I}}$. As we demonstrate, $(U_E - A_E) \sqcap D'_E \sqcap D''_E \neq \phi_E$. Since D'_E is soft ideal dense, by Theorem 4, $(U_E - A_E) \sqcap D'_E \neq \phi_E$. Since $(X_E, \tau, \overline{\mathcal{I}})$ is soft ideal semi- $\mathcal{IRS}$, there exists a non-null soft open set V'_E and $B'_E \in \overline{\mathcal{I}}$ such that $\phi_E \neq (V'_E - B'_E) \sqsubseteq (U_E - A_E) \sqcap D'_E$. Again, since D''_E is soft ideal dense, there exists a non-null soft open set V''_E and $B''_E \in \overline{\mathcal{I}}$ such that $\phi_E \neq (V_E'' - B_E'') \sqsubseteq (V_E' - B_E') \sqcap D_E''$. Hence, $\phi_E \neq V_E'' - B_E'' \sqsubseteq (U_E - A_E) \sqcap D_E' \sqcap D_E''$. Therefore, $(U_E - A_E) \sqcap (D_E' \sqcap D_E'') \neq \phi_E$ and, by Theorem 4, $D_E' \sqcap D_E''$ is soft ideal dense.

Conversely, assume that the intersection of soft ideal dense sets is soft ideal dense. Assume that $(X_E, \tau, \overline{\mathcal{I}})$ is not soft ideal semi- $\mathcal{IRS}$. Then, there exists a soft ideal dense set D_E', and a non-null soft open set U_E and $A_E \in \overline{\mathcal{I}}$, where $\phi_E \neq U_E - A_E$, such that $(U_E - A_E) \sqcap D_E'$ does not contain $V_E - B_E$, for any non-null soft open set V_E and $B_E \in \overline{\mathcal{I}}$. Consider the set $D_E'' = (X_E - (U_E - A_E)) \sqcup ((U_E - A_E) - (U_E - A_E) \sqcap D_E')$. By Theorem 4, D_E'' is soft ideal dense since $(V_E - B_E) \sqcap D_E'' \neq \phi_E$. But $(U_E - A_E) \sqcap D_E' \sqcap D_E'' = \phi_E$. This contradicts the reality that the intersection of two soft ideal dense sets is a soft ideal dense set. Hence, $(X_E, \tau, \overline{\mathcal{I}})$ must be soft ideal semi- $\mathcal{IRS}$. This concludes the theorem's proof. □

Example 2. *Let $(X_E, \tau, \overline{\mathcal{I}})$ be a $\mathcal{SITS}$, where $X = \{h_1, h_2, h_3\}$, $E = \{e\}$. Consider $\tau = \{X_E, \phi_E, \{(e, \{h_1, h_2\})\}$ and $\overline{\mathcal{I}} = \{\phi_E, \{(e, \{h_2\})\}, \{(e, \{h_3\})\}, \{(e, \{h_2, h_3\})\}\}$. Then, we have the following.*

1. $\tau \sqcap \overline{\mathcal{I}} = \phi_E$.
2. *The collection of all soft ideal dense sets are X_E, $\{(e, \{h_1\})\}$, $\{(e, \{h_1, h_2\})\}$ and $\{(e, \{h_1, h_3\})\}$.*
3. *The soft intersection of any soft ideal dense sets is soft ideal dense.*

Hence, by Theorem 12, $(X_E, \tau, \overline{\mathcal{I}})$ is soft ideal semi- $\mathcal{IRS}$.

Theorem 13. *Let $(X_E, \tau, \overline{\mathcal{I}})$ be a $\mathcal{SITS}$ and $\tau \sqcap \overline{\mathcal{I}} = \phi_E$. If $(X_E, \tau, \overline{\mathcal{I}})$ is soft ideal semi- $\mathcal{IRS}$, then $(Y_E, \tau_{Y_E}, \overline{\mathcal{I}}_{Y_E})$ is soft ideal semi- $\mathcal{IRS}$ whenever $Y_E = U_E - A_E$, for every non-null soft open set U_E and $A_E \in \overline{\mathcal{I}}$.*

Proof. Assume that D_E and G_E are soft ideal dense sets in $(Y_E, \tau_{Y_E}, \overline{\mathcal{I}}_{Y_E})$. Then, by Theorem 11, $D_E = (U_E - A_E) \sqcap D_E'$ and $G_E = (U_E - A_E) \sqcap D_E''$, where D_E' and D_E'' are soft ideal dense sets in $(X_E, \tau, \overline{\mathcal{I}})$. Hence, $D_E \sqcap G_E = (U_E - A_E) \sqcap D_E' \sqcap D_E''$ and, since $D_E' \sqcap D_E''$ is a soft ideal dense set in $(X_E, \tau, \overline{\mathcal{I}})$, once more by Theorem 11, $D_E \sqcap G_E$ is soft ideal dense in $(Y_E, \tau_{Y_E}, \overline{\mathcal{I}}_{Y_E})$. So, by Theorem 12, $(Y_E, \tau_{Y_E}, \overline{\mathcal{I}}_{Y_E})$ is soft ideal semi-$\mathcal{IRS}$. □

Definition 10. *A $\mathcal{SITS}$ $(X_E, \tau, \overline{\mathcal{I}})$ is said to be soft ideal semi-$\mathcal{HC}$ if each $U_E - A_E \neq \phi_E$, where U_E is a soft open set and $A_E \in \overline{\mathcal{I}}$ is a soft ideal dense set.*

Theorem 14. *A $\mathcal{SITS}$ $(X_E, \tau, \overline{\mathcal{I}})$ is soft ideal semi-$\mathcal{HC}$ iff it is soft ideal $\mathcal{HC}$ and $\tau \sqcap \overline{\mathcal{I}} = \phi_E$.*

Proof. Let $(X_E, \tau, \overline{\mathcal{I}})$ be soft ideal semi-$\mathcal{HC}$. Clearly, $(X_E, \tau, \overline{\mathcal{I}})$ is soft ideal $\mathcal{HC}$. Let $U_E \neq \phi_E$ be a non-null soft open set and a member of the soft ideal $\overline{\mathcal{I}}$. Then, $\overline{U_E}^* = X_E$ since $(X_E, \tau, \overline{\mathcal{I}})$ is soft ideal $\mathcal{HC}$. Conversely, yet, since $U_E \in \overline{\mathcal{I}}$, $\overline{U_E}^* = \phi_E$, it is paradoxical. So $\tau \sqcap \overline{\mathcal{I}} = \phi_E$.

Conversely let $(X_E, \tau, \overline{\mathcal{I}})$ be a soft ideal $\mathcal{HC}$ and $\tau \sqcap \overline{\mathcal{I}} = \phi_E$. Let $U_E - A_E$, where U_E is a non-null soft open set and $A_E \in \overline{\mathcal{I}}$. Then $U_E - A_E \neq \phi_E$ because $\tau \sqcap \overline{\mathcal{I}} = \phi_E$. We show that $U_E - A_E$ is soft ideal dense. Let $x_e \in X_E$ and V_E be a soft open set containing x_e. By Lemma 2, (X_E, τ) is soft $\mathcal{HC}$ and $V_E \sqcap (U_E - A_E) \neq \phi_E$ because $V_E \sqcap (U_E - A_E) = V_E \sqcap U_E - A_E \neq \phi_E$ and $\tau \sqcap \overline{\mathcal{I}} = \phi_E$. Thus, $(X_E, \tau, \overline{\mathcal{I}})$ is soft ideal semi-$\mathcal{HC}$. □

Example 3. *Let $(X_E, \tau, \overline{\mathcal{I}})$ be a $\mathcal{SITS}$, where $X = \{h_1, h_2, h_3\}$, $E = \{e\}$. Consider $\tau = \{X_E, \phi_E, \{(e, \{h_1, h_2\})\}$ and $\overline{\mathcal{I}} = \{\phi_E, \{(e, \{h_2\})\}, \{(e, \{h_3\})\}, \{(e, \{h_2, h_3\})\}\}$. Then*

1. $\tau \sqcap \overline{\mathcal{I}} = \phi_E$.
2. *Every non-null soft open set is soft ideal dense. So, $(X_E, \tau, \overline{\mathcal{I}})$ is soft ideal $\mathcal{HC}$.*

Hence, by Theorem 14, $(X_E, \tau, \overline{\mathcal{I}})$ is soft ideal semi- $\mathcal{IRS}$.

Theorem 15. *If a $\mathcal{SITS}$ $(X_E, \tau, \overline{\mathcal{I}})$ is soft ideal semi-$\mathcal{HC}$ and soft ideal $\mathcal{IRS}$, then it is soft ideal semi-$\mathcal{IRS}$.*

Proof. By Theorem 14, $\tau \sqcap \overline{\mathcal{I}} = \phi_E$. Let $D_E^{'}$ and $D_E^{''}$ be two soft ideal dense sets in $(X_E, \tau, \overline{\mathcal{I}})$. We demonstrate that $D_E^{'} \cap D_E^{''}$ is soft ideal dense. By Theorem 4, it suffices to demonstrate that $(D_E^{'} \cap D_E^{''}) \sqcap (U_E - A_E) \neq \phi_E$ for all non-null soft open sets U_E and $A_E \in \overline{\mathcal{I}}$. So, since $(X_E, \tau, \overline{\mathcal{I}})$ is soft ideal $\mathcal{IRS}$, by Corollary 1, there exists a non-null soft open set V_E and $B_E \in \overline{\mathcal{I}}$ such that $\phi_E \neq V_E - B_E \sqsubseteq D_E^{'}$. Similarly, there exists a non-null soft open set W_E and $C_E \in \overline{\mathcal{I}}$ such that $\phi_E \neq W_E - C_E \sqsubseteq D_E^{''}$. Now, (X_E, τ) is soft $\mathcal{HC}$ by Lemma 2 and Theorem 14; we have $V_E \sqcap W_E \neq \phi_E$. Since $\tau \sqcap \overline{\mathcal{I}} = \phi_E$, $(V_E - B_E) \sqcap (W_E - C_E) = (V_E \sqcap W_E) - (B_E \sqcup C_E) \neq \phi_E$ and, hence, $(V_E \sqcap W_E) - (B_E \sqcup C_E) \sqsubseteq D_E^{'} \sqcap D_E^{''}$. Therefore, by the soft ideal semi-$\mathcal{HC}$ property of $(X_E, \tau, \overline{\mathcal{I}})$, $(V_E \sqcap W_E) - (B_E \sqcup C_E)$ is soft ideal dense and, by Theorem 4, we have $\phi_E \neq (U_E - A_E) \sqcap [(V_E \sqcap W_E) - (B_E \sqcup C_E)]$ and, hence, $(U_E - A_E) \sqcap (D_E^{'} \sqcap D_E^{''}) \neq \phi_E$. Therefore, $D_E^{'} \sqcap D_E^{''}$ is soft ideal dense. So, by Theorem 12, $(X_E, \tau, \overline{\mathcal{I}})$ is soft ideal semi-$\mathcal{IRS}$. □

Remark 3. *For a $\mathcal{SITS}$ $(X_E, \tau, \overline{\mathcal{I}})$, if $\tau \sqcap \overline{\mathcal{I}} \neq \phi_E$. Then, no soft ideal dense set exists, because, if $\tau \sqcap \overline{\mathcal{I}} \neq \phi_E$ and there exists D_E, any soft ideal dense, then $\overline{D}_E^{*} = X_E$, so by Remark 1 we have $\overline{X}_E^{*} = X_E$. Hence, by Theorem 1, $\tau \sqcap \overline{\mathcal{I}} = \phi_E$, which is a contradiction. Therefore, if $\tau \sqcap \overline{\mathcal{I}} \neq \phi_E$ then no soft ideal dense set exists.*

Question: Is there any example of soft ideal topological space such that $\tau \sqcap \overline{\mathcal{I}} \neq \phi_E$, and Theorems 10–14 are true?

7. Conclusions and Future Work

As an extension of the classical (crisp) topology, the idea of a soft topology on a universal set was independently proven by Shabir and Naz [3], and Çağman et al. [30]. The study of this topological generalization has becoming more fascinating. Numerous techniques for building soft topologies have been documented in the literature. We have added to the body of knowledge in soft topology by delving into the ideas of soft hyperconnected modulo ideal, soft ideal resolvable, and soft ideal semi-irresolvable spaces. This research is based on the hyperconnectedness and resolvability of soft ideal spaces. We spoken about several fundamental operations on soft ideal spaces. A concept of a soft ideal semi-irresolvable space and an overview of its properties are provided. Furthermore, we have determined the basic characteristics of soft ideal resolvable spaces and connections between the other concepts. The findings presented in this work are preliminary and further research will examine additional aspects of the soft ideal resolvable space. By integrating these two approaches, our work creates opportunities for potential contributions to this trend using hyperconnectedness and resolvability structures with generalized rough approximation spaces, as well as the resolvability of primal soft topologies and the resolvability of fuzzy soft topologies in classical and soft settings.

Author Contributions: Writing—original draft, A.A.-O.; Writing—review & editing, A.A.-O. and W.A. All authors have read and agreed to the published version of the manuscript.

Funding: This research received no external funding.

Data Availability Statement: No data were used to support this study.

Conflicts of Interest: The authors declare no conflict of interest.

Abbreviations

The following abbreviations are utilized in this document:

$\mathcal{SITS}$	soft ideal topological space
$\mathcal{HC}$	hyperconnected
$\mathcal{IRS}$	irresolvable
$\mathcal{RS}$	resolvable

References

1. Molodtsov, D. Soft set theory-first results. *Comput. Math. Appl.* **1999**, *37*, 19–31. [CrossRef]
2. Molodtsov, D.; Leonov, V.Y.; Kovkov, D.V. Soft sets technique and its application. *Nechetkie Sist. Myagkie Vychisleniya* **2006**, *1*, 8–39.
3. Shabir, M.; Naz, M. On soft topolgical spaces. *Comput. Math. Appl.* **2011**, *61*, 1786–1799. [CrossRef]
4. Kandil, A.; Tantawy, O.A.E.; El-Sheikh, S.A.; Abd El-latif, A.M. Soft ideal theory, Soft local function and generated soft topological spaces. *Appl. Math. Inf. Sci.* **2014**, *8*, 1595–1603. [CrossRef]
5. Aktas, H.; Çağman, N. Soft sets and soft groups. *Inf. Sci.* **2007**, *177*, 2726–2735. [CrossRef]
6. Acar, U.; Koyuncu, F.; Tanay, B. Soft sets and soft rings. *Comput. Math. Appl.* **2010**, *59*, 3458–3463. [CrossRef]
7. Al-shami, T.M.; Ameen, Z.A.; Abu-Gdairi, R.; Mhemdi, A. On Primal Soft Topology. *Mathematics* **2023**, *11*, 2329. [CrossRef]
8. Al-shami, T.M.; Ameen, Z.A.; Mhemdi, A. The connection between ordinary and soft s-algebras with applications to information structures. *AIMS Math.* **2023**, *8*, 14850–14866. [CrossRef]
9. Ameen, Z.A.; Al-shami, T.M.; Abu-Gdairi, R.; Mhemdi, A. The Relationship between Ordinary and Soft Algebras with an Application. *Mathematics* **2023**, *11*, 2035. [CrossRef]
10. Sardar, S.K.; Gupta, S. Soft category theory—An introduction. *J. Hyperstruct.* **2013**, *2*, 118–135.
11. Jankovic, D.; Hamlett, T.R. New topologies from old via ideals. *Am. Math. Mon.* **1990**, *97*, 295–310. [CrossRef]
12. Dontchev, J.; Ganster, M.; Rose, D. Ideal resolvability. *Topol. Appl.* **1999**, *93*, 1–16. [CrossRef]
13. Mahmoud, R.A. Remarks on soft topological spaces with soft grill. *Far East J. Math. Sci.* **2014**, *86*, 111–128.
14. Gilbert, R.M. Soft resolvable topological spaces. *Int. J. Comput. Appl. Math.* **2017**, *12*, 630–634.
15. Al-Saadi, H.S.; Aygün, H.; Al-Omari, A. Some notes on soft hyperconnected spaces. *J. Anal.* **2020**, *28*, 351–362. [CrossRef]
16. Al-Omari, A. Soft topology in ideal topological spaces. *Hacet. J. Math. Stat.* **2019**, *48*, 1277–1285. [CrossRef]
17. Kandil, A.; Tantawy, O.A.E.; El-Sheikh, S.A.; Abd El-latif, A.M. Soft Connectedness Via Soft Ideals. *J. New Results Sci.* **2014**, *4*, 90–108.
18. Al Ghour, S.; Ameen, Z.A. On soft submaximal spaces. *Heliyon* **2022**, *8*, e10574. [CrossRef]
19. Al-shami, T.M.; Kočinac, L.D.R. Almost soft Menger and weakly soft Menger spaces. *Appl. Comput. Math.* **2022**, *21*, 35–51.
20. Alcantud, J.C.R.; Al-shami, T.M.; Azzam, A.A. Caliber and Chain Conditions in Soft Topologies. *Mathematics* **2021**, *9*, 2349. [CrossRef]
21. Maji, P.K.; Biswas, R.; Roy, A.R. Soft set theory. *Comput. Math. Appl.* **2003**, *45*, 555–562. [CrossRef]
22. Zorlutuna, I.; Akdağ, M.; Min, W.K.; Atmaca, S. Remarks on soft topological spaces. *Ann. Fuzzy Math. Inform.* **2012**, *3*, 171–185.
23. Al-shami, T.M.; Mhemdi, A.; Abu-Gdairid, R. Novel framework for generalizations of soft open sets 512 and its applications via soft topologies. *Mathematics* **2023**, *11*, 840. [CrossRef]
24. Ameen, Z.A.; Al-Ghour, S. Extensions of soft topologies. *Filomat* **2023**, *36*, 5279–5287. [CrossRef]
25. Al-Omari, A.; Noiri, T. Regular Γ-irresolvable spaces. *Hacet. J. Math. Stat.* **2022**, *51*, 95–100.
26. Al-Omari, A.; Acharjee, S.; Özkoç, M. A new operator of primal topological spaces. *Mathematica* **2023**, *65*, 175–183.
27. Ali, M.I.; Feng, F.; Liu, X.; Min, W.K.; Shabir, M. On some new operations in soft set theory. *Comput. Math. Appl.* **2009**, *57*, 1547–1553. [CrossRef]
28. Ameen, Z.A.; Asaad, B.A.; AL-shami, T.M. Soft somewhat continuous and soft somewhat open functions. *Twms J. Appl. Eng. Math.* **2023**, *13*, 792–806.
29. Ameen, Z.A.; Al Ghour, S. Cluster soft sets and cluster soft topologies. *Comput. Appl. Math.* **2023**, *42*, 337. [CrossRef]
30. Çağman, N.; Karataş, S.; Enginoglu, S. Soft topology. *Comput. Math. Appl.* **2011**, *62*, 351–358. [CrossRef]

mathematics

Article

Calculating Insurance Claim Reserves with an Intuitionistic Fuzzy Chain-Ladder Method

Jorge De Andrés-Sánchez

Social and Business Research Laboratory, Universitat Rovira i Virgili, Campus de Bellissens, 43204 Reus, Spain; jorge.deandres@urv.cat

Abstract: Estimating loss reserves is a crucial activity for non-life insurance companies. It involves adjusting the expected evolution of claims over different periods of active policies and their fluctuations. The chain-ladder (CL) technique is recognized as one of the most effective methods for calculating claim reserves in this context. It has become a benchmark within the insurance sector for predicting loss reserves and has been adapted to estimate variability margins. This variability has been addressed through both stochastic and possibilistic analyses. This study adopts the latter approach, proposing the use of the CL framework combined with intuitionistic fuzzy numbers (IFNs). While modeling with fuzzy numbers (FNs) introduces only epistemic uncertainty, employing IFNs allows for the representation of bipolar data regarding the feasible and infeasible values of loss reserves. In short, this paper presents an extension of the chain-ladder technique that estimates the parameters governing claim development through intuitionistic fuzzy regression, such as symmetric triangular IFNs. Additionally, it compares the results obtained with this method with those derived from the stochastic chain ladder by England and Verrall.

Keywords: loss reserving; chain ladder; probability–possibility transformation; intuitionistic fuzzy numbers; symmetric triangular intuitionistic fuzzy numbers; intuitionistic fuzzy regression

MSC: 91G05; 62P05; 90C05; 62A86; 90C70

Citation: Andrés-Sánchez, J.D. Calculating Insurance Claim Reserves with an Intuitionistic Fuzzy Chain-Ladder Method. *Mathematics* **2024**, *12*, 845. https://doi.org/10.3390/math12060845

Academic Editor: Michael Voskoglou

Received: 21 February 2024
Revised: 10 March 2024
Accepted: 11 March 2024
Published: 13 March 2024

1. Introduction

The estimation of loss reserves is a fundamental process in the management of insurance companies. It consists of setting a prudent value on claims not yet made on active policies, which will ultimately impact the financial statements and the required capital to continue with the current insurance portfolio [1]. Thus, a prudent estimation of these provisions, which ultimately requires the application of so-called actuarial judgement, needs to use a value of maximum reliability but, at the same time, estimate the possible variability around that expected value [2]. The final estimated value for reserves, although it should tend to overestimate them and cover possible unfavorable deviations from their expected value, should not be excessive [3].

Within claim-reserving methods, the actuarial literature often distinguishes between deterministic and stochastic methods. While the former provides a point value of reserves that can be considered the "expected" or maximum confidence value, stochastic methods allow the variability around that reasonable value to be measured [2]. To this commonly accepted typology, we can add fuzzy methods [4].

Among the various applications that fuzzy set theory (FST) has had in insurance mathematics, we can outline the modeling of uncertain and vague parameters with possibility distributions [5,6]. In these applications, fuzzy modeling allows the quantification of epistemic uncertainty, that is, a measure of the reliability with which a certain variable A takes a specific value x [7]. In the context of determining loss reserves, this vagueness may be induced, first, by the imprecision of some of the data available to the insurance company [8].

An additional source to consider is the scarcity of the sample used for reserve calculation; since it is not advisable to use data too far from the present, it can bias estimates due to factors such as changes in judicial practices and public awareness of liability issues [9].

The literature on the variability of loss reserves starts from a scheme used in practice that allows loss reserves to be obtained as a point value. A very common scheme for calculating the value of reliable mathematical reserves is the chain-ladder (CL) method, or variants of this method, such as the London CL or the Bornhuetter–Ferguson methods [10]. The chain-ladder method has been the subject of adaptations that allow modeling of the variability of reserves stochastically [11,12] but also with possibility distributions [13–15].

As shown in Table 1, among the most commonly used schemes for quantifying loss reserves, in addition to the CL method, we can highlight the geometric separation method [16] and methods that model incremental claims in a two-way manner, such as in [17]. The methodology for adjusting the parameters governing the evolution of claims over time can be performed heuristically [4,14,15,18] or with fuzzy regression methods that apply both the principle of minimum fuzziness [19,20] and the fuzzy least-squares approach [21,22].

Table 1. A revision of contributions to claim reserve modeling with fuzzy mathematics.

Method to Fit Fuzzy Parameters	Note Extensions	Taylor's Separation Method	Two-Way Methods
Heuristically	[4,14,15,18]	---	---
FR-MFP	[3,13]	[23,24]	[19,20,25]
FR-FLS	[26]	[21]	[22]

Note: FR-MFP stands for fuzzy regression with the minimum fuzziness principle, and FR-FLS stands for fuzzy least squares.

All of the methods reviewed in Table 1 model the uncertainty of parameters with type-one fuzzy numbers, i.e., simple fuzzy numbers (FNs), that is, through possibility distributions that allow introducing epistemic uncertainty about the real value of the parameters [27]. However, FNs do not allow the introduction of negative information about these parameters that the evaluator might have, i.e., about what the parameters "are not". This paper extends fuzzy loss reserving to the use of bipolar information, i.e., imprecise estimations about the values that the parameters of interest can take and about those they cannot take. Bipolarity does not introduce additional uncertainty but provides new information [28].

Our paper uses the chain-ladder scheme to capture the dynamics of claiming processes and the concept of intuitionistic fuzzy numbers (IFNs) that model uncertain quantities [29] within Atanassov's theory of intuitionistic fuzzy sets [30,31]. Thus, this work expands the practical applications of IFNs, which are relatively scarce in finance and insurance. Among such applications, we can highlight the following:

1. Capital budgeting [32–35];
2. Option pricing [36–38];
3. Productivity measurements [39–41];
4. Actuarial field: while Uzhga-Rebrov and Grabusts [42] use intuitionistic fuzzy values to address environmental risk analysis, Andrés-Sánchez [43] does so to price the life contingencies of people with impaired life expectancies.

This paper falls within the fourth domain, specifically in the field of claim reserving. In this regard, our aim is threefold. First, we demonstrate that the estimation of stochastic loss reserves can be interpreted as estimates made through possibility distributions with type-one fuzzy numbers. Subsequently, we introduce intuitionistic fuzzy regression in claim-reserving calculations. Although fuzzy regression has been applied in several areas of actuarial analysis, such as mortality adjustment [44,45], the use of intuitionistic fuzzy regression in actuarial science is nonexistent. We do so by employing the intuitionistic fuzzy regression method [46], which extends the possibilistic regression models [47–49].

Similarly, we compare the results of the proposed method to those obtained with the stochastic chain-ladder (SCL) method [12].

2. Intuitionistic Fuzzy Numbers

2.1. Fuzzy Numbers and Intuitionistic Fuzzy Numbers

Definition 1. *A fuzzy set (FS) in a referential set X,* $\ddot{A}$*, is defined as follows [50]:*

$$\ddot{A} = \{\langle x, \mu_A(x)\rangle,\ x \in X\}, \tag{1}$$

where $\mu_A : X \longrightarrow [0,1]$ *is the membership function of* $\ddot{A}$.

Definition 2. *The fuzzy set* $\ddot{A}$ *can be represented through level sets or* α*-cuts,* A_α *[50]:*

$$A_\alpha = \{x|\mu_A(x) \geq \alpha,\ 0 < \alpha \leq 1\}. \tag{2}$$

Definition 3. *A fuzzy number (FN),* $\ddot{A}$*, is a fuzzy subset of the real line [51] such that*

i. *is normal, i.e.,* $\exists x|\mu_A(x) = 1$;

ii. *is convex, i.e.,* $\forall x_1, x_2 \in \mathbb{R}, 0 \leq \lambda \leq 1,\ \mu_A(\lambda x_1, (1-\lambda)x_2) \geq \min(\mu_A(x_1), \mu_A(x_2))$.

Remark 1. *As a consequence, the* α*-cuts of* $\ddot{A}$ *and* A_α *are confidence intervals:*

$$A_\alpha = \{x|\mu_A(x) \geq \alpha,\ 0 < \alpha \leq 1\} = [\underline{A}_\alpha, \overline{A}_\alpha], \tag{3}$$

where $\underline{A}_\alpha$ *is an increasing function of* α *and* $\overline{A}_\alpha$ *is a decreasing function.*

Remark 2. *The membership function of* $\ddot{A}$, $\mu_A(x)$ *is also called the possibility distribution function.*

Fuzzy set theory commonly relies on fuzzy numbers (FNs) to represent imprecise quantities [51]. Specifically, triangular fuzzy numbers are very common in practical applications because the grading of the membership level is linear. This approach is reasonable because it applies the principle of parsimony when dealing with vague information [52].

Definition 4. *A symmetric triangular fuzzy number (STFN) is a particular case in which a triangular fuzzy number (TFN) can be represented by the couple* $\ddot{A} = (A, r_A)$, $r_A \geq 0$. *Then, the membership function is*

$$\mu_A(x) = \begin{cases} 1 - \frac{|x-A|}{r_A} & |x - A| < r_A \\ 1 & x = A \\ 0 & otherwise \end{cases}, \tag{4}$$

with the following being its α*-cut representation:*

$$A_\alpha = [\underline{A}_\alpha, \overline{A}_\alpha] = [A - r_A(1-\alpha), A + r_A(1-\alpha)],\ 0 \leq \alpha \leq 1. \tag{5}$$

Within TFNs, shapes are of special interest when the available information about the reference variable is scarce and can be summarized in a center and plausible deviations from it [53,54]. Symmetric triangular fuzzy numbers (STFNs) allow for a good balance between comprehensiveness in capturing the available information and the use of the parsimony principle [54]. In insurance modeling, the usefulness of STFNs has been shown in several papers [13,14,55].

Definition 5. *Let us take a continuous random variable* $\mathbf{A}$ *and a family of confidence intervals* A_α*, such that* $P(x \in A_\alpha) \geq 1 - \alpha$ *and* $P(\cdot)$ *is a probability measure. Therefore, an equivalent fuzzy quantity* $\ddot{A}$ *has the following* α*-cut,* A_α *[56]:*

$$A_\alpha = \left[\underline{A}_\alpha, \overline{A}_\alpha\right] = \left[\left\{x|F(\mathbf{A} \leq x) = \frac{\alpha}{2}\right\}, \left\{x|F(\mathbf{A} \leq x) = 1 - \frac{\alpha}{2}\right\}\right], \tag{6}$$

where $F(\cdot)$ *is the distribution function.*

Remark 3. *Consequently, the possibility distribution function of* $\ddot{A}$ *equivalent to* $\mathbf{A}$ *is* $\mu_A(x) = sup\{\alpha|x\epsilon A_\alpha\}$.

It should be emphasized that the interpretation of probabilistic confidence intervals as α-level sets of possibility distributions has been widely argued in the literature [53,54,56–61]. Buckley [58] justified the transformation of a set of probabilistic confidence intervals into fuzzy numbers with the fact that in subsequent calculations, more information is used than simple point estimates or confidence intervals.

Definition 6. *The intuitionistic fuzzy set (IFS)* $\widetilde{A}$ *defined in a referential set X is*

$$\widetilde{A} = \{\langle x, \mu_A(x), v_A(x)\rangle, \ x \in X\}, \tag{7}$$

where $\mu_A : X \longrightarrow [0,1]$ *measures the membership of x in* $\widetilde{A}$ *and* $v_A : X \longrightarrow [0,1]$ *is nonmembership. These functions must accomplish* $0 \leq \mu_A(x) + v_A(x) \leq 1$.

Remark 4. *The degree of hesitancy,* $h_A(x)$*, of* $\widetilde{A}$ *is* $h_A(x) = 1 - \mu_A(x) - v_A(x)$.

Remark 5. *An IFS generalizes the concept of an FS such that if* $h_A(x) = 0 \, \forall x$*,* $\widetilde{A}$ *is a conventional FS* $\ddot{A}$.

Definition 7. *An IFN can be expressed using* $\langle\alpha, \beta\rangle$*-levels or* $\langle\alpha, \beta\rangle$*-cuts, as* $A_{\langle\alpha,\beta\rangle}$*:*

$$A_{\langle\alpha,\beta\rangle} = \{x|\mu_A(x) \geq \alpha, \ v_A(x) \leq \beta, 0 \leq \alpha + \beta \leq 1, \alpha, \beta \in [0,1]\}. \tag{8}$$

Remark 6. $A_{\langle\alpha,\beta\rangle}$ *can be decoupled into two level sets [62], such as* $A_\alpha = \{x|\mu_A(x) \geq \alpha\}$ *and* $A^*_\beta = \{x|v_A(x) \leq \beta\}$*, in such a way that*

$$A_{\langle\alpha,\beta\rangle} = \left\langle A_\alpha = \{x|\mu_A(x) \geq \alpha\}, \ A^*_\beta = \{x|v_A(x) \leq \beta\}, 0 \leq \alpha + \beta \leq 1, \alpha, \beta \in [0,1]\right\rangle. \tag{9}$$

Definition 8. *An intuitionistic fuzzy number (IFN) is an IFS defined on real numbers, such that*

i. *is normal, i.e.,* $\exists x|\mu_A(x) = 1 \Rightarrow v_A(x) = h_A(x) = 0$;
ii. $\mu_A(x)$ *is convex,* $\forall x_1, x_2 \in \mathbb{R}, 0 \leq \lambda \leq 1, \mu_A(\lambda x_1, (1-\lambda)x_2) \geq \min(\mu_A(x_1), \mu_A(x_2))$;
iii. $v_A(x)$ *is concave,* $\forall x_1, x_2 \in \mathbb{R}, 0 \leq \lambda \leq 1, v_A(\lambda x_1, (1-\lambda)x_2) \leq \max(v_A(x_1), v_A(x_2))$.

Remark 7. *The* $\langle\alpha, \beta\rangle$*-cuts of* $\widetilde{A}$ *and* $A_{\langle\alpha,\beta\rangle}$ *can be decoupled as follows:* $A_\alpha = \{x|\mu_A(x) \geq \alpha\} = \left[\underline{A}_\alpha, \overline{A}_\alpha\right]$ *and* $A^*_\beta = \{v_A(x) \leq \beta\} = \left[\underline{A^*}_\beta, \overline{A^*}_\beta\right]$, $0 \leq \alpha + \beta \leq 1, \ \alpha, \beta \in (0,1)$.

Remark 8. *Thus, from Remark 7, an* $\langle\alpha, \beta\rangle$*-level of* $A_{\langle\alpha,\beta\rangle}$ *can be represented as*

$$A_{\langle\alpha,\beta\rangle} = \left\langle A_\alpha = \left[\underline{A}_\alpha, \overline{A}_\alpha\right], A^*{}_\beta = \left[\underline{A^*}_\beta, \overline{A^*}_\beta\right], 0 \leq \alpha + \beta \leq 1, \alpha, \beta \in (0,1)\right\rangle, \tag{10}$$

where $\underline{A}_\alpha$ and $\overline{A^*}_\beta$ increase with their arguments, α and β, respectively. Similarly, $\overline{A}_\alpha$ and $\underline{A^*}_\beta$ are decreasing with respect to these arguments.

Remark 9. *In an IFN, $\mu_A(x)$ can be interpreted as the lower possibility distribution function of the quantity of interest A, and $\mu_{A^*}(x) = 1 - v_A(x)$ is the upper distribution function of that quantity.*

The functions $\mu_{A^*}(x)$ and $\mu_A(x)$ can be interpreted as bipolar possibility distribution measurements, in such a way that $\mu_{A^*}(x)$ accounts for the potential possibility and $\mu_A(x)$ quantifies the real possibility of A being x [28].

Definition 9. *A symmetric triangular intuitionistic fuzzy number (STIFN) is a particular case of a triangular intuitionistic fuzzy number (TIFN) that can be denoted as $\tilde{A} = (A, r_A, r_A^*)$, with membership and nonmembership functions:*

$$\mu_A(x) = \begin{cases} 1 - \frac{|x-A|}{r_A} & |x - A| < r_A \\ 1 & x = A \\ 0 & otherwise \end{cases}, \quad (11)$$

and

$$v_A(x) = \begin{cases} \frac{|x-A|}{r_A^*} & |x - A| < r_A \\ 0 & x = A \\ 1 & otherwise \end{cases}, \quad (12)$$

where $r_A \le r_A^*$. Figure 1 depicts the shape of an STIFN and the relationship between the embedded functions $\mu_A(x)$ (the actual possibility distribution function), $v_A(x)$, $\mu_{A^*}(x)$ (the potential possibility distribution function), and $h_A(x)$.

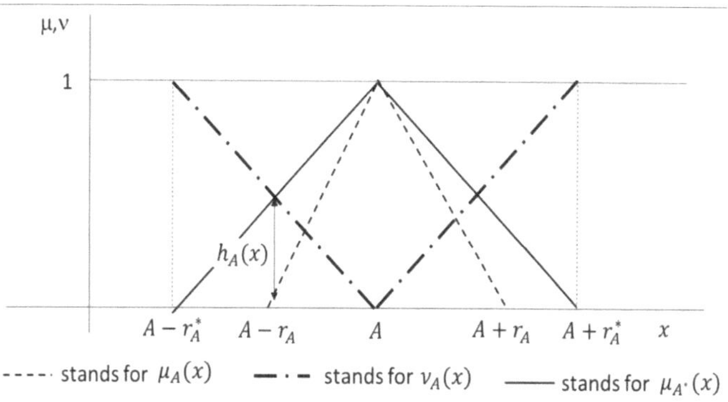

Figure 1. Triangular intuitionistic fuzzy numbers.

Remark 10. *The level sets $A_{\langle\alpha,\beta\rangle}$ of a TIFN can be decoupled into*

$$A_\alpha = \left[\underline{A}_\alpha, \overline{A}_\alpha\right] = [A - r_A(1-\alpha), A + r_A(1-\alpha)], \quad (13)$$

$$A^*_\beta = \left[\underline{A^*}_\beta, \overline{A^*}_\beta\right] = [A - r_A^*\beta, A + r_A^*\beta]. \quad (14)$$

Thus, STIFNs are an extension of STFNs such that if $r_A = r_A^*$, we deal with conventional TFNs [63]. Thus, the use of symmetrical TFNs based on the principle of parsimony to justify their use can be extended to the use of STIFNs.

2.2. Intuitionistic Fuzzy Number Arithmetic

The fuzzy loss-reserving methods in Table 1 calculate provisions based on the assumption that the parameters governing the claiming process are determined by fuzzy numbers. Performing arithmetic operations with FNs requires the application of Zadeh's extension principle, which can be implemented through α-cuts [64].

Zadeh's extension principle and its compatibility with α-cuts arithmetic can be extended to the evaluation of functions defined in real numbers when the parameters are IFNs instead of FNs [65]. This paper considers the case of continuous and differentiable functions $y = f(x_1, x_2, \ldots, x_n)$, such that the values of the input variables are given as the means of IFNs $\tilde{A}_{(i)}$, $i = 1, 2, \ldots, n$. This generates an IFN $\tilde{B}$, $\tilde{B} = f\left(\tilde{A}_{(1)}, \tilde{A}_{(2)}, \ldots, \tilde{A}_{(n)}\right)$.

Thus, the membership and nonmembership functions of $\tilde{B}$ are as follows:

$$\mu_B(y) = \max_{y=f(x_1,x_2,\ldots,x_n)} \min\left\{\mu_{A_{(1)}}(x_1), \mu_{A_{(2)}}(x_2), \ldots, \mu_{A_{(n)}}(x_n)\right\}, \tag{15}$$

$$\upsilon_B(y) = \min_{y=f(x_1,x_2,\ldots,x_n)} \max\left\{\upsilon_{A_{(1)}}(x_1), \upsilon_{A_{(2)}}(x_2), \ldots, \upsilon_{A_{(n)}}(x_n)\right\}. \tag{16}$$

Therefore, if $\tilde{A}_{(i)}$, $i = 1, 2, \ldots, n$ are FNs, it is only necessary to obtain $\mu_B(y)$ using the usual max/min principle. However, we can fit $\tilde{B}$ thoughout $B_{\langle\alpha,\beta\rangle}$ from $A_{(i)}{}_{\langle\alpha,\beta\rangle}$ by calculating $B_{\langle\alpha,\beta\rangle} = f\left(A_{(1)}{}_{\langle\alpha,\beta\rangle}, A_{(2)}{}_{\langle\alpha,\beta\rangle}, \ldots, A_{(n)}{}_{\langle\alpha,\beta\rangle}\right)$. Thus, given that f is continuous, the $\langle\alpha,\beta\rangle$-cuts of $\tilde{B}$ are defined as $B_{\langle\alpha,\beta\rangle} = \left\langle B_\alpha = \left[\underline{B}_\alpha, \overline{B}_\alpha\right], B^*{}_\beta = \left[\underline{B}^*{}_\beta, \overline{B}^*{}_\beta\right], 0 \leq \alpha + \beta \leq 1, \alpha, \beta \in [0,1]\right\rangle$, where

$$\underline{B}_\alpha = \inf\left\{y \middle| y = f(x_1, \ldots, x_n), x_i \in A_{(i)}{}_\alpha\right\}, \overline{B}_\alpha = \sup\left\{y \middle| y = f(x_1, \ldots, x_n), x_i \in A_{(i)}{}_\alpha\right\}, \tag{17}$$

$$\underline{B}^*{}_\beta = \inf\left\{y \middle| y = f(x_1, \ldots, x_n), x_i \in A^*_{(i)}{}_\beta\right\}, \overline{B}^*{}_\beta = \sup\left\{y \middle| y = f(x_1, \ldots, x_n), x_i \in A^*_{(i)}{}_\beta\right\}. \tag{18}$$

Following [66], when f monotonically increases with respect to x_i, $i = 1, 2, \ldots m$ and monotonically decreases in x_i, $i = m+1, m+2, \ldots, n$, $m \leq n$, $B_\alpha = \left[\underline{B}_\alpha, \overline{B}_\alpha\right]$ is as follows:

$$\begin{aligned} \underline{B}_\alpha &= f\left(\underline{A_{(1)}}_\alpha, \underline{A_{(2)}}_\alpha, \ldots, \underline{A_{(m)}}_\alpha, \overline{A_{(m+1)}}_\alpha, \ldots, \overline{A_{(n)}}_\alpha\right) \text{ and} \\ \overline{B}_\alpha &= f\left(\overline{A_{(1)}}_\alpha, \overline{A_{(2)}}_\alpha, \ldots, \overline{A_{(m)}}_\alpha, \underline{A_{(m+1)}}_\alpha, \ldots, \underline{A_{(n)}}_\alpha\right). \end{aligned} \tag{19}$$

By analogy, the β-cut representation of $B^*{}_\beta = \left[\underline{B}^*{}_\beta, \overline{B}^*{}_\beta\right]$ is

$$\begin{aligned} \underline{B}^*{}_\beta &= f\left(\underline{A^*_{(1)}}_\beta, \underline{A^*_{(2)}}_\beta, \ldots, \underline{A^*_{(m)}}_\beta, \overline{A^*_{(m+1)}}_\beta, \ldots, \overline{A^*_{(n)}}_\beta\right) \text{ and} \\ \overline{B}^*{}_\beta &= f\left(\overline{A^*_{(1)}}_\beta, \overline{A^*_{(2)}}_\beta, \ldots, \overline{A^*_{(m)}}_\beta, \underline{A^*_{(m+1)}}_\beta, \ldots, \underline{A^*_{(n)}}_\beta\right). \end{aligned} \tag{20}$$

The linear combination of STIFNs is also an STIFN. Therefore, from the STIFNs $\tilde{A}_{(i)} = \left(A_{(i)}, r_{A_{(i)}}, r^*_{A_{(i)}}\right)$, $\tilde{B} = (B,\ r_B,\ r^*_B\ )$, where [46]

$$B = \sum_{i=1}^{n} \lambda_i A_{(i)}, \ r_B = \sum_{i=1}^{n} |\lambda_i| \cdot r_{A_{(i)}}, \ r^*_B = \sum_{i=1}^{n} |\lambda_i| \cdot r^*_{A_{(i)}}. \tag{21}$$

The evaluation of nonlinear functions using STIFNs does not produce a new STIFN. Despite this limitation, we feel that maintaining a linear shape is relevant. Following the argument in [67] justifying the use of approximating linear fuzzy numbers, complicated forms of IFNs may cause drawbacks in processing imprecise information modeled by these fuzzy structures, and the interpretation of the results becomes more difficult. The same argument, based on the parsimony principle, can be used to maintain the symmetrical structure of the input data.

Thus, we evaluate the approximation to $\widetilde{B} = f\left(\widetilde{A}_{(1)}, \widetilde{A}_{(2)}, \ldots, \widetilde{A}_{(n)}\right)$ with an STIFN $\widetilde{B}^T = (B, r_B, r_B^*)$ when the inputs are $\widetilde{A}_{(i)} = \left(A_{(i)}, r_{A_{(i)}}, r^*_{A_{(i)}}\right), i = 1, 2, \ldots, n$. To do this, we rely on the results of [51] to approximate an LR fuzzy number to the result of a nonlinear function of LR fuzzy numbers, which is based on the linear approximation of α-cuts with a Taylor expansion. In the field of FNs, this methodology produces an STFN that approximates the functions of STFNs, as shown in several actuarial applications [13–15,55].

The extremes of the α-cuts $B_\alpha = \left[\underline{B}_\alpha, \overline{B}_\alpha\right]$ in (19) are approximated by means of a Taylor expansion to the first grade from $\alpha = 1$ to any $\alpha \in [0, 1]$. To do this, we use the gradient $\nabla f(\boldsymbol{A}) = \left(\frac{\partial f}{\partial x_1}(\boldsymbol{A}), \frac{\partial f}{\partial x_2}(\boldsymbol{A}), \ldots, \frac{\partial f}{\partial x_n}(\boldsymbol{A})\right)$, such that $\boldsymbol{A} = (A_1, A_2, \ldots, A_n)$. Therefore, $\underline{B}_\alpha$ can be developed as follows:

$$\begin{aligned}\underline{B}_\alpha \approx \underline{B^T}_\alpha &= f(\boldsymbol{A}) + \left(\textstyle\sum_{i=1}^{m} \frac{\partial f}{\partial x_i}(\boldsymbol{A}) \cdot r_{A_{(i)}}\right)(\alpha - 1) - \left(\textstyle\sum_{i=m+1}^{n} \frac{\partial f}{\partial x_i}(\boldsymbol{A}) \cdot r_{A_{(i)}}\right)(\alpha - 1) \\ &= f(\boldsymbol{A}) - \left(\sum_{i=1}^{n} \left|\frac{\partial f}{\partial x_i}(\boldsymbol{A})\right| \cdot r_{A_{(i)}}\right)(1 - \alpha).\end{aligned} \tag{22}$$

Analogously, we develop $\overline{B}_\alpha$ as follows:

$$\begin{aligned}\overline{B}_\alpha \approx \overline{B^T}_\alpha &= f(\boldsymbol{A}) - \left(\sum_{i=1}^{m} \frac{\partial f}{\partial x_i}(\boldsymbol{A}) \cdot r_{A_{(i)}}\right)(\alpha - 1) + \left(\sum_{i=m+1}^{n} \frac{\partial f}{\partial x_i}(\boldsymbol{A}) \cdot r_{A_{(i)}}\right)(\alpha - 1) \\ &= f(\boldsymbol{A}) + \left(\sum_{i=1}^{n} \left|\frac{\partial f}{\partial x_i}(\boldsymbol{A})\right| \cdot r_{A_{(i)}}\right)(1 - \alpha).\end{aligned} \tag{23}$$

Similarly, $B^*{}_\beta = \left[\underline{B}^*{}_\beta, \overline{B}^*{}_\beta\right]$, whose exact values are given in (20), can also be determined via Taylor expansion to the first grade from $\beta = 0$ to $\beta \in (0, 1]$. Therefore, for $\underline{B}^*{}_\beta$, we state

$$\begin{aligned}\underline{B}^*{}_\beta \approx \underline{B^{T*}}_\beta &= f(\boldsymbol{A}) - \left(\sum_{i=1}^{m} \frac{\partial f}{\partial x_i}(\boldsymbol{A}) \cdot r^*_{A_{(i)}}\right)\beta + \left(\sum_{i=m+1}^{n} \frac{\partial f}{\partial x_i}(\boldsymbol{A}) \cdot r^*_{A_{(i)}}\right)\beta \\ &= f(\boldsymbol{A}) - \left(\sum_{i=1}^{n} \left|\frac{\partial f}{\partial x_i}(\boldsymbol{A})\right| \cdot r^*_{A_{(i)}}\right)\beta.\end{aligned} \tag{24}$$

In the same manner, we expand $\overline{B}^*{}_\beta$ as follows:

$$\begin{aligned}\overline{B}^*{}_\beta \approx \overline{B^{T*}}_\beta &= f(\boldsymbol{A}) + \left(\sum_{i=1}^{m} \frac{\partial f}{\partial x_i}(\boldsymbol{A}) \cdot r^*_{A_{(i)}}\right)\beta - \left(\sum_{i=m+1}^{n} \frac{\partial f}{\partial x_i}(\boldsymbol{A}) \cdot r^*_{A_{(i)}}\right)\beta \\ &= f(\boldsymbol{A}) + \left(\sum_{i=1}^{n} \left|\frac{\partial f}{\partial x_i}(\boldsymbol{A})\right| \cdot r^*_{A_{(i)}}\right)\beta.\end{aligned} \tag{25}$$

Consequently, from (22), (23), (24), and (25), we find that

$$B = f(\boldsymbol{A}),\ r_B = \sum_{i=1}^{n} \left|\frac{\partial f}{\partial x_i}(\boldsymbol{A})\right| \cdot r_{A_{(i)}},\ r_B^* = \sum_{i=1}^{n} \left|\frac{\partial f}{\partial x_i}(\boldsymbol{A})\right| \cdot r^*_{A_{(i)}}. \tag{26}$$

Analogous to [68], we evaluate the relative error measurement in the bounds of $B_{\langle\alpha,\beta\rangle}$, whose exact value can be calculated with (19)–(20), by those of its symmetrical triangular approximation, $B^T_{\langle\alpha,\beta\rangle}$, which must be stated by applying (26) in (11) and (12). Thus, the deviations in $B_\alpha = \left[\underline{B}_\alpha, \overline{B}_\alpha\right]$ are

$$\underline{\varepsilon}_\alpha = \frac{\left|\underline{B}_\alpha - \underline{B^T}_\alpha\right|}{\underline{B}_\alpha}, \overline{\varepsilon}_\alpha = \frac{\left|\overline{B}_\alpha - \overline{B^T}_\alpha\right|}{\overline{B}_\alpha}, \tag{27}$$

and for $B^*_\beta = \left[\underline{B^*}_\beta, \overline{B^*}_\beta\right]$,

$$\underline{\varepsilon^*}_\beta = \frac{\left|\underline{B^*}_\beta - \underline{B^{T*}}_\beta\right|}{\underline{B^*}_\beta}, \overline{\varepsilon^*}_\beta = \frac{\left|\overline{B^*}_\beta - \overline{B^{T*}}_\beta\right|}{\overline{B^*}_\beta}. \tag{28}$$

2.3. Intuitionistic Linear Regression with the Minimum Fuzziness Principle and Symmetric Coefficients

Within the fuzzy field, there are a large number of regression methodologies that can be divided into two main groups. In the first type, we can group those based on the minimum fuzziness principle (MFP), and the second includes those based on the minimization of the distance between observations and predictions, such as models that can be labeled fuzzy least-squares models [69].

This dichotomy between the minimum fuzziness principle and distance minimization is also observed in intuitionistic fuzzy regression models. For example, [46] extended the minimum fuzziness principle to an intuitionistic regression setting, and [70] developed a least-squares intuitionistic fuzzy regression methodology. Our paper uses the first approach. Therefore, our model is based on fuzzy regression models with symmetric parameters.

Let us suppose that the equation to be fitted has a dependent factor dependent on m real-value explanatory variables x_i , i = 0, 1, 2, ..., m, where $x_0 = 1$ and $x_i \epsilon \mathbb{R}$, $i = 1, 2, \ldots, n$. The outcome is then a linear function of intuitionistic coefficients $\widetilde{A}_{(i)} = \left(A_{(i)}, r_{A_{(i)}}, r^*_{A_{(i)}}\right)$, $i = 0, 1, \ldots, m$ and, thus, an STIFN $\widetilde{Y} = (Y, r_Y, r^*_Y)$. This is obtained from (21), as follows:

$$Y = \sum_{j=0}^{m} A_{(i)} x_i, \; r_Y = \sum_{i=0}^{n} r_{A_{(i)}} |x_i|, \; r^*_Y = \sum_{i=0}^{n} r^*_{A_{(i)}} |x_i|. \tag{29}$$

Moreover, both the observations of the input variables and the output variable are crisp, which is a common hypothesis in intuitionistic fuzzy regression models. Thus, for the jth observation, the outcome is the crisp number y_j, generated by the crisp income $(1, x_{1j}, x_{2j}, \ldots, x_{ij}, \ldots, x_{im})$. Therefore, y_j is a possible value of a TIFN $\widetilde{Y}_j = \left(Y_j, r_{Y_j}, r^*_{Y_j}\right)$, whose membership function $\mu_{Y_j}(y_j)$ and nonmembership function $\nu_{Y_j}(y_j)$ in (11)–(12) are determined from (29)

$$Y_j = \sum_{i=0}^{m} A_{(i)} x_{ij}, \; r_{Y_j} = \sum_{i=0}^{m} r_{A_{(i)}} |x_{ij}|, \; r^*_{Y_j} = \sum_{i=0}^{m} r^*_{A_{(i)}} |x_{ij}|. \tag{30}$$

The objective is to fit for $\widetilde{A}_{(i)}$, $i = 0, 1, 2, \ldots, m$, an STIFN estimate $\widetilde{a}_{(i)} = \left(a_{(i)}, r_{a_{(i)}}, r^*_{a_{(i)}}\right)$, $i = 0, 1, 2, \ldots, m$ that simultaneously maximizes the membership of the observations in the fitted system and minimizes the uncertainty of that system. Therefore, to find $\widetilde{a}_{(i)}$, the following multiple-objective programming problem must be implemented:

$$\underset{A_{(i)}, r_{A_{(i)}} r^*_{A_{(i)}}, i=0,1,\ldots,n}{\text{minimize}} \left(-\alpha, \; \beta, \; z_1 = \sum_{j=1}^{n} r_{Y_j}, \; z_2 = \sum_{j=1}^{n} r^*_{Y_j}\right),$$

which is subject to

$$\mu_{Y_j}(y_j) \geq \alpha, \; \nu_{Y_j}(y_j) \leq \beta, \; j = 1, 2, \ldots, n, r_{A_{(i)}}, r^*_{A_{(i)}} \geq 0, \; i = 0, 1, \ldots, m. \tag{31}$$

$$0 \leq \alpha + \beta \leq 1, \alpha, \beta \in [0, 1].$$

To solve (31), we implement the following steps:

Step 1: We state a minimum reachable value $\alpha = g$ and $\beta = 1 - g - h$. Like in possibilistic regression models, $g \in [0, 1)$ scales the total fuzziness of the estimated system. If $g = 0$, the uncertainty of the system is minimal; conversely, the inclusiveness of the observations may be low. On the other hand, a higher g causes all observations to be included with greater intensity, and the predictions of the fitted system are less specific [49].

The value of $h \in [0, 1 - g)$ reflects the level of hesitancy in the system. For $h = 0$, the actual and potential possibility of a particular value are identical; therefore, we have a conventional possibilistic regression. At this step, we decouple (31) as follows:

$$\underset{A_{(i)}, r_{A_{(i)}}, i=0,1,\ldots,n}{\text{minimize}} \quad z_1 = \sum_{j=1}^{n} r_{Y_j} \ ,$$

subject to

$$\mu_{Y_j}(y_j) \geq g, \ j = 1, 2, \ldots, n, \ r_{A_{(i)}} \geq 0, i = 0, 1, \ldots, m, \tag{32}$$

and

$$\underset{A_{(i)}, r^*_{A_{(i)}}, i=0,1,\ldots,n}{\text{minimize}} \quad z_2 = \sum_{j=1}^{n} r^*_{Y_j} \ ,$$

subject to

$$\nu_{Y_j}(y_j) \leq 1 - g - h, \ = 1, 2, \ldots, n, \ r^*_{A_{(i)}} \geq 0, \ i = 0, 1, \ldots, m. \tag{33}$$

Step 2: We initially state for (32)–(33) that $g = h = 0$. This implies the minimum fuzziness level and no hesitancy. Thus, we adjust a possibilistic regression model and $r_{A_{(i)}} = r^*_{A_{(i)}}$. This leads us to obtain the estimates of $A_{(i)}$ and $r_{A_{(i)}}$, which we denote as $a^{(0)}_{(i)}$ and $r^{(0)}_{a_{(i)}}$, respectively, where $i = 0, 1, \ldots, m$. Thus, we must solve the following:

$$\underset{A_{(i)}, r_{A_{(i)}}, i=0,1,\ldots,n}{\text{minimize}} \quad z_1 = z_2 = \sum_{i=0}^{m} r_{A_{(i)}} \sum_{j=1}^{n} |x_{ij}| \ ,$$

subject to

$$\sum_{i=0}^{m} A_{(i)} x_{ij} - \sum_{i=0}^{m} r_{A_{(i)}} |x_{ij}| \leq y_j \leq \sum_{i=0}^{m} A_{(i)} x_{ij} + \sum_{i=0}^{m} r_{A_{(i)}} |x_{ij}|, \ j = 1, 2, \ldots, n \tag{34}$$

$$A_{(i)}, r_{A_{(i)}} \geq 0, \ i = 0, 1, \ldots, m.$$

Step 3: To fit the centers in (34), $a^{(0)}_{(i)}$ for $A_{(i)}$ and $r^{(0)}_{a_{(i)}}$ for $r_{A_{(i)}}$ $i = 0, 1, \ldots, m$, the literature proposes two alternatives:

- Alternative 1. The values of $a^{(0)}_{(i)}$ and $r^{(0)}_{a_{(i)}}$ are those that are solved in a unique step (34). In this case, the centers $a^{(0)}_{(i)}$ are those that are obtained in a quantile regression at the median, identical to [71].
- Alternative 2. The value $a^{(0)}_{(i)}$ in the first step is obtained by using ordinary least squares [72]. However, there is no reason why any other method, such as the maximum likelihood or weighted least-squares methods, cannot be used. In the second step, $r^{(0)}_{a_{(i)}}$ is obtained by solving (34) and taking into account that this linear programming problem is as follows, after independently stating $a^{(0)}_{(i)}$:

$$\underset{r_{A_{(i)}}, i=0,1,\ldots,n}{\text{minimize}} \ z_1 = z_2 = \sum_{i=0}^{m} r_{A_{(i)}} \sum_{j=1}^{n} |x_{ij}| \ ,$$

subject to

$$-\sum_{i=0}^{n} r_{A_{(i)}}|x_{ij}| \leq y_j - \sum_{i=0}^{n} a_{(i)}^{(0)} x_{ij} \leq \sum_{i=0}^{n} r_{A_{(i)}}|x_{ij}|,\ j = 1,2,\ldots,n \tag{35}$$

$$r_{A_{(i)}} \geq 0,\ i = 0,1,\ldots,m.$$

Step 4: We establish the optimal value of g based on this criterion. This value optimizes what these authors refer to as the credibility of the system [73]. To achieve this, we define the estimation of $\widetilde{Y}_j$, obtained from the parameters adjusted in Step 1 and Step 3 as $\widetilde{y}_j^{(0)} = \left(y_j^{(0)}, r_{y_j}^{(0)}, r_{y_j}^{(0)}\right)$, i.e., $\widetilde{y}_j^{(0)}$ is an STFN where $y_j^{(0)} = \sum_{i=0}^{m} a_{(i)} x_{ij}$, and $r_{y_j}^{(0)} = \sum_{i=0}^{m} r_{a_{(i)}}^{(0)}|x_{ij}|$. So,

$$g = \begin{cases} \frac{1}{2}\left(1 - \frac{\gamma^{(0)}}{\delta^{(0)}}\right) & \gamma^{(0)} < \delta^{(0)} \\ 0 & otherwise \end{cases}, \tag{36}$$

where $\gamma^{(0)} = \sum_{j=1}^{n} \frac{\mu_{y_j^{(0)}}(y_j)}{r_{y_j}^{(0)}}$, $\delta^{(0)} = \sum_{j=1}^{n} \frac{1-\mu_{y_j^{(0)}}(y_j)}{r_{y_j}^{(0)}}$ and then we state that

$$r_{a_{(i)}} = \frac{r_{a_{(i)}}^{(0)}}{1-g}. \tag{37}$$

Step 5: We subsequently proceed to obtain the estimates of $r_{a_{(i)}}^{*}$. To achieve this, the decision maker must determine the degree of hesitancy in the system, where $h \epsilon [0, 1-g)$. In the case where $h = 0$, there is no hesitancy; if $h \to 1-g$, the level of hesitancy tends to be at its maximum. Thus,

$$r_{a_{(i)}}^{*} = \frac{r_{a_{(i)}}^{(0)}}{1-g-h}. \tag{38}$$

3. An Intuitionistic Chain Ladder for Claim Reserving

3.1. Claim Reserving with the Chain-Ladder Method and Stochastic Variability and a Probability–Possibility Transformation

The historical data illustrating the evolution of claims are typically presented in a run-off triangle format, similar to Table 2 [10]. In this table, $C_{i,j}$ represents the accumulated claim cost of insurance contracts originating in the ith development period ($i = 0, 1, \ldots, n$) during the jth claiming period ($j = 0, 1, \ldots, n$). Therefore, the accumulated claims $C_{i,j}$, $i = 1, 2, \ldots, n$; $j = n - i + 1, n - i + 2, \ldots, n$ are unknown and must be fitted.

Table 2. Run-off triangle of accumulated claims.

		Development/Payment Period						
	$i \mid j$	0	1	…	$j = n - i$	…	$n-1$	n
Occurrence/Origin Period	0	$C_{0,0}$	$C_{0,1}$	…	$C_{0,j}$	…	$C_{0,n-1}$	$C_{0,n}$
	1	$C_{1,0}$	$C_{1,1}$	…	$C_{1,j}$	…	$C_{1,n-1}$	
	⋮	⋮	⋮	⋮	⋮	⋮		
	i	$C_{i,0}$	$C_{i,1}$	…	$C_{i,n-i}$	…		
	⋮	⋮	⋮	⋮				
	$n-1$	$C_{n-1,0}$	$C_{n-1,1}$	…				
	n	$C_{n,0}$		…				

An alternative way to present historical data consists of the run-off triangle of incremental claims, in a way similar to Table 3. Table 3 can be obtained from Table 2 by taking into account that $S_{i,j} = C_{i,j} - C_{i,j-1}$, $i = 0, 1, 2, \ldots, n-1$, $j = 1, 2, \ldots, n-i$, and $S_{i,0} = C_{i,0}$.

Therefore, the incremental claims $S_{i,j}$, $i = 1, 2, \ldots, n$; $j = n - i + 1, n - i + 2, \ldots, n$ are unknown and must be fitted.

Table 3. Run-off triangle of incremental claims.

		Development/Payment Period						
		0	**1**	...	$j = n - i$	...	$n - 1$	n
Occurrence/Origin Period	0	$S_{0,0}$	$S_{0,1}$	...	$S_{0,j}$	...	$S_{0,n-1}$	$S_{0,n}$
	1	$S_{1,0}$	$S_{1,1}$	...	$S_{1,j}$	...	$S_{1,n-1}$	
	⋮	⋮	⋮	⋮	⋮	⋮		
	i	$S_{i,0}$	$S_{i,1}$	...	$S_{i,n-i}$	...		
	⋮	⋮	⋮	⋮				
	$n - 1$	$S_{n-1,0}$	$S_{n-1,1}$	...				
	n	$S_{n,0}$		...				

The triangle of accumulated claims (Table 2) is the input of several common methods to fit claim reserves, such as the chain-ladder method or the Bornhuetter–Ferguson method. The key concept of the CL method is the so-called link ratio between development year j and $j + 1$, F_j, which allows us to obtain the cumulative claims of the $(j + 1)$th development period from those of the jth period:

$$C_{i,j+1} = F_j \cdot C_{i,j} \Longrightarrow F_j = \frac{C_{i,j+1}}{C_{i,j}}, \tag{39}$$

where the available observations of F_j are as follows:

$$f_{i,j} = \frac{C_{i,j+1}}{C_{i,j}}, \; i = 0, 1, \ldots, n - j - 1 \tag{40}$$

To obtain an average value of F_j, f_j, we consider the widely used CL, which provides an unbiased estimator of F_j [11]. Thus, the average development factor for the jth year is

$$f_j = \frac{\sum_{i=0}^{n-j-1} C_{i,j+1}}{\sum_{i=0}^{n-j-1} C_{i,j}}. \tag{41}$$

The terminal value of accumulated claims for the ith origin year $C_{i,n}$, $i = 1, 2, \ldots, n$ is approximated by $c_{i.n}$, as follows:

$$c_{i.n} = C_{i,n-i} \prod_{j=n-i}^{n-1} f_j, \tag{42}$$

and $c_{i.n}$ is an increasing function of development factors, since the partial derivative $\frac{\partial c_{i.n}}{\partial f_j}$ is

$$\frac{\partial c_{i.n}}{\partial f_j} = C_{i,n-i} \prod_{\substack{k=n-i \\ k \neq j}}^{n-1} f_k. \tag{43}$$

Thus, the reserves are linked with the origin year $i = 1, 2, \ldots, n$, RO_i:

$$RO_i = c_{i.n} - C_{i,n-i} = C_{i,n-i}\left(\prod_{j=n-i}^{n-1} f_j - 1\right). \tag{44}$$

So, the overall provisions, R, are

$$R = \sum_{i=1}^{n} RO_i. \tag{45}$$

The classical chain-ladder method is deterministic. However, this methodology is flexible enough to generate stochastic estimates of fluctuations by applying the SCL method, which is implemented in the following six steps:

1. Obtain the estimates of the observations $C_{i,j}$, $c_{i,j}$, $i = 0, 1, \ldots, n; j < n - i$ by using f_j backwards from $C_{i,n-i}$.
2. Calculate an estimate of observed incremental claims (Table 2) by stating $s_{i,j} = c_{i,j} - c_{i,j-1}$, in the case of $s_{i,0} = c_{i,0}$.
3. Calculate the descaled Pearson residuals due to fitting the real incremental claims in Table 2, $S_{i,j}$, with $s_{i,j}$:

$$m_{i,j} = \frac{S_{i,j} - s_{i,j}}{\sqrt{s_{i,j}}}, i = 0, 1, \ldots, n; j \leq n - i.$$

4. Resample $m_{i,j}$, $i = 0, 1, \ldots, n; j \leq n - i$. Therefore, we find $m^b_{i,j}$, $i = 0, 1, \ldots, n; j \leq n - i$.
5. Calculate the incremental claims $s^b_{i,j} = s_{i,j} + \sqrt{s_{i,j}} m^b_{i,j}$, $i = 0, 1, \ldots, n; j \leq n - i$. This implies adjusting a new Table 3.
6. From Table 3, in the above step, we can resample the accumulated claims and construct Table 2. This new table allows us to obtain the development factors (40) and reserves (44) and (45). These six steps can be implemented B times in such a way that predictions of claiming reserves can be obtained as confidence intervals.

Note that Steps 1–6 allow B simulations of loss reserves to be obtained for every origin year $RO_i^{(b_i)}$, $b_i = 1, 2, \ldots, B$ and the whole reserve $R^{(b)}$ and $b = 1, 2, \ldots, B$. Without losing generality, let us suppose that in all the cases, $RO_i^{(b_i)} \leq RO_i^{(b_i+1)}$. Then, the reserve RO_i is contained with a probability $1 - \alpha$ in the interval $RO_{i\alpha}$, such that

$$RO_{i\alpha} = \left[\underline{RO_{i}}_{\alpha}, \overline{RO_{i\alpha}}\right] = \left[RO_i^{(round[B \cdot \frac{\alpha}{2}])}, RO_i^{(round[B \cdot (1 - \frac{\alpha}{2})])}\right], \tag{46}$$

which can be interpreted as the α-cuts of a possibilistic estimate of the reserves of the ith year $\ddot{RO}_i$.

Therefore, we can estimate a confidence interval for the overall reserves in two ways. A conservative estimate, R'_α, is $R'_\alpha = \sum_{i=1}^{n} RO_{i\alpha}$, such that R'_α can be considered the α-cuts of the possibility distribution $\ddot{R}\prime$:

$$R'_\alpha = \left[\underline{R'_\alpha}, \overline{R\prime_\alpha}\right] = \left[\sum_{i=1}^{n} \underline{RO_{i}}_{\alpha}, \sum_{i=1}^{n} \overline{RO_{i\alpha}}\right] \tag{47}$$

A more specific approximation of the overall reserves implies inducing a confidence interval with a probability level $1 - \alpha$, R_α from $R^{(b)} \leq R^{(b+1)}$, $b = 1, 2, \ldots, B$ by calculating the following:

$$R_\alpha = \left[\underline{R}_\alpha, \overline{R}_\alpha\right] = \left[R^{(round[B \cdot \frac{\alpha}{2}])}, R^{(round[B \cdot (1 - \frac{\alpha}{2})])}\right]. \tag{48}$$

Therefore, from the probabilistic confidence interval R_α, we can induce a possibility distribution function $\ddot{R}$ by considering Definition 5.

3.2. *An Intuitionistic Fuzzy Chain-Ladder Method*

3.2.1. Fitting Symmetrical Intuitionistic Triangular Fuzzy Development Factors

Let us express relation (39), in which, from a known accumulated claim amount in the *j*th development period, we must obtain the accumulated quantity in the (*j* + 1)th development period, which is uncertain because the development factor is an STIFN. So,

$$\widetilde{C}_{i,j+1} = \widetilde{F}_{(j)} \cdot C_{i,j} \tag{49}$$

where $\widetilde{C}_{i,j+1} = \left(C_{i,j+1}, r_{C_{i,j+1}}, r^{*}_{C_{i,j+1}}\right)$ and $\widetilde{F}_{(j)} = \left(F_{(j)}, r_{F_{(j)}}, r^{*}_{F_{(j)}}\right)$. Therefore, from (21), $C_{i,j+1} = F_{(j)} \cdot C_{i,j}$, $r_{C_{i,j+1}} = C_{i,j} \cdot r_{F_{(j)}}$ and $r^{*}_{C_{i,j+1}} = C_{i,j} \cdot r^{*}_{F_{(j)}}$.

To fit $\widetilde{F}_{(j)}$ by means of $\widetilde{f}_{(j)} = \left(f_{(j)}, r_{f_{(j)}}, r^{*}_{f_{(j)}}\right)$, we consider the data in Table 2. The couples (y,x) are defined as $\left(C_{i,j+1}, C_{i,j}\right), i = 0, 1, \ldots, n-j-1$. Therefore, $\widetilde{f}_{(j)} = \left(f_{(j)}, r_{f_{(j)}}, r^{*}_{f_{(j)}}\right)$ is first fitted, where $f^{(0)}_{(j)} = f_{(j)}$ and $r^{(0)}_{f_{(j)}} = r_{f_{(j)}} = r^{*}_{f_{(j)}}$ are the optimum values of the arguments in the programming problem (32)–(33) for $g = h = 0$. Therefore, we must solve the version of (34) for relation (49):

$$\underset{F_{(j)}, r_{F_{(j)}}}{\text{minimize}} z_1 = z_2 = r_{F_{(j)}} \sum_{i=0}^{n-j-1} C_{i,j},$$

which is subject to

$$F_{(j)} C_{i,j} - C_{i,j} r_{F_{(j)}} \leq C_{i,j+1} \leq F_{(j)} C_{i,j} + C_{i,j} r_{F_{(j)}}, \ i = 0, 1, \ldots, n-j-1. \tag{50}$$

$$r_{F_{(j)}} \geq 0.$$

By dividing the inclusion constraints in (50) by $C_{i,j}$, $i = 0, 1, \ldots, n-j-1$, the independent terms turn into (40), $f_{i,j} = \frac{C_{i,j+1}}{C_{i,j}}$. Likewise, the cost function of (50) has only one argument. Therefore, the linear pro-gramming problem becomes

$$\underset{F_{(j)}, r_{F_{(j)}}}{\text{minimize}} z_1 = z_2 = r_{F_{(j)}},$$

which is subject to

$$F_{(j)} - r_{F_{(j)}} \leq f_{i,j} \leq F_{(j)} + r_{F_{(j)}}, \ i = 0, 1, \ldots, n-j-1. \tag{51}$$

$$r_{F_{(j)}} \geq 0.$$

To solve (51), we can follow Alternatives 1 and 2 in Section 2.3. By using Alternative 1, the solution of that linear programming problem allows us to obtain $f^{(0)}_{(j)}$ as the result of the quantile regression at the median and, simultaneously, $r^{(0)}_{f_{(j)}}$. Models (51) can be implemented by Alternative 2 in Section 2.3 by prefixing $f^{(0)}_{(j)}$ with the CL formula (41). In this case, the linear programming problem (51) becomes

$$\underset{r_{F_{(j)}}}{\text{minimize}} z_1 = z_2 = r_{F_{(j)}},$$

which is subject to

$$-r_{F_{(j)}} \leq f_{i,j} - f^{(0)}_{(j)} \leq r_{F_{(j)}}, \ i = 0, 1, \ldots, n-j-1. \tag{52}$$

$$r_{F_{(j)}} \geq 0,$$

and so,

$$r^{(0)}_{f_{(j)}} = \max_{i=0,1,\ldots,n-i-1}\left|f_{i,j} - f^{(0)}_{(j)}\right|. \tag{53}$$

Then, the empirical estimates of $\widetilde{F}_{(j)} = \left(F_{(j)}, r_{F_{(j)}}, r^*_{F_{(j)}}\right)$, $\widetilde{f}_{(j)} = \left(f_{(j)}, r_{f_{(j)}}, r^*_{f_{(j)}}\right)$, $j = 0, 1, \ldots, n-1$, are obtained as follows:

i. Considering that $f_{(j)} = f^{(0)}_{(j)}$,
ii. $r_{f_{(j)}}$ is obtained by calculating g in Step 4 of Section 2.3 with (36) and (37).
iii. Finally, $r^*_{f_{(j)}}$ is adjusted in Step 5 of Section 2.3 by subjectively stating the degree of system hesitancy, h, and using (38).

The structure of the data in Table 2 leads us to obtain the last development factor $\widetilde{f}_{(n-1)}$ with only the pair $(C_{0,n}, C_{0,n-1})$. Therefore, it is easy to verify that $f_{(j)} = f^{(0)}_{(j)} = \frac{C_{0,n}}{C_{0,n-1}}$, but this approach also leads to the unrealistic conclusion that it is a certain parameter, i.e., $r_{f_{(j)}} = r^*_{f_{(j)}} = 0$. Mack [11], in his stochastic free-distribution modeling of reserves over the CL model, addresses this issue based on the intuition that the absolute uncertainty of the development factors tends to decrease over time, as does the expected value of these factors. Thus, the standard deviation of the development factor F_{n-1} is estimated as the minimum of the standard deviation of F_{n-3} and F_{n-2} and the ratio between the variance of F_{n-3} and the standard deviation of F_{n-2}. Taking this idea into consideration and considering that k times the standard deviation of random quantities can be interpreted as the radius of an equivalent STFN [54,56], $\widetilde{f}_{(n-1)} = \left(f_{(n-1)}, r_{f_{(n-1)}}, r^*_{f_{(n-1)}}\right)$, where

$$f_{(n-1)} = \frac{C_{0,n}}{C_{0,n-1}}, \tag{54}$$

and

$$r_{f_{(n-1)}} = \min\left\{\frac{r_{f_{(n-3)}}^{\;2}}{r_{f_{(n-2)}}}, r_{f_{(n-3)}}, r_{f_{(n-2)}}\right\},\; r^*_{f_{(n-1)}} = \min\left\{\frac{r^{*\;2}_{f_{(n-3)}}}{r^*_{f_{(n-2)}}}, r^*_{f_{(n-3)}}, r^*_{f_{(n-2)}}\right\}. \tag{55}$$

3.2.2. Fitting Reserves with Symmetric Triangular Intuitionistic Fuzzy Development Factors

To state the reserves, we must estimate the terminal value of the claims in every origin year $i = 1, 2, \ldots, n$, $\widetilde{c}_{i,n}$, which can be expressed through its $\langle\alpha,\beta\rangle$-cuts as follows:

$$c_{i,n\,\langle\alpha,\beta\rangle} = \left\langle c_{i,n_\alpha} = \left[\underline{c_{i,n}}_\alpha, \overline{c_{i,n}}_\alpha\right], c^*_{i,n_\beta} = \left[\underline{c^*_{i,n}}_\beta, \overline{c^*_{i,n}}_\beta\right], 0 \le \alpha+\beta \le 1, \alpha,\beta \in (0,1)\right\rangle. \tag{56}$$

Specifically, $c_{i,n\,\langle\alpha,\beta\rangle}$ is obtained from $C_{i,n-i}$ and the $\langle\alpha,\beta\rangle$-cuts of $\widetilde{f}_{(j)}$, $f_{(j)\,\langle\alpha,\beta\rangle}$, $j = n-i, n-i+1, \ldots, n-1$ by adapting (42) to an intuitionistic setting:

$$c_{i,n\,\langle\alpha,\beta\rangle} = C_{i,n-i}\prod_{j=n-i}^{n-1} f_{(j)\,\langle\alpha,\beta\rangle}, \tag{57}$$

and thus, $c_{i,n_\alpha} = \left[\underline{c_{i,n}}_\alpha, \overline{c_{i,n}}_\alpha\right]$ is obtained considering that (42) is an increasing function of development factors:

$$\begin{aligned} c_{i,n_\alpha} &= \left[C_{i,n-i}\prod_{j=n-i}^{n-1}\underline{f_{(j)}}_\alpha, C_{i,n-i}\prod_{j=n-i}^{n-1}\overline{f_{(j)}}_\alpha\right] \\ &= \left[C_{i,n-i}\prod_{j=n-i}^{n-1}\left(f_{(j)} - r_{f_{(j)}}(1-\alpha)\right), C_{i,n-i}\prod_{j=n-i}^{n-1}\left(f_{(j)} + r_{f_{(j)}}(1-\alpha)\right)\right]. \end{aligned} \tag{58}$$

Similarly, $c^*_{i,n\beta} = \left[\underline{c^*_{i,n}}_\beta, \overline{c^*_{i,n}}_\beta\right]$ is calculated as follows:

$$\begin{aligned} c^*_{i,n\beta} &= \left[C_{i,n-i}\prod_{j=n-i}^{n-1}\underline{f^*_{(j)}}_\beta, C_{i,n-i}\prod_{j=n-i}^{n-1}\overline{f^*_{(j)}}_\beta\right] \\ &= \left[C_{i,n-i}\prod_{j=n-i}^{n-1}\left(f_{(j)} - r^*_{f_{(j)}}\beta\right), C_{i,n-i}\prod_{j=n-i}^{n-1}\left(f_{(j)} + r^*_{f_{(j)}}\beta\right)\right]. \end{aligned} \tag{59}$$

Note that $\tilde{c}_{i,n}$ is not an STIFN. However, by using derivatives (43) and (22)–(25), we can approximate $\tilde{c}_{i,n} \approx \tilde{c}^T_{i,n} = \left(c_{i,n}, , r_{c_{i,n}}, r^*_{c_{i,n}}\right)$, where the center is

$$c_{i,n} = C_{i,n-i}\prod_{j=n-i}^{n-1} f_{(j)}, \tag{60}$$

and the radii are

$$r_{c_{i,n}} = C_{i,n-i}\sum_{j=n-i}^{n-1}\left(\prod_{\substack{k=n-i \\ k\neq j}}^{n-1} f_k\right) r_{f_{(j)}}, r^*_{c_{i,n}} = C_{i,n-i}\sum_{j=n-i}^{n-1}\left(\prod_{\substack{k=n-i \\ k\neq j}}^{n-1} f_k\right) r^*_{f_{(j)}}. \tag{61}$$

Therefore, by using (44), we can obtain the intuitionistic reserves for the ith origin year $\tilde{RO}_i$ through $RO_{i\langle\alpha,\beta\rangle} = \left\langle RO_{i\alpha} = \left[\underline{RO_i}_\alpha, \overline{RO_{i\alpha}}\right], RO^*_{i\beta} = \left[\underline{RO^*_i}_\beta, \overline{RO^*_{i\beta}}\right], 0 \le \alpha+\beta \le 1, \alpha,\beta \in (0,1)\right\rangle$ by calculating:

$$RO_{i\langle\alpha,\beta\rangle} = c_{i,n\langle\alpha,\beta\rangle} - C_{i,n-i}. \tag{62}$$

Then,

$$\begin{aligned} RO_{i\alpha} &= \left[C_{i,n-i}\left(\prod_{j=n-i}^{n-1}\left(f_{(j)} - r_{f_{(j)}}(1-\alpha)\right) - 1\right), C_{i,n-i}\left(\prod_{j=n-i}^{n-1}\left(f_{(j)} + r_{f_{(j)}}(1-\alpha)\right) - 1\right)\right], \\ RO^*_{i\beta} &= \left[C_{i,n-i}\left(\prod_{j=n-i}^{n-1}\left(f_{(j)} - r^*_{f_{(j)}}(1-\alpha)\right) - 1\right), C_{i,n-i}\left(\prod_{j=n-i}^{n-1}\left(f_{(j)} + r^*_{f_{(j)}}(1-\alpha)\right) - 1\right)\right]. \end{aligned} \tag{63}$$

The intuitionistic fuzzy estimate of reserves of the ith year is not an STIFN. However, an STIFN approximate $\tilde{RO}_i \approx \tilde{RO}^T_i = \left(RO_i, r_{RO_i}, r^*_{RO_i}\right)$ is obtained by the following:

$$\tilde{RO}^T_i = c^T_{i,n} - C_{i,n-i} = \left(c_{i,n} - C_{i,n-i}, r_{c_{i,n}}, r^*_{c_{i,n}}\right), \tag{64}$$

and so, considering (60) and (61),

$$\begin{aligned} RO_i &= \tilde{c}^T_{i,n} - C_{i,n-i} = C_{i,n-i}\left(\prod_{j=n-i}^{n-1} f_j - 1\right) \\ r_{RO_i} &= C_{i,n-i}\sum_{j=n-i}^{n-1}\left(\prod_{\substack{k=n-i \\ k\neq j}}^{n-1} f_k\right) r_{f_{(j)}}, r^*_{RO_i} = C_{i,n-i}\sum_{j=n-i}^{n-1}\left(\prod_{\substack{k=n-i \\ k\neq j}}^{n-1} f_k\right) r^*_{f_{(j)}}. \end{aligned} \tag{65}$$

Similarly, an intuitionistic fuzzy estimate of the overall reserve $\tilde{R}$ is obtained with (45) through $R_{\langle\alpha,\beta\rangle} = \left\langle R_\alpha = \left[\underline{R}_\alpha, \overline{R}_\alpha\right], R^*_\beta = \left[\underline{R^*}_\beta, \overline{R^*}_\beta\right], 0 \le \alpha+\beta \le 1, \alpha,\beta \in (0,1)\right\rangle$. By implementing $R_{\langle\alpha,\beta\rangle} = \sum_{i=1}^{n} RO_{i\langle\alpha,\beta\rangle}$. Then,

$$R_\alpha = \left[\sum_{i=1}^{n} \underline{RO}_{i\alpha}, \sum_{i=1}^{n} \overline{RO}_{i\alpha}\right], R^*_\beta = \left[\sum_{i=1}^{n} \underline{RO}^*_{i\beta}, \sum_{i=1}^{n} \overline{RO}^*_{i\beta}\right]. \tag{66}$$

Therefore, an STIFN approximate to $\tilde{R} \approx \tilde{R}^T = (R, r_R, r^*_R)$ is obtained simply as follows:

$$\tilde{R}^T = \sum_{i=1}^{n} \tilde{RO}_i^T = \left(\sum_{i=1}^{n} RO_i, \sum_{i=1}^{n} r_{RO_i}, \sum_{i=1}^{n} r^*_{RO_i}\right). \tag{67}$$

4. Empirical Application

4.1. Estimating Loss Reserves with Deterministic and Stochastic Chain-Ladder Method

Below, we present an empirical application based on the run-off triangle of accumulated claims shown in Table 4. These data were utilized in [74,75]. Table 4 also illustrates the development factors found using (41). Thus, we observe that a crisp development factor f_0 = 1.899 is estimated, indicating that the accumulated claims from development years zero to one increase on average by 89.90% for all origin years. Similarly, we can interpret the estimates of the development factors f_1, f_2, f_3, and f_4.

Table 5 presents the individual reserves obtained for each of the origin years i = 1, 2, ..., 5 and the total reserves with a deterministic CL. Thus, we can observe that as the origin year increases, the reserve to be allocated increases, as claims from more development years are pending. It can be noted that in both Tables 4 and 5, we obtain the expected values of the link ratios and reserves, but we do not have any estimation of their variability. This analysis is carried out in Tables 6 and 7, where reserves are estimated using the SCL method, and the obtained possibilistic confidence intervals are interpreted as possibility distributions, using Definition 5 of Section 2.

Table 6 displays a table of incremental claims analogous to Table 3 that is deduced from Table 4. Table 4 also shows the theoretical table of incremental claims that are deduced from the development factors of the chain-ladder method. The difference between the observed and theoretical tables of incremental claims through descaled Pearson residuals allows the implementation of the SCL method, described in Section 3.1, to fit the variability of reserves by origin year and total reserves.

Table 7 presents the results obtained with $B = 5000$ bootstrapping resamples. The confidence intervals were calculated with Equations (46)–(48). The upper endpoints of the confidence intervals obtained for probability levels α = 0, 0.01, 0.05, and 0.1 are the 100%, 99.5%, 97.5%, and 95% estimated percentiles for the reserves, respectively. These quantiles are commonly used to estimate extreme claim scenarios.

Within the total reserves, we distinguished two confidence intervals: R'_α (47) and R_α (48). The former arises from adding the confidence intervals associated with the reserves of each origin year. Thus, as shown in Table 7, for a confidence level of 100% ($\alpha = 0$), we obtained the overall reserves $R'_0 = [63.68, 97.77]$ + [526.48, 628.62] + [1507.29, 1677.46] + [2720.66, 2997.42] + [4641.72, 5105.40] = [9459.82, 10,506.67]. The most prudent reserve value would be 10506.67 since it arises from the sum of the estimates of the value that accumulates 100% probability of the reserves from each origin year. In contrast, R_α arises from the application of (45) in each of the B = 5000 simulations, making it a narrower confidence interval. Table 7 shows that $R_0 = [9533.03, 10,481.08]$, so the prudent value for the reserve based on this confidence interval is 10,481.08.

Table 7 also shows that the reserves of each origin year, and the total reserves can be estimated through a possibility distribution by gathering and fitting successive confidence intervals (46)–(48) from $\alpha = \varepsilon$ ($\varepsilon \approx 0$) to $\alpha = 1$. By applying Definition 5 and Remark 3, we can adjust the reserves of the fifth period to a possibility distribution $\ddot{RO}_5$ whose core is 4826.23 and support [4641.72, 5105.40]. Likewise, Table 6 also shows that we can obtain a possible estimate of overall reserves $\ddot{R}\prime = \sum_{i=1}^{5} \ddot{RO}_i$ whose center is 9899.31, supporting [9459.82, 10,506.67].

Table 4. Run-off triangle of accumulated claims used in this paper.

$i \mid j$	0	1	2	3	4	5
0	1001	1855	2423	2988	3335	3403
1	1113	2103	2774	3422	3844	
2	1265	2433	3233	3977		
3	1490	2873	3883			
4	1725	3261				
5	1889					
f_j	1.899	1.329	1.232	1.120	1.020	

Source: Faculty and Institute of Actuaries [74].

Table 5. Deterministic loss reserves obtained by using the chain-ladder method.

RO_1	RO_2	RO_3	RO_4	RO_5	R
78.38	567.93	1584.67	2842.10	4826.23	9899.31

Table 6. Run-off triangles of observed incremental claims and theoretical incremental claims with chain-ladder development factors (41).

Observed Incremental Claims							Theoretical Incremental Claims						
$i \mid j$	0	1	2	3	4	5	$i \mid j$	0	1	2	3	4	5
0	1001	854	568	565	347	68	0	957.27	861.02	598.44	561.04	357.24	68
1	1113	990	671	648	422		1	1103.37	992.43	689.78	646.66	411.76	
2	1265	1168	800	744			2	1278.49	1149.95	799.26	749.30		
3	1490	1383	1010				3	1538.06	1383.41	961.53			
4	1725	1536					4	1716.81	1544.19				
5	1889						5	1889					

Source: Own elaboration from the Faculty and Institute of Actuaries [74].

Table 7. Estimates of reserves with bootstrapping confidence intervals and chain-ladder development factors.

α	$RO1_\alpha$	$RO2_\alpha$	$RO3_\alpha$	$RO4_\alpha$
1	[78.38, 78.38]	[567.93, 567.93]	[1584.67, 1584.67]	[2842.10, 2842.10]
0.25	[76.94, 79.83]	[564.14, 571.63]	[1577.02, 1592.89]	[2830.92, 2852.36]
0.5	[75.08, 81.62]	[560.41, 576.65]	[1569.64, 1602.17]	[2820.37, 2866.04]
0.75	[71.78, 87.40]	[554.77, 583.26]	[1558.79, 1613.60]	[2804.07, 2883.77]
0.1	[69.09, 91.11]	[548.46, 589.15]	[1547.12, 1625.22]	[2787.26, 2901.24]
0.05	[68.06, 92.87]	[544.98, 593.35]	[1539.65, 1633.24]	[2775.83, 2915.09]
0.01	[66.74, 94.64]	[537.02, 602.96]	[1522.32, 1651.93]	[2751.60, 2942.85]
0	[63.68, 97.77]	[526.48, 628.62]	[1507.29, 1677.46]	[2720.66, 2997.42]

α	$RO5_\alpha$	R'_α	R_α
1	[4826.23, 4826.23]	[9899.31, 9899.31]	[9899.31, 9899.31]
0.25	[4808.51, 4838.96]	[9857.53, 9935.67]	[9866.55, 9930.80]
0.5	[4792.94, 4859.91]	[9818.44, 9986.38]	[9834.38, 9972.34]
0.75	[4768.92, 4887.95]	[9758.33, 10,055.97]	[9786.68, 10,028.49]
0.1	[4739.83, 4918.17]	[9691.76, 10,124.88]	[9733.84, 10,078.13]
0.05	[4721.56, 4937.74]	[9650.07, 10,172.29]	[9702.70, 10,107.32]
0.01	[4682.60, 4994.47]	[9560.29, 10,286.87]	[9644.19, 10,193.22]
0	[4641.72, 5105.40]	[9459.82, 10,506.67]	[9533.03, 10,481.08]

Note: (a) $1-\alpha$ represents the confidence level of the probabilistic confidence interval, which can be interpreted as the α-cut of the equivalent fuzzy number; (b) R'_α is the overall reserve calculated by summing the confidence intervals $\sum_{i=1}^{5} RO_{i\alpha}$ and R_α, which are the confidence intervals of the reserves, by applying bootstrapping.

4.2. Estimating Loss Reserves with a Symmetric Triangular Intuitionistic Fuzzy Chain Ladder

Next, we put into work the methodology developed in Section 3.2, which allows us to estimate the claim reserves with STIFNs, with the data of the run-off triangle in Table 4. We also compare the results obtained with those of the bootstrap estimates using the SCL method in Table 6, which we reinterpret as α-cuts of possibility distributions. Therefore, to obtain the estimates of $\widetilde{F}_{(0)} = \left(F_{(0)}, r_{F_{(0)}}, r^*_{F_{(0)}}\right)$ and $\widetilde{f}_{(0)} = \left(f_{(0)}, r_{f_{(0)}}, r^*_{f_{(0)}}\right)$, we solve the linear programming problem (51), whose constraints are built up with the link ratios of each origin year $i = 1, 2, \ldots, 5$, as shown in Table 8:

$$\underset{F_{(0)}, r_{F_{(0)}}}{\text{minimize}} z_1 = z_2 = r_{F_{(0)}},$$

which is subject to

$$\begin{gathered} F_{(0)} - r_{F_{(0)}} \leq 1.853 \leq F_{(0)} + r_{F_{(0)}}, \\ F_{(0)} - r_{F_{(0)}} \leq 1.889 \leq F_{(0)} + r_{F_{(0)}}, \\ F_{(0)} - r_{F_{(0)}} \leq 1.923 \leq F_{(0)} + r_{F_{(0)}}, \\ F_{(0)} - r_{F_{(0)}} \leq 1.928 \leq F_{(0)} + r_{F_{(0)}}, \\ F_{(0)} - r_{F_{(0)}} \leq 1.890 \leq F_{(0)} + r_{F_{(0)}}, \\ r_{F_{(0)}} \geq 0. \end{gathered}$$

Table 8. Run-off triangle of individual link ratios, $f_{i,j}$, $i = 0, 1, \ldots, 4$; $j = 0, 1, \ldots, n-i-1$.

$i \mid j$	0	1	2	3	4	5
0	1.853	1.306	1.233	1.116	1.020	
1	1.889	1.319	1.234	1.123		
2	1.923	1.329	1.230			
3	1.928	1.352				
4	1.890					
5						

Table 9 shows the STIFNs adjusted to development factors for $j = 0, 1, 2, 3, 4$. Thus, if the estimate $F_{(0)}$ is not prefixed with (41), we obtain $f_{(0)}^{(0)} = 1.891$ and $r_{f_{(0)}}^{(0)} = 0.038$, and (36) and (37) allow us to obtain an optimum uncertainty level for membership functions of development factor $g = 0.14$. Thus, from (38), $r_{f_{(0)}} = 0.044$. The degree of system hesitancy, h, must be estimated subjectively by the decision maker. This may be linked, for example, to the perceived reliability of the data or the predictability of the insurance environment. The calculations in this numerical application are performed with $h = 0.1$, so we obtain $r^*_{f_{(0)}} = 0.049$.

In Section 3.2, we also state that $f_{(0)}^{(0)}$ can be predefined with the deterministic CL shown in Table 4. Therefore, $f_{(0)}^{(0)} = 1.899$, and by using (51), $r_{f_{(j)}}^{(0)} = 0.046$. Equations (36) and (37) allow us to obtain an optimum uncertainty degree $g = 0$. Therefore, from (38) $r_{f_{(0)}} = 0.046$ and by using the hesitancy level $h = 0.1$, $r^*_{f_{(0)}} = 0.051$.

Note that the spreads of $\widetilde{f}_{(4)}$, $r_{f_{(4)}}$ and $r^*_{f_{(4)}}$ cannot be obtained from the sample in Table 4 since only one individual link ratio exists. To fit these spreads, we use (55) and then set the following:

$$r_{f_{(4)}} = \min\left\{\frac{0.0035^2}{0.0067}; 0.0035; 0.0067\right\} = 0.0035$$

$$r^*_{f_{(4)}} = \min\left\{\frac{0.0042^2}{0.0081}; 0.0042; 0.0081\right\} = 0.0042.$$

Table 9. Symmetric triangular intuitionistic fuzzy number estimation of development factors with $h = 0.1$.

Parameters of Intuitionistic Fuzzy Regression (Alternative 1)					
j	0	1	2	3	4
$f_{(j)}$	1.891	1.329	1.232	1.120	1.020
$r^{(0)}_{f_{(j)}}$	0.038	0.023	0.002	0.004	---
g	0.140	0.179	0.457	0.500	---
$r_{f_{(j)}}$	0.044	0.028	0.003	0.007	0.003
$r^*_{f_{(j)}}$	0.049	0.031	0.004	0.009	0.004
Parameters of Intuitionistic Fuzzy Regression (Alternative 2)					
j	0	1	2	3	4
$f_{(j)}$	1.8995	1.3291	1.2321	1.1200	1.0204
$r^{(0)}_{f_{(j)}}$	0.0463	0.0229	0.0020	0.0038	---
g	0.0000	0.0000	0.4179	0.4274	---
$r_{f_{(j)}}$	0.0463	0.0229	0.0035	0.0067	0.0035
$r^*_{f_{(j)}}$	0.0515	0.0255	0.0042	0.0081	0.0042

Table 10 shows the estimates of the overall loss reserves of the intuitionistic claim reserves calculated with the two alternatives proposed in Section 3.2, $\tilde{R}$. Thus, first, we compute the "exact" $\langle\alpha,\beta\rangle$-cuts of both methods. This involves using (58) and (59) to determine the terminal accumulated claims; (63) to find $\tilde{RO}_i$; and $i = 1, 2, \ldots, 5$ and (66) to determine the total value. Table 10 also shows the STIFN approximation of the total reserve, $\tilde{R}^T$, which is obtained using the sequential use of (60), (61), (65), and (67). Table 10 also shows the errors calculated with (27) and (28). Their values suggest that the symmetric triangular approximation is almost perfect. Note that the maximum error lies in the β-cuts of the nonmembership function at $\beta = 1$ and does not exceed 0.15% in any case.

The results of Table 7, which come from bootstrapping resamples, can be interpreted as α-level sets of possibility distributions. Therefore, they can be compared with fuzzy intuitionistic estimates, which are constructed through two possibility distributions. In other words, the probabilistic intervals obtained with bootstrapping and the $\langle\alpha,\beta\rangle$-cuts can be interpreted by the actuary in a similar manner. Thus, according to Table 7, the value of reserves that includes 100% of their possible values could be given as 10,506.67 if we sum the 100th percentile of the reserves associated with all origin years, and 10,481.08 if we consider the 100th percentile of the bootstrap simulations of overall reserves. These results are similar and comparable to those obtained with the membership function of the overall reserves obtained in Table 10. We can observe in the α-cuts of the reserves, R^T_α, that if they are calculated with Alternative 1, their prudent estimate can range between 10,391.15 (at the 0.25-cut) and 10,565.45 (at the 0-cut). The conclusions we can draw from the fit obtained with Alternative 2 are similar, as the upper end of the 0-cut is 10,563.24 and that of the 0.25-cut is 10,397.25.

The β-cuts of the nonmembership functions complement the information provided by the α-cuts of the membership functions, introducing the existence of bipolarity. Thus, in Table 10, Alternative 1 for estimating the development factors offers an upper bound at the 0-cut for the loss reserves of $\overline{R^T}_0 = 10{,}565.45$ and an upper limit of the 1-cut of the nonmembership function, $\overline{R^{T^*}}_1 = 10{,}688.71$. Thus, the use of IFNs in reserve estimation allows us to first obtain an estimation of the most extreme possible scenario (10,565.45), whose adjustment does not use subjective information at any time but rather uses only run-off triangle data. That is, the meaning of the estimation is analogous to that obtained with stochastic simulation or what we would obtain with the use of possibilistic regression. However, the use of IFNs also allows us to obtain an estimation of the scenario that we could classify as potentially more extreme through the higher value of the 1-cut of the nonmembership function. The quantification of this scenario requires the participation of the decision maker, who must indicate a perceived degree of hesitancy, which in this numerical application was $h = 0.1$.

Table 10. $\langle\alpha,\beta\rangle$-cuts of the intuitionistic fuzzy estimates of overall reserves with the two methodologies proposed in this paper.

		Alternative 1				Alternative 2			
α	β	$\underline{R}_\alpha$	$\overline{R}_\alpha$	$\underline{R^*}_\beta$	$\overline{R^*}_\beta$	$\underline{R}_\alpha$	$\overline{R}_\alpha$	$\underline{R^*}_\beta$	$\overline{R^*}_\beta$
1	0	9868.25	9868.25	9868.25	9868.25	9899.31	9899.31	9899.31	9899.31
0.75	0.25	9694.52	10,043.12	9663.92	10,074.16	9733.86	10,065.82	9708.72	10,091.30
0.5	0.5	9521.94	10,219.16	9461.17	10,281.66	9569.46	10,233.40	9519.52	10,284.69
0.25	0.75	9350.50	10,396.36	9260.00	10,490.77	9406.10	10,402.04	9331.70	10,479.50
0	1	9180.19	10,574.72	9060.38	10,701.50	9243.80	10,571.76	9145.26	10,675.72
		$\tilde{R}^T = (9868.25, 697.21, 820.46)$				$\tilde{R}^T = (9899.31, 663.93, 765.15)$			
α	β	$\underline{R^T}_\alpha$	$\overline{R^T}_\alpha$	$\underline{R^{T*}}_\beta$	$\overline{R^{T*}}_\beta$	$\underline{R^T}_\alpha$	$\overline{R^T}_\alpha$	$\underline{R^{T*}}_\beta$	$\overline{R^{T*}}_\beta$
1	0	9868.25	9868.25	9868.25	9868.25	9899.31	9899.31	9899.31	9899.31
0.75	0.25	9693.94	10,042.55	9663.13	10,073.36	9733.33	10,065.29	9708.02	10,090.60
0.5	0.5	9519.64	10,216.85	9458.01	10,278.48	9567.35	10,231.27	9516.73	10,281.88
0.25	0.75	9345.34	10,391.15	9252.90	10,483.59	9401.36	10,397.25	9325.45	10,473.17
0	1	9171.04	10,565.45	9047.78	10,688.71	9235.38	10,563.24	9134.16	10,664.46
α	β	$\underline{\varepsilon}_\alpha$	$\overline{\varepsilon}_\alpha$	$\underline{\varepsilon^*}_\beta$	$\overline{\varepsilon^*}_\beta$	$\underline{\varepsilon}_\alpha$	$\overline{\varepsilon}_\alpha$	$\underline{\varepsilon^*}_\beta$	$\overline{\varepsilon^*}_\beta$
1	0	0.00%	0.00%	0.00%	0.00%	0.00%	0.00%	0.00%	0.00%
0.75	0.25	0.01%	0.01%	0.01%	0.01%	0.01%	0.01%	0.01%	0.01%
0.5	0.5	0.02%	0.02%	0.03%	0.03%	0.02%	0.02%	0.03%	0.03%
0.25	0.75	0.06%	0.05%	0.08%	0.07%	0.05%	0.05%	0.07%	0.06%
0	1	0.10%	0.09%	0.14%	0.12%	0.09%	0.08%	0.12%	0.11%

Note: The errors $\overline{\varepsilon^*}_\beta$, $\overline{\varepsilon}_\alpha$, and $\underline{\varepsilon^*}_\beta$, $\overline{\varepsilon^*}_\beta$ are obtained with (27) and (28).

Using other types of modeling for the underlying link ratios in the run-off triangle, such as LR or adaptive functions, allows us to obtain the same <0,1>-cut and <1,0>-cut as our method if the IFN estimates have the same centers and radii. However, the rest of the $\langle\alpha,\beta\rangle$-cuts, which can be assimilated to structured simulations of the variables involved in the analysis, would change, varying their amplitude. In the case of using adaptive functions, the linear functions used in this paper can be considered as a baseline, with an order of $m = 1$. From this baseline, $m < 1$ implies a dilation of the $\langle\alpha,\beta\rangle$-levels, and thus, they will incorporate more uncertainty. In contrast, $m > 1$ indicates a contraction of the results compared to those obtained with STIFNs. Thus, the $\langle\alpha,\beta\rangle$-cuts will have a smaller width.

Table 11 shows the estimated reserves associated with the five origin years and the overall reserves through the STIFNs. The use of this type of IFN can be very useful for applying the actuarial judgement required to set a definite crisp value for the loss reserves. In the case of total reserves, if we take Alternative 2 from Section 3.2 as a reference for decision making, the most reliable value is 9899.31, which coincides with (40). Possible deviations of up to 663.93 are estimated, and deviations exceeding 765.15 are considered not possible. Regarding deviations between 663.93 and 765.15, there is hesitancy about their feasibility. When considering only the data in the run-off triangle, the conclusion must be that they are not possible. On the other hand, they are possible based on the degree of hesitancy perceived by the decision maker.

Table 11. Symmetrical triangular intuitionistic fuzzy estimates of reserves.

	Alternative 1	Alternative 2
$\tilde{RO}_1^T$	(78.38, 12.28, 15.05)	(78.38, 13.34, 16.11)
$\tilde{RO}_2^T$	(567.93, 43.40, 53.90)	(567.93, 42.66, 51.62)
$\tilde{RO}_3^T$	(1584.67, 66.38, 82.21)	(1584.67, 66.72, 80.69)
$\tilde{RO}_3^T$	(2842.10, 200.87, 236.11)	(2842.10, 179.74, 207.03)
$\tilde{RO}_4^T$	(4795.16, 374.28, 433.19)	(4826.23, 361.47, 409.70)
$\tilde{R}$	(9868.25, 697.21, 820.46)	(9899.31, 663.93, 765.15)

5. Conclusions and Further Research

The determination of insurance loss reserves must be prudent, necessitating the quantification of their expected value and potential deviations from that value. To ascertain the most plausible value, a statistical method such as the chain-ladder (CL) method is utilized to estimate the expected claim evolution. Subsequently, it is necessary to estimate possible deviations from these values with greater reliability. The contributions of this work include providing tools for estimating and interpreting such values using fuzzy set theory and intuitionistic fuzzy set theory.

The first contribution of this work is to show that the information obtained through stochastic models such as bootstrapping and the use of conventional fuzzy numbers are similar. In fact, we can reinterpret the value and variability of reserves obtained with the stochastic CL (SCL) methodology with possibility distributions. Therefore, both instruments capture epistemic uncertainty.

The second and main contribution of our work is the generalization of developments in claim reserving with fuzzy numbers to the use of intuitionistic fuzzy numbers (IFNs). This tool allows the introduction of bipolar information about possible reserve variability into the estimation, i.e., both "positive" information about feasible parameter values and negative information about those that cannot be taken in any case.

This work assumes that the parameters governing the evolution of claims are symmetrical and triangular IFNs (STIFNs). Special attention is given to the approximation of each IFN to be of the same nature as the results that arise from its functional handling. Linear shapes often provide effective resolution in practical applications of fuzzy set theory. Moreover, symmetry often allows for a good balance between parsimony and comprehensiveness in capturing available information and facilitates interpretability of the results by end-users who may not necessarily have knowledge of fuzzy logic. The value of loss reserves when the development factors are estimated using the STIFN technique can be easily approximated through the most likely scenario, obtained with conventional chain-ladder methodology, and by evaluating the deviations from this value with the gradient function of the terminal value of claims from each origin year in the spreads of the membership and nonmembership functions of the link ratios.

The results provided by the proposed method can be very useful in actuarial practice since they can be interpreted very intuitively by the person responsible for establishing reserves, as there is no need for knowledge of fuzzy set theory. While the center of an STIFN quantifies, in a very synthetic way, the most reliable value of reserves, the two spreads provide an approximation of the maximum deviations from this value, the maximum achievable deviation, and the first not-achievable deviation. On the other hand, representing reserves through $\langle\alpha, \beta\rangle$-cuts allows for the structuring of simulations on their appropriate value in multiple scenarios, which can be of great help to decision makers.

Certainly, the limitation of using STIFNs is that they do not account for asymmetry in the link ratios, and similarly, they do not allow for the introduction of more refined calibration of possibility distributions, such as adaptive membership functions. This latter issue implies that introducing nuances, such as concentration and dilation, is not possible.

However, the proposed scheme can be adapted to accommodate more sophisticated forms of membership and nonmembership functions.

Our extension of intuitionistic regression can be applied in other financial and actuarial contexts where possibilistic regression has already been used, such as, for example, estimating the implied moments of options [76,77]. A natural extension of this work would involve introducing intuitionistic uncertainty into the analysis of non-life insurance claims, expanding the results obtained with fuzzy numbers to calculate discounted reserves [78], the discounted values of non-life insurance liabilities [79], or the terminal values of an insurance company [80,81].

Funding: This research benefited from the Research Project of the Spanish Science and Technology Ministry "Sostenibilidad, digitalizacion e innovacion: nuevos retos en el derecho del seguro" (PID2020-117169GB-I00).

Institutional Review Board Statement: Not applicable.

Data Availability Statement: The data used in the paper have been referenced.

Conflicts of Interest: The authors declare no conflicts of interest.

References

1. Hindley, D. Introduction. In *Claims Reserving in General Insurance. International Series on Actuarial Science*; Hindley, D., Ed.; Cambridge University Press: Cambridge, UK, 2017; pp. 1–15.
2. Hindley, D. Stochastic Reserving Methods. In *Claims Reserving in General Insurance. International Series on Actuarial Science*; Hindley, D., Ed.; Cambridge University Press: Cambridge, UK, 2017; pp. 146–319.
3. Andrés Sánchez, J. Calculating insurance claim reserves with fuzzy regression. *Fuzzy Sets Syst.* **2006**, *157*, 3091–3108. [CrossRef]
4. Bastos, I.S.; Vana, L.B.; Novo, C.C. Estimating IBNR claim reserves using Gaussian Fuzzy Numbers. *Context. Rev. Cont. Econ. Gest.* **2023**, *21*, e83343. [CrossRef]
5. Shapiro, A.F. Fuzzy logic in insurance. *Insur. Math. Econ.* **2004**, *35*, 399–424. [CrossRef]
6. Derrig, R.A.; Ostaszewski, K.M. Fuzzy Set Theory. In *Encyclopedia of Actuarial Science*; Teugels, J.F., Sundt, B., Asmussen, S., Eds.; John Willey and Sons Ltd.: Chichester, NH, USA, 2006.
7. Dubois, D.; Prade, H. The three semantics of fuzzy sets. *Fuzzy Sets Syst.* **1997**, *90*, 141–150. [CrossRef]
8. Hindley, D. Data. In *Claims Reserving in General Insurance. International Series on Actuarial Science*; Hindley, D., Ed.; Cambridge University Press: Cambridge, UK, 2017; pp. 16–39.
9. Straub, E. *Nonlife Insurance Mathematics*; Springer: Berlin/Heidelberg, Germany, 1997; pp. 102–115.
10. Schmidt, K.D.; Zocher, M. Additive Method. In *Handbook on Loss Reserving. EAA Series*; Radtke, M., Schmidt, K.D., Schnaus, A., Eds.; Springer: Cologne, Germany, 2016.
11. Mack, T. Distribution-free Calculation of the Standard Error of Chain Ladder Reserve Estimates. *Astin Bullet.* **1993**, *23*, 213–225. [CrossRef]
12. England, P.D.; Verrall, R. Analytic and bootstrap estimates of prediction errors in claims reserving. *Insur. Math. Econ.* **1999**, *25*, 281–293. [CrossRef]
13. Andrés-Sanchez, J.; Gómez, A.T. Applications of fuzzy regression in actuarial analysis. *J. Risk Insur.* **2003**, *70*, 665–699. [CrossRef]
14. Heberle, J.; Thomas, A. Combining chain-ladder claims reserving with fuzzy numbers. *Insur. Math. Econ.* **2014**, *55*, 96–104. [CrossRef]
15. Heberle, J.; Thomas, A. The fuzzy Bornhuetter–Ferguson method: An approach with fuzzy numbers. *Ann. Actuar. Sci.* **2016**, *10*, 303–321. [CrossRef]
16. Taylor, G.C. Separation of inflation and other effects from the distribution of nonlife insurance claim delays. *Astin Bullet.* **1977**, *10*, 219–230. [CrossRef]
17. Kremer, E. IBNR-claims and the two-way model of ANOVA. *Scand. Actuar. J.* **1982**, *1*, 47–55. [CrossRef]
18. Yan, C.; Liu, T.; Dong, Q.; Liu, W. Payments Per Claim Method Based on Fuzzy Numbers. In Proceedings of the 14th International Conference on Natural Computation, Fuzzy Systems and Knowledge Discovery (ICNC-FSKD), Huangshan, China, 28–30 July 2018; pp. 643–648.
19. Kim, J.H.; Kim, J. Fuzzy regression towards a general insurance application. *J. Appl. Math. Inform.* **2014**, *32*, 343–357. [CrossRef]
20. Woundjiagué, A.; Mbele Bidima, M.L.D.; Waweru Mwangi, R. An Estimation of a Hybrid Log-Poisson Regression Using a Quadratic Optimization Program for Optimal Loss Reserving in Insurance. *Adv. Fuzzy Syst.* **2019**, 1393946. [CrossRef]
21. Apaydin, A.; Baser, F. Hybrid fuzzy least-squares regression analysis in claims reserving with geometric separation method. *Insur. Math. Econ.* **2010**, *47*, 113–122. [CrossRef]
22. Woundjiagué, A.; Mbele Bidima, M.L.D.; Waweru Mwangi, R. A fuzzy least-squares estimation of a hybrid log-Poisson regression and its goodness of fit for optimal loss reserves in insurance. *Int. J. Fuzzy Syst.* **2019**, *21*, 930–944.

23. Andrés-Sánchez, J. Claim reserving with fuzzy regression and Taylor's geometric separation method. *Insur. Math. Econ.* **2007**, *40*, 145–163. [CrossRef]
24. Yan, C.; Liu, Q.; Liu, J.; Liu, W.; Li, M.; Qi, M. Payments per claim model of outstanding claims reserve based on fuzzy linear regression. *Int. J. Fuzzy Syst.* **2019**, *21*, 1950–1960. [CrossRef]
25. Andrés-Sánchez, J. Claim reserving with fuzzy regression and the two ways of ANOVA. *Appl. Soft Comput.* **2012**, *12*, 2435–2441. [CrossRef]
26. Baser, F.; Apaydin, A. Calculating insurance claim reserves with hybrid fuzzy least squares regression analysis. *Gazi Univ. J. Sci.* **2010**, *23*, 163–170.
27. Dubois, D.; Prade, H. An overview of the asymmetric bipolar representation of positive and negative information in possibility theory. *Fuzzy Sets Syst.* **2009**, *160*, 1355–1366. [CrossRef]
28. Dubois, D.; Prade, H. Gradualness, uncertainty and bipolarity: Making sense of fuzzy sets. *Fuzzy Sets Syst.* **2012**, *192*, 3–24. [CrossRef]
29. Mitchell, H.B. Ranking-intuitionistic fuzzy numbers. *Int. J. Uncertain. Fuzziness Knowl.-Based Syst* **2004**, *12*, 377–386. [CrossRef]
30. Atanassov, K.T. Intuitionistic fuzzy sets. *Fuzzy Sets Syst.* **1986**, *20*, 87–96. [CrossRef]
31. Atanassov, K.T. More on intuitionistic fuzzy sets. *Fuzzy Sets Syst.* **1989**, *33*, 37–45. [CrossRef]
32. Kumar, G.; Bajaj, R.K. Implementation of intuitionistic fuzzy approach in maximizing net present value. *Int. J. Math. Comput. Sci.* **2014**, *8*, 1069–1073.
33. Kahraman, C.; Çevik Onar, S.; Öztayşi, B. Engineering economic analyses using intuitionistic and hesitant fuzzy sets. *J. Intell. Fuzzy Syst.* **2015**, *29*, 1151–1168. [CrossRef]
34. Boltürk, E.; Kahraman, C. Interval-valued and circular intuitionistic fuzzy present worth analyses. *Informatica* **2022**, *33*, 693–711. [CrossRef]
35. Haktanır, E.; Kahraman, C. Intuitionistic fuzzy risk adjusted discount rate and certainty equivalent methods for risky projects. *Int. J. Prod. Econ.* **2023**, *257*, 108757. [CrossRef]
36. Wu, L.; Liu, J.F.; Wang, J.T.; Zhuang, Y.M. Pricing for a basket of LCDS under fuzzy environments. *SpringerPlus* **2016**, *5*, 1–12. [CrossRef]
37. Ersen, H.Y.; Tas, O.; Kahraman, C. Intuitionistic fuzzy real-options theory and its application to solar energy investment projects. *Eng. Econ.* **2018**, *29*, 140–150. [CrossRef]
38. Ersen, H.Y.; Tas, O.; Ugurlu, U. Solar energy investment valuation with intuitionistic fuzzy trinomial lattice real option model. *IEEE Trans. Eng. Manag.* **2023**, *70*, 2584–2593. [CrossRef]
39. Puri, J.; Yadav, S.P. Intuitionistic fuzzy data envelopment analysis: An application to the banking sector in India. *Expert Syst. Appl.* **2015**, *42*, 4982–4998. [CrossRef]
40. Arya, A.; Yadav, S.P. Development of intuitionistic fuzzy data envelopment analysis models and intuitionistic fuzzy input–output targets. *Soft Comp.* **2019**, *23*, 8975–8993. [CrossRef]
41. Davoudabadi, R.; Mousavi, S.M.; Mohagheghi, V. A new decision model based on DEA and simulation to evaluate renewable energy projects under interval-valued intuitionistic fuzzy uncertainty. *Renew. Energ.* **2021**, *164*, 1588–1601. [CrossRef]
42. Uzhga-Rebrov, O.; Grabusts, P. Methodology for Environmental Risk Analysis Based on Intuitionistic Fuzzy Values. *Risks* **2023**, *11*, 88. [CrossRef]
43. Andrés-Sánchez, J. Pricing Life Contingencies Linked to Impaired Life Expectancies Using Intuitionistic Fuzzy Parameters. *Risks* **2024**, *12*, 29. [CrossRef]
44. Koissi, M.C.; Shapiro, A.F. Fuzzy formulation of the Lee–Carter model for mortality forecasting. *Insur. Math. Econ.* **2006**, *39*, 287–309. [CrossRef]
45. Szymański, A.; Rossa, A. The modified fuzzy mortality model based on the algebra of ordered fuzzy numbers. *Biom. J.* **2021**, *63*, 671–689. [CrossRef]
46. Parvathi, R.; Malathi, C.; Akram, M.; Atanassov, K. Intuitionistic fuzzy linear regression analysis. *Fuzzy Optim Decis Making* **2013**, *12*, 215–229. [CrossRef]
47. Tanaka, H.; Ishibuchi, H. A possibilistic regression analysis based on linear programming. In *Fuzzy Regression Analysis*; Kacprzuk, J., Fedrizzi, M., Eds.; Physica-Verlag: Heildelberg, Germany, 1992; pp. 47–60.
48. Lee, H.; Tanaka, H. Upper and lower approximation models in interval regression using regression quantile techniques. *Eur. J. Oper. Res.* **1999**, *116*, 653–666. [CrossRef]
49. Savic, D.; Predrycz, W. Fuzzy linear models: Construction and evaluation. In *Fuzzy Regression Analysis*; Kacprzuk, J., Fedrizzi, M., Eds.; Physica-Verlag: Heildelberg, Germany, 1992; pp. 91–100.
50. Zadeh, L.A. Fuzzy Sets. *Inf. Control* **1965**, *8*, 338–353. [CrossRef]
51. Dubois, D.; Prade, H. Fuzzy numbers: An overview. *Read. Fuzzy Sets Intell. Syst.* **1993**, 112–148.
52. Kreinovich, V.; Kosheleva, O.; Shahbazova, S.N. Why Triangular and Trapezoid Membership Functions: A Simple Explanation. In *Recent Developments in Fuzzy Logic and Fuzzy Sets. Studies in Fuzziness and Soft Computing*; Shahbazova, S., Sugeno, M., Kacprzyk, J., Eds.; Springer: Cologne, Germany, 2020; Volume 391, pp. 25–51.
53. Mauris, G.; Lasserre, V.; Foulloy, L. A fuzzy approach for the expression of uncertainty in measurement. *Measurement* **2001**, *29*, 165–177. [CrossRef]

54. Dubois, D.; Folloy, L.; Mauris, G.; Prade, H. Probability–possibility transformations, triangular fuzzy sets, and probabilistic inequalities. *Reliab. Comput.* **2004**, *10*, 273–297. [CrossRef]
55. Andrés-Sánchez, J.; Gonzalez-Vila, L.G.V. The valuation of life contingencies: A symmetrical triangular fuzzy approximation. *Insur. Math. Econ.* **2017**, *72*, 83–94. [CrossRef]
56. Mauris, G. Possibility distributions: A unified representation of usual direct-probability-based parameter estimation methods. *Int. J. Approx. Reason.* **2011**, *52*, 1232–1242. [CrossRef]
57. Couso, I.; Montes, S.; Gil, P. The necessity of the strong α-cuts of a fuzzy set. *Int. J. Uncertain. Fuzziness Knowl. Based Syst.* **2001**, *9*, 249–262. [CrossRef]
58. Buckley, J.J. Fuzzy statistics: Regression and prediction. *Soft Comput.* **2005**, *9*, 769–775. [CrossRef]
59. Sfiris, D.S.; Papadopoulos, B.K. Non-asymptotic fuzzy estimators based on confidence intervals. *Inf. Sci.* **2014**, *279*, 446–459. [CrossRef]
60. Dubois, D.; Prade, H. Practical methods for constructing possibility distributions. *Inte. J. Intell. Syst.* **2016**, *31*, 215–239. [CrossRef]
61. Adjenughwure, K.; Papadopoulos, B. Fuzzy-statistical prediction intervals from crisp regression models. *Evolv. Syst.* **2020**, *11*, 201–213. [CrossRef]
62. Yuan, X.H.; Li, H.X.; Zhang, C. The theory of intuitionistic fuzzy sets based on the intuitionistic fuzzy special sets. *Inf. Sci.* **2014**, *277*, 284–298. [CrossRef]
63. Kumar, P.S.; Hussain, R.J. A method for solving unbalanced intuitionistic fuzzy transportation problems. *Notes Intuition. Fuzzy Sets* **2015**, *21*, 54–65.
64. Mukherjee, A.K.; Gazi, K.H.; Salahshour, S.; Ghosh, A.; Mondal, S.P. A brief analysis and interpretation on arithmetic operations of fuzzy numbers. *Res. Contr. Optim.* **2023**, *13*, 100312. [CrossRef]
65. Bayeg, S.; Mert, R. On intuitionistic fuzzy version of Zadeh's extension principle. *Notes Intuition. Fuzzy Sets* **2021**, *27*, 9–17. [CrossRef]
66. Buckley, J.J.; Qu, Y. On using α-cuts to evaluate fuzzy equations. *Fuzzy Sets Syst.* **1990**, *38*, 309–312. [CrossRef]
67. Grzegorzewski, P.; Pasternak-Winiarska, K. Natural trapezoidal approximations of fuzzy numbers. *Fuzzy Sets Syst.* **2014**, *250*, 90–109. [CrossRef]
68. Andrés-Sánchez, J.; González-Vila Puchades, L. Life settlement pricing with fuzzy parameters. *Appl. Soft Comput.* **2023**, *148*, 110924. [CrossRef]
69. Chukhrova, N.; Johannssen, A. Fuzzy regression analysis: Systematic review and bibliography. *Appl. Soft Comput.* **2019**, *84*, 105708. [CrossRef]
70. Arefi, M.; Taheri, S.M. Least-Squares Regression Based on Atanassov's Intuitionistic Fuzzy Inputs–Outputs and Atanassov's Intuitionistic Fuzzy Parameters. *IEEE Trans. Fuzzy. Syst.* **2014**, *23*, 1142–1154. [CrossRef]
71. Koenker, R.; Bassett Jr, G. Regression quantiles. *Econometrica* **1978**, *46*, 33–50. [CrossRef]
72. Ishibuchi, H.; Nii, M. Fuzzy regression using asymmetric fuzzy coefficients and fuzzified neural networks. *Fuzzy Sets Syst.* **2001**, *119*, 273–290. [CrossRef]
73. Chen, F.; Chen, Y.; Zhou, J.; Liu, Y. Optimizing h value for fuzzy linear regression with asymmetric triangular fuzzy coeffi-cients. *Eng. Appl. Artif. Intell.* **2016**, *47*, 16–24. [CrossRef]
74. The Faculty and Institute of Actuaries. *Claims Reserving Manual*, 2nd ed.; The Faculty and Institute of Actuaries: London, UK, 1997.
75. Schmidt, K.D.; Zocher, M. The Bornhuetter-Ferguson. *Variance* **2008**, *2*, 85–110. Available online: https://www.casact.org/sites/default/files/2021-07/Bornhuetter-Ferguson-Schmidt-Zocher.pdf (accessed on 9 March 2024).
76. Muzzioli, S.; Gambarelli, L.; De Baets, B. Option implied moments obtained through fuzzy regression. *Fuzzy Optim. Decis. Making* **2020**, *19*, 211–238. [CrossRef]
77. Muzzioli, S.; Ruggieri, A.; De Baets, B. A comparison of fuzzy regression methods for the estimation of the implied volatility smile function. *Fuzzy Sets Syst.* **2015**, *266*, 131–143. [CrossRef]
78. Andrés-Sánchez, J. Fuzzy claim reserving in nonlife insurance. *Comput. Sci. Inf. Syst.* **2014**, *11*, 825–838.
79. Cummins, D.J.; Derrig, R.A. Fuzzy financial pricing of property-liability insurance. *N. Am. Actuar. J.* **1997**, *1*, 21–40. [CrossRef]
80. Mircea, I.; Covrig, M. A discrete time insurance model with reinvested surplus and a fuzzy number interest rate. *Procedia Econ. Financ.* **2015**, *32*, 1005–1011. [CrossRef]
81. Ungureanu, D.; Vernic, R. On a fuzzy cash flow model with insurance applications. *Decis. Econ. Financ.* **2015**, *38*, 39–54. [CrossRef]

mathematics

Article

Dominations in Intutionistic Fuzzy Directed Graphs with Applications towards Influential Graphs

Hao Guan [1,2], Waheed Ahmad Khan [3,*], Amna Fida [3], Khadija Ali [3], Jana Shafi [4] and Aysha Khan [5]

1 Institute of Computing Science and Technology, Guangzhou University, Guangzhou 510006, China; guanhao@gzhu.edu.cn
2 School of Computer Science of Information Technology, Qiannan Normal University for Nationalities, Duyun 558000, China
3 Division of Science and Technology, Department of Mathematics, University of Education Lahore, Attock Campus, Attock 43600, Pakistan; bsf1800783@ue.edu.pk (A.F.); bsf1800810@ue.edu.pk (K.A.)
4 Department of Computer Engineering and Information, College of Engineering in Wadi Alddawasir, Prince Sattam Bin Abdulaziz University, Wadi Alddawasir 11991, Saudi Arabia; j.jana@psau.edu.sa
5 Department of Mathematics, Prince Sattam Bin Abdulaziz University, Al-Kharj 16278, Saudi Arabia; a.aysha@psau.edu.sa
* Correspondence: sirwak2003@yahoo.com

Abstract: In this manuscript, we introduce a few new types of dominations in intuitionistic fuzzy directed graphs (IFDGs) based on different types of strong arcs (SAs). Our work is not only a direct extension of domination in directed fuzzy graphs (DFGs) but also fills the gap that exists in the literature regarding the dominations in different extended forms of fuzzy graphs (FGs). In the beginning, we introduce several types of strong arcs in IFDGs, like semi-β strong arcs, semi-δ strong arcs, etc. Then, we introduce the concepts of domination in IFDGs based on these strong arcs and discuss its various useful characteristics. Moreover, the dominating set (DS), minimal dominating set (MDS), etc., are described with some fascinating results. We also introduce the concept of an independent set in IFDGs and investigate its relations with the DS, minimal independent set (MIS) and MDS. We also provide numerous important characterizations of domination in IFDGs based on minimal and maximal dominating sets. In this context, we discuss the lower and upper dominations of some IFDGs. In addition, we introduce the terms status and structurally equivalent and examine a few relationships with the dominations in IFDGs. Finally, we investigate the most expert (influential) person in the organization by utilizing the concepts of domination in IFGs.

Keywords: IFDGs; strong arcs; domination in IFDG; independent set; minimal and maximal dominating sets

MSC: 03E72; 05C72

Citation: Guan, H.; Khan, W.A.; Fida, A.; Ali, K.; Shafi, J.; Khan, A. Dominations in Intutionistic Fuzzy Directed Graphs with Applications towards Influential Graphs. *Mathematics* **2024**, *12*, 872. https://doi.org/10.3390/math12060872

Academic Editor: Michael Voskoglou

Received: 5 February 2024
Revised: 5 March 2024
Accepted: 8 March 2024
Published: 16 March 2024

1. Introduction

The term fuzzy sets (FSs) was first introduced by Zadeh [1] in 1965. The theory of FSs has become useful in different areas, such as management sciences, medical and life sciences, management sciences, social sciences, statistics, artificial intelligence, multiagent systems, expert systems, etc. In FSs, each element has some membership value allocated from the interval [0, 1]. Due to the flexibility of FSs, numerous generalizations of them has been introduced. The very first generalization of FSs, named interval-valued fuzzy sets (IVFSs), was introduced by Zadeh in [2]. In IVFSs, the membership value is a subinterval of [0, 1] instead of a fixed number. Since the concept of the non-membership value is not considered in FSs, it was also observed that in order to describe the particular type of information, one component (i.e., a membership value) is not sufficient. To explain such circumstances, Atanassov [3] introduced the concept of intuitionistic fuzzy sets (IFs), in which both the membership and non-membership values are considered, with the restriction that their sum is less than 1.

On the other hand, fuzzy logic becomes more beneficial and important in describing real-life problems with uncertainties. Recently, different types of networking have been dealt with through fuzzy logic. Consequently, fuzzy graph (FG) theory has become an important mathematical tool to address real-time issues more accurately. This new concept includes the fuzziness of the vertices and edges in fuzzy graphs (FGs). FGs were first introduced by Rosenfeld [4] and Kauffman [5]. They also introduced various graph theoretic tools, such as paths, cycles, bridges, trees, connectedness, etc., in their articles. As compared to classical graph theory, FGs are more effective because of their flexibility. In the literature, numerous applications of FGs have been investigated because of their flexibility. In the theory of FGs, many new terms were introduced by Bhattacharya [6]. In [7], some new operations were initiated and applied to FGs. The notion of Cayley IVFGs was described in [8]. In [9], the term complement of FGs was discussed. Poulik et al. [10] shifted the term average connectivity from classical graphs to FGs. Overall, FGs have become useful in several fields, like networking, modelling, social sciences, the recognition of different patterns, etc. Among the other types of FGs, fuzzy directed graphs (FDGs) or fuzzy digraphs have their own importance. Mordeson and Nair [11] introduced the notion of FDG. FDGs were further discussed in [12]. Numerous new terms related to FDGs, along with their applications, have been explored. Akram, Muhammad et al. [13] discussed the concept of bipolar FDGs in decision support systems. In continuation, a generalization of FGs, termed intuitionistic fuzzy graphs (IFGs), was introduced in [14]. Similarly, the notion of complex intuitionistic fuzzy graphs, along with their application to networking, was explored in [15]. Akram et al. [16–18] introduced many new terms, which included strong IFGs, IF hypergraphs, IF cycles, and IF trees. Afterwards, Akram et al. [19] introduced the concept of intuitionistic fuzzy digraphs (IFDGs) and their application in decision support systems. The application of IFGs in a water supply system was explored in [20]. Interval-valued intuitionistic fuzzy competition graphs were explored in [21]. IVIF-(s, t) graphs were discussed in [22,23]. The concepts of m-polar IFGs were introduced in [24]. Singh, Suneet et al. [25] discussed an interval-valued intuitionistic fuzzy directed graph with application towards transportation systems. Nithyanandham et al. [26] discussed an energy-based bipolar IFDG and presented its application in decision making theory. Some of the main components of picture fuzzy graphs (PFGs) were explored in [27].

In classical graph theory, the term domination has its own importance. Many researchers have presented several extended forms of domination in graphs, such as double Roman domination [28], triple Roman domination [29], broadcast domination [30], outer-convex domination [31], paired domination [32], etc. Kosari and Asgharsharghi introduced different domination numbers of graphs [33]. The notion of influence graphs has also been described in the literature to solve "influential problems" like the influence maximization problem for unknown social networks [34,35], etc. Alternatively, the term domination in FGs based on effective edges was introduced in [36]. The domination in FGs using strong arcs (SAs) was discussed by Nagoorgani et al. [37]. The notion of global domination in FGs based on SAs was discussed in [38]. Similarly, Shanmugam et al. [39] presented the idea of bridge domination in FGs. In [40], domination in FDGs was examined. Recently, in [41], the notions of broadcasts and dominating broadcasts were introduced, and they also provided applications of these concepts in a transportation model. The concept of domination in rough fuzzy digraphs was described by [42]. Similarly, domination in several types of vague graphs was discussed in [43–46]. Domination in IFGs was discussed by Parvathi [47], while double domination in IFGs was described by Nagoorgani [48]. The concept of domination in bipolar picture fuzzy graphs (BPPFGs) with application in social networks was introduced in [49].

In this study, we introduce various types of domination based on different strong arcs in intuitionistic fuzzy digraphs (IFDGs). Firstly, we describe various types of strong arcs in IFDGs. Then, based on these arcs, we introduce the concepts of domination in IFDGs.

These concepts are direct generalizations of the dominations in FDGs. We also provide some important characteristics of dominations in IFDGs based on minimal and maximal dominating sets. In addition, we introduce the terms status, structurally equivalent, and the lower and upper domination number, etc., in the framework of IFDGs. At the end, we provide the application of domination in IFDGs towards an organization in order to identify the most influential person through domination in IFDGs.

Motivations and Novelty:

In an IFG, the membership and non-membership values extend the domain as compared to the other extensions of FGs and make the circumstances more flexible to express problems with uncertainties. The term domination in FGs, IFGs, and BPFGs has been established in the literature, which motivated us to extend these terms towards IFDGs, along with their application. Our study also fills the gaps existing in the literature. We can summarize the novelty of our work as in the following points.

1. Firstly, we introduce different types of strong arcs in IFDGs, like semi-β strong arcs, semi-δ strong arcs, etc. Then, we introduce the concepts of domination in IFDGs based on these strong arcs. Different characterizations of some special IFDGs are also explored.
2. We also provide numerous important characterizations of domination in IFDGs based on minimal and maximal dominating sets. The lower and upper dominations of some IFDGs are also investigated.
3. We introduce the terms status and structurally equivalent and find few relationships with the dominations in IFDGs.
4. To demonstrate the usefulness of the terms that we have introduced, we offer their application in the context of influence graphs.

This article consists of five sections. In Section 2, we add some useful definitions and explanations related to FSs, FGs, FDGs, IFGs, etc. In Section 3, we introduce the concept of domination in an intuitionistic fuzzy digraph (IFDG) based on different types of SAs, which is a direct generalization of domination in FDGs. In the beginning, we introduce different types of SAs, like semi-β strong arcs, semi-δ strong arcs, etc. Then, we provide some important characterizations of domination in IFDGs based on minimal and maximal dominating sets. We also introduce the terms status, structurally equivalent, and the lower and upper domination number, etc., in the framework of IFDGs. At the end, we provide the application of domination in IFDGs towards an organization in order to identify the most influential person through domination in IFDGs. In Section 5, we provide the conclusions, which also include the future prospects of our work.

2. Preliminaries

In this section, we provide some useful terms related to FSs and FGs and their extensions. For the basics of classical graph theory, one may consult [50].

Definition 1 ([49]). *An FS F described on a non-empty set Y is a pair $F = \{(s,\sigma(s)) : s \in Y, \sigma(s) \in [0, 1]\}$, where $\sigma(s)$ is the membership function from Y to [0, 1].*

Definition 2 ([51]). *An intutionistic fuzzy set (IFS) N on a non-empty set Y is a pair $N = (\beta_N, \delta_N) : Y \to [0, 1]$, where $\beta_N : Y \to [0, 1]$ is said to be the degree of membership and $\delta_N : Y \to [0, 1]$ is the degree of non-membership satisfying the condition $0 \leq \beta_N(s) + \delta_N(s) \leq 1$, for all $s \in Y$.*

Definition 3 ([51]). *A function $N = (\beta_N, \delta_N) : Y \times Y \to [0, 1] \times [0, 1]$ is said to be an intutionistic fuzzy relation (IFR) on Y if $\beta_N(s,t) + \delta_N(s,t) \leq 1$, for all $(s,t) \in Y \times Y$.*

Definition 4 ([51]). *Let $N = (\beta_N, \delta_N)$ and $M = (\beta_M, \delta_M)$ be IFSs on the set Y. If $N = (\beta_N, \delta_N)$ is an IFR on a set Y, then $N = (\beta_N, \delta_N)$ is called an IFR on $M = (\beta_M, \beta_M)$, if $\beta_N(s,t) \leq min\{\beta_M(s), \delta_M(t)\}$ and $\delta_N(s,t) \geq max\{\delta_M(s), \delta_M(t)\}$, for all $s, t \in Y$. An IFR N on Y is said* *to be symmetric if $\beta_N(s,t) = \beta_N(t,s)$ and $\delta_N(s,t) = \delta_N(t,s)$, for all $s,t \in Y$.*

Definition 5 ([49])**.** *A fuzzy graph (FG) on a set V is a pair $G^\bullet = (A,B)$, where $A = \{\rho_A\}$ and $B = \{\rho_B\}$, where $\rho_A : V \to [0,1]$ and $\rho_B : V \times V \to [0,1]$ with $\rho_B(s,t) \leq \rho_A(s) \wedge \rho_A(t)$, for all $s,t \in V$.*

Definition 6 ([49])**.** *Let $G^\bullet = (A,B)$, where $A = \{\rho_A\}$ and $B = \{\rho_B\}$, is the FG of a crisp graph $G=(V,E)$. We say that s dominates t in the $G^\bullet$, if $\rho_B(st) = \rho_A(s) \wedge \rho_A(t)$, for $s,t \in V$. A subset V_1 of V is said to be a dominating set (DS) of the FG $G^\bullet$ if, for each $s \in V_1$, there is $t \in V - V_1$ such that s dominates t. A DS A_1 in an FG $G^\bullet$ is a minimal dominating set (MDS) if A_1 has no proper dominating subset. A DS in FG $G^\bullet$ having the minimum (fuzzy) cardinality is known as the domination number (DN) of FG $G^\bullet$.*

Definition 7 ([49])**.** *Let $G^\bullet$ be an FG without an isolated vertex. Then, the DS V_1 is known as the total dominating set (TDS) if a vertex in V_1 dominates all vertices of V. The minimum (fuzzy) cardinality of the TDS is known as the total domination number (TDN).*

Definition 8 ([49])**.** *Two vertices s and t are called neighbors (Ns) in an FG $G^\bullet$ if $\rho(s,t) > 0$. The set of all Ns of s is denoted by $Nbhd(s)$.*

Definition 9 ([49])**.** *A vertex s is known as a strong neighbor (SN) if the arc (s,t) is strong. The collection of all strong neighbors (SNs) of s is said to be a strong neighborhood (SNbhd) of s and is represented by $Nbhd_S(s)$.*

Definition 10. *The closed strong neighborhood (CSNbhd) is defined as $Nbhd_S[s] = Nbhd_S(s) \cup \{s\}$.*

Definition 11 ([51])**.** *An IFG with underlying set V is described as $\hat{G} = (N,M)$, where $N = \{\beta_N, \delta_N\}$ and $M = \{\beta_M, \delta_M\}$, where*
(i) the function $\beta_N : V \to [0,1]$ represents the degree of membership of any element $s \in V$ and $\delta_N : V \to [0,1]$ represents the degree of non-membership of any element $s \in V$ such that $\beta_N(s) + \delta_N(s) \leq 1$, for all $s \in V$;
(ii) the function $\beta_M : E \subseteq V \times V \to [0,1]$ is the degree of membership of any element $(s,t) \in E$, while $\delta_M : E \subseteq V \times V \to [0,1]$ is the degree of non-membership of any element $(s,t) \in E$ satisfying $\beta_M(s,t) \leq min\{\beta_N(s), \beta_N(t)\}$ and $\delta_M(s,t) \geq max\{\delta_N(s), \delta_N(t)\}$ such that $0 \leq \delta_M(s,t) + \delta_M(s,t) \leq 1$, for all $(s,t) \in E$.

Definition 12 ([51])**.** *If s,t are any two vertices of the IFG $\hat{G} = (N,M)$, where $N = \{\beta_N, \delta_N\}$ and $M = \{\beta_M, \delta_M\}$, then the β_M-strength of connectedness between s and t is $\beta_M^\infty(s,t)$, where*

$$\beta_M^\infty(s,t) = sup\{\beta_M^k : k = 0,1,2,3......n\}$$

and the δ_M-strength of connectedness between s and t is

$$\delta_M^\infty(s,t) = inf\{\delta_M^k : k = 0,1,2,3......n\}.$$

If y and z are connected by means of paths of length k, then

$$\beta_M^k(s,t) = sup\{\beta_M(s,t_1) \wedge \beta_M(t_1,t_2) \wedge ....\beta_M(t_{k-1},t) : s,t_1,t_2,....,t_{k-1},t \in V\}$$

and

$$\delta_M^k(s,t) = inf\{\delta_M(s,t_1) \wedge \delta_M(t_1,t_2) \wedge ....\delta_M(t_{k-1},t) : s,t_1,t_2,....,t_{k-1},t \in V\}.$$

Definition 13 ([51])**.** *If deleting any vertex s of connected IFG $\hat{G}$ decreases the strength of connectedness between several pairs of vertices (nodes), then such a vertex s is called a cut vertex.*

Definition 14 ([51]). *Let* $\hat{G}=(N, M)$ *be an IFG. Then,* $|N| = \sum_{s \in N} \frac{1+\beta_N(s)-\delta_N(s)}{2}$ *is known as the vertex cardinality of N,* $|M| = \sum_{(s,t) \in M} \frac{1+\beta_M(s,t)-\delta_M(s,t)}{2}$ *is the edge cardinality of M, and* $|T| = |N| + |M|$ *is the cardinality of IFG* $\hat{G}$.

Definition 15 ([40]). *A directed simple graph is represented by* $G_D = (\tilde{V}, \tilde{E})$, *where* $\tilde{V}$ *is a non-empty finite set of vertices and* $\tilde{E} = \{(s,t) : s, t \in \tilde{V}, s \neq t\}$ *is a set of directed edges. A pair* $G_D^{\bullet} = (A, B)$ *is called a fuzzy digraph (FDG), where* $A = \{\rho_A\}$ *and* $B = \{\rho_B\}$ *are the mappings* $\rho_A : \tilde{V} \to [0,1]$ *and* $\rho_B : \tilde{E} \to [0,1]$, *such that* $\rho_B(s,t) \leq \rho_A(s) \wedge \rho_A(t)$, *for all* $s, t \in \tilde{V}$ *and* $(s,t) \in \tilde{E}$. *We call a digraph* $G_D = (\tilde{V}, \tilde{E})$ *a hidden directed graph of a fuzzy directed graph* $G_D^{\bullet} = (A, B)$.

Definition 16 ([40]). *The sequence of strong arcs such that the end vertex of every arc is the same as the starting vertex of the next arc in a sequence is called a fuzzy dipath (FDP) P.*

Definition 17 ([40]). *A dipath (DP) that begins and ends with the same vertex is called a fuzzy dicycle (FDC) C.*

Definition 18 ([19]). *An intuitionistic fuzzy digraph (IFDG) of a digraph* $G_D = (\tilde{V}, \tilde{E})$ *is a pair* $G_D^{\circ} = (N, M)$, *where* $N = (\tilde{V}, \beta_N, \delta_N)$ *represents an IFS in* $\tilde{V}$ *and* $M = (\tilde{V} \times \tilde{V}, \beta_M, \delta_M)$ *represents an IF relation on* $\tilde{V}$ *such that*

$$\beta_M(st) \leq min(\beta_N(s), \delta_N(t))$$

$$\beta_M(st) \geq max(\beta_N(s), \delta_N(t))$$

and $0 \leq \beta_M(st) + \delta_M(st) \leq 1$, *for all* $s, t \in \tilde{V}$. *We note that M may not be a symmetric relation.*

3. Domination in Intutionistic Fuzzy Digraphs

In this section, firstly, we introduce the concepts of strong arcs and their types in IFDGs. Based on these strong arcs, we present the concepts of domination in IFDGs. Moreover, the dominating set (DS), minimal dominating set (MDS), etc., are also described with some interesting results. Then, we also introduce the concept of an independent set in an IFDG and its relations with the DS, minimal independent set (MIS) and MDS. At the end of this section, we present the terms status and structurally equivalent and explore some relations among these terms and the domination in IFDGs.

We begin our discussion with the definition of the degree of a vertex in an IFDG.

Definition 19. *Let* $G_D = (\tilde{V}, \tilde{E})$ *be a hidden digraph of an IFDG* $G_D^{\circ} = (N, M)$. *Then, the order q of* G_D° *is defined as*

$$q = (\sum_{s \in \tilde{V}} \beta_N(s), \sum_{s \in \tilde{V}} \delta_N(s)).$$

Example 1. *In the IFDG shown in Figure 1, we have* $q = (2, 0.6)$.

Now, we present the definition of the size of an IFDG.

Definition 20. *Let* $G_D = (\tilde{V}, \tilde{E})$ *be a hidden digraph of* $G_D^{\circ} = (N, M)$. *The size p of* G_D° *is defined as*

$$p = (\sum_{s \neq t} \beta_M(s,t), \sum_{s \neq t} \delta_M(s,t))$$

for all $(s,t) \in \tilde{E}$.

Example 2. *Referring to the IFDG shown in Figure 1, we have* $p = (1.6, 1.6)$.

Here, we present the definition of a strong arc in an IFDG, which plays a crucial role in the rest of this paper.

Definition 21. *An arc (s,t) of an IFDG G_D° is said to be a strong arc if $\beta_M(s,t) = \beta_M^{\infty}(s,t)$ and $\delta_M(s,t) = \delta_M^{\infty}(s,t)$; otherwise, the arc (s,t) is non-strong.*

Afterwards, we present different types of strong arcs in IFDGs, such as semi β-strong arcs, semi δ-strong arcs, etc.

Definition 22. *An arc (s,t) of an IFDG G_D° is a semi β-strong arc if $\beta_M(s,t) = \beta_M^{\infty}(s,t)$ and $\delta_M(s,t) \neq \delta_M^{\infty}(s,t)$.*

Definition 23. *An arc (s,t) of an IFDG G_D° is a semi δ-strong arc if $\beta_M(s,t) \neq \beta_M^{\infty}(s,t)$ and $\delta_M(s,t) = \delta_M^{\infty}(s,t)$.*

In Example 3, we analyze the strong arcs among those depicted in the IFDG given in Figure 1.

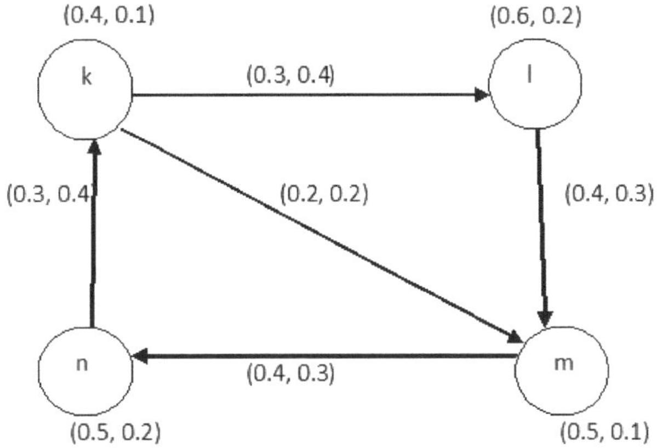

Figure 1. Intuitionistic fuzzy digraph.

Example 3. *We determine which arcs in the IFDG shown in Figure 1 are considered strong arcs and which ones are not.*
Case (i) *Consider the arc (k,l); $\beta_M(k,l) = 0.3$ and $\delta_M(k,l) = 0.4$. Now, $\beta_M^{\infty}(k,l) = sup\{\beta_N(k,l)\} = 0.3$ and $\delta_M^{\infty}(k,l) = sup\{\delta_N(k,l)\} = 0.4$. Therefore, $\beta_M(k,l) = \beta_M^{\infty}(k,l) = 0.3$ and $\delta_M(k,l) = \delta_M^{\infty}(k,l) = 0.3$. Hence, the arc (k,l) is a strong arc.*
Case (ii) *Let us consider an arc (l,m); $\beta_M(l,m) = 0.4$ and $\delta_M(l,m) = 0.3$. Now, $\beta_M^{\infty}(l,m) = sup\{\beta_N(l,m)\} = 0.4$ and $\delta_M^{\infty}(l,m) = inf\{\delta_N(l,m)\} = 0.3$. Therefore, $\beta_M(l,m) = \beta_M^{\infty}(l,m) = 0.4$ and $\delta_M(l,m) = \delta_M^{\infty}(l,m) = 0.3$. Hence, the arc (l,m) is a strong arc.*
Case (iii) *Let us consider the arc (m,n); $\beta_M(m,n) = 0.4$ and $\delta_M(m,n) = 0.3$. Now, $\beta_2^{\infty}(m,n) = sup\{\beta_1(m,n)\} = 0.4$ and $\delta_M^{\infty}(m,n) = inf\{\delta_N(m,n)\}$ =0.3. Therefore, $\beta_M(m,n) = \beta_M^{\infty}(m,n) = 0.4$ and $\delta_M(m,n) = \delta_M^{\infty}(m,n) = 0.3$. Hence, the arc (m,n) is a strong arc.*
Case (iv) *Let us consider the arc (n,k); $\beta_M(n,k) = 0.3$ and $\delta_M(n,k) = 0.4$. Now, $\beta_M^{\infty}(n,k) = sup\{\beta_N(n,k)\} = 0.3$ and $\delta_M^{\infty}(n,k) = inf\{\delta_M(n,k)\} = 0.4$. Therefore, $\beta_M(n,k) = \beta_M^{\infty}(n,k) = 0.3$ and $\delta_M(n,k) = \delta_M^{\infty}(n,k) = 0.4$. Hence, the arc (n,k) is a strong arc.*
Case (v) *Consider the arc (k,m); $\beta_M(k,m) = 0.2$ and $\delta_M(k,m) = 0.2$. Now, $\beta_M^{\infty}(m,k) = sup\{\beta_N(k,l) \wedge \beta_N(l,m)\} = sup\{0.3, 0.4\} = 0.4$ and $\delta_M^{\infty}(k,m) = inf\{\delta_N(k,l) \vee \delta_N(l,m)\} = inf\{0.4, 0.3\} = 0.3$. Therefore, $\beta_M(k,m) \neq \beta_M^{\infty}(k,m)$ and $\delta_M(k,m) = \delta_m^{\infty}(k,m) = 0.3$. Hence, the arc (k,m) is not a strong arc.*

In Definition 24, we introduce the terms strong neighborhood (SNbhd) and closed neighborhood (CNbhd) along with their types and cardinalities.

Definition 24. *Let $G_D = (\tilde{V}, \tilde{E})$ be a hidden digraph of an IFDG $G_D^\circ = (N, M)$. Then,*
(i) $Nbhd_S(s) = \{t \in \tilde{V} : arc(s,t)$ is strong arc$\}$ is the SNbhd of $s \in \tilde{V}$. Similarly, the CNbhd of s is $Nbhd_S[s] = Nbhd_S(s) \cup \{s\}$.
(ii) $Nbhd_{\beta S}(s) = \{t \in \tilde{V} : arc\ (s,t)$ is semi β-strong arc$\}$ is known as the semi β-SNbhd of $s \in \tilde{V}$ and CNbhd of s is $Nbhd_{\beta S}[s] = Nbhd_{\beta S}(s) \cup \{s\}$.
(iii) $Nbhd_{\delta S}(s) = \{t \in \tilde{V} : arc(s,t)$ is semi δ-strong arc$\}$ is known as the semi δ-SNbhd of $s \in \tilde{V}$ and CNbhd of s is$Nbhd_{\delta S}[s] = Nbhd_{\delta S}(s) \cup \{s\}$.
(iv) $\eta_S(G_D^\circ) = min\{|Nbhd_S(s)| : s \in \tilde{V}(G_D^\circ)\}$ is the minimum cardinality of the SNbhd.
(v) $\theta_S(G_D^\circ) = max\{|Nbhd_S(s)| : s \in \tilde{V}(G_D^\circ)\}$ is the maximum cardinality of the SNbhd.

Theorem 1. *If two nodes of an IFDG G_D° are linked by one dipath, then every arc of G_D° is a strong arc.*

Proof. Let G_D° be a connected IFDG with n nodes. If we take $n = 2$, then s and t must be adjacent by one arc (because G_D° is a connected IFDG). Clearly, $\beta_M(s,t) = \beta_M{}^\infty(s,t)$ and $\delta_M(s,t) = \delta_M{}^\infty(s,t)$. Hence, an arc (s,t) is a strong arc. Let $n > 2$. In any IF dipath, $\beta_M{}^\infty(s,t) = \beta_M(s,t)$ and $\delta_M{}^\infty(s,t) = \delta_M(s,t)$ for any arc in the dipath (s,t), as they are connected through the same dipath. Thus, it is proven that $\beta_M(s,t) = \beta_M{}^\infty(s,t)$ and $\delta_M(s,t) = \delta_M{}^\infty(s,t)$ for any number of arcs in a given dipath. Hence, all the arcs are strong. □

Corollary 1. *In an IF dipath, each arc is a strong arc.*

Theorem 2. *In a non-trivial connected IFDG G_D° with n nodes such that $n \geq 2$, G_D° has at least one strong arc.*

Proof. Let G_D° be a connected IFDG with vertices $n \geq 2$. Assume that s and t are the two nodes of G_D°.
Case(i) : When $n = 2$: Because G_D° is a connected IFDG, s and t are two nodes such that (s,t) is an arc. From Theorem 1, only one strongest dipath between s and t exists such that $\beta_M(s,t) = \beta_M{}^\infty(s,t)$ and $\delta_M(s,t) = \delta_M{}^\infty(s,t)$. Hence, (s,t) is a strong arc.
Case(ii) : When $n > 2$: Assume that G_D° has at least one strong arc. Because G_D° is connected with $n > 2$, there exists more than one dipath between s and t such that at least one strong dipath exists. Thus, $\beta_M(s,t) = \beta_M{}^\infty(s,t)$ and $\delta_M(s,t) = \delta_M{}^\infty(s,t)$ (from Theorem 1). If this does not hold, there is no dipath between s and t. Hence, G_D° is a disconnected digraph, which contradicts our hypothesis that G_D° is connected. Therefore, if $n \geq 2$, then non-trivial connected IFDG G_D° has at least one strong arc. □

Theorem 3. *Let (s,t) be the arc of IFDG G_D°. Then, the following conditions are equivalent.*
(i) In G_D°, an arc (s,t) is a strong arc.
(ii) An arc (s,t) must be semi β-strong and semi δ-strong.
(iii) The membership degree and non-membership degree of arc (s,t) must be in between the closed interval $[\beta_{SM}, \delta_{LM}]$, where the smallest value of the membership degree of the IFDG G_D° is β_{SM}, and the largest value of the non-membership degree of the IFDG G_D° is δ_{LM}.

Definition 25. *Let G_D° be an IFDG and s, t be any two vertices of G_D°. Then, s dominates t, if the arc (s,t) is a strong arc.*

Example 4. *Referring to the IFDG given in Figure 1, the arcs (k,l), (l,m), (m,n), (n,k) are strong arcs but the arc (m,k) is a non-strong arc. Thus, l dominates m, m dominates n and n dominates k, but m does not dominate k.*

Definition 26. *A DS of IFDG G_D° is a subset N_1 of $\tilde{V}$ if, for each $t \in \tilde{V} - N_1$, there exists $s \in N_1$ such that s dominates t. A DS N_1 is an MDS if there is no proper subset of N_1 that is a DS. The minimum cardinality from all MDSs is a lower DN of G_D° and it is abbreviated as $L_D(G_D^\circ)$. The maximum cardinality from all MDSs is an upper DN of G_D° and is abbreviated as $U_D(G_D^\circ)$. The minimum fuzzy cardinality from all DSs of an IFDG is known as the strong arc DN and is* *symbolically written as $\omega_S(G^\circ_D)$. The corresponding DS is known as the minimum strong arc DS and the number of elements in the minimum strong arc DS is known as $n[\omega_S(G^\circ_D)]$.*

Example 5. *Consider a set of vertices $N = \{a, b, c, d\}$ in an IFDG, as shown in Figure 2. Let $N_1 = \{a, c\}$ be the DS lying in N. Let $\{b, d\}$ be the set of vertices other than N_1, such that each of its vertices dominates at least one vertex in N, which implies that N_1 is a DS. Again, consider that $N_2 = \{b, d\}$ is the DS lying in N. Let $\{a, c\}$ be the set other than N_2 such that each of its vertices dominates at least one vertex in N, which implies that N_2 is a DS. Thus, the DSs are $\{a, c\}$ and $\{b, d\}$, while $\{b, d\}$ is the MDS of minimum cardinality 1.25 and $\{a, c\}$ is the MDS of maximum cardinality 1.35.*

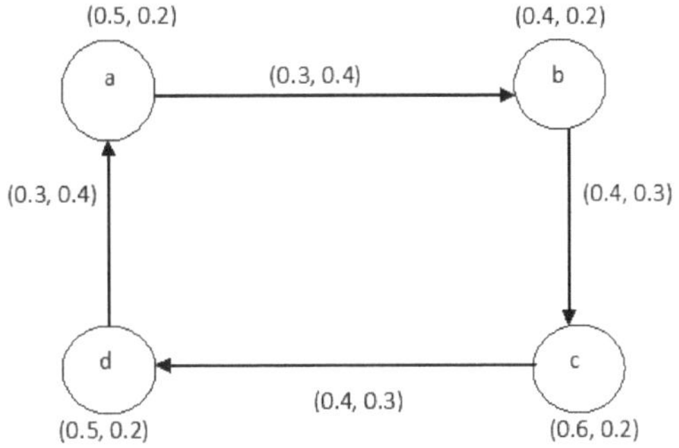

Figure 2. Intuitionistic fuzzy digraph.

Definition 27. *The open Nbhd of s in an IFDG G°_D is represented as $ONbhd(s)$ and is defined as $ONbhd(s) = \{t \in \tilde{V} : \beta(s,t) > 0, \delta(s,t) > 0\}$. The vertex t is known as the SN of s if an arc (s,t) is a strong arc, and the set of all SNs of s is known as the SNbhd of s and is abbreviated as $Nbhd_S(s)$. Similarly, $Nbhd_S[s] = Nbhd_S(s) \cup \{s\}$ is the CSNbhd of s.*

Example 6. *Referring to the IFDG given in Figure 1, one can easily deduce that the arcs $(k, l), (l, m), (m, n), (n, k)$ are strong arcs, while the arc (k, m) is a non-strong arc. The SN of k is l. Thus, $Nbhd_S[k] = \{l\} \cup \{k\} = \{l, k\}$ is the CSNbhd of k.*

Definition 28. *Let G°_D be an IFDG and s, t be any two vertices of G°_D. Then,*
(i) s semi β- dominates t, if the arc (s,t) is a semi β-strong arc;
(ii) s semi δ- dominates t, if an arc (s,t) is a semi δ-strong arc.

Remark 1. *(i) Semi β- strong arc DN is $\omega_{\beta S}(G^\circ_D)$. The number of elements in the minimum semi β- strong arc DS is symbolically written as $n[\omega_{\beta S}(G^\circ_D)]$.*
(ii) Semi δ - strong arc DN is described as $\omega_{\delta S}(G^\circ_D)$. The number of elements in the minimum semi δ - strong arc DS is represented as $n[\omega_{\delta S}(G^\circ_D)]$.

Definition 29. *Two vertices s and t of an IFDG $G^\circ_D = (N, M)$ are called isolated vertices if $\beta_M(s,t) = 0$ and $\delta_M(s,t) = 0$. Secondly, $Nbhd(s) = \emptyset$, which implies that there does not exist any Nbhd of s. Thus, an isolated vertex cannot dominate any other vertex of G°_D.*

Theorem 4. *In an IFDG $G^\circ_D = (N, M)$, a DS N_1 is an MDS if, for each $s \in N_1$, one of the following conditions holds.*
(i) s is not an SN of any vertex in N_1;
(ii) there exists a vertex $t \in N - N_1$ such that $Nbhd(t) \cap N_1 = \{s\}$.

Proof. Assume that N_1 is an MDS of G°_D. For each vertex $s \in N_1$, $N_1 - s$ is not a DS. Then, $t \in (N_1 - s)$ exists and is not dominated by any vertex in $N_1 - s$. If $t = s$, then t is not an SN of any vertex in N_1. If $t \neq s$, t is not dominated by $N_1 - t$, but it is dominated by N_1, and there is a vertex t that is the only SN of s in N_1. Hence, $Nbhd(t) \cap N_1 = s$.

Conversely, consider that N_1 is a DS. For every vertex $s \in N_1$, one of the two given conditions holds true. Assume that N_1 is not an MDS. Thus, there exists a vertex $s \in N_1$, $N_1 - s$ that is a DS. Hence, s is an SN to one of the vertices in $N_1 - s$, so condition (i) does not hold true. If $N_1 - s$ is a DS, then each vertex of $N - N_1$ is an SN to one of the vertices in $N_1 - s$, and condition (ii) also does not hold true. This is a contradiction of our hypothesis that one of the two conditions holds true. Thus, N_1 is an MDS. □

Theorem 5. *Let $G^\circ_D = (N, M)$ be an IFDG with no isolated vertex. Let N_1 be an MDS. Then, $N - N_1$ is a DS of G°_D.*

Proof. Assume that N_1 is an MDS. Consider that t is a vertex of N_1. As G°_D does not have isolated vertices and there exists a vertex $s \in Nbhd(t)$, t is dominated by one of the vertices in $N_1 - t$, i.e., $N_1 - t$ is a DS. From Theorem 4, $s \in N - N_1$. Thus, each vertex in N_1 is dominated by one of the vertices in $N - N_1$ and $N - N_1$ is a DS. □

Corollary 2. *If there is no isolated vertex in an IFDG $G^\circ_D = (N, M)$, then $L_D(G^\circ_D) \leq q(G^\circ_D)/2$.*

Proof. Let G°_D be an IFDG with no isolated vertex. Then, it has two disjoint DSs, i.e., $L_D(G^\circ_D) \leq q(G^\circ_D)/2$. □

Definition 30. *Two vertices s and t of an IFDG $G^\circ_D = (N, M)$ are called independent if there is no strong edge between these two vertices. A subset N_2 of N is known as an independent set (IS) of an IFDG G°_D if the following conditions hold:*

$$\beta_M(s,t) < \beta^\infty_M(s,t) \text{ and } \delta_M(s,t) < \delta^\infty_M(s,t)$$

for all $(s,t) \in N_2$.

Definition 31. *An IS $N_2 \subseteq N$ in an IFDG $G^\circ_D = (N, M)$ is called a maximal independent set (MIS) if the set $N \cup \{s\}$ is not independent for every $s \in N - N_2$. The minimum cardinality between the MISs is called the lower independent number of an IFDG G°_D, represented by $i(G^\circ_D)$. The maximum cardinality between the MISs is called the upper independent number of an IFDG G°_D, represented as $I(G^\circ_D)$.*

Theorem 6. *An IS is an MIS in an IFDG $G^\circ_D = (N, M)$ if and only if it is an IS and DS.*

Proof. Let N_2 be an MIS of IFDG G°_D. Then, for each vertex $s \in (N - N_2)$, the set $N_2 \cup s$ is not independent. Moreover, for each vertex $s \in (N - N_2)$, there exists a vertex $t \in N_2$ such that t is an SN of s. Hence, N_2 is a DS. Thus, N_2 is both a DS and IS.

Conversely, let N_2 be an IS and DS. If N_2 is not an MIS, there is a vertex $s \in N - N_2$ such that the set $N_2 \cup \{s\}$ is independent. If $N_2 \cup \{s\}$ is independent, then there is no vertex in N_2 that is an SN of s. Hence, N_2 is not a DS, which contradicts our assumption. Thus, N_2 is an MIS. □

Theorem 7. *Every MIS in an IFDG $G^\circ_D = (N, M)$ is an MDS.*

Proof. Let N_2 be an MIS of an IFDG. By assumption, N_2 is a DS but not an MDS. Then, there exists at least one vertex $s \in N_2$ such that $N_2 - \{s\}$ is a DS. If $N_2 - \{s\}$ dominates $N - \{N_2 - (s)\}$, then there is at least one vertex in $N_2 - \{s\}$ that is necessarily an SN of t, which contradicts our assumption. Hence, N_2 is an MDS. □

Definition 32. *In IFDG G°_D, a subset of vertex set N is known as status S if each vertex $g, h \in S$ obeys the property that the vertex g dominates the vertices in $N - S$ and is equal to the set of vertices in $N - S$ that is dominated by h.*

Remark 2. *Each vertex in status S dominates the same set of vertices outside the status. It can be seen that the status must contain at least two vertices.*

Theorem 8. *If a status S of a connected non-trivial IFDG G°_{D} is an MDS, then S is an independent DS with cardinality 2.*

Proof. Let S be a status that is an MDS. As G°_{D} is connected with no isolated vertex, then there exists at least one vertex $g \in N - S$. As S is an MDS, g is adjoint at least in the S, and since S is the status, each node of S is adjoint to the g. Additionally, every vertex of S is adjoint to the each vertex in $N - S$. Thus, $|S| \geq 2$, because S is the status. Now, consider $|S| \geq 3$ and assume that h belongs to S and g belongs to $N - S$. Since S is the status, it implies that h is adjoint to each vertex of $C - S$ and g is adjoint to every other vertex of S. Hence, the DS is $\{g, h\}$, which contradicts our assumption that S is the minimal set. Thus, $|S| = 2$. However, if h is adjoint to the g, then the DS of G°_{D} is g, which is again a contradiction that S is the minimal set. Consequently, $|S| = 2$ is an IS. □

Definition 33. *Let g and h be any two vertices of an IFDG. Then, these two vertices are called structurally equivalent if either $Nbhd_S(g) = Nbhd_S(h)$ or $Nbhd_S[g] = Nbhd_S[h]$. A set S is called structurally equivalent if each of the two vertices in S is structurally equivalent.*

Corollary 3. *Let G°_{D} be a connected IFDG. Let S be an MDS that is structurally equivalent. Then, the set S has two independent vertices such that each vertex has a degree $q(G^{\circ}_{D}) - 1$.*

4. Application of Domination in IFDGs towards Social Networks

Graphs have various applications in many areas of science, such as chemistry, physics, biology, mathematics, computer science and others. In the organization model, it has been noted that, in a group, there is a connection between two workers. It is also necessary to conclude that, in a graph, one worker is more dominant or influential. Using the graph,we can draw this scenario. In a specific group, we can draw a graph in which each vertex represents each worker. In the graph, the directed edges show the relationship between two workers from one particular vertex (worker) to another. Multiple edges or loops are not needed in these types of graphs. In classical graph theory, every vertex has equal importance. It is not possible to draw such types of graphs in an organization model accurately. Additionally, in classical graph theory, every organization in a social unit (individual or organization) should have equal importance, but the situation is different in real life. Similarly, in classical graph theory, every directed edge has equal strength. Thus, the influence of the worker has fuzzy directed boundaries. It is useful to represent these situations in fuzzy directed graphs. Every vertex represents a worker and the strength of his influence in the organization model, and it is represented by the membership value in the fuzzy directed influential graph. Since the developed form of FS is the IFS, domination in IFDGs provides better results as compared to fuzzy directed graphs.

4.1. Fuzzy Influence Digraph

Let us consider an organization with workers and their designations. Let S = {BOD, CEO, CTO, DM, DPD, DHR, Stt } be the set of workers for this organization, as shown in Table 1. By conducting research on the organization, we conclude the following.

- (i) The CEO has worked with the DM for about 8 years, and, on strategic initiatives, he gives importance to his input.
- (ii) The BOD has been chaired for about 8 years and is associated with the DM. Similarly to the CEO, the BOD also values the DM.
- (iii) In reorganization, the whole marketing scheme is vital but the DHR is more vital.
- (iv) There is a history of disputes between the CTO and DHR.
- (v) The CTO has more influence on the DPD.

Table 1. Designations of workers in an organization and abbreviations used for their designations.

Designation	Abbreviation
Board of Directors	BOD
Chief Executive officer	CEO
Chief Technology officer	CTO
Director of Marketing	DM
Director of Product Development	DPD
Director of Human Resources	DHR
Staff	Stt

An influence digraph can be drawn by observing the above-mentioned points, but this type of digraph does not show the power of the workers in an organization and also the degree of influence of workers on one another. It is important to show them in fuzzy sets as their influence and power have no definite limits. The influence of workers on one another can be represented through a fuzzy digraph, but there exists hesitation in evaluating their influence. We consider a fuzzy directed influential graph of this organization, shown in Figure 3. The organization is represented by the nodes and its membership value represents the degree of influence. The degree of membership represents how influential the worker is? in the organization. The BOD has an 80% level of influence. In the digraph, the directed edges show the influence level of one worker on the other workers within the organization. The membership degree of the directed edges is considered as a positive percentage of influence, e.g., the DM has a 50% influence on both the BOD and CEO. Thus, the DM dominates both the BOD and CEO, which is why it is busier and more influential than the others.

While dealing with the above circumstances through FDGs, we have only the degree of acceptance and there is no information about the degree of non-acceptance of the lower staff members. Hence, there is a lack of information that can be properly manipulated through the IFDGs.

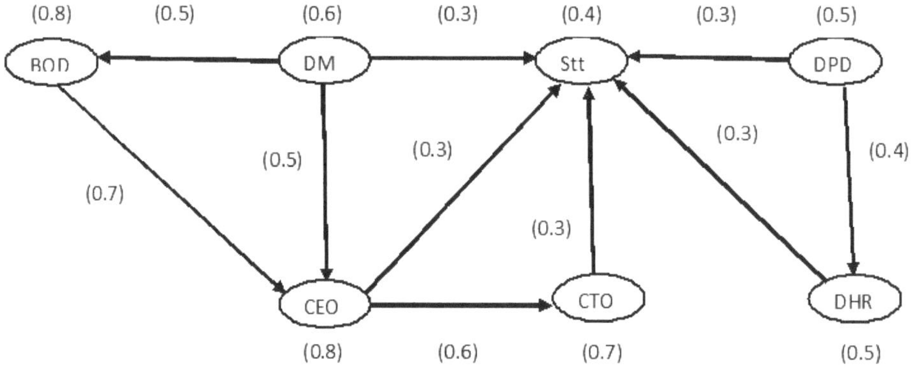

Figure 3. Fuzzy directed influence graph.

4.2. *Intuitionistic Fuzzy Influence Digraph*

Since the power and influence of workers cannot be properly described in fuzzy digraphs, we use an IFDG, which gives better results as compared to FGs. In an IFDG, the directed edges are used to show the influence. The resulting IFDG is shown in Figure 4, and Table 2 shows the allocated membership and non-membership values. In the IFDG, the vertices also represent the workers along with their power in terms of membership and non-membership degrees, which are described by percentages. For instance, the CEO has 80% power in the organization. Likewise, in the IFDG, the directed edges show the influence of one worker on another. The membership and non-membership degrees can also be referred to as a positive influence and negative influence, respectively. For instance, the BOD has a 50% influence on the DM's opinion but he does not follow his opinion 30% of the time. In Figure 4, it can be seen that the DM has an influence on both the BOD and CEO. As the membership degrees in both cases are 0.5, which is 50%, his influence on both of them is the same. In the case of the CEO, the hesitation degree is 0.2, which is $(\pi = 1 - 0.5 - 0.3)$, but it is 0.1 in the case of the BOD, which is $(\pi = 1 - 0.5 - 0.4)$, which shows that the CEO has more hesitation than the BOD. It is clear that the most influential worker within the organization is the DM. He has a great influence on both the BOD and CEO; each has 80% power. Clearly, all the arcs are strong but the DM dominates the BOD, CEO and Stt. Hence, the most influential worker in the organization is the DM.

Table 2. Power of workers allocated in terms of membership and non-membership degrees.

	BOD	CEO	CTO	DM	DPD	DHR	Stt
β_N	0.8	0.8	0.7	0.6	0.5	0.5	0.4
δ_N	0.1	0.1	0.2	0.2	0.2	0.3	0.2

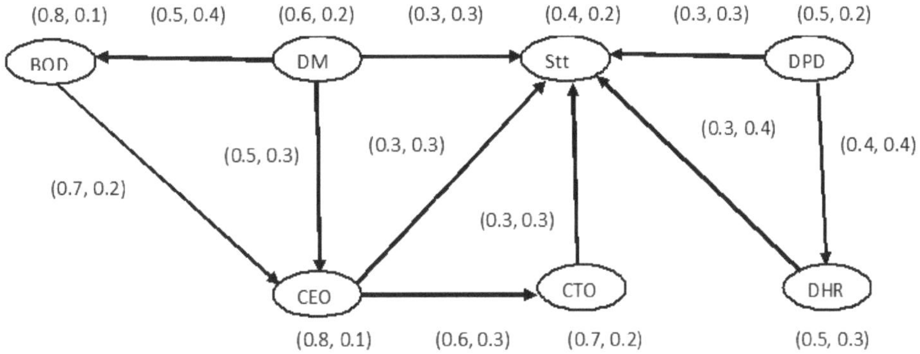

Figure 4. Intuitionistic fuzzy directed influence graph

5. Conclusions

In this article, we have introduced the notion of domination in IFDGs based on SAs, along with several fundamental properties and applications. We have extended the concepts of domination in FDGs. Since dominations in picture fuzzy graphs and bipolar picture fuzzy graphs were introduced in the literature, but the concept of domination in IFDGs was missing, we have also filled this gap the literature related to domination. At the beginning of our study, we introduced several types of strong arcs in IFDGs, like semi-β strong arcs, semi-δ strong arcs, etc. Then, we introduced the concept of domination in IFDGs based on these strong arcs and discussed its various useful characteristics. Moreover, the dominating set (DS), minimal dominating set (MDS), etc., were described with some fascinating results. We have also introduced the concept of an independent set in an IFDG and investigated its relations with the DS, minimal independent set (MIS) and MDS. We have also provided numerous important characterizations of domination in IFDGs based on the minimal and maximal dominating sets. In this context, we have discussed the lower and upper dominations of some IFDGs. In addition, we have introduced the terms status and structurally equivalent and explored a few relationships with the dominations in IFDGs. Finally, we have investigated the most expert (influential) person in the organization by using the concepts of domination in IFGs. One could extend these concepts towards other extended forms of FGs, like spherical picture fuzzy graphs.

Author Contributions: Conceptualization, H.G., W.A.K., A.F., K.A., J.S. and A.K.; methodology, H.G., W.A.K., A.F., K.A., J.S. and A.K.; validation, H.G., W.A.K. and A.F.; formal analysis, H.G., W.A.K., A.F., K.A., J.S. and A.K.; investigation, W.A.K., A.F. and K.A.; writing—original draft preparation, H.G., W.A.K., A.F., K.A., J.S. and A.K.; writing—review and editing, J.S. and A.K.; supervision, H.G. and W.A.K. All authors have read and agreed to the published version of the manuscript.

Funding: This research received no external funding.

Data Availability Statement: Data are contained within the article.

Conflicts of Interest: The authors declare no conflicts of interest.

References

1. Zadeh, L.A. Fuzzy sets. *Inform. Control.* **1965**, *8*, 338–353. [CrossRef]
2. Zadeh, L.A. The concept of a linguistic variable and its application to approximate reasoning-I. *Inform. Sci.* **1975**, *8*, 199–249. [CrossRef]
3. Atanassov, K.T.; Stoeva, S. Intuitionistic fuzzy sets. *Fuzzy Sets Syst.* **1986**, *20*, 87–96. [CrossRef]
4. Rosenfield, A. *Fuzzy Graphs, Fuzzy Sets and Their Applications to Cognitive and Decision Processes*; Academic Press: New York, NY, USA, 1975; pp. 77–95.
5. Kauffman, A. *Introduction a 1a Theories des Sous-Emsembles Flous*; Masson et cie: Paris, France, 1973; p. 1.
6. Bhattacharya, P. Some remarks on fuzzy graphs. *Pattern Recognit. Lett.* **1987**, *6*, 297–302. [CrossRef]
7. Mordeson, J.N.; Peng, C.S. Operations on fuzzy graphs. *Inform. Sci.* **1994**, *79*, 159–170. [CrossRef]
8. Borzooei, R.A.; Rashmanlou, H. Cayley interval-valued fuzzy graphs. *Upb Sci. Bull. Ser. Appl. Math. Phys.* **2016**, *78*, 83–94.
9. Sunitha, M.S.; Vijayakumar, A. Complement of a fuzzy graphs. *Indian J. Pure Appl. Math.* **2002**, *33*, 1451–1464.
10. Poulik, S.; Ghorial, G. Estimation of most effected cycles and busiest network route based on complexity function of graph in fuzzy environment. *Artif. Intell. Rev.* **2022**, *55*, 4557–4574. [CrossRef]
11. Mordeson, J.; Nair, P. Successor and source of (fuzzy) finite state machines and (fuzzy) directed graphs. *Inf. Sci.* **1996**, *95*, 113–124. [CrossRef]
12. Kumar, P.K.K.; Lavanya, S. On fuzzy digraphs. *Int. J. Pure Appl. Math.* **2017**, *115*, 599–606. [CrossRef]
13. Akram, M.; Alshehri, N.; Davvaz, B.; Ashraf, A. Bipolar Fuzzy Digraphs in Decision Support Systems. *J. Mult. Valued Log. Soft Comput.* **2016**, *27*, 553–572.
14. Shannon, A.; Atanassov, K.T. A first step to a theory of the intuitionistic fuzzy graphs. In Proceedings of the FUBEST, Sofia, Bulgaria, 28–30 September 1994; Lakov, D., Ed.; Sofia: Paris, France, 1994; pp. 59–61.
15. Yaqoob, N.; Gulistan, M.; Kadry, S.; Wahab, H.A. Complex Intuitionistic Fuzzy Graphs with Application in Cellular Network Provider Companies. *Mathematics* **2019**, *7*, 35. [CrossRef]
16. Akram, M.; Davvaz, B. Strong intuitionistic fuzzy graphs. *Filomat* **2012**, *26*, 177–195. [CrossRef]
17. Akram, M.; Dudek, W.A. Intuitionistic fuzzy hypergraphs with applications. *Inform. Sci.* **2013**, *218*, 182–193. [CrossRef]
18. Akram, M.; Al-Shehrie, N.O. Intuitionistic fuzzy cycles and intuitionistic fuzzy trees. *Sci. World J.* **2014**, *2014*, 305836. [CrossRef] [PubMed]
19. Akram, M.; Ashraf, A.; Sarwar, M. Novel applications of intuitionistic fuzzy digraphs in decision support systems. *Sci. World J.* **2014**, *2014*, 904606. [CrossRef] [PubMed]
20. Shao, Z.; Kosari, S.; Rashmanlou, H.; Shoaib, M. New concepts in intuitionistic fuzzy graph with application in water supplier systems. *Mathematics* **2020**, *8*, 1241. [CrossRef]
21. Talebi, A.A.; Rashmanlou, H.; Sadati, S.H. Interval-valued Intuitionistic Fuzzy Competition Graph. *J. Mult. Valued Log. Soft Comput.* **2020**, *34*, 335.
22. Rashmanlou, H.; Borzooei, R.A.; Samanta, S.; Pal, M. Properties of interval valued intuitionistic (s, t)–fuzzy graphs. *Pac. Sci. Rev. Nat. Sci. Eng.* **2016**, *18*, 30–37. [CrossRef]
23. Rashmanlou, H.; Borzooei, R.A. New concepts of interval-valued intuitionistic (S, T)-fuzzy graphs. *J. Intell. Fuzzy Syst.* **2016**, *30*, 1893–1901. [CrossRef]
24. Talebi, A.A.; Rashmanlou, H.; Sadati, S.H. New concepts on m-polar interval-valued intuitionistic fuzzy graph. *TWMS J. Appl. Eng. Math.* **2020**, *10*, 806–818.
25. Singh, S.; Barve, A.; Muduli, K.; Kumar, A.; Luthra, S. Evaluating roadblocks to implementing a green freight transportation system an interval valued intuitionistic fuzzy digraph matrix approach. *IEEE Trans. Eng. Manag.* **2022**, *71*, 2758–2771. [CrossRef]
26. Nithyanandham, D.; Augustin, F.; Micheal, D.R.; Pillai, N.D. Energy based bipolar intuitionistic fuzzy digraph decision-making system in selecting COVID-19 vaccines. *Appl. Soft Comput.* **2023**, *147*, 110793. [CrossRef]
27. Shi, X.; Kosari, S.; Talebi, A.A.; Sadati, S.H.; Rashmanlou, H. Investigation of the main energies of picture fuzzy graph and its applications. *Int. J. Comput. Intell. Syst.* **2022**, *15*, 31. [CrossRef]
28. Yue, J.; Wei, M.; Li, M.; Liu, G. On the double Roman domination of graphs. *Appl. Math. Comput.* **2018**, *338*, 669–675. [CrossRef]
29. Ahangar, H.A.; Álvarez, M.; Chellali, M.; Sheikholeslami, S.; Valenzuela-Tripodoro, J. Triple Roman domination in graphs. *Appl. Math. Comput.* **2021**, *391*, 125444.

30. Henning, M.A.; MacGillivray, G.; Yang, F. Broadcast domination in graphs. In *Structures of Domination in Graphs*; Haynes, T.W., Hedetniemi, S.T., Henning, M.A., Eds.; Springer International Publishing: Cham, Switzerland, 2021; pp. 15–46.
31. Dayap, J.A.; Enriquez, E.L. Outer-convex domination in graphs. *Discret. Math. Algorithms Appl.* **2019**, *12*, 2050008. [CrossRef]
32. Desormeaux, W.J.; Haynes, T.W.; Henning, M.A. Paired Domination in Graphs. In *Topics in Domination in Graphs*; Springer International Publishing: Cham, Switzerland, 2020; pp. 31–77.
33. Kosari, S.; Asgharsharghi, L. The l-distance k-rainbow domination numbers of graphs. *Asian-Eur. J. Math.* **2023**, *16*, 2350040. [CrossRef]
34. Mihara, S.; Tsugawa, S.; Ohsaki, H. Influence maximization problem for unknown social networks. In Proceedings of the 2015 IEEE/ACM International Conference on Advances in Social Networks Analysis and Mining 2015, Paris, France, 25–28 August 2015; pp. 1539–1546.
35. Chen, W.; Wang, Y.; Yang, S. Efficient influence maximization in social networks. In Proceedings of the 15th ACM SIGKDD International Conference on Knowledge Discovery and Data Mining, Paris, France, 28 June–1 July 2009; pp. 199–208.
36. Somasundaram, A.; Somasundaram, S. Domination in fuzzy graphs-I. *Pattern Recognit. Lett.* **1998**, *19*, 787–791. [CrossRef]
37. Nagoorgani, A.; Chandrasekaran, V.T. Domination in Fuzzy graph. *Adv. Fuzzy Syst.* **2006**, *1*, 17–26.
38. Manjusha, O.T. Global domination in Fuzzy graphs using Strong arcs. *J. Fuzzy Ext. Appl.* **2023**, *4*, 8–17.
39. Shanmugam, S.; Aishwarya, T.P.; Shreya, N. Bridge domination in fuzzy graphs. *J. Fuzzy Ext. Appl.* **2023**, *4*, 148–154.
40. Enriquez, E.; Estrada, G.; Loquias, C.; Bacalso, R.J.; Ocampo, L. Domination in fuzzy directed graphs. *Mathematics* **2021**, *9*, 2143. [CrossRef]
41. Noppakaew, P.; Hengthonglert, K.; Sakuntasathien, S. Dominating broadcasts in fuzzy graphs. *Mathematics* **2022**, *10*, 281. [CrossRef]
42. Ahmad, U.; Batool, T. Domination in rough fuzzy digraphs with application. *Soft Comput.* **2023**, *27*, 2425–2442. [CrossRef]
43. Qiang, X.; Akhoundi, M.; Kou, Z.; Liu, X.; Kosari, S. Novel concepts of domination in vague graphs with application in medicine. *Math. Probl. Eng.* **2021**, *2021*, 6121454. [CrossRef]
44. Shi, X.; Kosari, S. Certain properties of domination in product vague graphs with an application in medicine. *Front. Phys.* **2021**, *9*, 680634. [CrossRef]
45. Kosari, S.; Shao, Z.; Rao, Y.; Liu, X.; Cai, R.; Rashmanlou, H. Some Types of Domination in Vague Graphs with Application in Medicine. *J. Mult. Valued Log. Soft Comput.* **2023**, *41*, 203.
46. Shao, Z.; Kosari, S.; Rao, Y.; Rashmanlou, H.; Mofidnakhaei, F. New Kind of Vague Graphs With Novel Application. *J. Mult. Valued Log. Soft Comput.* **2023**, *40*, 323.
47. Parvathi, R.; Thamizhendhi, G. Domination in intuitionistic fuzzy graphs. *Notes Intuitionistic Fuzzy Sets* **2010**, *16*, 39–49.
48. Nagoorgani, A.; Akram, M.; Anupriya, S. Double domination on intuitionistic fuzzy graphs. *J. Appl. Math. Comput.* **2016**, *52*, 515–528. [CrossRef]
49. Khan, W.A.; Taouti, A. Dominations in bipolar picture fuzzy graphs and social networks. *Results Nonlinear Anal.* **2023**, *6*, 60–74.
50. Diestel, R. *Graph Theory*; Springer: New York, NY, USA, 2000.
51. Senthilkumar, V. Types of domination in intuitionistic fuzzy graph by strong arc and effective arc. *Bull. Pure Appl. Sci. Math. Stat.* **2018**, *37*, 490–498. [CrossRef]

mathematics MDPI

Article

On Soft ω_δ-Open Sets and Some Decomposition Theorems

Dina Abuzaid [1], Samer Al-Ghour [2,*] and Monia Naghi [1]

[1] Department of Mathematics, Faculty of Science, King Abdulaziz University, Jeddah 21589, Saudi Arabia
[2] Department of Mathematics and Statistics, Jordan University of Science and Technology, Irbid 22110, Jordan
* Correspondence: algore@just.edu.jo

Abstract: In this paper, we present a novel family of soft sets named "soft ω_δ-open sets". We find that this class constitutes a soft topology that lies strictly between the soft topologies of soft δ-open sets and soft ω^0-open sets. Also, we introduce certain sufficient conditions for the equivalence between this new soft topology and several existing soft topologies. Moreover, we verify several relationships that contain soft covering properties, such as soft compactness and soft Lindelofness, which are related to this new soft topology. Furthermore, in terms of the soft interior operator in certain soft topologies, we define four classes of soft sets. Via them, we obtain new decomposition theorems for soft δ-openness and soft θ-openness, and we characterize the soft topological spaces that have the soft "semi-regularization property". In addition, via soft ω_δ-open sets, we introduce and investigate a new class of soft functions named "soft ω_δ-continuous functions". Finally, we look into the connections between the newly proposed soft concepts and their counterparts in classical topological spaces.

Keywords: soft δ-open sets; soft θ-open sets; soft ω^0-open sets; super-continuity; soft generated soft topological spaces

MSC: 54A10; 54A40; 54D1

Citation: Abuzaid, D.; Al-Ghour, S.; Naghi, M. On Soft ω_δ-Open Sets and Some Decomposition Theorems. *Mathematics* **2024**, *12*, 924. https://doi.org/10.3390/math12060924

Academic Editor: Michael Voskoglou

Received: 18 February 2024
Revised: 16 March 2024
Accepted: 19 March 2024
Published: 21 March 2024

1. Introduction and Preleminaries

In today's complex world, accurate modeling and management of many types of uncertainty are essential to tackle difficult issues in different fields, including environmental science, economics, engineering, social sciences, and medicine. While well-known techniques like probability theory, fuzzy sets [1], and rough sets [2] help handle ambiguity and uncertainty, they are not without limitations. These mathematical methods all share the same flaw, which is insufficient parameterization capabilities. In 1999, Molodtsov [3] introduced soft set theory as a solution to the shortcomings of earlier uncertainty-handling techniques. After that, the interpretation of soft sets for modeling uncertainty has been conducted; advancements in this area are described in [4,5]. Equipped with soft sets, parameter sets offer a defined framework that is naturally adaptable, facilitating the modeling of unclear data. Soft set theory and related fields have advanced greatly as a result very soon. As may be observed in [6–12], this has led to several applications of soft sets in real-world fields.

Numerous mathematicians have used soft set theory to introduce various mathematical structures, including soft group theory [13], soft ring theory [14], soft convex structures [15], and soft ideals [16]. These papers highlight the use of soft set theory in handling challenging mathematical problems.

Shabir and Naz [17] created soft topology first, and since then, a lot of researchers have focused on extending the topological concepts to include the field of soft topology. For instance, soft metric spaces [18–20], soft connected spaces [21], soft covering properties [22–24], and generalized soft open sets [25–29] are a few of the notions mentioned.

Recent papers [30–37] show that research in soft topology is currently ongoing and that there is still an opportunity for important contributions.

The generalizations of soft open sets play an effective role in the structure of soft topology by using them to redefine and investigate some soft topological concepts such as soft continuity, soft compactness, and soft separation axioms. This paper follows this area of research.

The arrangement of this article is as follows:

In Section 2, we define soft ω_δ-open sets. We study the features of sets and show how they relate to well-known other classes of soft sets, like soft δ-open sets and soft ω^0-open sets. Furthermore, we investigate the links between this class of soft sets and its classical topology analogs. We also investigate several relationships that contain soft covering properties, such as soft compactness and soft Lindelofness.

In Section 3, we define four new classes of soft sets. We use them to provide novel decomposition theorems for soft δ-openness and soft θ-openness, as well as characterize semi-regularized soft topological spaces.

In Section 4, via soft ω_δ-open sets, we define soft ω_δ-continuous functions as a new class of soft functions and investigate some of their properties. We give several characterizations of it. Also, we investigate the links between this class of soft functions and its analogs in general topology. Moreover, we show that soft ω_δ-continuity is strictly weaker than soft ω^0-continuity.

In Section 5, we give some findings and potential future studies.

Throughout this paper, we will use the concepts and terminology as they appear in [38,39].

Here, we recall some basic definitions and results that will be needed in this sequel.

Let M be an initial universe and Z be a set of parameters. A soft set over M relative to Z is a function $T : Z \longrightarrow \mathcal{P}(M)$, where $\mathcal{P}(M)$ is the power set of M. The collection of all soft sets over M relative to Z is denoted by $SS(M,Z)$. Let $G \in SS(M,Z)$. If $G(a) = \emptyset$ for every $a \in Z$, then G is called the null soft set over M relative to Z and denoted by 0_Z. If $G(a) = M$ for all $a \in Z$, then G is called the absolute soft set over M relative to Z and denoted by 1_Z. If there exist $x \in M$ and $a \in Z$ such that $G(a) = \{x\}$ and $G(b) = \emptyset$ for all $b \in Z - \{a\}$, then G is called a soft point over M relative to Z and denoted by a_x. The collection of all soft points over M relative to Z is denoted by $SP(M,Z)$. If for some $a \in Z$ and $X \subseteq M$, $G(a) = X$ and $G(b) = \emptyset$ for all $b \in Z - \{a\}$, then G will be denoted by a_X. If for some $X \subseteq M$, $G(a) = X$ for all $a \in Z$, then G will be denoted by C_X. G is called a countable soft set over M relative to Z if $G(a)$ is countable for all $a \in Z$. The collection of all countable soft sets over M relative to Z will be denoted by $C(M,Z)$. If $G \in SS(M,Z)$ and $a_x \in SP(M,Z)$, then a_x is said to belong to G (notation: $a_x \widetilde{\in} G$) if $x \in G(a)$.

Soft topological spaces were defined in [17] as follows: A triplet $(M,\mathcal{Y},Z)$, where $\mathcal{Y} \subseteq SS(M,Z)$, is called a soft topological space if $0_Z, 1_Z \in \mathcal{Y}$, and $\mathcal{Y}$ is closed under finite soft intersections and arbitrary soft unions.

Let $(M,\mathcal{Y},Z)$ be a soft topological space, and let $H \in SS(M,Z)$. Then the members of $\mathcal{Y}$ are called soft open sets. The soft complements of the members of $\mathcal{Y}$ are called soft closed sets in $(M,\mathcal{Y},Z)$. The family of all soft closed sets in $(M,\mathcal{Y},Z)$ will be denoted by $\mathcal{Y}^c$. The soft interior and the soft closure of H in $(M,\mathcal{Y},Z)$ will be denoted by $Int_{\mathcal{Y}}(H)$ and $Cl_{\mathcal{Y}}(H)$, respectively. Let (M,λ) be a topological space, and let $U \subseteq M$. The interior and the closure of U in (M,λ) will be denoted by $Int_\lambda(U)$ and $Cl_\lambda(U)$, respectively.

Definition 1 ([40])**.** *Let (M,λ) be a topological space, and $V \subseteq M$. Then V is said to be a δ-open set in (M,λ) if for every $x \in V$, we find $D \in \lambda$ such that $x \in D \subseteq Int_\lambda(Cl_\lambda(D)) \subseteq V$. λ_δ denotes the family of all δ-open sets in (M,λ).*

It is well known that (M,λ_δ) is a topological space with $\lambda_\delta \subseteq \lambda$.

Definition 2 ([41]). *Let (M, λ) be a topological space, and $V \subseteq M$. Then V is said to be a ω_δ-open set in (M, λ) if for every $x \in V$, we find $D \in \lambda$ such that $x \in D$ and $D - Int_{\lambda_\delta}(V)$ is a countable set. λ_{ω_δ} denotes the family of all ω_δ-open sets in (M, λ).*

It is proved in [41] that $(M, \lambda_{\omega_\delta})$ is a topological space.

Definition 3 ([41]). *A function $g : (M, \lambda) \longrightarrow (N, \gamma)$ between the topological spaces (M, λ) and (N, γ) is called ω_δ-continuous if $g^{-1}(V) \in \lambda_{\omega_\delta}$ for every $V \in \gamma$.*

Definition 4 ([39]). *Let $(M, \mathcal{Y}, Z)$ be a soft topological space and $K \in SS(M, Z)$. Then*

(a) K is a soft ω-open set in $(M, \mathcal{Y}, Z)$ if for any $z_m \widetilde{\in} K$, we find $G \in \mathcal{Y}$ such that $z_m \widetilde{\in} G$ and $G - K \in C(M, Z)$. $\mathcal{Y}_\omega$ will denote the family of all soft ω-open sets in $(M, \mathcal{Y}, Z)$.

(b) K is a soft ω-closed set in $(M, \mathcal{Y}, Z)$ if $1_Z - K \in \mathcal{Y}_\omega$.

It is proved in [39] that $(M, \mathcal{Y}_\omega, Z)$ is a soft topological space, $\mathcal{Y} \subseteq \mathcal{Y}_\omega$, and $\mathcal{Y} \neq \mathcal{Y}_\omega$ in general.

Definition 5. *Let $(M, \mathcal{Y}, Z)$ be a soft topological space and $H \in SS(M, Z)$. Then*

Ref. [42] (a) H is a soft θ-open set in $(M, \mathcal{Y}, Z)$ if for any $z_m \widetilde{\in} H$, we find $G \in \mathcal{Y}$ such that $z_m \widetilde{\in} G \widetilde{\subseteq} Cl_{\mathcal{Y}}(G) \widetilde{\subseteq} H$. The family of all soft θ-open sets in $(M, \mathcal{Y}, Z)$ will be denoted by $\mathcal{Y}_\theta$.

Ref. [43] (b) H is a soft δ-open set in $(M, \mathcal{Y}, Z)$ if for any $z_m \widetilde{\in} H$, we find $G \in \mathcal{Y}$ such that $z_m \widetilde{\in} G \widetilde{\subseteq} Int_{\mathcal{Y}}(Cl_{\mathcal{Y}}(G)) \widetilde{\subseteq} H$.

Ref. [39] (c) H is a soft ω-open set in $(M, \mathcal{Y}, Z)$ if for any $z_m \widetilde{\in} H$, we find $G \in \mathcal{Y}$ such that $z_m \widetilde{\in} G$ and $G - H \in C(M, Z)$.

Ref. [44] (d) H is a soft ω^0-open set in $(M, \mathcal{Y}, Z)$ if for any $z_m \widetilde{\in} H$, we find $G \in \mathcal{Y}$ such that $z_m \widetilde{\in} G$ and $G - Int_{\mathcal{Y}}(H) \in C(M, Z)$.

Ref. [45] (e) H is a soft ω_θ-open set in $(M, \mathcal{Y}, Z)$ if for any $z_m \widetilde{\in} H$, we find $G \in \mathcal{Y}$ such that $z_m \widetilde{\in} G$ and $G - Int_{\mathcal{Y}_\theta}(H) \in C(M, Z)$.

Ref. [46] (f) H is a soft regular-open set in $(M, \mathcal{Y}, Z)$ if $H = Int_{\mathcal{Y}}(Cl_{\mathcal{Y}}(H))$.

$\mathcal{Y}_\delta$ ($\mathcal{Y}_\omega$, $\mathcal{Y}_{\omega^0}$, $\mathcal{Y}_{\omega_\theta}$, and $RO(\mathcal{Y})$) will denote the family of all soft δ-open (resp. ω-open, ω^0-open, ω_θ-open, and regular open) sets in $(M, \mathcal{Y}, Z)$.

It is known that $\mathcal{Y}_\theta$, $\mathcal{Y}_\delta$, $\mathcal{Y}_\omega$, $\mathcal{Y}_{\omega^0}$, and $\mathcal{Y}_{\omega_\theta}$ are all soft topologies such that $\mathcal{Y}_\theta \subseteq \mathcal{Y}_\delta \subseteq \mathcal{Y} \subseteq \mathcal{Y}_{\omega^0} \subseteq \mathcal{Y}_\omega$ and $\mathcal{Y}_\theta \subseteq \mathcal{Y}_{\omega_\theta} \subseteq \mathcal{Y}_{\omega^0}$.

Definition 6. *A soft topological space $(M, \mathcal{Y}, Z)$ is called:*

Ref. [39] (a) Soft locally countable if it has a soft base $\mathcal{K} \subseteq C(M, Z)$.

Ref. [39] (b) Soft anti-locally countable (soft A-L-C) if $\mathcal{Y} \cap C(M, Z) = \{0_Z\}$.

Ref. [24] (c) Soft Lindelof if for every $\mathcal{H} \subseteq \mathcal{Y}$ such that $\widetilde{\cup}_{H \in \mathcal{H}} H = 1_Z$, there is a countable subcollection $\mathcal{H}_1 \subseteq \mathcal{H}$ such that $\widetilde{\cup}_{H \in \mathcal{H}_1} H = 1_Z$.

Ref. [47] (d) Soft nearly compact if for every $\mathcal{H} \subseteq RO(\mathcal{Y})$ such that $\widetilde{\cup}_{H \in \mathcal{H}} H = 1_Z$, there is a finite subcollection $\mathcal{H}_1 \subseteq \mathcal{H}$ such that $\widetilde{\cup}_{H \in \mathcal{H}_1} H = 1_Z$.

Ref. [47] (e) Soft nearly Lindelof if for every $\mathcal{H} \subseteq RO(\mathcal{Y})$ such that $\widetilde{\cup}_{H \in \mathcal{H}} H = 1_Z$, there is a countable subcollection $\mathcal{H}_1 \subseteq \mathcal{H}$ such that $\widetilde{\cup}_{H \in \mathcal{H}_1} H = 1_Z$.

Ref. [48] (f) Soft regular if for every $a_x \in SP(M, Z)$ and every $G \in \mathcal{Y}$ such that $a_x \widetilde{\in} G$, there exists $H \in \mathcal{Y}$ such that $a_x \widetilde{\in} H \widetilde{\subseteq} Cl_{\mathcal{Y}}(H) \widetilde{\subseteq} G$.

Ref. [49] (g) Soft semi-regularization topology if $\mathcal{Y} = \mathcal{Y}_\delta$.

Definition 7 ([50]). *A soft function $f_{qv} : (M, \mathcal{Y}, Z) \longrightarrow (N, \mathcal{X}, W)$ is called soft ω^0-continuous if $f_{qv}^{-1}(K) \in \mathcal{Y}_{\omega^0}$ for every $K \in \mathcal{X}$.*

Theorem 1 ([17]). *For any soft topological space $(M, \mathcal{Y}, Z)$ and any $a \in Z$, the family*

$$\{G(a) : G \in \mathcal{Y}\}$$

forms a topology on M. This topology is denoted by $\mathcal{Y}_a$.

Theorem 2 ([38]). *For any family of topological spaces $\{(M, \beta_a) : a \in A\}$, the family*

$$\{G \in SS(M, A) : G(a) \in \beta_a \text{ for all } a \in A\}$$

forms a soft topology on M relative to A. This soft topology is denoted by $\oplus_{a \in A}\beta_a$.

Theorem 3 ([38]). *For any topological space (M, λ) and any set of parameters Z, the family $\{G \in SS(M, Z) : G(z) \in \lambda \text{ for all } z \in Z\}$ defines a soft topology on M relative to Z. $\tau(\lambda)$ denotes this soft topology.*

2. Soft ω_δ-Open Sets

Definition 8. *Let $(M, \mathcal{Y}, Z)$ be a soft topological space and $K \in SS(M, Z)$. Then*

(a) K is a soft ω_δ-open set in $(M, \mathcal{Y}, Z)$ if for any $z_m \widetilde{\in} K$, we find $G \in \mathcal{Y}$ such that $z_m \widetilde{\in} G$ and $G - Int_{\mathcal{Y}_\delta}(K) \in C(M, Z)$. $\mathcal{Y}_{\omega_\delta}$ will denote the family of all soft ω_δ-open sets in $(M, \mathcal{Y}, Z)$.

(b) K is a soft ω_δ-closed set in $(M, \mathcal{Y}, Z)$ if $1_Z - K \in \mathcal{Y}_{\omega_\delta}$.

Theorem 4. *Let $(M, \mathcal{Y}, Z)$ be a soft topological space and $H \in SS(M, Z)$. Then $H \in \mathcal{Y}_{\omega_\delta}$ if and only if for each $z_m \widetilde{\in} H$, we find $G \in \mathcal{Y}$ and $R \in C(M, Z)$ such that $z_m \widetilde{\in} G$ and $G - R \widetilde{\subseteq} Int_{\mathcal{Y}_\delta}(H)$.*

Proof. *Necessity*. Suppose that $H \in \mathcal{Y}_{\omega_\delta}$. Let $z_m \widetilde{\in} H$. Then we find $G \in \mathcal{Y}$ such that $z_m \widetilde{\in} G$ and $G - Int_{\mathcal{Y}_\delta}(H) \in C(M, Z)$. Let $R = G - Int_{\mathcal{Y}_\delta}(H)$. Then $R \in C(M, Z)$ and $G - R = Int_{\mathcal{Y}_\delta}(H) \widetilde{\subseteq} Int_{\mathcal{Y}_\delta}(H)$.

Sufficiency. Suppose that for each $z_m \widetilde{\in} H$, we find $G \in \mathcal{Y}$ and $R \in C(M, Z)$ such that $z_m \widetilde{\in} G$ and $G - R \widetilde{\subseteq} Int_{\mathcal{Y}_\delta}(H)$. Let $z_m \widetilde{\in} H$. Then, by assumption, we find $G \in \mathcal{Y}$ and $R \in C(M, Z)$ such that $z_m \widetilde{\in} G$ and $G - R \widetilde{\subseteq} Int_{\mathcal{Y}_\delta}(H)$. Since $G - R \widetilde{\subseteq} Int_{\mathcal{Y}_\delta}(H)$, then $G - Int_{\mathcal{Y}_\delta}(H) \widetilde{\subseteq} R \in C(M, Z)$, and thus, $G - Int_{\mathcal{Y}_\delta}(H) \in C(M, Z)$. Therefore, $H \in \mathcal{Y}_{\omega_\delta}$. □

Theorem 5. *For any soft topological space $(M, \mathcal{Y}, Z)$, $\mathcal{Y}_\delta \subseteq \mathcal{Y}_{\omega_\delta} \subseteq \mathcal{Y}_{\omega^0}$.*

Proof. To see that $\mathcal{Y}_\delta \subseteq \mathcal{Y}_{\omega_\delta}$, let $G \in \mathcal{Y}_\delta$ and $z_m \widetilde{\in} G$. Since $G \in \mathcal{Y}_\delta$, then $Int_{\mathcal{Y}_\delta}(G) = G$. Thus, we have $z_m \widetilde{\in} G \in \mathcal{Y}$ such that $G - Int_{\mathcal{Y}_\delta}(G) = 0_Z \in C(M, Z)$, and hence $G \in \mathcal{Y}_{\omega_\delta}$.

To prove that $\mathcal{Y}_{\omega_\delta} \subseteq \mathcal{Y}_{\omega^0}$, let $G \in \mathcal{Y}_{\omega_\delta}$ and $z_m \widetilde{\in} G$. Then we find $H \in \mathcal{Y}$ such that $z_m \widetilde{\in} H$ and $H - Int_{\mathcal{Y}_\delta}(G) \in C(M, Z)$. Since $Int_{\mathcal{Y}_\delta}(G) \widetilde{\subseteq} Int_{\mathcal{Y}}(G)$, then $H - Int_{\mathcal{Y}}(G) \widetilde{\subseteq} H - Int_{\mathcal{Y}_\delta}(G)$, and so $H - Int_{\mathcal{Y}}(G) \in C(M, Z)$. Hence, $G \in \mathcal{Y}_{\omega^0}$. □

Theorem 6. *For any soft topological space $(M, \mathcal{Y}, Z)$, $(M, \mathcal{Y}_{\omega_\delta}, Z)$ is a soft topological space.*

Proof. Since by Proposition 4.2 of [43], $(M, \mathcal{Y}_\delta, A)$ is a soft topological space, then 0_Z, $1_Z \in \mathcal{Y}_\delta$. Thus, by Theorem 5, $0_Z, 1_Z \in \mathcal{Y}_{\omega_\delta}$.

Let $K, N \in \mathcal{Y}_{\omega_\delta}$ and $z_m \widetilde{\in} K \widetilde{\cap} N$. Then $z_m \widetilde{\in} K \in \mathcal{Y}_{\omega_\delta}$ and $z_m \widetilde{\in} N \in \mathcal{Y}_{\omega_\delta}$. So, we find $H, L \in \mathcal{Y}$ such that $z_m \widetilde{\in} H \widetilde{\cap} L \in \mathcal{Y}$ and $H - Int_{\mathcal{Y}_\delta}(K)$, $L - Int_{\mathcal{Y}_\delta}(N) \in C(M, Z)$. Since $Int_{\mathcal{Y}_\delta}(K \widetilde{\cap} N) = Int_{\mathcal{Y}_\delta}(K) \widetilde{\cap} Int_{\mathcal{Y}_\delta}(N)$, then

$$\begin{aligned} (H \widetilde{\cap} L) - (Int_{\mathcal{Y}_\delta}(K \widetilde{\cap} N)) &= (H \widetilde{\cap} L) - \left(Int_{\mathcal{Y}_\delta}(K) \widetilde{\cap} Int_{\mathcal{Y}_\delta}(N)\right) \\ &= \left((H \widetilde{\cap} L) - Int_{\mathcal{Y}_\delta}(K)\right) \widetilde{\cup} \left((H \widetilde{\cap} L) - Int_{\mathcal{Y}_\delta}(N)\right) \in C(M, Z). \end{aligned}$$

Hence, $K \widetilde{\cap} N \in \mathcal{Y}_{\omega_\delta}$.

Let $\{G_\alpha : \alpha \in \Delta\} \subseteq \mathcal{Y}_{\omega_\delta}$ and $z_m \widetilde{\in} \cup_{\alpha \in \Delta} G_\alpha$. Then there exists $\alpha_\circ \in \Delta$ such that $z_m \widetilde{\in} G_{\alpha_\circ}$. So, by Theorem 4 , we find $H \in \mathcal{Y}$ and $R \in C(M, Z)$ such that $z_m \widetilde{\in} H$ and $H - R \widetilde{\subseteq} Int_{\mathcal{Y}_\delta}(G_{\alpha_\circ}) \widetilde{\subseteq} Int_{\mathcal{Y}_\delta}(\widetilde{\cup}_{\alpha \in \Delta} G_{\alpha_\circ})$. Hence, $\widetilde{\cup}_{\alpha \in \Delta} G_{\alpha_\circ} \in \mathcal{Y}_{\omega_\delta}$. □

Theorem 7. *If $(M, \mathcal{Y}, Z)$ is soft locally countable, then $\mathcal{Y}_{\omega_\delta} = SS(M, Z)$.*

Proof. Let $(M, \mathcal{Y}, Z)$ be soft locally countable. Let $H \in SS(M, Z)$ and $z_m \widetilde{\in} H$. Choose $K \in C(M, Z) \cap \mathcal{Y}$ such that $z_m \widetilde{\in} K \widetilde{\subseteq} H$. Thus, we have $K \in C(M, Z)$, $z_m \widetilde{\in} K \in \mathcal{Y}$, and $K - Int_{\mathcal{Y}_\delta}(H) \in C(M, Z)$. Hence, $H \in \mathcal{Y}_{\omega_\delta}$. □

Theorem 8. *If $(M, \mathcal{Y}, Z)$ is a soft semi-regularization topology, then $\mathcal{Y}_{\omega_\delta} = \mathcal{Y}_{\omega^0}$.*

Proof. By Theorem 5, it is sufficient to see that $\mathcal{Y}_{\omega^0} \subseteq \mathcal{Y}_{\omega_\delta}$. Let $H \in \mathcal{Y}_{\omega^0}$ and $z_m \widetilde{\in} H$. Then we find $G \in \mathcal{Y}$ such that $z_m \widetilde{\in} G$ and $G - Int_{\mathcal{Y}}(H) \in C(M, Z)$. Since $(M, \mathcal{Y}, Z)$ is a soft semi-regularization topology, then $\mathcal{Y}_\delta = \mathcal{Y}$, and so $Int_{\mathcal{Y}_\delta}(H) = Int_{\mathcal{Y}}(H)$. This shows that $H \in \mathcal{Y}_{\omega_\delta}$. □

Theorem 9. *For any soft topological space $(M, \mathcal{Y}, Z)$, $\mathcal{Y}_{\omega_\theta} \subseteq \mathcal{Y}_{\omega_\delta}$.*

Proof. Let $G \in \mathcal{Y}_{\omega_\theta}$ and $z_m \widetilde{\in} G$. Then we find $H \in \mathcal{Y}$ such that $z_m \widetilde{\in} H$ and $H - Int_{\mathcal{Y}_\theta}(G) \in C(M, Z)$. Since $Int_{\mathcal{Y}_\theta}(G) \widetilde{\subseteq} Int_{\mathcal{Y}_\delta}(G)$, then $H - Int_{\mathcal{Y}_\delta}(G) \widetilde{\subseteq} H - Int_{\mathcal{Y}_\theta}(G)$, and so $H - Int_{\mathcal{Y}_\delta}(G) \in C(M, Z)$. Hence, $G \in \mathcal{Y}_{\omega_\delta}$. □

Lemma 1. *Let $(M, \mathcal{Y}, Z)$ be a soft topological space, and $K \in SS(M, Z)$. Then, for each $a \in Z$, $\left(Int_{\mathcal{Y}_\delta}(K)\right)(a) \subseteq Int_{(\mathcal{Y}_a)_\delta}(K(a))$.*

Proof. Let $m \in \left(Int_{\mathcal{Y}_\delta}(K)\right)(a)$. Then $a_m \widetilde{\in} Int_{\mathcal{Y}_\delta}(K)$, and so, we find $G \in \mathcal{Y}_\delta$ such that $a_m \widetilde{\in} G \widetilde{\subseteq} K$. Thus, we have $m \in G(a) \subseteq K(a)$ and $G(a) \in (\mathcal{Y}_\delta)_a$. Since, by Theorem 30 of [51], $G(a) \in (\mathcal{Y}_a)_\delta$, then $m \in Int_{(\mathcal{Y}_a)_\delta}(K(a))$. □

Theorem 10. *Let $(M, \mathcal{Y}, Z)$ be a soft topological space. Then, for every $a \in Z$, $(\mathcal{Y}_{\omega_\delta})_a \subseteq (\mathcal{Y}_a)_{\omega_\delta}$.*

Proof. Let $a \in Z$. Let $V \in (\mathcal{Y}_{\omega_\delta})_a$ and $m \in V$. Then, there exists $K \in \mathcal{Y}_{\omega_\delta}$ such that $V = K(a)$. Thus, $a_m \widetilde{\in} K \in \mathcal{Y}_{\omega_\delta}$, and by Theorem 4, we find $G \in \mathcal{Y}$ and $R \in C(M, Z)$ such that $a_m \widetilde{\in} G$ and $G - R \widetilde{\subseteq} Int_{\mathcal{Y}_\delta}(K)$. So, we have $m \in G(a) \in \mathcal{Y}_a$, $R(a)$ is a countable set, and $G(a) - R(a) = (G - R)(a) \subseteq \left(Int_{\mathcal{Y}_\delta}(K)\right)(a)$. On the other hand, by Lemma 1, $\left(Int_{\mathcal{Y}_\delta}(K)\right)(a) \subseteq Int_{(\mathcal{Y}_a)_\delta}(K(a))$. This shows that $V \in (\mathcal{Y}_a)_{\omega_\delta}$. □

Corollary 1. *Let $(M, \mathcal{Y}, Z)$ be a soft topological space, and $K \in \mathcal{Y}_{\omega_\delta}$. Then $K(a) \in (\mathcal{Y}_a)_{\omega_\delta}$ for all $z \in Z$.*

Proof. Let $s \in S$. Since $G \in \mathcal{Y}_{\omega_\delta}$, then $G(s) \in (\mathcal{Y}_{\omega_\delta})_s$. Thus, by Theorem 9, $G(s) \in (\mathcal{Y}_s)_{\omega_\delta}$. □

Theorem 11. *Let $\{(M, \beta_z) : z \in Z\}$ be a collection of topological spaces. Then $(\oplus_{z \in Z} \beta_z)_{\omega_\delta} = \oplus_{z \in Z} (\beta_z)_{\omega_\delta}$.*

Proof. To show that $(\oplus_{z \in Z} \beta_z)_{\omega_\delta} \subseteq \oplus_{z \in Z} (\beta_z)_{\omega_\delta}$, let $H \in (\oplus_{z \in Z} \beta_z)_{\omega_\delta}$. Let $b \in Z$. We will show that $H(b) \in (\beta_b)_{\omega_\delta}$. Let $m \in H(b)$. Then $b_m \widetilde{\in} H$. Since $H \in (\oplus_{z \in Z} \beta_z)_{\omega_\delta}$, we find $G \in \oplus_{z \in Z} \beta_z$ and $R \in C(M, Z)$ such that $b_m \widetilde{\in} G$ and $G - R \widetilde{\subseteq} Int_{(\oplus_{z \in Z} \beta_z)_\delta}(H)$. Now, by Theorem 31 of [51], $(\oplus_{z \in Z} \beta_z)_\delta = \oplus_{z \in Z} (\beta_z)_\delta$. Thus, $G - R \widetilde{\subseteq} Int_{\oplus_{z \in Z} (\beta_z)_\delta}(H)$ and so $G(b) - R(b) = (G - R)(b) \subseteq \left(Int_{\oplus_{z \in Z} (\beta_z)_\delta}(H)\right)(b)$. In contrast, by Lemma 4.9 of [52], $\left(Int_{\oplus_{z \in Z} (\beta_z)_\delta}(H)\right)(b) = Int_{(\beta_b)_\delta}(H(b))$. Therefore, we have $m \in G(b) \in \beta_b$, $R(b)$ is a countable set, and $G(b) - R(b) = Int_{(\beta_b)_\delta}(H(b))$. Hence, $H(b) \in (\beta_b)_{\omega_\delta}$.

To show that $\oplus_{z \in Z} (\beta_z)_{\omega_\delta} \subseteq (\oplus_{z \in Z} \beta_z)_{\omega_\delta}$, let $H \in \oplus_{z \in Z} (\beta_z)_{\omega_\delta}$. Let $b_m \widetilde{\in} H$. Then $m \in H(b) \in (\beta_b)_{\omega_\delta}$. So, we find $V \in \beta_b$ such that $m \in V$ and $V - Int_{(\beta_b)_\delta}(H(b))$ is a countable set. By Lemma 4.9 of [52], $\left(Int_{\oplus_{z \in Z} (\beta_z)_\delta}(H)\right)(b) = Int_{(\beta_b)_\delta}(H(b))$ and so $\left(b_V - \left(Int_{\oplus_{z \in Z} (\beta_z)_\delta}(H)\right)\right)(b) = V - \left(Int_{\oplus_{z \in Z} (\beta_z)_\delta}(H)\right)(b)$ is a countable set. Therefore, we have $b_m \tilde{\in} b_V \in \oplus_{z\in Z}\beta_z$ and $b_V - \left(Int_{\oplus_{z\in Z}(\beta_z)_\delta}(H)\right) \in C(M,Z)$. This shows that $H \in (\oplus_{z\in Z}\beta_z)_{\omega_\delta}$. □

Corollary 2. *For any topological space (M,β) and any set of parameters Z, $(\tau(\beta))_{\omega_\delta} = \tau(\beta_{\omega_\delta})$.*

Proof. Let $\beta_z = \beta$ for every $z \in Z$. Then $\tau(\beta) = \oplus_{z\in Z}\beta_z$. Thus, by Theorem 11,

$$\begin{aligned}(\tau(\beta))_{\omega_\delta} &= (\oplus_{z\in Z}\beta_z)_{\omega_\delta} \\ &= \oplus_{z\in Z}(\beta_z)_{\omega_\delta} \\ &= \tau(\beta_{\omega_\delta}).\end{aligned}$$

□

The following examples show that equality cannot be used to replace either of the two soft inclusions in Theorem 5:

Example 1. *Let $M = \mathbb{Q}$, $A = \mathbb{N}$, $\mathcal{Y} = \{0_A\} \cup \{K \in SS(M,A) : M - K(a)$ is a finite set for every $a \in A\}$. Since $(M,\mathcal{Y},A)$ is soft locally countable, then by Theorem 7, $\mathcal{Y}_{\omega_\delta} = SS(M,A)$. Therefore, $C_{\mathbb{Z}} \in \mathcal{Y}_{\omega_\delta} - \mathcal{Y}_\delta$.*

Example 2. *Let $M = \mathbb{R}$, $Z = \{a,b,d\}$, and $\mathcal{Y} = \left\{0_Z, 1_Z, b_{(0,\infty)}\right\}$. Suppose that $Int_{\mathcal{Y}_\delta}\left(b_{(0,\infty)}\right) \neq 0_Z$. Then we find $m \in (0,\infty)$ such that $b_m \tilde{\in} Int_{\mathcal{Y}_\delta}\left(b_{(0,\infty)}\right)$. So, we find $K \in \mathcal{Y}$ such that $b_m \tilde{\in} K \tilde{\subseteq} Int_{\mathcal{Y}}(Cl_{\mathcal{Y}}(K)) \tilde{\subseteq} b_{(0,\infty)}$. Thus, $K = b_{(0,\infty)}$, and so $Int_{\mathcal{Y}}(Cl_{\mathcal{Y}}(K)) = Int_{\mathcal{Y}}(1_Z) = 1_Z \tilde{\subseteq} b_{(0,\infty)}$. Hence, $Int_{\mathcal{Y}_\delta}\left(b_{(0,\infty)}\right) = 0_Z$. Suppose that $b_{(0,\infty)} \in \mathcal{Y}_{\omega_\delta}$, then we find $H \in \mathcal{Y}$ such that $b_1 \tilde{\in} H$ and $H - Int_{\mathcal{Y}_\delta}\left(b_{(0,\infty)}\right) = H \in C(M,Z)$. Since $H \in \mathcal{Y} - \{0_Z\}$, then $H \in \left\{1_Z, b_{(0,\infty)}\right\}$. But $\left\{1_Z, b_{(0,\infty)}\right\} \cap C(M,Z) = \emptyset$. Therefore, $b_{(0,\infty)} \notin \mathcal{Y}_{\omega_\delta}$. In contrast, by Theorem 5 of [44], $b_{(0,\infty)} \in \mathcal{Y}_{\omega^0}$.*

Additionally, Example 2 demonstrates that $\mathcal{Y}$ need not always be a subset of $\mathcal{Y}_{\omega_\delta}$.

The inclusion in Theorem 9 need not be equality in general:

Example 3. *Let $M = \mathbb{R}$, $Z = \mathbb{N}$, and*

$\mathcal{Y} = \{K \in SS(M,Z) : K(a) \in \{\emptyset, M, \mathbb{Q} \cap (1,2), \mathbb{R} - \mathbb{Q}, (\mathbb{Q} \cap (1,2)) \cup (\mathbb{R} - \mathbb{Q})\}$ for all $a \in Z\}$.

Then $C_{\mathbb{R}-\mathbb{Q}} \in \mathcal{Y}_{\omega_\delta} - \mathcal{Y}_{\omega_\theta}$.

Theorem 12. *Let $(M,\mathcal{Y},Z)$ be a soft topological space. If $C_V \in (\mathcal{Y} \cap \mathcal{Y}_{\omega_\delta}) - \{0_Z\}$, then $(\mathcal{Y}_{\omega_\delta})_V \subseteq (\mathcal{Y}_V)_{\omega_\delta}$.*

Proof. Let $K \in (\mathcal{Y}_{\omega_\delta})_V$ and $z_m \tilde{\in} K$. Choose $T \in \mathcal{Y}_{\omega_\delta}$ such that $K = T \tilde{\cap} C_V$. Since $C_V \in \mathcal{Y}_{\omega_\delta}$, then $K \in \mathcal{Y}_{\omega_\delta}$. So, we find $D \in \mathcal{Y}$ and $E \in C(M,Z)$ such that $z_m \tilde{\in} D$ and $D - E \tilde{\subseteq} Int_{\mathcal{Y}_\delta}(K)$. So, we have $z_m \tilde{\in} D \tilde{\cap} C_V \in \mathcal{Y}_V$, $E \tilde{\cap} C_V \in C(V,A)$, and $(D \tilde{\cap} C_V) - (E \tilde{\cap} C_V) \tilde{\subseteq} (D - E) \tilde{\cap} C_V \tilde{\subseteq} Int_{\mathcal{Y}_\delta}(K) \tilde{\cap} C_V \tilde{\subseteq} Int_{(\mathcal{Y}_V)_\delta}(K)$. This shows that $K \in (\mathcal{Y}_V)_{\omega_\delta}$. □

Corollary 3. *Let $(M,\mathcal{Y},Z)$ be a soft topological space. If $C_V \in \mathcal{Y}_\delta - \{0_Z\}$, then $(\mathcal{Y}_{\omega_\delta})_V \subseteq (\mathcal{Y}_V)_{\omega_\delta}$.*

Theorem 12 requires the condition "$C_V \in \mathcal{Y} \cap \mathcal{Y}_{\omega_\delta}$", as the following example demonstrates.

Example 4. *Let $M = \mathbb{R}$, $V = \mathbb{R} - \mathbb{Q}$, $Z = \mathbb{N}$, λ be the usual topology on M, and $\mathcal{Y} = \{C_W : W \in \lambda\}$. Since $C_{(3,\infty)} \in \mathcal{Y}$, then by Theorem 5 of [44], $C_{(3,\infty)} \in \mathcal{Y}_{\omega^0}$. Since $(M, \mathcal{Y}, Z)$ is soft regular and $C_{(3,\infty)} \in \mathcal{Y}$, then by Theorem 8, $C_{(3,\infty)} \in \mathcal{Y}_{\omega_\delta}$. Thus, $C_{(3,\infty)} \tilde{\cap} C_V = C_{(3,\infty)\cap(\mathbb{R}-\mathbb{Q})} \in (\mathcal{Y}_{\omega_\delta})_V$. Suppose that $C_{(3,\infty)\cap(\mathbb{R}-\mathbb{Q})} \in (\mathcal{Y}_V)_{\omega_\delta}$. Let $a = 1$. Then we find $W \in \lambda$ and $K \in C(V, A)$ such that $a_{\sqrt{11}} \in C_W$ and $C_W - K \tilde{\subseteq} Int_{(\mathcal{Y}_V)_\delta}\left(C_{(3,\infty)\cap(\mathbb{R}-\mathbb{Q})}\right) \tilde{\subseteq} Int_{\mathcal{Y}_V}\left(C_{(3,\infty)\cap(\mathbb{R}-\mathbb{Q})}\right) = 0_Z$. Thus, $C_W \tilde{\subseteq} K$, and hence $C_W \in C(V, A)$. Therefore, W is a countable set, which is impossible. This shows that $C_{(3,\infty)\cap(\mathbb{R}-\mathbb{Q})} \notin (\mathcal{Y}_V)_{\omega_\delta}$.*

Theorem 13. *Let $(M, \mathcal{Y}, Z)$ be soft Lindelof. Then for every $W \in \mathcal{Y}_{\omega_\delta} \cap \mathcal{Y}^c$, we have $W - Int_{\mathcal{Y}_\delta}(W) \in C(M, Z)$.*

Proof. Let $W \in \mathcal{Y}_{\omega_\delta} \cap \mathcal{Y}^c$. Since $W \in \mathcal{Y}_{\omega_\delta}$, for every $z_m \tilde{\in} W$, we find $T_{z_m} \in \mathcal{Y}$ such that $z_m \tilde{\in} T_{z_m}$ and $T_{z_m} - Int_{\mathcal{Y}_\delta}(W) \in C(M, Z)$. Since $W \in \mathcal{Y}^c$, W is a soft Lindelof subset of $(M, \mathcal{Y}, Z)$. Set $\ominus = \{T_{z_m} : z_m \tilde{\in} K\}$. Since $W \tilde{\subseteq} \tilde{\cup}_{z_m \tilde{\in} K} T_{z_m}$, then we find a countable subfamily $\ominus_1 \subseteq \ominus$ such that $W \tilde{\subseteq} \tilde{\cup}_{S \in \ominus_1} S$. Since $\ominus_1$ is countable, then $\tilde{\cup}_{S \in \ominus_1}(S - Int_{\mathcal{Y}_\delta}(W)) \in C(M, Z)$. Since $W - Int_{\mathcal{Y}_\delta}(W) \tilde{\subseteq} \tilde{\cup}_{S \in \ominus_1}(S - Int_{\mathcal{Y}_\delta}(W))$, $W - Int_{\mathcal{Y}_\delta}(W) \in C(M, Z)$. □

Theorem 14. *Let $(M, \mathcal{Y}, Z)$ be a soft topological space, and $K \in (\mathcal{Y}_{\omega_\delta})^c$. Then we find $H \in \mathcal{Y}^c$ and $T \in C(M, Z)$ such that $Cl_{\mathcal{Y}_\delta}(K) \tilde{\subseteq} H \tilde{\cup} T$.*

Proof. If $K = 1_Z$, then $K \tilde{\subseteq} 1_Z \tilde{\cup} 0_Z$ with $1_Z \in \mathcal{Y}^c$ and $0_Z \in C(M, Z)$. If $K \neq 1_Z$, then we find $z_m \tilde{\in} 1_Z - K \in \mathcal{Y}_{\omega_\delta}$. So, we find $G \in \mathcal{Y}$ and $T \in C(M, Z)$ such that $z_m \tilde{\in} G$ and $G - T \tilde{\subseteq} Int_{\mathcal{Y}_\delta}(1_Z - K) = 1_Z - Cl_{\mathcal{Y}_\delta}(K)$ and thus $Cl_{\mathcal{Y}_\delta}(K) \tilde{\subseteq} 1_Z - (G - T) = (1_Z - G) \tilde{\cup} T$. Let $H = 1_Z - G$. Then $H \in \mathcal{Y}^c$ and $Cl_{\mathcal{Y}_\delta}(K) \tilde{\subseteq} H \tilde{\cup} T$. □

Theorem 15. *A soft topological space $(M, \mathcal{Y}, Z)$ is soft A-L-C if and only if $(M, \mathcal{Y}_{\omega_\delta}, A)$ is soft A-L-C.*

Proof. *Necessity*. Let $(M, \mathcal{Y}, Z)$ be soft A-L-C. To show that $(M, \mathcal{Y}_{\omega_\delta}, A)$ is soft A-L-C, on the contrary, we find $K \in (\mathcal{Y}_{\omega_\delta} \cap C(M, Z)) - \{0_Z\}$. Pick $z_m \tilde{\in} K$. Since $K \in \mathcal{Y}_{\omega_\delta}$, then we find $T \in \mathcal{Y}$ and $N \in C(M, Z)$ such that $z_m \tilde{\in} T$ and $T - N \tilde{\subseteq} Int_{\mathcal{Y}_\delta}(K) \tilde{\subseteq} K$. Thus, $T \tilde{\subseteq} K \tilde{\cup} N$, and hence $T \in C(M, Z)$. Since $z_m \tilde{\in} T$, then $T \in \mathcal{Y} - \{0_Z\}$. Since $(M, \mathcal{Y}, Z)$ is soft A-L-C, then $T \notin C(M, Z)$, a contradiction.

Sufficiency. Clear. □

Theorem 16. *Let $(M, \mathcal{Y}, Z)$ be soft A-L-C. Then, for every $K \in \mathcal{Y}_{\omega_\delta}$, $Cl_{\mathcal{Y}}(K) \tilde{\subseteq} Cl_{\mathcal{Y}_{\omega_\delta}}(K)$.*

Proof. Let $K \in \mathcal{Y}_{\omega_\delta}$. By Theorem 5, $\mathcal{Y}_{\omega_\delta} \subseteq \mathcal{Y}_{\omega^0}$, and thus $Cl_{\mathcal{Y}_{\omega^0}}(K) \tilde{\subseteq} Cl_{\mathcal{Y}_{\omega_\delta}}(K)$. Since $(M, \mathcal{Y}, Z)$ is soft A-L-C and $H \in \mathcal{Y}_{\omega_\delta} \subseteq \mathcal{Y}_{\omega^0}$, then by Theorem 21 of [44], $Cl_{\mathcal{Y}_{\omega^0}}(K) = Cl_{\mathcal{Y}}(K)$. Hence, $Cl_{\mathcal{Y}}(K) \tilde{\subseteq} Cl_{\mathcal{Y}_{\omega_\delta}}(K)$. □

Corollary 4. *Let $(M, \mathcal{Y}, Z)$ be soft A-L-C. Then for each $K \in (\mathcal{Y}_{\omega_\delta})^c$, then $Int_{\mathcal{Y}_{\omega_\delta}}(K) \tilde{\subseteq} Int_{\mathcal{Y}}(K)$.*

Theorem 17. *If $(M, \mathcal{Y}, Z)$ is soft Lindelof, then $(M, \mathcal{Y}_{\omega_\delta}, Z)$ is soft Lindelof.*

Proof. Let $\mathcal{K} \subseteq \mathcal{Y}_{\omega_\delta}$ such that $1_Z = \tilde{\cup}_{K \in \mathcal{K}} K$. For each $z_m \tilde{\in} 1_Z$, choose $K_{z_m} \in \mathcal{K}$ such that $z_m \tilde{\in} K_{z_m}$. For each $z_m \tilde{\in} 1_Z$, choose $H_{z_m} \in \mathcal{Y}$ and $T_{z_m} \in C(M, Z)$ such that $z_m \tilde{\in} H_{z_m}$ and $H_{z_m} - T_{z_m} \tilde{\subseteq} Int_{\mathcal{Y}_{\omega_\delta}}(K_{z_m}) \tilde{\subseteq} K_{z_m}$. Since $(M, \mathcal{Y}, Z)$ is soft Lindelof and $1_Z = \tilde{\cup}_{z_m \tilde{\in} 1_Z} H_{z_m}$, then there exists a countable subset $R \subseteq SP(M, Z)$ such that $1_Z = \tilde{\cup}_{z_m \tilde{\in} R} H_{z_m}$ and so

$$1_Z = \tilde{\cup}_{z_m \tilde{\in} R} H_{z_m} = \left(\tilde{\cup}_{z_m \tilde{\in} R}(H_{z_m} - T_{z_m})\right) \tilde{\cup} \left(\tilde{\cup}_{z_m \tilde{\in} R} T_{z_m}\right) \tilde{\subseteq} \left(\tilde{\cup}_{z_m \tilde{\in} R} K_{z_m}\right) \tilde{\cup} \left(\tilde{\cup}_{z_m \tilde{\in} R} T_{z_m}\right).$$

Put $S = \tilde{\cup}_{z_m \tilde{\in} R} T_{z_m}$. Then $S \in C(M, Z)$. For each $b_x \tilde{\in} S$, choose $K_{b_x} \in \mathcal{K}$ such that $b_x \tilde{\in} K_{b_x}$. Put $\mathcal{N} = \{K_{z_m} : z_m \in R\} \cup \{K_{b_x} : b_x \tilde{\in} S\}$. Then $\mathcal{N}$ is a countable subcollection of $\mathcal{K}$ such that $1_Z = \tilde{\cup}_{N \in \mathcal{N}} N$. Therefore, $(M, \mathcal{Y}_{\omega_\delta}, Z)$ is soft Lindelof. □

But the converse of Theorem 17 is not always true:

Theorem 18. *Let $M = \mathbb{R}$, $Z = \mathbb{N}$, and $Y = \{0_Z\} \tilde{\cup} \{K \in SS(M, Z) : (-\infty, 1) \subseteq K(z)$ for all $z \in Z\}$. Let $\mathcal{H} = \left\{C_{(-\infty,1) \cup \{m\}} : m \in [1, \infty)\right\}$. Then $\mathcal{H} \subseteq \mathcal{Y}$, $\tilde{\cup}_{H \in \mathcal{H}} H = 1_Z$, and for any countable subcollection $\mathcal{H}_1 \subseteq \mathcal{H}$, $\tilde{\cup}_{H \in \mathcal{H}_1} H \neq 1_Z$. Therefore, $(M, \mathcal{Y}, Z)$ is not soft Lindelof. In contrast, since for any $G \in \mathcal{Y} - \{0_Z\}$, $Cl_{\mathcal{Y}}(G) = 1_Z$, then $\mathcal{Y}_\delta = \{0_Z, 1_Z\}$ and so $\mathcal{Y}_{\omega_\delta} = \{0_Z, 1_Z\}$. Hence, $(M, \mathcal{Y}_{\omega_\delta}, Z)$ is soft Lindelof.*

Theorem 19. *If $(M, \mathcal{Y}_{\omega_\delta}, Z)$ is soft Lindelof, then $(M, \mathcal{Y}, Z)$ is soft nearly Lindelof.*

Proof. Let $\mathcal{K} \subseteq RO(\mathcal{Y})$ such that $1_Z = \tilde{\cup}_{K \in \mathcal{K}} K$. Then $\mathcal{K} \subseteq \mathcal{Y}_\delta$, and by Theorem 5, $\mathcal{K} \subseteq \mathcal{Y}_{\omega_\delta}$. Since $(M, \mathcal{Y}_{\omega_\delta}, Z)$ is soft Lindelof, then we find a countable subfamily $\mathcal{K}_1 \subseteq \mathcal{K}$ such that $1_Z = \tilde{\cup}_{K \in \mathcal{K}_1} K$. This shows that $(M, \mathcal{Y}, Z)$ is soft nearly Lindelof. □

In general, Theorem 19 cannot be reversed:

Theorem 20. *Let $M = \mathbb{R}$, $Z = \mathbb{N}$, and*
$\mathcal{Y} = \{0_Z\} \tilde{\cup} \{K \in SS(M, Z) : 1 \in K(z)$ for all $z \in Z\}$.
Since $\mathcal{Y}_\delta = \{0_Z, 1_Z\}$, then $(M, \mathcal{Y}, Z)$ is soft nearly Lindelof. Since for each $z_m \in SP(M, Z)$, $z_m \tilde{\in} z_{\{1,m\}} \in \mathcal{Y} \cap C(M, Z)$, then $(M, \mathcal{Y}, Z)$ is soft locally countable. Thus, by Theorem 7, $\mathcal{Y}_{\omega_\delta} = SS(M, Z)$. Since $1_Z = \tilde{\cup}_{z_m \in SP(M,Z)} z_m$ and for any countable subfamily $\mathcal{H} \subseteq SP(M, Z)$, $1_Z \neq \tilde{\cup}_{z_m \in \mathcal{H}} z_m$, then $(M, \mathcal{Y}_{\omega_\delta}, Z)$ is not soft Lindelof.

Theorem 21. *If $(M, \mathcal{Y}_{\omega_\delta}, Z)$ is soft compact, then $(M, \mathcal{Y}, Z)$ is soft nearly compact.*

Proof. Let $\mathcal{K} \subseteq RO(\mathcal{Y})$ such that $1_Z = \tilde{\cup}_{K \in \mathcal{K}} K$. Then $\mathcal{K} \subseteq \mathcal{Y}_\delta$, and by Theorem 5, $\mathcal{K} \subseteq \mathcal{Y}_{\omega_\delta}$. Since $(M, \mathcal{Y}_{\omega_\delta}, Z)$ is soft compact, then we find a finite subfamily $\mathcal{K}_1 \subseteq \mathcal{K}$ such that $1_Z = \tilde{\cup}_{K \in \mathcal{K}_1} K$. This shows that $(M, \mathcal{Y}, Z)$ is soft nearly compact. □

In general, Theorem 21 cannot be reversed.

Example 5. *Let $M = \mathbb{Q}$, $Z = \{a, b\}$, and $\mathcal{Y} = \{0_Z, 1_Z\}$. Then $\mathcal{Y}_\delta = \{0_Z, 1_Z\}$, and thus $(M, \mathcal{Y}, Z)$ is soft nearly compact. Since $(M, \mathcal{Y}, Z)$ is soft locally countable, then by Theorem 7, $\mathcal{Y}_{\omega_\delta} = SS(M, Z)$. Since $1_Z = \tilde{\cup}_{z_m \in SP(M,Z)} z_m$ and for any finite subfamily $\mathcal{H} \subseteq SP(M, Z)$, $1_Z \neq \tilde{\cup}_{z_m \in \mathcal{H}} z_m$, then $(M, \mathcal{Y}_{\omega_\delta}, Z)$ is not soft compact.*

Example 5 and the following example show that the soft compactness of a soft topological space $(M, \mathcal{Y}, Z)$ is neither implied nor imply by the soft compactness of $(M, \mathcal{Y}_{\omega_\delta}, Z)$.

Example 6. *Let $M = \mathbb{R}$, $Z = \{a\}$ and*
$\mathcal{Y} = \{0_Z\} \tilde{\cup} \{K \in SS(M, Z) : \mathbb{R} - K(a)$ is countable$\}$.
Since $\mathcal{Y}_\delta = \{0_Z, 1_Z\} = \mathcal{Y}_{\omega_\delta}$, then $(M, \mathcal{Y}_{\omega_\delta}, Z)$ is soft compact. In contrast, it is clear that $(M, \mathcal{Y}, Z)$ is not soft compact.

3. Decompositions

Definition 9. *Let $(M, \mathcal{Y}, Z)$ be a soft topological space and $K \in SS(M, Z)$. Then K is*
(a) Soft ω_δ^δ-open set in $(M, \mathcal{Y}, Z)$ if $Int_{\mathcal{Y}_{\omega_\delta}}(K) = Int_{\mathcal{Y}_\delta}(K)$.
(b) Soft ω_δ^0 open set in $(M, \mathcal{Y}, Z)$ if $Int_{\mathcal{Y}_{\omega_\delta}}(K) = Int_{\mathcal{Y}}(K)$.
(c) Soft ω_δ^θ-open set in $(M, \mathcal{Y}, Z)$ if $Int_{\mathcal{Y}_{\omega_\delta}}(K) = Int_{\mathcal{Y}_\theta}(K)$.
(d) Soft ω_δ^ω-open set in $(M, \mathcal{Y}, Z)$ if $Int_{\mathcal{Y}_{\omega_\delta}}(K) = Int_{\mathcal{Y}_\omega}(K)$.

In a soft topological space $(M, \mathcal{Y}, Z)$, the collections of soft ω_δ^δ-open sets, soft ω_δ^0-open set, soft ω_δ^θ-open sets, and soft ω_δ^ω-open sets will be denoted by $\omega_\delta^\delta(\mathcal{Y})$, $\omega_\delta^0(\mathcal{Y})$, $\omega_\delta^\theta(\mathcal{Y})$, and $\omega_\delta^\omega(\mathcal{Y})$, respectively.

Theorem 22. *Let $(M, \mathcal{Y}, Z)$ be a soft topological space. Then*
(a) $\mathcal{Y}_{\omega_\delta} \subseteq \omega_\delta^\omega(\mathcal{Y})$.
(b) $\mathcal{Y}_\delta \subseteq \omega_\delta^\omega(\mathcal{Y}) \cap \omega_\delta^\delta(\mathcal{Y}) \cap \omega_\delta^0(\mathcal{Y})$.
(c) $\mathcal{Y}_\theta \subseteq \omega_\delta^\delta(\mathcal{Y}) \cap \omega_\delta^0(\mathcal{Y}) \cap \omega_\delta^\omega(\mathcal{Y}) \cap \omega_\delta^\theta(\mathcal{Y})$.
(d) $\omega_\delta^\theta(\mathcal{Y}) \subseteq \omega_\delta^\delta(\mathcal{Y})$.

Proof. (a) Let $K \in \mathcal{Y}_{\omega_\delta}$. Then $Int_{\mathcal{Y}_{\omega_\delta}}(K) = K$. Also, by Theorem 5 and Theorem 5 of [44], $K \in \mathcal{Y}_\omega$, and so $Int_{\mathcal{Y}_\omega}(K) = K$. Therefore, $Int_{\mathcal{Y}_{\omega_\delta}}(K) = Int_{\mathcal{Y}_\omega}(K)$. Hence, $K \in \omega_\delta^\omega(\mathcal{Y})$.

(b) Since by Theorem 5, $\mathcal{Y}_\delta \subseteq \mathcal{Y}_{\omega_\delta}$. Then, by (a), $\mathcal{Y}_\delta \subseteq \omega_\delta^\omega(\mathcal{Y})$. Let $K \in \mathcal{Y}_\delta$. Then $Int_{\mathcal{Y}_\delta}(K) = K$. By Theorem 5, $K \in \mathcal{Y}_{\omega_\delta}$, and thus, $Int_{\mathcal{Y}_{\omega_\delta}}(K) = K$. Also, since $\mathcal{Y}_\delta \subseteq \mathcal{Y}$, then $K \in \mathcal{Y}$, and so $Int_{\mathcal{Y}}(K) = K$. Therefore, we have $Int_{\mathcal{Y}_\omega}(K) = Int_{\mathcal{Y}_\delta}(K) = Int_{\mathcal{Y}}(K)$. This shows that $K \in \omega_\delta^\delta(\mathcal{Y}) \cap \omega_\delta^0(\mathcal{Y})$.

(c) Since $\mathcal{Y}_\theta \subseteq \mathcal{Y}_\delta$, then by (c), $\mathcal{Y}_\theta \subseteq \omega_\delta^\delta(\mathcal{Y}) \cap \omega_\delta^0(\mathcal{Y}) \cap \omega_\delta^\omega(\mathcal{Y})$. Let $K \in \mathcal{Y}_\theta$. Then $Int_{\mathcal{Y}_\theta}(K) = K$. Since $\mathcal{Y}_\theta \subseteq \mathcal{Y}_\delta$, then by Theorem 2.3, $K \in \mathcal{Y}_{\omega_\delta}$, and so $Int_{\mathcal{Y}_{\omega_\delta}}(K) = K$. Therefore, $Int_{\mathcal{Y}_{\omega_\delta}}(K) = Int_{\mathcal{Y}_\theta}(K)$, and hence $K \in \omega_\delta^\theta(\mathcal{Y})$.

(d) Let $K \in \omega_\delta^\theta(\mathcal{Y})$. Then $Int_{\mathcal{Y}_{\omega_\delta}}(K) = Int_{\mathcal{Y}_\theta}(K)$. In contrast, by Theorem 5, we have $\mathcal{Y}_\theta \subseteq \mathcal{Y}_\delta \subseteq \mathcal{Y}_{\omega_\delta}$, then $Int_{\mathcal{Y}_\theta}(K) \tilde{\subseteq} Int_{\mathcal{Y}_\delta}(K) \tilde{\subseteq} Int_{\mathcal{Y}_{\omega_\delta}}(K)$. Therefore, we have $Int_{\mathcal{Y}_\delta}(K) = Int_{\mathcal{Y}_{\omega_\delta}}(K)$ and hence $K \in \omega_\delta^\delta(\mathcal{Y})$. □

As the next two examples show, in general, none of the inclusions in Theorem 22 can be replaced by equality:

Example 7. *Let $M = \mathbb{R}$, $A = \{a\}$, and $\mathcal{Y} = \{0_A, 1_A, a_{\mathbb{R}-\mathbb{Q}}\}$. Let $K = a_{\mathbb{N}}$. Suppose that $Int_{\mathcal{Y}_\omega}(K) \neq 0_A$. Then there exists $x \in M$ such that $a_x \tilde{\in} Int_{\mathcal{Y}_\omega}(K) \in \mathcal{Y}_\omega$. So, we find $G \in \mathcal{Y}$ such that $a_x \tilde{\in} G$ and $G - K \in C(M, A)$, which is impossible. Therefore, $Int_{\mathcal{Y}}(K) = Int_{\mathcal{Y}_\omega}(K) = 0_A$. In contrast, since $\mathcal{Y}_\delta = \mathcal{Y}_\theta = \mathcal{Y}_{\omega_\delta} = \{0_A, 1_A\}$, then $Int_{\mathcal{Y}_{\omega_\delta}}(K) = Int_{\mathcal{Y}_\delta}(K) = Int_{\mathcal{Y}_\theta}(K) = 0_A$ and $K \notin \mathcal{Y}_\theta \cup \mathcal{Y}_\delta \cup \mathcal{Y}_{\omega_\delta}$. This shows that none of the inclusions in Theorem 22 (a), (b), and (c), cannot be replaced by equality in general.*

Example 8. *Let $M = \mathbb{R}$, $Z = \{a\}$, and*
$\mathcal{Y} = \{K \in SS(M, Z) : K(a) \in \{\emptyset, M, \mathbb{Q} \cap (1,2), \mathbb{R} - \mathbb{Q}, (\mathbb{Q} \cap (1,2)) \cup (\mathbb{R} - \mathbb{Q})\}\}$.
Then $a_{\mathbb{R}-\mathbb{Q}} \in \omega_\delta^\delta(\mathcal{Y}) - \omega_\delta^\theta(\mathcal{Y})$. As a result, equality in general cannot replace the inclusion in Theorem 22 (d).

For a soft topological space $(M, \mathcal{Y}, Z)$, the first and second components of each of the ordered pairs of classes of soft sets below are not comparable in general, as demonstrated by the following three examples:

1. $(\mathcal{Y}, \omega_\delta^\delta(\mathcal{Y}))$.
2. $(\mathcal{Y}, \omega_\delta^0(\mathcal{Y}))$.
3. $(\mathcal{Y}, \omega_\delta^\theta(\mathcal{Y}))$.
4. $(\omega_\delta^\delta(\mathcal{Y}), \omega_\delta^0(\mathcal{Y}))$.
5. $(\omega_\delta^\delta(\mathcal{Y}), \omega_\delta^\omega(\mathcal{Y}))$.
6. $(\omega_\delta(\mathcal{Y}), \omega_\delta^\delta(\mathcal{Y}))$.
7. $(\omega_\delta(\mathcal{Y}), \omega_\delta^0(\mathcal{Y}))$.
8. $(\omega_\delta(\mathcal{Y}), \omega_\delta^\theta(\mathcal{Y}))$.
9. $(\omega_\delta^0(\mathcal{Y}), \omega_\delta^\omega(\mathcal{Y}))$.
10. $(\mathcal{Y}_\omega, \omega_\delta^\omega(\mathcal{Y}))$.

Example 9. *Let* $M = \{1,2\}$, $Z = \{a\}$, *and* $\mathcal{Y} = \{K \in SS(M,Z) : K(a) \in \{\emptyset, M, \{1\}\}\}$. *Then* $a_{\{1\}} \in (\mathcal{Y} \cap \omega_\delta(\mathcal{Y}) \cap \omega_\delta^0(\mathcal{Y}) \cap \omega_\delta^\omega(\mathcal{Y})) - (\omega_\delta^\theta(\mathcal{Y}) \cup \omega_\delta^\delta(\mathcal{Y}))$ *and* $a_{\{2\}} \in \omega_\delta(\mathcal{Y}) - (\omega_\delta^0(\mathcal{Y}) \cup \omega_\delta^\delta(\mathcal{Y}))$.

Example 10. *Let* $(M,\mathcal{Y},Z)$ *be as in Example 6. Then* $a_{\mathbb{R}-\mathbb{N}} \in \omega_\delta^\delta(\mathcal{Y}) - (\omega_\delta^0(\mathcal{Y}) \cup \omega_\delta^\omega(\mathcal{Y}))$.

Example 11. *Let* $M = \{1,2\}$, $Z = \{a\}$, β *be the usual topology on* $\mathbb{R}$, *and* $\mathcal{Y} = \{K \in SS(M,Z) : K(a) \in \beta\}$. *Then* $a_{\{1\}} \in (\omega_\delta^\delta(\mathcal{Y}) \cap \omega_\delta^0(\mathcal{Y}) \cap \omega_\delta^\omega(\mathcal{Y}) \cap \omega_\delta^\theta(\mathcal{Y})) - \mathcal{Y}_\omega$.

Theorem 23. *Let* $(M,\mathcal{Y},Z)$ *be a soft topological space. Then*
(a) $\mathcal{Y}_{\omega_\delta} = \mathcal{Y}_\omega \cap \omega_\delta^\omega(\mathcal{Y})$.
(b) $\mathcal{Y}_\delta = \mathcal{Y}_{\omega_\delta} \cap \omega_\delta^\delta(\mathcal{Y})$.
(c) $\mathcal{Y}_\theta = \mathcal{Y}_{\omega_\delta} \cap \omega_\delta^\theta(\mathcal{Y})$.
(d) $\mathcal{Y}_\theta = \mathcal{Y}_{\omega_\theta} \cap \omega_\delta^\theta(\mathcal{Y})$.
(e) $\mathcal{Y} \cap \omega_\delta^0(\mathcal{Y}) \subseteq \mathcal{Y}_{\omega_\delta}$.
(f) $\mathcal{Y}_{\omega_\delta} \cap \omega_\delta^0(\mathcal{Y}) \subseteq \mathcal{Y}$.
(g) $\mathcal{Y} \cap \omega_\delta^0(\mathcal{Y}) = \mathcal{Y}_{\omega_\delta} \cap \omega_\delta^0(\mathcal{Y})$.

Proof. (a) By Theorem 5 and Theorem 5 of [44], $\mathcal{Y}_{\omega_\delta} \subseteq \tau_\omega$. In contrast, by Theorem 22 (a), $\mathcal{Y}_{\omega_\delta} \subseteq \omega_\delta^\omega(\mathcal{Y})$. Thus, $\mathcal{Y}_{\omega_\delta} \subseteq \mathcal{Y}_\omega \cap \omega_\delta^\omega(\mathcal{Y})$. To see that $\mathcal{Y}_\omega \cap \omega_\delta^\omega(\mathcal{Y}) \subseteq \mathcal{Y}_{\omega_\delta}$, let $K \in \mathcal{Y}_\omega \cap \omega_\delta^\omega(\mathcal{Y})$. Since $K \in \tau_\omega$, then $K = Int_{\mathcal{Y}_\omega}(K)$. Since $K \in \omega_\delta^\omega(\mathcal{Y})$, then $Int_{\mathcal{Y}_{\omega_\delta}}(K) = Int_{\mathcal{Y}_\omega}(K)$. Thus, $Int_{\mathcal{Y}_{\omega_\delta}}(K) = K$, and hence $K \in \mathcal{Y}_{\omega_\delta}$.

(b) By Theorem 5 and Theorem 22 (b), we have $\mathcal{Y}_\delta \subseteq \mathcal{Y}_{\omega_\delta} \cap \omega_\delta^\delta(\mathcal{Y})$. To see that $\mathcal{Y}_{\omega_\delta} \cap \omega_\delta^\delta(\mathcal{Y}) \subseteq \mathcal{Y}_\delta$, let $K \in \mathcal{Y}_{\omega_\delta} \cap \omega_\delta^\delta(\mathcal{Y})$. Then $K = Int_{\mathcal{Y}_{\omega_\delta}}(K)$ and $Int_{\mathcal{Y}_{\omega_\delta}}(K) = Int_{\mathcal{Y}_\delta}(K)$. Thus, $K = Int_{\mathcal{Y}_\delta}(K)$, and hence $K \in \mathcal{Y}_\delta$.

(c) By Theorem 5, we have $\mathcal{Y}_\theta \subseteq \mathcal{Y}_\delta \subseteq \mathcal{Y}_{\omega_\delta}$. Also, by Theorem 22 (c), $\mathcal{Y}_\theta \subseteq \omega_\delta^\theta(\mathcal{Y})$. Thus, $\mathcal{Y}_\theta \subseteq \mathcal{Y}_{\omega_\delta} \cap \omega_\delta^\theta(\mathcal{Y})$. To see that $\mathcal{Y}_{\omega_\delta} \cap \omega_\delta^\theta(\mathcal{Y}) \subseteq \mathcal{Y}_\theta$, let $K \in \mathcal{Y}_{\omega_\delta} \cap \omega_\delta^\theta(\mathcal{Y})$. Then $K = Int_{\mathcal{Y}_{\omega_\delta}}(K)$ and $Int_{\mathcal{Y}_{\omega_\delta}}(K) = Int_{\mathcal{Y}_\theta}(K)$. Thus, $K = Int_{\mathcal{Y}_\theta}(K)$, and hence $K \in \mathcal{Y}_\theta$.

(d) By Theorem 5 of [45], $\mathcal{Y}_\theta \subseteq \mathcal{Y}_{\omega_\theta}$. Also, by (c), $\mathcal{Y}_\theta \subseteq \omega_\delta^\theta(\mathcal{Y})$. Thus, $\mathcal{Y}_\theta \subseteq \mathcal{Y}_{\omega_\theta} \cap \omega_\delta^\theta(\mathcal{Y})$. In contrast, by Theorem 9 and (c), $\mathcal{Y}_{\omega_\theta} \cap \omega_\delta^\theta(\mathcal{Y}) \subseteq \mathcal{Y}_{\omega_\delta} \cap \omega_\delta^\theta(\mathcal{Y}) = \mathcal{Y}_\theta$.

(e) Let $K \in \mathcal{Y} \cap \omega_\delta^0(\mathcal{Y})$. Then $K = Int_{\mathcal{Y}}(K)$ and $Int_{\mathcal{Y}_{\omega_\delta}}(K) = Int_{\mathcal{Y}}(K)$. Thus, $K = Int_{\mathcal{Y}_{\omega_\delta}}(K)$, and hence $K \in \mathcal{Y}_{\omega_\delta}$.

(f) Let $K \in \mathcal{Y}_{\omega_\delta} \cap \omega_\delta^0(\mathcal{Y})$. Then $K = Int_{\mathcal{Y}_{\omega_\delta}}(K)$ and $Int_{\mathcal{Y}_{\omega_\delta}}(K) = Int_{\mathcal{Y}}(K)$. Thus, $K = Int_{\mathcal{Y}}(K)$, and hence $K \in \mathcal{Y}$.

(g) We have $\mathcal{Y} \cap \omega_\delta^0(\mathcal{Y}) \subseteq \omega_\delta^0(\mathcal{Y})$. Also, by (e), $\mathcal{Y} \cap \omega_\delta^0(\mathcal{Y}) \subseteq \mathcal{Y}_{\omega_\delta}$. Hence, $\mathcal{Y} \cap \omega_\delta^0(\mathcal{Y}) \subseteq \mathcal{Y}_{\omega_\delta} \cap \omega_\delta^0(\mathcal{Y})$. In contrast, we have $\mathcal{Y}_{\omega_\delta} \cap \omega_\delta^0(\mathcal{Y}) \subseteq \omega_\delta^0(\mathcal{Y})$. Also, by (f), $\mathcal{Y}_{\omega_\delta} \cap \omega_\delta^0(\mathcal{Y}) \subseteq \mathcal{Y}$. Hence, $\mathcal{Y}_{\omega_\delta} \cap \omega_\delta^0(\mathcal{Y}) \subseteq \mathcal{Y} \cap \omega_\delta^0(\mathcal{Y})$. □

Corollary 5. *Let* $(M,\mathcal{Y},Z)$ *be a soft topological space and* $K \in \omega_\delta^0(\mathcal{Y})$. *Then* $K \in \mathcal{Y}$ *if and only if* $K \in \mathcal{Y}_{\omega_\delta}$.

Proof. The proof follows from Theorem 23 (g). □

Theorem 24. *Let* $(M,\mathcal{Y},Z)$ *be a soft topological space. Then* $(M,\mathcal{Y},Z)$ *is a soft semi-regularization topology if and only if* $\mathcal{Y} \subseteq \omega_\delta^0(\mathcal{Y}) \cap \omega_\delta^\delta(\mathcal{Y})$.

Proof. *Necessity.* Let $(M,\mathcal{Y},Z)$ be a soft semi-regularization topology. Then $\mathcal{Y}_\delta = \mathcal{Y}$. Thus, by Theorem 22 (b), $\mathcal{Y} \subseteq \omega_\delta^0(\mathcal{Y}) \cap \omega_\delta^\delta(\mathcal{Y})$.

Sufficiency. Let $\mathcal{Y} \subseteq \omega_\delta^0(\mathcal{Y}) \cap \omega_\delta^\delta(\mathcal{Y})$. To see that $\mathcal{Y} \subseteq \mathcal{Y}_\delta$, let $K \in \mathcal{Y}$. Then $K \in \mathcal{Y} \cap \omega_\delta^0(\mathcal{Y}) \cap \omega_\delta^\delta(\mathcal{Y})$. So, we have $Int_{\mathcal{Y}}(K) = K$, $Int_{\mathcal{Y}_{\omega_\delta}}(K) = Int_{\mathcal{Y}}(K)$, and $Int_{\mathcal{Y}_{\omega_\delta}}(K) = Int_{\mathcal{Y}_\delta}(K)$. Thus, $Int_{\mathcal{Y}_\delta}(K) = K$. Hence, $K \in \mathcal{Y}_\delta$. □

Theorem 25. *A soft topological space* $(M,\mathcal{Y},Z)$ *is soft regular if and only if* $\mathcal{Y} \subseteq \omega_\delta^0(\mathcal{Y}) \cap \omega_\delta^\theta(\mathcal{Y})$.

Proof. *Necessity.* Let $(M,\mathcal{Y},Z)$ be soft regular. Then $\mathcal{Y}_\theta = \mathcal{Y}$. Thus, by Theorem 22 (c), $\mathcal{Y} \subseteq \omega_\delta^0(\mathcal{Y}) \cap \omega_\delta^\theta(\mathcal{Y})$.

Sufficiency. Let $\mathcal{Y} \subseteq \omega_\delta^0(\mathcal{Y}) \cap \omega_\delta^\theta(\mathcal{Y})$. To see that $\mathcal{Y} \subseteq \mathcal{Y}_\theta$, let $K \in \mathcal{Y}$. Then $K \in \mathcal{Y} \cap \omega_\delta^0(\mathcal{Y}) \cap \omega_\delta^\theta(\mathcal{Y})$. So, we have $Int_{\mathcal{Y}}(K) = K$, $Int_{\mathcal{Y}_{\omega_\delta}}(K) = Int_{\mathcal{Y}}(K)$, and $Int_{\mathcal{Y}_{\omega_\delta}}(K) = Int_{\mathcal{Y}_\theta}(K)$. Thus, $Int_{\mathcal{Y}_\theta}(K) = K$. Hence, $K \in \mathcal{Y}_\theta$. □

4. Soft ω_δ-Continuity

Definition 10. *A soft function $f_{qv} : (M,\mathcal{Y},Z) \longrightarrow (N,\mathcal{X},W)$ is called soft ω_δ-continuous if $f_{qv}^{-1}(K) \in \mathcal{Y}_{\omega_\delta}$ for every $K \in \mathcal{X}$.*

Theorem 26. *For a soft function $f_{qv} : (M,\mathcal{Y},Z) \longrightarrow (N,\mathcal{X},W)$, the following are equivalent:*

(1) $f_{qv} : (M,\mathcal{Y},Z) \longrightarrow (N,\mathcal{X},W)$ is soft ω_δ-continuous.

(2) $f_{qv}^{-1}(T) \in (\mathcal{Y}_{\omega_\delta})^c$ for every $T \in \mathcal{X}^c$.

(3) $Cl_{\mathcal{Y}_{\omega_\delta}}\left(f_{qv}^{-1}(A)\right) \widetilde{\subseteq} f_{qv}^{-1}(Cl_{\mathcal{X}}(A))$ for each $A \in SS(N,W)$.

(4) $f_{qv}^{-1}(Int_{\mathcal{X}}(A)) \widetilde{\subseteq} Int_{\mathcal{Y}_{\omega_\delta}}\left(f_{qv}^{-1}(A)\right)$ for each $A \in SS(N,W)$.

(5) $f_{qv} : (M,\mathcal{Y}_{\omega_\delta},Z) \longrightarrow (N,\mathcal{X},W)$ is soft continuous.

(6) For each $z_m \in SP(M,Z)$ and each $G \in \mathcal{X}$ such that $f_{qv}(z_m) \widetilde{\in} G$, we find $H \in \mathcal{Y}_{\omega_\delta}$ such that $z_m \widetilde{\in} H$ and $f_{qv}(H) \widetilde{\subseteq} G$.

Proof. (1)⟶(2): Let $T \in \mathcal{X}^c$. Then $1_W - T \in \mathcal{X}$. So, by (1), $f_{qv}^{-1}(1_W - T) = 1_Z - f_{qv}^{-1}(T) \in \mathcal{Y}_{\omega_\delta}$. Hence, $f_{qv}^{-1}(T) \in (\mathcal{Y}_{\omega_\delta})^c$.

(2)⟶(3): Let $A \in SS(N,W)$. Then $Cl_{\mathcal{X}}(A) \in \mathcal{X}^c$. So, by (2), $f_{qv}^{-1}(Cl_{\mathcal{X}}(A)) \in (\mathcal{Y}_{\omega_\delta})^c$. Since $f_{qv}^{-1}(A) \widetilde{\subseteq} f_{qv}^{-1}(Cl_{\mathcal{X}}(A)) \in (\mathcal{Y}_{\omega_\delta})^c$, then $Cl_{\mathcal{Y}_{\omega_\delta}}\left(f_{qv}^{-1}(A)\right) \widetilde{\subseteq} f_{qv}^{-1}(Cl_{\mathcal{X}}(A))$.

(3)⟶(4): Let $A \in SS(N,W)$. Then, by (3),

$$\begin{aligned}
1_Z - Int_{\mathcal{Y}_{\omega_\delta}}\left(f_{qv}^{-1}(A)\right) &= Cl_{\mathcal{Y}_{\omega_\delta}}\left(1_Z - f_{qv}^{-1}(A)\right) \\
&= Cl_{\mathcal{Y}_{\omega_\delta}}\left(f_{qv}^{-1}(1_W - A)\right) \\
&\widetilde{\subseteq} f_{qv}^{-1}(Cl_{\mathcal{X}}(1_W - A)) \\
&= f_{qv}^{-1}(1_W - Int_{\mathcal{X}}(A)) \\
&= 1_Z - f_{qv}^{-1}(Int_{\mathcal{X}}(A))
\end{aligned}$$

and so $f_{qv}^{-1}(Int_{\mathcal{X}}(A)) \widetilde{\subseteq} Int_{\mathcal{Y}_{\omega_\delta}}\left(f_{qv}^{-1}(A)\right)$.

(4)⟶(5): Let $K \in \mathcal{X}$. Then $Int_{\mathcal{X}}(K) = K$, and by (4), $f_{qv}^{-1}(K) \widetilde{\subseteq} Int_{\mathcal{Y}_{\omega_\delta}}\left(f_{qv}^{-1}(K)\right)$. Thus, $f_{qv}^{-1}(K) = Int_{\mathcal{Y}_{\omega_\delta}}\left(f_{qv}^{-1}(K)\right)$. Hence, $f_{qv}^{-1}(K) \in \mathcal{Y}_{\omega_\delta}$. This shows that $f_{qv} : (M,\mathcal{Y}_{\omega_\delta},Z) \longrightarrow (N,\mathcal{X},W)$ is soft continuous.

(5)⟶(6): Let $z_m \in SP(M,Z)$ and $G \in \mathcal{X}$ such that $f_{qv}(z_m) \widetilde{\in} G$. Then, by (5), $f_{qv}^{-1}(G) \in \mathcal{Y}_{\omega_\delta}$. Put $H = f_{qv}^{-1}(G)$. Then $H \in \mathcal{Y}_{\omega_\delta}$ such that $z_m \widetilde{\in} H$ and $f_{qv}(H) = f_{qv}\left(f_{qv}^{-1}(G)\right) \widetilde{\subseteq} G$.

(6)⟶(1): Let $K \in \mathcal{X}$. To show that $f_{qv}^{-1}(K) \in \mathcal{Y}_{\omega_\delta}$, let $z_m \widetilde{\in} f_{qv}^{-1}(K)$. Then $f_{qv}(z_m) \widetilde{\in} K$, and by (6), we find $H \in \mathcal{Y}_{\omega_\delta}$ such that $z_m \widetilde{\in} H$ and $f_{qv}(H) \widetilde{\subseteq} K$. Thus, we have $z_m \widetilde{\in} H \widetilde{\subseteq} f_{qv}^{-1}$ $(f_{qv}(H)) \widetilde{\subseteq} f_{qv}^{-1}(K)$. Hence, $f_{qv}^{-1}(K) \in \mathcal{Y}_{\omega_\delta}$. □

Theorem 27. *If $f_{qv} : (M,\mathcal{Y},Z) \longrightarrow (N,\mathcal{X},W)$ is soft ω_δ-continuous, then $q : (M,\mathcal{Y}_a) \longrightarrow \left(N,\mathcal{X}_{v(a)}\right)$ is ω_δ-continuous for every $a \in Z$.*

Proof. Suppose that $f_{qv} : (M,\mathcal{Y},Z) \longrightarrow (N,\mathcal{X},W)$ is soft ω_δ-continuous, and let $a \in Z$. By Theorem 4.2 (5), $f_{qv} : (M,\mathcal{Y}_{\omega_\delta},Z) \longrightarrow (N,\mathcal{X},W)$ is soft continuous. So, by Proposition 3.8 of [38], $q : (M,(\mathcal{Y}_{\omega_\delta})_a) \longrightarrow \left(N,\mathcal{X}_{v(a)}\right)$ is continuous. Since, by Theorem 10, $(\mathcal{Y}_{\omega_\delta})_a \subseteq$

$(\mathcal{Y}_a)_{\omega_\delta}$, then $q : (M, (\mathcal{Y}_a)_{\omega_\delta}) \longrightarrow \left(N, \mathcal{X}_{v(a)}\right)$ is continuous. Hence, by Theorem 4.2 (5) of [41], $q : (M, \mathcal{Y}_a) \longrightarrow \left(N, \mathcal{X}_{v(a)}\right)$ is ω_δ-continuous. □

Theorem 28. *Let $\{(M, \beta_z) : z \in Z\}$ and $\{(N, \alpha_w) : w \in W\}$ be two collections of topological spaces. Let $q : M \longrightarrow N$ and $v : Z \longrightarrow W$ be functions where v is bijective. Then $f_{qv} : (M, \oplus_{z\in Z}\beta_z, Z) \longrightarrow (N, \oplus_{w\in W}\alpha_w, W)$ is soft ω_δ-continuous if and only if $q : (M, \beta_a) \longrightarrow \left(N, \alpha_{v(a)}\right)$ is ω_δ-continuous for all $a \in Z$.*

Proof. *Necessity*. Let $f_{qv} : (M, \oplus_{z\in Z}\beta_z, Z) \longrightarrow (N, \oplus_{w\in W}\alpha_w, W)$ be soft ω_δ-continuous. Let $a \in Z$. Then, by Theorem 27, $q : (M, (\oplus_{z\in Z}\beta_z)_a) \longrightarrow \left(N, (\oplus_{w\in W}\alpha_w)_{v(a)}\right)$ is ω_δ-continuous. But by Theorem 3.11 of [38], $(\oplus_{z\in Z}\beta_z)_a = \beta_a$ and $(\oplus_{w\in W}\alpha_w)_{v(a)} = \alpha_{v(a)}$. Hence, $q : (M, \beta_a) \longrightarrow \left(N, \alpha_{v(a)}\right)$ is ω_δ-continuous.

Sufficiency. Let $q : (M, \beta_a) \longrightarrow \left(N, \alpha_{v(a)}\right)$ be ω_δ-continuous for all $a \in Z$. Let $K \in \oplus_{w\in W}\alpha_w$. By Theorem 11, it is sufficient to show that $\left(f_{qv}^{-1}(K)\right)(a) \in (\beta_a)_{\omega_\delta}$ for all $a \in Z$. Let $a \in Z$. Since $q : (M, \beta_a) \longrightarrow \left(N, \alpha_{v(a)}\right)$ is ω_δ-continuous and $K(v(a)) \in \alpha_{v(a)}$, then $\left(f_{qv}^{-1}(K)\right)(a) = q^{-1}(K(v(a))) \in (\beta_a)_{\omega_\delta}$. □

Corollary 6. *Let $q : (M, \xi) \longrightarrow (N, \phi)$ and $v : Z \longrightarrow W$ be two functions where v is a bijection. Then $q : (M, \xi) \longrightarrow (N, \phi)$ is ω_δ-continuous if and only if $f_{qv} : (M, \tau(\xi), Z) \longrightarrow (N, \tau(\phi), W)$ is soft ω_δ-continuous.*

Proof. For each $z \in Z$ and $w \in W$, put $\beta_z = \xi$ and $\alpha_w = \phi$. Then $\tau(\alpha) = \oplus_{z\in Z}\beta_z$ and $\tau(\phi) = \oplus_{w\in W}\alpha_w$. By using Theorem 28, we get the result. □

Theorem 29. *Let $f_{qv} : (M, \mathcal{Y}, Z) \longrightarrow (N, \mathcal{X}, W)$ be soft ω_δ-continuous and surjective. If $(M, \mathcal{Y}_{\omega_\delta}, Z)$ is soft Lindelof, then $(N, \mathcal{X}, W)$ is soft Lindelof.*

Proof. Let $\mathcal{H} \subseteq \mathcal{X}$ such that $\widetilde{\cup}_{H\in\mathcal{H}} H = 1_W$. Then $f_{qv}^{-1}(\widetilde{\cup}_{H\in\mathcal{H}} H) = \widetilde{\cup}_{H\in\mathcal{H}} f_{qv}^{-1}(H) = f_{qv}^{-1}(1_W) = 1_Z$. Since $f_{qv} : (M, \mathcal{Y}, Z) \longrightarrow (N, \mathcal{X}, W)$ is soft ω_δ-continuous, then $\left\{f_{qv}^{-1}(H) : H \in \mathcal{H}\right\} \subseteq \mathcal{Y}_{\omega_\delta}$. Since $(M, \mathcal{Y}_{\omega_\delta}, Z)$ is soft Lindelof, then we find a countable subfamily $\mathcal{H}_1 \subseteq \mathcal{H}$ such that $\widetilde{\cup}_{H\in\mathcal{H}_1} f_{qv}^{-1}(H) = f_{qv}^{-1}(\widetilde{\cup}_{H\in\mathcal{H}_1} H) = 1_Z$. So, $f_{qv}\left(f_{qv}^{-1}(\widetilde{\cup}_{H\in\mathcal{H}_1} H)\right) = f_{qv}(1_Z)$. Since f_{qv} is surjective, then $f_{qv}(1_Z) = 1_W$. Thus, $1_W = f_{qv}\left(f_{qv}^{-1}(\widetilde{\cup}_{H\in\mathcal{H}_1} H)\right) \widetilde{\subseteq} \widetilde{\cup}_{H\in\mathcal{H}_1} H$, and hence $1_W = \widetilde{\cup}_{H\in\mathcal{H}_1} H$. This shows that $(N, \mathcal{X}, W)$ is soft Lindelof. □

Corollary 7. *Let $f_{qv} : (M, \mathcal{Y}, Z) \longrightarrow (N, \mathcal{X}, W)$ be soft ω_δ-continuous and onto. If $(M, \mathcal{Y}, Z)$ is soft Lindelof, then $(N, \mathcal{X}, W)$ is soft Lindelof.*

Proof. The proof follows from Theorems 17 and 29. □

Theorem 30. *Every soft ω_δ-continuous function is soft ω^0-continuous.*

The following illustration shows that Theorem 30 's converse need not always hold true:

Example 12. *Let $(M, \mathcal{Y}, Z)$ be as in Example 2.14. Let $q : M \longrightarrow M$ and $v : Z \longrightarrow Z$ be the identity functions. Since $f_{qv}^{-1}\left(b_{(0,\infty)}\right) = b_{(0,\infty)} \in \mathcal{Y}_{\omega^0} - \mathcal{Y}_{\omega_\delta}$, then $f_{qv} : (M, \mathcal{Y}, Z) \longrightarrow (M, \mathcal{Y}, Z)$ is soft ω^0-continuous but not soft ω_δ-continuous.*

5. Conclusions

We introduced five types of soft sets. Also, we introduced soft ω_δ-continuous functions as a new class of soft functions. We gave several characterizations, relationships, and decomposition theorems. In addition, we investigated the links between our novel soft topological notions and their classical topological analogs.

We intend to do the following in the next work: (1) To define soft separation axioms via our new classes of soft sets; (2) To define new soft classes of functions via our new classes of soft sets.

Author Contributions: Conceptualization, D.A., S.A.-G. and M.N.; Methodology, D.A., S.A.-G. and M.N.; Formal analysis, D.A., S.A.-G. and M.N.; Writing—original draft, D.A., S.A.-G. and M.N.; Writing—review and editing, D.A., S.A.-G. and M.N.; Funding acquisition, S.A.-G. All authors have read and agreed to the published version of the manuscript.

Funding: This research received no external funding.

Data Availability Statement: No new data were created in this study. Data sharing does not apply to this article.

Conflicts of Interest: The authors declare no conflicts of interest.

References

1. Zadeh, L. Fuzzy sets. *Inf. Control* **1965**, *8*, 338–353. [CrossRef]
2. Pawlak, Z. Rough sets. *Int. J. Comput. Inf. Sci.* **1982**, *11*, 341–356. [CrossRef]
3. Molodtsov, D. Soft set theory—First results. Comput. *Math. Appl.* **1999**, *37*, 19–31.
4. Yang, J.; Yao, Y. Semantics of soft sets and three-way decision with soft sets. *Knowl. Based Syst.* **2020**, *194*, 105538. [CrossRef]
5. Alcantud, J.C.R. The semantics of *N*-soft sets, their applications, and a coda about three-way decision. *Inf. Sci.* **2022**, *606*, 837–852. [CrossRef]
6. Akguller, O. A soft set theoretic approach to network complexity and a case study for Turkish Twitter users. *Appl. Soft Comput.* **2023**, *143*, 110344. [CrossRef]
7. Gwak, J.; Garg, H.; Jan, N. Hybrid integrated decision-making algorithm for clustering analysis based on a bipolar complex fuzzy and soft sets. *Alex. Eng. J.* **2023**, *67*, 473–487. [CrossRef]
8. Dalkılıc O.; Demirta¸s, N. Algorithms for COVID-19 outbreak using soft set theory: Estimation and application. *Soft Comput.* **2022**, *27*, 3203–3211. [CrossRef]
9. Qin, H.; Fei, Q.; Ma, X.; Chen, W. A new parameter reduction algorithm for soft sets based on chi-square test. *Appl. Intell.* **2021**, *51*, 7960–7972. [CrossRef]
10. Ma, X.; Qin, H. Soft set based parameter value reduction for decision making application. *IEEE Access* **2019**, *7*, 35499–35511. [CrossRef]
11. Yuksel, S.; Dizman, T.; Yildizdan, G.; Sert, U. Application of soft sets to diagnose the prostate cancer risk. *J. Inequal. Appl.* **2013**, *2013*, 229. [CrossRef]
12. Maji, P.; Roy, A.R.; Biswas, R. An application of soft sets in a decision making problem. *Comput. Math. Appl.* **2002**, *44*, 1077–1083. [CrossRef]
13. Aktas, H.; Çagman, N. Soft sets and soft groups. *Inf. Sci.* **2007**, *177*, 2726–2735. [CrossRef]
14. Acar, U.; Koyuncu, F.; Tanay, B. Soft sets and soft rings. *Comput. Math. Appl.* **2010**, *59*, 3458–3463. [CrossRef]
15. Alcantud, J.C.R. Convex soft geometries. *J. Comput. Cogn. Eng.* **2022**, *1*, 2–12. [CrossRef]
16. Kandil, A.; Tantawy, O.A.E.; El-Sheikh, S.A.; M Abd El-latif, A. Soft ideal theory soft local function and generated soft topological spaces. *Appl. Math. Inf. Sci.* **2014**, *8*, 1595–1603. [CrossRef]
17. Shabir, M.; Naz, M. On soft topological spaces. *Comput. Math. Appl.* **2011**, *61*, 1786–1799. [CrossRef]
18. Das, S.; Samanta, S.K. Soft metric. *Ann. Fuzzy Math. Inform.* **2013**, *6*, 77–94.
19. Cetkin, V.; Guner, E.; Aygün, H. On 2S-metric spaces. *Soft Comput.* **2020**, *24*, 12731–12742. [CrossRef]
20. Badyakar, U.; Nazmul, S. Some fixed soft point results on soft *S*-metric spaces. *Math. Sci.* **2021**, *15*, 283–291. [CrossRef]
21. Lin, F. Soft connected spaces and soft paracompact spaces. *Int. J. Math. Comput. Sci.* **2013**, *7*, 277–283.
22. Al-shami, T.M.; Kocinac, L.D. Almost soft Menger and weakly soft Menger spaces. *Appl. Comput. Math.* **2022**, *21*, 35–51.
23. Al-shami, T.M.; Mhemdi, A.; Rawshdeh, A.A.; Al-Jarrah, H.H. Soft version of compact and Lindelof spaces using soft somewhere dense sets. *AIMS Math.* **2021**, *6*, 8064–8077. [CrossRef]
24. Aygunoglu, A.; Aygun, H. Some notes on soft topological spaces. *Neural Comput. Appl.* **2012**, *21*, 113–119. [CrossRef]
25. Chen, B. Soft semi-open sets and related properties in soft topological spaces. *Appl. Math. Inf. Sci.* **2013**, *7* , 287–294. [CrossRef]
26. Akdag, M.; Ozkan, A. Soft α-open sets and soft α -continuous functions. *Abstr. Appl. Anal.* **2014**, *2014*, 891341. [CrossRef]
27. Al-shami, T.M. Soft somewhere dense sets on soft topological spaces. *Commun. Korean Math. Soc.* **2018**, *33*, 1341–1356.

28. Al-shami, T.M.; Mhemdi, A. On soft parametric somewhat-open sets and applications via soft topologies. *Heliyon* **2023**, *9*, e21472. [CrossRef]
29. Al-shami, T.M.; Mhemdi, A.; Rawshdeh, A.; Al-Jarrah. H.H. On weakly soft somewhat open sets. *Rocky Mountain J. Math.* **2024**, *54*, 13–30. [CrossRef]
30. Al-Mufarrij, J.; Saleh, S. New results on soft generalized topological spaces. *J. Math. Comput. Sci.* **2024**, *32*, 43–53. [CrossRef]
31. Goldar, S.; Ray, S. On soft Lebesgue measure. *J. Uncertain Syst.* **2023**, *16*, 2350005. [CrossRef]
32. Bayramov, S.; Aras, C.G.; Kocinac, L.D.R. Interval-Valued Topology on Soft Sets. *Axioms* **2023**, *12*, 692. [CrossRef]
33. Al-shami, T.M.; Mhemdi, A. A weak form of soft α-open sets and its applications via soft topologies. *AIMS Math.* **2023**, *8*, 11373–11396. [CrossRef]
34. Demir, I.; Okurer, M. A new approach to N-soft topological structers. *Rocky Mt. J. Math.* **2023**, *53*, 1789–1805. [CrossRef]
35. Al-shami, T.M.; Mhemdi, A.; Abu-Gdairi, R. A Novel framework for generalizations of soft open sets and its applications via soft topologies. *Mathematics* **2023**, *11*, 840. [CrossRef]
36. Rawshdeh, A.A.; Al-Jarrah, H.H.; Al-shami, T.M. Soft expandable spaces. *Filomat* **2023**, *37*, 2845–2858. [CrossRef]
37. Alzahran, S.; EL-Maghrabi, A.I.; AL-Juhani, M.A.; Badr, M.S. New approach of soft M-open sets in soft topological spaces. *J. King Saud Univ. Sci.* **2023**, *35*, 102414. [CrossRef]
38. Al Ghour, S.; Bin-Saadon, A. On some generated soft topological spaces and soft homogeneity. *Heliyon* **2019**, *5*, e02061. [CrossRef]
39. Al Ghour, S.; Hamed, W. On two classes of soft sets in soft topological spaces. *Symmetry* **2020**, *12*, 265. [CrossRef]
40. Velicko, N.V. H-closed Topological Spaces. *Amer. Math. Soc. Trans.* **1968**, *78*, 103–118.
41. Darwesh, H.M. A new topology from an old one. *J. Chungcheong Math. Soc.* **2012**, *25*, 401. [CrossRef]
42. Georgiou, D.N.; Megaritis, A.C.; Petropoulos, V.I. On soft topological spaces. *Appl. Math. Inf. Sci.* **2013**, *7*, 1889–1901. [CrossRef]
43. Mohammed, R.A.; Sayed, O.R.; Eliow, A. Some properties of soft delta-topology. *Acad. J. Nawroz Univ.* **2019**, *8*, 352–361. [CrossRef]
44. Al Ghour, S. Between the classes of soft open sets and soft omega open sets. *Mathematics* **2022**, *10*, 719. [CrossRef]
45. Al Ghour, S. Between soft θ-openness and soft ω^0-openness. *Axioms* **2023**, *12*, 311. [CrossRef]
46. Yuksel, S.; Tozlu, N.; Ergul, Z.G. Soft regular generalized closed sets in soft topological spaces. *Int. J. Math. Anal.* **2014**, *8*, 355–367. [CrossRef]
47. Debnath, B. A note on soft nearly compact and soft nearly paracompactness in soft topological spaces. *Int. J. Innov. Res. Sci. Eng. Technol.* **2017**, *6*, 15906–15914.
48. Hussain, S.; Ahmad, B. Soft separation axioms in soft topological spaces. *Hacet. J. Math. Stat.* **2015**, *44*, 559–568. [CrossRef]
49. Al Salem, S.M. Soft regular generalized b-closed sets in soft topological spaces. *J. Linear Topol. Algebra* **2014**, 3, 195–204.
50. Al Ghour, S. On some weaker forms of soft continuity and their decomposition theorems. *J. Math. Comput. Sci.* **2023**, *29*, 317–328. [CrossRef]
51. Al Ghour, S. Soft $R\omega$-open sets and the soft topology of soft δ_ω-open sets. *Axioms* **2022**, *11*, 177. [CrossRef]
52. Al Ghour, S. Strong form of soft semi-open sets in soft topological spaces. *Int. J. Fuzzy Log. Intell. Syst.* **2021**, *21*, 159–168. [CrossRef]

mathematics

Article

Innovative Methods of Constructing Strict and Strong Fuzzy Negations, Fuzzy Implications and New Classes of Copulas

Panagiotis Georgiou Mangenakis and Basil Papadopoulos *

Department of Civil Engineering, Section of Mathematics and Informatics, Democritus University of Thrace, 67100 Kimeria, Greece; pmangena@civil.duth.gr
* Correspondence: papadob@civil.duth.gr; Tel.: +30-2541079747

Abstract: This paper presents new classes of strong fuzzy negations, fuzzy implications and Copulas. It begins by presenting two theorems with function classes involving the construction of strong fuzzy negations. These classes are based on a well-known equilibrium point theorem. After that, a construction of fuzzy implication is presented, which is not based on any negation. Finally, moving on to the area concerning copulas, we present proof about the third property of copulas. To conclude, we will present two original constructions of copulas. All the above constructions are motivated by a specific formula. For some specific conditions of the variables x, y and other conditions for the function f(x), the formula presented produces strict and strong fuzzy negations, fuzzy implications and copulas.

Keywords: fuzzy negation; fuzzy logic; fuzzy sets; strong fuzzy negation; rational function; formula $f(f^{-1}(y) * x)$; fuzzy implication; copula

MSC: 03B52

Citation: Mangenakis, P.G.; Papadopoulos, B. Innovative Methods of Constructing Strict and Strong Fuzzy Negations, Fuzzy Implications and New Classes of Copulas. *Mathematics* **2024**, *12*, 2254. https://doi.org/10.3390/math12142254

Academic Editor: Michael Voskoglou

Received: 6 June 2024
Revised: 12 July 2024
Accepted: 15 July 2024
Published: 19 July 2024

1. Introduction

It is well known that one of the most rapidly growing branches of modern applied mathematics is fuzzy logic and its objects. More and more applications of fuzzy implication and fuzzy negations are widespread; negations either through these implications or autonomously. Fuzzy implication is the generalization of classical (Boolean) implication in the interval [0, 1]. It plays perhaps the most important role in the field of fuzzy logic, decision theory and fuzzy control. The article presents new methods for constructing fuzzy negations [1–4]. Furthermore, the creation of new fuzzy implications [5–14], and through them, new fuzzy negations is necessary. Using the knowledge and information gained through the study of relevant writings [15–19], the article proceeds to study other areas of fuzzy logic. Other interesting objects of fuzzy logic are copulas [20–25]. Since new classes of negations and implications can be defined, the generated negations will be used to construct, additionally, two new classes of copulas.

Methodologically, this article's analysis begins in Section 2 by listing all the theorems and remarks that will be useful in the proof of the constructions below. Those definitions are listed in the order they are used. Definitions 1–5 relate to the construction of the fuzzy negations, Definitions 6 and 7 relate to the construction of fuzzy implications and Definitions 8–12 are helpful in the construction of copulas.

Therefore, for practical reasons, the first object to deal with is the construction of strong negations [1–4]. Some of the areas that strong negations apply are as follows:

1. Artificial Intelligence (AI): Particularly in designing systems that handle uncertain or imprecise information.
2. Control Systems: For instance, in developing controllers for complex systems like washing machines, air conditioners and automotive systems.

3. Decision Making: Assisting in multi-criteria decision-making processes where inputs are not clear-cut.
4. Pattern Recognition: Helping in classifying patterns that are not crisply defined.
5. Robotics: Enabling robots to handle ambiguous or uncertain environments.
6. Data Mining: For analyzing and interpreting data that are noisy or incomplete.
7. Natural Language Processing (NLP): Managing the inherent ambiguity and imprecision in human language.
8. Medical Diagnosis: Supporting systems that need to deal with uncertain or imprecise medical data.

All the fuzzy negations that will be presented will have the form of a multi-branch function and will be based on Definition 5 [1]. This definition constructs negations with the help of the equilibrium point. Two classes of strong fuzzy negations will be constructed. And every class of negations is followed by one example. The second example presents a class of negations with a special property: it makes it very easy to calculate the equilibrium point. This calculation will be obtained by solving a simple secondary equation.

What follows is the construction of a fuzzy implication [8–13,20,21,24] with an alternative way, without the use of fuzzy negations.

This will be achieved with the use of the **formula** $\mathbf{f\left(f^{-1}(y) * x\right)}$. For every x, y into the interval [0, 1] and the use of a decreasing function f(x), the formula $f\left(f^{-1}(y) * x\right)$ helps to construct fuzzy implications. In addition, the formula constructs one branch of a strong fuzzy negation (Remark 1) and, autonomously, a strict fuzzy negation (Remark 2). The construction of the implication will be achieved with the use of Definitions 6 and 7. Let us mention some of the areas where fuzzy implications are important:

1. Artificial Intelligence (AI) and Machine Learning (Expert System, Knowledge Representation) 2. Control Systems (Fuzzy Control) 3. Decision Support System (Multi-Criteria Decision Making (MCDM), Risk Assessment) 4. Pattern Recognition and Image Processing (Classification, Image Segmentation) 5. Robotics (Autonomous Navigation, Sensor Fusion) 6. Natural Language Processing (NLP) (Semantic Analysis, Text Mining) 7. Medical Diagnosis and Healthcare (Diagnostic Systems, Treatment Planning) 8. Economics and Finance (Forecasting, Credit Scoring).

Finally, with the use of the fuzzy negations, newly constructed classes of copulas are built. Making some adjustments to the functions used in the construction of the negations, three-dimensional copulas [20–24] will be generated. Again, the formula $f\left(f^{-1}(y) * x\right)$ will participate in the construction of a class of copulas, with some minor modifications. It is well known that copulas find huge applications in economic problems, portfolio management and risk analysis, specifically in the banking, insurance and investing fields.

In conclusion, this article aims to answer the following questions:

(1) Is there an easy way to calculate the equilibrium point in a two-branch strong negation?
(2) Are there real functions that can provide at the same time the construction of strong negations, implications and copulas?
(3) Is there a point of convergence in the construction of fuzzy negations, fuzzy implications and copulas?
(4) Can the formula $f\left(f^{-1}(y) * x\right)$ provide more alternative options?
(5) Can this article provide knowledge for future use in robotics kai AI technology?

The paper is organized as follows: Section 2 is a reminder of the basic concepts and definitions used in the paper. Section 3 analyzes the newly constructed methods of strong fuzzy negations, fuzzy implications and copulas. One example for every theorem given is presented. Section 4 is about the discussion of the results, and Section 5 is the conclusion.

2. Materials and Methods

Some theorems of fuzzy logic and some definitions will be listed here. This will be conducted so that the theorems concerning the upcoming constructions will be explained and proved. To help the readers get familiar with the theory, some of the concepts and results employed in the rest of the paper shall be recalled below.

In this section all the theorems and propositions necessary to be able to present and fully prove the constructions we have mentioned above will be given.

Theorems from the whole range of the literature concerning the structural definitions of fuzzy negations, fuzzy implications and copulas will be given. In particular, Definitions 1–5 are concerned exclusively with the construction of negations, Definitions 6 and 7 are concerned with the construction of fuzzy implications, and Definitions 8–12 are concerned with the constructions to be presented in the area of copulas.

Note also that between Definitions 5 and 6 there is a table with reference to the most important and best-known classes of fuzzy negations.

At this point, a special bibliographical reference could be made to the articles on the construction of copulas, their properties, Archimedeans and fuzzy copulas [21,24,26].

Definition 1. **(see [1–4,8–14] Definition 1.4.1).** *The function* $N : [0,1] \to [0,1]$ *is a fuzzy negation if the following properties are applied:*

$$N(0) = 1, N(1) = 0 \tag{1}$$

$$N: \text{ is decreasing} \tag{2}$$

Definition 2. **(see [1–4,8–14] Definition 1.4.2 (i)).** *A fuzzy negation N is called strict if the following properties are applied:*

$$N \text{ is strictly decreasing} \tag{3}$$

$$N \text{ is continuous} \tag{4}$$

Definition 3. **(see [1–4,8–14] Definition 1.4.2 (ii)).** *A fuzzy negation N is called strong if*

$$N(N(x)) = x \tag{5}$$

Definition 4. **(see [1–4,8–14] Definition 1.4.2 (ii)).** *The solution of the equation* $N(x) = x$ *is called the equilibrium point of N. If the function N is continuous, the equilibrium point is unique.*

Definition 5 **([1]).** *Strong branching fuzzy negations can be produced, while in every branch is a decreasing function. If* N_1 *is a fuzzy negation, which is not necessary, a strong negation and* $N_1(\varepsilon) = \varepsilon$ *where* ε *is the equilibrium point of* N_1*. So, if* N_1 *is any continuous fuzzy negation in the interval [0, 1], then the following form [12] product is strong fuzzy negations* N_2 *and, in our case, rational fuzzy negations (Figure 1).*

$$N_2(x) = \begin{cases} N_1(x) & , x \in [0, \varepsilon] \\ N_1^{-1}(x) & , x \in (\varepsilon, 1] \end{cases} \tag{6}$$

The above formula will be generalized by using two functions (f, g), one decreasing and one increasing.

Below is Table 1 listing the most well-known classes of fuzzy negations.

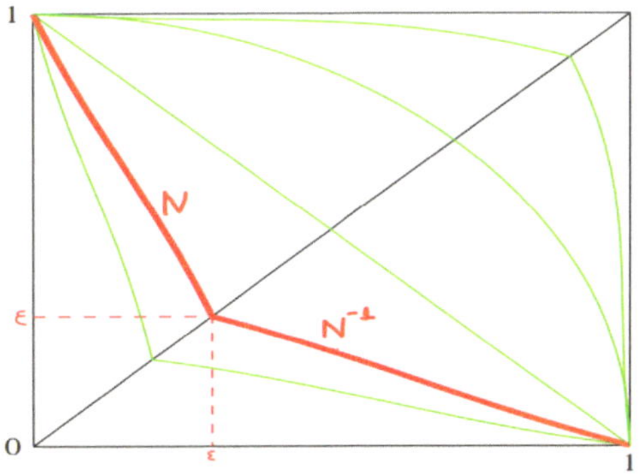

Figure 1. A random example of the form of the negation $N_2(x)$.

Table 1. Some examples of known negation classes.

Name	Fuzzy Negations
Yager class	$N^w(x) = (1 - x^w)^{\frac{1}{w}}$, $w > 0$
Threshold class	$N^t(x) = \begin{cases} 1, & \alpha\nu\ x < t \\ 1\ \acute{\eta}\ 0, & \alpha\nu\ x = t, \quad t \in (0,1) \\ 0, & \alpha\nu\ x > t \end{cases}$
Standard negation	$N(x) = 1 - x$
The least fuzzy negation	$N_{D1}(x) = \begin{cases} 1, & if\ x = 0 \\ 0, & if\ x \in (0,1] \end{cases}$
The greatest fuzzy negation	$N_{D2}(x) = \begin{cases} 0, & if\ x = 1 \\ 1, & if\ x \in [0,1) \end{cases}$
Sugeno Class	$N_\delta(x) = \frac{1-x}{1+\delta x}$, $\delta > -1$

Fuzzy implications have probably become the most important operations in fuzzy logic, approximate reasoning and fuzzy control. These operators not only model fuzzy conditionals but also make inferences in any fuzzy rule-based system. These operators are defined as follows:

Definition 6 (see [8–14] Definition 1.1.1). *A function $I : [0,1]^2 \to [0,1]$ is called a fuzzy implication if it satisfies, for all $x, x_1, x_2, y, y_1, y_2 \in [0,1]$, the following conditions:*

$$x_1 \le x_2 \Leftrightarrow I(x_1, y) \ge I(x_2, y), \text{ i.e., } I(\cdot, y) \text{ is decreasing.} \tag{7}$$

$$y_1 \le y_2 \Leftrightarrow I(x, y_1) \le I(x, y_2), \text{ i.e., } I(x, \cdot) \text{ is increasing.} \tag{8}$$

$$I(0,0) = 1 \tag{9}$$

$$I(1,1) = 1 \tag{10}$$

$$I(1,0) = 0 \tag{11}$$

Definition 7 (see [8–14] Definition 1.4.15 (ii)). *If I is a fuzzy implication, then the function $N_I : [0,1] \to [0,1]$ with the form $N_I(x) = I(x, 0)$ is called natural negation of I.*

Definition 8 ([26]). *Let I be a nonempty interval of R. A function f from I to R is convex if, and only if, $\frac{\partial^2 f}{\partial x^2} \ge 0$.*

Definition 9 **([20–24,26]).** *A function* $C : [0,1]^2 \rightarrow [0,1]$ *is called a copula if it satisfies the following properties:*

$$C(0,t) = C(t,0) = 0 \quad \textit{for each } 0 \leq t \leq 1 \tag{12}$$

$$C(1,t) = C(t,1) = t \quad \textit{for each } 0 \leq t \leq 1 \tag{13}$$

The C-volume of a rectangle must be not negative, e.g.,

$$V_H = C(x_1, y_1) - C(x_1, y_2) - C(x_2, y_1) + C(x_2, y_2) \geq 0 \tag{14}$$

for each $x_1 \leq x_2$ *and* $y_1 \leq y_2$ *where* $0 \leq x_1, x_2, y_1, y_2 \leq 1$.

Definition 10 **([20–24,26]).** *If the function C is a copula, then the function in form* $C^*(x,y) = x + y - 1 + C(1-x, 1-y)$ *for each* $0 \leq x, y \leq 1$ *is also a copula, and it is called survival copula.*

Definition 11 **([20–24,26]).** *If f is a decreasing function where* $f(1) = 0$*, then we define the pseudo-inverse of function f*

$$\text{Given by } f^{[-1]} = \begin{cases} f^{-1}(x) & ,if \;\; 0 \leq x \leq f(0) \\ 0 & ,if \;\; f(0) \leq x \leq \infty \end{cases} \tag{15}$$

Definition 12 **([20–24,26]).** *Let* $f : [0,1] \rightarrow [0,\infty]$ *be a continuous, strictly decreasing and convex function such that* $f(1) = 0$*, and let* $f^{[-1]}$ *be the pseudo-inverse. Let* $C : [0,1] \rightarrow [0,1]$*, defined by*

$$C(x,y) = f^{[-1]}(f(x) + f(y)) \tag{16}$$

Then, C is an Archimedean Copula.

3. Results

In this section, this article will present all the constructions resulting from the use of the definitions in the previous section. All the proofs will be presented in detail, with mathematical relations and explanations. In total, five theorems and an interesting proof on the third property of copulas (increasing with respect to the variables x, y) will be presented.

The first theorem proves that a class of multi-branching functions will be a strong fuzzy negation. An example of this follows. The second theorem presents another class of possible fuzzy negations. This second class with some adjustments presents the formula $\mathrm{f}\left(\mathrm{f}^{-1}(\mathrm{y}) * \mathrm{x}\right)$. The following example gives a class of strong fuzzy negations that presents great ease in finding the equilibrium point.

The third proof concerns the presentation of a fuzzy implication using the same formula $\mathrm{f}\left(\mathrm{f}^{-1}(\mathrm{y}) * \mathrm{x}\right)$, avoiding the use of some fuzzy negation.

This article then moves on to the spectrum of copulas.

First, a proof of some classes of copulas will be presented.

This will be followed by the proofs of two propositions on the definition of copulas and, finally, another proof of a class of copulas containing the formula $\mathrm{f}\left(\mathrm{f}^{-1}(\mathrm{y}) * \mathrm{x}\right)$.

3.1. New Forms of Strong Fuzzy Negations

Strong branching fuzzy negations can be produced [1] while in every branch there is a decreasing function. Let N_1 be a fuzzy negation, not necessarily a strong negation, and $\mathrm{N}_1(\varepsilon) = \varepsilon$ where ε is the equilibrium point of N_1. So, if N_1 is any continuous fuzzy negation in the interval [0, 1], then the following form [12] produces strong fuzzy negations N_2 and, in our case, rational fuzzy negations.

$$N_2(x) = \begin{cases} \boldsymbol{N_1(x)} & , \boldsymbol{x \in [0, \varepsilon]} \\ \boldsymbol{N_1^{-1}(x)} & , \boldsymbol{x \in (\varepsilon, 1]} \end{cases} \tag{17}$$

In the Figure 2 below, consider $\boldsymbol{N_1(x) = f(x)}$ and $\boldsymbol{N_1^{-1}(x) = f^{-1}(x)}$

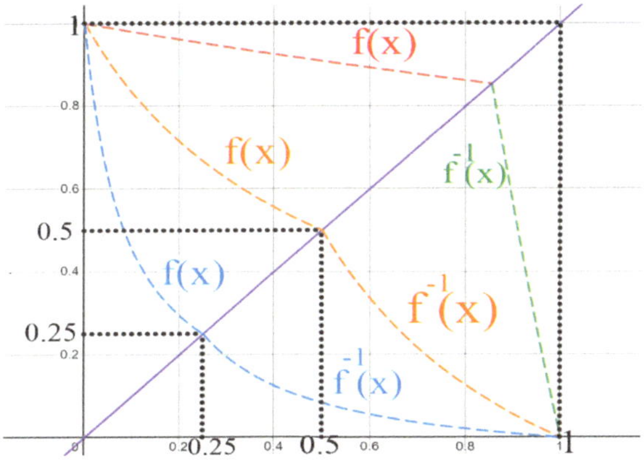

Figure 2. The graph of the negation $N_2(x)$ for three random values of the ε when ε = 0.25, ε = 0.5 and ε = 1.

The above formula will be generalized using two functions (f, g), one decreasing and one increasing.

Generating Classes of Strong Fuzzy Negations

Theorem 1. *Let ε the equilibrium point of N_{PM1}, $f : [0,1] \to [0,+\infty)$ continuous decreasing function and $g : [0,1] \to [0,+\infty)$ continuous increasing function with the conditions: f^{-1}, g^{-1} well defined, $f(0) = 1$ and $g(0) = 0$ and k > 0 positive real number. Then, the following form is a class of strong fuzzy negations:*

$$\boldsymbol{N_{PM1}(x)} = \begin{cases} \boldsymbol{f(g(x)*k)}, & \boldsymbol{0 \le x \le \varepsilon} \\ \boldsymbol{g^{-1}\left(\frac{f^{-1}(x)}{k}\right)}, & \boldsymbol{\varepsilon < x \le 1} \end{cases} \tag{18}$$

Proof of Theorem 1. The proof that the class of strong negations above is a continuous function will be given first. It is obvious that what is examined is the continuity in the equilibrium point. Assuming that all the values x of the equilibrium points are the solution of the equation $N_{PM1}(x) = x$, then it implies:

$f(g(x) * k) = x \Leftrightarrow f^{-1}(f(g(x) * k)) = f^{-1}(x) \Leftrightarrow g(x) * k = f^{-1}(x)$, for k > 0 implies that $g(x) = \frac{f^{-1}(x)}{k}$ and, finally, $x = g^{-1}\left(\frac{f^{-1}(x)}{k}\right)$. That proves that the two multi-branched functions intersect on the line y = x at the equilibrium point. That proves that the negation $N_{PM1}(x)$ is a continuous function in the interval [0, 1].

Boundary conditions

- For x ≤ ε implies that $N_{PM1}(x) = f(g(x) * k)$

$$N_{PM1}(0) = f(g(0) * k) = f(0) = 1$$

- For x > ε implies that $N_{PM1}(1) = g^{-1}\left(\frac{f^{-1}(1)}{k}\right) = g^{-1}(0) = 0$

  Monotony condition
- For $x \le \varepsilon$ implies that $N_{PM1}(x) = f(g(x) * k)$
  For every $x_1, x_2 \in [0, \varepsilon]$ where

$$x_1 \le x_2 \overset{g\nearrow}{\Leftrightarrow} g(x_1) \le g(x_2)$$

$$\text{thus } k > 0, g(x_1) * k \le g(x_2) * k \overset{f\searrow}{\Leftrightarrow} f(g(x_1) * k) \ge f(g(x_1) * k)$$
$$\Leftrightarrow N_{PM1}(x_1) \ge N_{PM1}(x_2)$$

  So that proves that N_{PM1} is decreasing when $x \le \varepsilon$.
- For $x > \varepsilon$ implies that $N_{PM1}(x) = g^{-1}\left(\frac{f^{-1}(x)}{k}\right)$
  For every $x_1, x_2 \in (\varepsilon, 1]$ where

$$\text{for } x_1 \le x_2 \Leftrightarrow f^{-1}(x_1) \ge f^{-1}(x_2) \text{ and for } \frac{1}{k} > 0 \text{ arises :}$$

$$: \frac{f^{-1}(x_1)}{k} \ge \frac{f^{-1}(x_2)}{k} \text{ and finally}$$

$$\overset{g^{-1}\nearrow}{\Leftrightarrow} g^{-1}\left(\frac{f^{-1}(x_1)}{k}\right) \ge g^{-1}\left(\frac{f^{-1}(x_2)}{k}\right).$$

  So $N_{PM1}(x_1) \ge N_{PM1}(x_2)$. That concludes that N_{PM1} is decreasing when x > ε.

  Synthesis condition

  The most important condition for a negation to be strong is as follows:

$$N_{PM1}(N_{PM1}(x)) = x$$

Because of the way the negation class is constructed, the set of values of one branch is mapped to the definition domain of the other branch. Thus, when synthesizing the negation with itself, the type of one branch inside the other is placed and vice versa.

That equals the following:

$$f\left(g\left(g^{-1}\left(\frac{f^{-1}(x)}{k}\right)\right) * k\right) = f\left(\frac{f^{-1}(x)}{k} * k\right) = f\left(f^{-1}(x)\right) = x.$$

And vice versa the following:

$$g^{-1}\left(\frac{f^{-1}(f(g(x) * k))}{k}\right) = g^{-1}\left(\frac{g(x) * k}{k}\right) = g^{-1}(g(x)) = x.$$

The class of negations is continuous as an operation of continuous functions, and it holds that for any $x \in [0, 1]$ then $N_{PM1}(N_{PM1}(x)) = x$. Therefore, this class of fuzzy negations is a strong one. □

Example 1. *One example of fuzzy negations is presented, generated by Theorem 1.*

Let the decreasing function f(x) be the function $f(x) = \frac{1}{x+1}$. It is easy to check that f(x) is positive, decreasing, f (0) = 1 and continuous. Let $g(x) = \sqrt{x}$, $g(x) \ge 0$ and increasing, g(0) = 0 and k > 0. This means that $f(g(x)*k) = \frac{1}{k*\sqrt{x}+1}$. Let us now construct the fuzzy negation proved before, which will be the following:

$$N^k{}_{PM1}(x) = \begin{cases} \frac{1}{k*\sqrt{x}+1}\,, & \mathbf{0 \leq x \leq \varepsilon} \\ \\ (\frac{1-x}{kx})^2, & \boldsymbol{\varepsilon < x \leq 1} \end{cases} \tag{19}$$

where ε is the equilibrium point. Quite easily can someone find out that $N^k{}_{PM1}(x)$ completes all the conditions needed.

Boundary conditions

$$N^k{}_{PM1}(0) = \frac{1}{k*\sqrt{0}+1} = 1/1 = 1 \text{ and } N^k{}_{PM1}(1) = \left(\frac{1-1}{k*1}\right)^2 = 0$$

Monotony conditions

- For $x \leq \varepsilon$, every $x_1 \leq x_2 \Leftrightarrow$

$$\sqrt{x_1} \leq \sqrt{x_2} \Leftrightarrow k*\sqrt{x_1} \leq k*\sqrt{x_2} \quad \Leftrightarrow k*\sqrt{x_1}+1 \leq k*\sqrt{x_2}+1 \Leftrightarrow$$

$$\frac{1}{k*\sqrt{x_1}+1} \geq \frac{1}{k*\sqrt{x_2}+1} \Leftrightarrow N^k{}_{PM1}(x_1) \geq N^k{}_{PM1}(x_2) \text{ so, it is decreasing.}$$

- For $\varepsilon < x$ every $x_1 \leq x_2 \Leftrightarrow$

$1 - x_1 \geq 1 - x_2$ (1) and again $x_1 \leq x_2 \Leftrightarrow k*x_1 \leq k*x_2 \Leftrightarrow \frac{1}{k*x_1} \geq \frac{1}{k*x_2}$ (2) I multiply (1) and (2):

$$\frac{1-x_1}{k*x_1} \geq \frac{1-x_2}{k*x_2} \Leftrightarrow (\frac{1-x_1}{kx_1})^2 \geq (\frac{1-x_2}{kx_2})^2 \Leftrightarrow N^k{}_{PM1}(x_1) \geq N^k{}_{PM1}(x_2)$$

it is decreasing.

Synthesis condition

The most important condition for a negation to be strong is the following:

$$N_{PM1}(N_{PM1}(x)) = x$$

Again, because of the way the negation class is constructed, the set of values of one branch is mapped to the definition domain of the other branch. Thus, when synthesizing the negation with itself, the type of one branch is placed inside the other and vice versa.

- For $\leq \varepsilon$:

$$N_{PM1}(N_{PM1}(x)) = \frac{1}{k*\sqrt{(\frac{1-x}{kx})^2}+1} = \frac{1}{k*\frac{1-x}{kx}+1} = \frac{1}{\frac{1-x}{x}+1} = \frac{1}{\frac{1}{x}} = x.$$

And vice versa:

- For $\varepsilon < x$

$$N_{PM1}(N_{PM1}(x)) = (\frac{1-\frac{1}{k*\sqrt{x}+1}}{k\frac{1}{k*\sqrt{x}+1}})^2 = (\frac{\frac{k*\sqrt{x}}{k*\sqrt{x}+1}}{k\frac{1}{k*\sqrt{x}+1}})^2 = (\sqrt{x})^2 = x$$

Theorem 2. *Let ε the equilibrium point of N_{PM2}, $f : [0,1] \to [0,+\infty)$ continuous decreasing function and $k > 0$ with the following conditions:*

f^{-1} well defined, $f(0) = 1$. Then, the following form is a class of strong fuzzy negations:

$$\boldsymbol{N_{PM2}(x)} = \begin{cases} \boldsymbol{f(k{*}x)}, & \boldsymbol{0 \leq x \leq \varepsilon} \\ \frac{\boldsymbol{f^{-1}(x)}}{\boldsymbol{k}}, & \boldsymbol{\varepsilon < x \leq 1} \end{cases} \tag{20}$$

Proof of Theorem 2. First of all, the proof that the class of strong negations above is a continuous function must be given. It is obvious that the continuity in the equilibrium point must be examined. So, let someone assume that all the values x of the equilibrium points are the solution of the equation $N_{PM2}(x) = x$. That implies the following:

$f(k * x) = x \Leftrightarrow f^{-1}(f(k * x)) = f^{-1}(x) \Leftrightarrow k * x = f^{-1}(x)$, for g(x) > 0 then $x = \frac{f^{-1}(x)}{k}$. That proves that the two bifurcated functions intersect on the line y = x at the equilibrium point. That proves that the negation $N_{PM2}(x)$ is a continuous function in the interval [0, 1].

Boundary conditions

- For $x \leq \varepsilon$ implies that

$$N_{PM2}(x) = f(k * x) \Leftrightarrow N_{PM2}(0) = f(k * 0) = f(0) = 1$$

- For $x > \varepsilon$ implies that $N_{PM2}(1) = \left(\frac{f^{-1}(1)}{k}\right) = \frac{0}{k} = 0$

Monotony condition

- For $x \leq \varepsilon$ implies that $N_{PM2}(x) = f(k * x)$
For every $x_1, x_2 \in [0, \varepsilon]$ where

$$x_1 \leq x_2$$

$$\text{and get } k * x_1 \leq k * x_2 \overset{f\searrow}{\Leftrightarrow} f(k * x_1) \geq f(k * x_1) \Leftrightarrow N_{PM2}(x_1) \geq N_{PM2}(x_2)$$

So, it is concluded that N_{PM2} is decreasing when $x \leq \varepsilon$.

- For $x > \varepsilon$ then $N_{PM2}(x) = \frac{f^{-1}(x)}{K}$
For every $x_1, x_2 \in (\varepsilon, 1]$ where

$$\text{for } x_1 \leq x_2 \overset{f^{-1}\searrow}{\Leftrightarrow} f^{-1}(x_1) \geq f^{-1}(x_2)$$

$$\text{so, we have}: \frac{f^{-1}(x_1)}{k} \geq \frac{f^{-1}(x_2)}{k} \text{ and finally,}$$

$$N_{PM2}(x_1) \geq N_{PM2}(x_2)$$

So, we conclude that N_{PM2} is decreasing when $x > \varepsilon$.

Synthesis condition

The most important condition for a negation to be strong is the following:

$$N_{PM2}(N_{PM2}(x)) = x$$

Again, because of the way the negation class we are studying is constructed, the set of values of one branch is mapped to the definition domain of the other branch. Thus, when we synthesize the negation with itself, we place the type of one branch inside the other and vice versa.

So, we have: $f\left(\frac{f^{-1}(x)}{k} * k\right) = f(f^{-1}(x)) = x$. And vice versa, it is the following:

$$\frac{f^{-1}(f(x * k))}{k} = \frac{x * k}{k} = x.$$

The class of negations is continuous as an operation of continuous functions, and it holds that for any $x \in [0, 1]$ then $N_{PM2}(N_{PM2}(x)) = x$. Therefore, this class of fuzzy negations is a strong one. □

Remark 1. *Let* $k = f^{-1}(y) > 0$*, for every* $0 \leq y < 1$ *then* $0 < f^{-1}(y) \leq 1$*, so the negation takes the following form:*

$$\mathbf{N_{PM2}(x)} = \begin{cases} \mathbf{f}\left(\mathbf{f}^{-1}(\mathbf{y}) * \mathbf{x}\right), & 0 \leq \mathbf{x} \leq \varepsilon \\ \frac{\mathbf{f}^{-1}(\mathbf{x})}{\mathbf{f}^{-1}(\mathbf{y})}, & \varepsilon < \mathbf{x} \leq \mathbf{1} \end{cases} \tag{21}$$

This is a strong fuzzy negation.

Remark 2. *For* $y = 0$ *and* $f(1) = 0$ *the function* $N_{PM2}(x) = f\left(f^{-1}(y) * x\right)$ *is a strict fuzzy negation.*

Remark 3. *We will examine later the form* $f\left(f^{-1}(y) * x\right)$*, which we will prove is a fuzzy implication. The same form of the g(x) function,* $g^{-1}(g(y) * x)$ *will take part in the construction of a copula.*

Example 2. *One example of fuzzy negations is presented, generated by Theorem 2.*

Let the decreasing function f(x) be the function $f(x) = \frac{1}{x+1}$. It is easy to check that f(x) is positive, decreasing, f (0) = 1 and continuous. Let k > 0. This means that $f(k*x) = \frac{1}{k*x+1}$. Let us now construct the fuzzy negation proved before, which will be the following:

$$N^k{}_{PM2}(x) = \begin{cases} \frac{1}{kx+1}, & 0 \leq x \leq \varepsilon \\ \frac{1-x}{kx}, & \varepsilon < x \leq 1 \end{cases} \tag{22}$$

where ε is the equilibrium point. This means that finding the point x=ε is the target. To achieve this someone has to solve the equation $\frac{1}{kx+1} = x \Leftrightarrow kx^2 + x - 1$, which is a second-degree equation. We use the type

$$x_{1,2} = \frac{-1 \pm \sqrt{4k+1}}{2k}$$

where the one solution is rejected $x_2 = \frac{-1-\sqrt{4k+1}}{2k}$ because it is negative. That means $\varepsilon = \frac{-1+\sqrt{4k+1}}{2k}$. So, the formula takes the form of: $if\ \varepsilon = \frac{-1 \pm \sqrt{4k+1}}{2k}$ then

$$N^k{}_{PM2}(x) = \begin{cases} \frac{1}{kx+1}, & 0 \leq x \leq \frac{-1+\sqrt{4k+1}}{2k} \\ \frac{1-x}{kx}, & \frac{-1+\sqrt{4k+1}}{2k} < x \leq 1 \end{cases} \tag{23}$$

In this way, a strong negation has been constructed in which someone can quite easily calculate the equilibrium point. That way, negations can exist that satisfy many types of implications or other problems while the class of negations created has a great range of values, easily calculated. For example (Figure 3):

- For k = 12, we calculate that ε = 0.25 and appears at the graph $N^{12}{}_{PM}(x)$.
- For k = 2, we calculate that ε = 0.5 and appears at the graph $N^{2}{}_{PM}(x)$.
- For k = 0.3125, we calculate that ε = 0.8 and appears at the graph $N^{0.3125}{}_{PM}(x)$

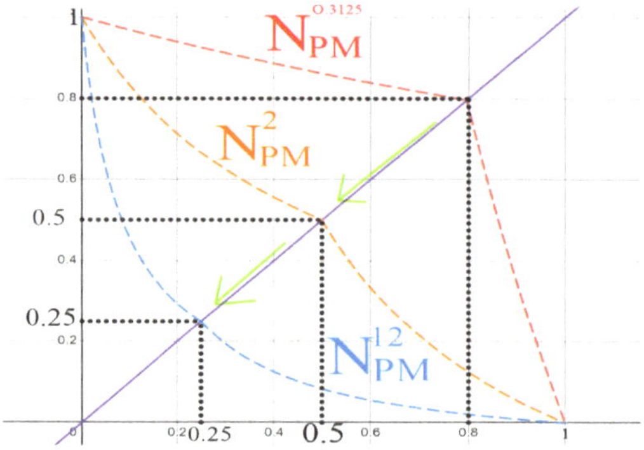

Figure 3. The graph of three specific examples of the negation $N^k{}_{PM2}(x)$.

3.2. *Constructing Non-Symmetric Fuzzy Implications without the Use of Fuzzy Negations*

Already mentioned above are the conditions that must be met for a function to be a fuzzy implication. In this section, there will be presented a construction of a fuzzy implication, non-symmetric and without the use of fuzzy negation. To perform this, it is necessary to use one of the two functions we have already used so far. The function f(x), which is strictly decreasing, is continuous, and f(0) = 1.

Theorem 3. *Let the function s f, f^{-1} continuous, well defined, then $I : [0,1]^2 \to [0,1]$ as* ***I(x,y) =*** $f\left(f^{-1}(y) * x\right)$*, and f(x) decreasing and f(0) = 1. Then, I(x,y) is a fuzzy implication.*

Definition 13 ([20–24,26]). *A function $I : [0,1]^2 \to [0,1]$ is called a fuzzy implication if it satisfies, for all $x, x_1, x_2, y, y_1, y_2 \in [0,1]$, the following conditions:*

$$(a)\ \ x_1 \leq x_2 \Leftrightarrow I(x_1, y) \geq I(x_2, y), \textit{ i.e., } I(\cdot, y) \textit{ is decreasing.}$$

$$(b)\ \ y_1 \leq y_2 \Leftrightarrow I(x, y_1) \leq I(x, y_2), \textit{ i.e., } I(x, \cdot) \textit{ is increasing.}$$

$$(c)\ \ I(0,0) = 1$$

$$(d)\ \ I(1,1) = 1$$

$$(e)\ \ I(1,0) = 0$$

Proof of Theorem 3.

(a) For every $x_1 \leq x_2 \Leftrightarrow f^{-1}(y)\, x_1 \leq f^{-1}(y) x_2$ *for* $f^{-1}(y) \geq 0 \overset{f\searrow}{\Leftrightarrow} f(f^{-1}(y)x_1) \geq f(f^{-1}(y)x_2)$ so, *I*(x_1,*y*)≥ *I*(x_2, *y*)

(b) For every $y_1 \leq y_2 \overset{f^{-1}\searrow}{\Leftrightarrow} f^{-1}(y_1) \geq f^{-1}(y_2) \Leftrightarrow f^{-1}(y_1)x \geq f^{-1}(y_2)x$ for $x \geq 0$ $\overset{f\searrow}{\Leftrightarrow} f(f^{-1}(y_1)x) \leq f(f^{-1}(y_2)x)$ so, *I*(*x*, y_1) ≤ *I*(*x*, y_2)

(c) *I*(0,0) = $f\left(f^{-1}(0) * 0\right) = f(0) = 1$

(d) *I*(1,1) = $f\left(f^{-1}(1) * 1\right) = f\left(f^{-1}(1)\right) = 1$

(e) *I*(1,0) = $f\left(f^{-1}(0) * 1\right) = f\left(f^{-1}(0)\right) = 0.$ □

This verifies all five properties of fuzzy implications. So, our function ***I(x,y)*** = $f\left(f^{-1}(y) * x\right)$ is a non-symmetric fuzzy implication.

Example 3. *Now, one example will be presented of the theorem above.*

Let the function f(x) = $\sqrt{1-(\frac{x}{2})}$, which is decreasing, f(0) = 1 and $f^{-1}(x) = 2*(1-x^2)$ be well defined in the interval [0, 1]. Let us prove that *I(x,y)* = $\sqrt{1-(1-y^2)*x}$ is a fuzzy implication.

(1) For every $x_1 \leq x_2 \Leftrightarrow 2*(1-y^2)*x_1 \leq 2*(1-y^2)*x_2 \overset{f\searrow}{\Leftrightarrow} \sqrt{1-(1-y^2)*x_1} \geq \sqrt{1-(1-y^2)*x_2}$ *so* $I(x_1,y) \geq I(x_2,y)$
(2) For every $y_1 \leq y_2 \overset{f^{-1}\searrow}{\Leftrightarrow} 2*(1-y_1{}^2)*x \geq 2*(1-y_2{}^2)*x$ *for* $x \geq 0 \overset{f\searrow}{\Leftrightarrow} \sqrt{1-(1-y_1{}^2)*x} \leq \sqrt{1-(1-y_2{}^2)*x}$ *so* $I(x,y_1) \leq I(x,y_2)$
(3) *I*(0,0) = $\sqrt{1-(1-0^2)*0} = \sqrt{1} = 1$
(4) *I*(1,1) = $\sqrt{1-(1-1^2)*1} = \sqrt{1} = 1$
(5) *I*(1,0) = $\sqrt{1-(1-0^2)*1} = \sqrt{1-1} = 0$. That means that *I(x,y)* = $\sqrt{1-(1-y^2)*x}$ is a fuzzy implication.

3.3. Generating Copulas Using the Same Functions

In this section, the construction of copulas will be given, functions that are known from their applications in economics and risk analysis, as well as in fuzzy logic in general. So far, our constructions were based on two specific functions called f(x) and g(x) and given some properties. Now, exactly the same functions will be used to construct the copulas. In some of these cases, some additional properties will be given.

Theorem 4. *Let the function* $g : [0,1] \to [0,+\infty)$ *be continuous, strictly increasing and convex, g(0) = 0, g(1) = 1, with* g^{-1} *continuous. The function* $C_1 : [0,1]^2 \to [0,1]$, *when* $C_1(x,y) = g(g^{-1}(x)*g^{-1}(y))$ *is a copula with the symmetric and incentive effect.*

Proof of Theorem 4. Let us remember that there are three conditions that make C(x, y) a copula.

(1) $C(0,t) = C(t,0) = 0$ *for each* $0 \leq t \leq 1$
(2) $C(1,t) = C(t,1) = t$ *for each* $0 \leq t \leq 1$
(3) The C-volume of a rectangle must be not negative, e.g.,

$$V_H = C(x_1, y_1) - C(x_1, y_2) - C(x_2, y_1) + C(x_2, y_2) \geq 0$$

for each $x_1 \leq x_2$ and $y_1 \leq y_2$ where $0 \leq x_1, x_2, y_1, y_2 \leq 1$.

For the proof of the first condition after replacing the following:

(1) $C_1(t,0) = g(g^{-1}(t)*g^{-1}(0)) = g(g^{-1}(t)*0) = g(0) = 0$
$C_1(0,t) = g(g^{-1}(0)*g^{-1}(t)) = g(0*g^{-1}(t)) = g(0) = 0$
(2) $C_1(t,1) = g(g^{-1}(t)*g^{-1}(1)) = g(g^{-1}(t)*1) = g(g^{-1}(t)) = t$
$C_1(1,t) = g(g^{-1}(1)*g^{-1}(t)) = g(1*g^{-1}(t)) = g(g^{-1}(t)) = t$
(3) There are two options for proving the third property. If the function g(x) is productive, then it is relatively easy to prove the third property, provided that the derivative $\frac{\partial^2 C(x,y)}{\partial xy} \geq 0$ is positive. But, if the function g(x) is not productive, then the proof becomes much more complex and difficult. Both cases will be listed. □

Proposition 1. *Knowing that for a function to be 2-increasing, must satisfy the inequality* $C(x_1,y_1) + C(x_2,y_2) - C(x_1,y_2) - C(x_2,y_1) \geq 0$. *This inequality is equivalent to* $\frac{\partial^2 C(x,y)}{\partial xy} \geq 0$ *when C is a differentiable function.*

Proof of Proposition 1. When someone applies the Mean Value Theorem for the function $C(x, y_1)$ in the interval $[x_1, x_2]$

$$\exists\, \xi_1 \in (x_1, x_2) : \frac{\partial C(\xi_1, y_1)}{\partial x} = \frac{C(x_2,y_1) - C(x_1,y_1)}{x_2 - x_1}$$

Applying the Mean Value Theorem for the function $C(x, y_2)$ in the interval $[x_1, x_2]$

$$\exists\, \xi_1 \in (x_1, x_2) : \frac{\partial C(\xi_1, y_2)}{\partial x} = \frac{C(x_2, y_2) - C(x_1, y_2)}{x_2 - x_1}$$

Let us suppose that $C(x_1, y_1) + C(x_2, y_2) - C(x_1, y_2) - C(x_2, y_1) \geq 0$ then

$$\frac{\partial C(\xi_1, y_2)}{\partial x} - \frac{\partial C(\xi_1, y_1)}{\partial x} \geq 0 \Leftrightarrow \frac{\partial^2 C(x, y)}{\partial xy} \geq 0.$$

□

(a) Considering $g(x)$ is convex, we have that $(g)''(x) \geq 0$. So, we have the following:

$$\frac{\partial C(x, y)}{\partial x} = (g)\prime\left(g^{-1}(x) * g^{(-1)}(y)\right) * \left[g^{-1}\right]\prime(x) * g^{-1}(y).$$

And then,

$$\frac{\partial^2 C(x,y)}{\partial xy} =$$
$$(g)''\left(g^{-1}(x) * g^{-1}(y)\right) * g^{-1}(x) * \left[g^{-1}\right]\prime(y) * \left[g^{-1}\right]\prime(x) * g^{-1}(y) +$$
$$(g)\prime\left(g^{-1}(x) * g^{-1}(y)\right) \left[g^{-1}\right]\prime(x) * \left[g^{-1}\right]\prime(y) =$$
$$\left[g^{-1}\right]\prime(x) * \left[g^{-1}\right]\prime(y) * \left[g^{-1}(x) * g^{-1}(y) * (g)''\left(g^{-1}(x) * g^{-1}(y)\right) +\right.$$
$$\left.(g)\prime\left(g^{-1}(x) * g^{-1}(y)\right)\right] \geq 0$$

Indeed, because $g(x) \geq 0$, $g'(x) \geq 0$, $(g^{-1})\prime \geq 0$, $(g)'' \geq 0$, $(g^{-1}) \geq 0$.

(b) If function g(x) is not productive, the proof of the third property becomes very difficult and interesting and comes with the help of the classical definition of convexity.

Definition 14. *A function $f : A \to \mathbb{R}$ is convex if, for all (x, y) in the domain of f, and for all t in [0, 1] when the inequality*

$$(f(t * x + (1 - t) * y) \leq t * f(x) + (1 - t) * f(y) \quad (24)$$

holds.

Knowing that the copula we constructed is a three-dimensional function, the definition is the following:

Definition 15. *A function $f : A^2 \to \mathbb{R}$ is convex if, for all points (x_1, y_1), (x_2, y_2) in the domain of f (x), and for all $t \in [0, 1]$ when the inequality*

$$f(t * x_1 + (1 - t) * x_2,\ t * y_1 + (1 - t) * y_2) \leq t * f(x_1, y_1) + (1 - t) * f(x_2, y_2) \text{ holds} \quad (25)$$

Proposition 2. *Knowing that for a function to be 2-increasing, must satisfy the inequality $C(x_1, y_1) + C(x_2, y_2) - C(x_1, y_2) - C(x_2, y_1) \geq 0$. If g(x) is convex and strictly increasing yet non-productive, then the function $C_1(x, y) = g\left(g^{-1}(x) * g^{-1}(y)\right)$ is 2-increasing.*

Proof of Proposition 2. First of all, let us give a proof that if $g(x)$ is convex, then C(x, y) is convex. Let

$C_1(x, y) = g\left(g^{-1}(x) * g^{-1}(y)\right)$, $0 \leq x \leq 1$, $0 \leq y \leq 1$, which also means that $0 \leq g^{-1}(x) \leq 1$, $0 \leq g^{-1}(y) \leq 1$.

Also, g(x) is strictly increasing $\overset{g\nearrow}{\Leftrightarrow}$, so let $g^{-1}(x) = u$ and $g^{-1}(y) = w$. That means that $0 \leq u * w \leq 1$.

So, let $u * w = v$. That makes $C_1(x, y) = g(g^{-1}(x) * g^{-1}(y)) = g(u * w) = g(v)$, which proves that if $g(x)$ is convex, then $C_1(x, y)$ is convex.

Due to the monotony conditions, it is proved that

For every pair of $y_1, y_2 \in A^2$, when

$$y_1 \le y_2 \overset{g^{-1}\nearrow}{\Leftrightarrow} g^{-1}(y_1) \le g^{-1}(y_2) \Leftrightarrow g^{-1}(x_1)g^{-1}(y_1) \le g^{-1}(x_1)\, g^{-1}(y_2) \overset{g^{-1}\nearrow}{\Leftrightarrow} g(g^{-1}(x_1) * g^{-1}(y_1)) \le g(g^{-1}(x_1) * g^{-1}(y_2)) \Leftrightarrow C_1(x_1, y_1) \le C_1(x_1, y_2) \tag{26}$$

For every pair of $x_1, x_2 \in A^2$, when

$$x_1 \le x_2 \overset{g^{-1}\nearrow}{\Leftrightarrow} g^{-1}(x_1) \le g^{-1}(x_2) \Leftrightarrow g^{-1}(x_1)g^{-1}(y_1) \le g^{-1}(x_2)\, g^{-1}(y_1) \overset{g\nearrow}{\Leftrightarrow} g(g^{-1}(x_1) * g^{-1}(y_1)) \le g(g^{-1}(x_2) * g^{-1}(y_1)) \Leftrightarrow C_1(x_1, y_1) \le C_1(x_2, y_1) \tag{27}$$

For every pair of $y_1, y_2 \in A^2$, when

$$y_1 \le y_2 \overset{g^{-1}\nearrow}{\Leftrightarrow} g^{-1}(y_1) \le g^{-1}(y_2) \Leftrightarrow g^{-1}(x_2)g^{-1}(y_1)g^{-1}(x_2)\, g^{-1}(y_2) \overset{g^{-1}\nearrow}{\Leftrightarrow} g(g^{-1}(x_2) * g^{-1}(y_1)) \le g(g^{-1}(x_2) * g^{-1}(y_2)) \Leftrightarrow C_1(x_2, y_1) \le C_1(x_2, y_2) \tag{28}$$

For every pair of $x_1, x_2 \in A^2$, when

$$x_1 \le x_2 \overset{g^{-1}\nearrow}{\Leftrightarrow} g^{-1}(x_1) \le g^{-1}(x_2) \Leftrightarrow g^{-1}(x_1)g^{-1}(y_2) \le g^{-1}(x_2)\, g^{-1}(y_2) \overset{g\nearrow}{\Leftrightarrow} g(g^{-1}(x_1) * g^{-1}(y_2)) \le g(g^{-1}(x_2) * g^{-1}(y_2)) \Leftrightarrow C_1(x_1, y_2) \le C_1(x_2, y_2) \tag{29}$$

Using the four inequalities above, someone can build the inequalities below:

$$C_1(x_1, y_1) \le C_1(x_1, y_2) \le C_1(x_2, y_2) \tag{30}$$

$$C_1(x_1, y_1) \le C_1(x_2, y_1) \le C_1(x_2, y_2) \tag{31}$$

multiplying relation (30) by t, $t \in [0, 1]$ and relation (31) by $(1 - t)$, by $(1 - t) \in [0, 1]$, and so

$$t * C_1(x_1, y_1) \le t * C_1(x_1, y_2) \le t * C_1(x_2, y_2) \tag{32}$$

$$(1-t) * C_1(x_1, y_1) \le (1-t) * C_1(x_2, y_1) \le (1-t) * C_1(x_2, y_2) \tag{33}$$

Adding by members the inequalities (32) and (33) it implies the following:

$$C_1(x_2, y_2) \ge t * C_1(x_1, y_2) + (1-t) * C_1(x_2, y_1) \ge C_1(x_1, y_1) \tag{34}$$

Knowing that the function C(x, y) is a continuous function inside the domain of $[x_1, y_1] \times [x_2, y_2]$, someone can make use of the intermediate value theorem, which means that for every $t \in [0, 1]$ there are points $(x_t, y_t) \in [x_1, y_1] \times [x_2, y_2]$ so that

$$C_1(x_t, y_t) = t * C_1(x_1, y_2) + (1-t) * C_1(x_2, y_1) \tag{35}$$

Remembering the definition of convexity for points (x_1, y_1), (x_2, y_2) in the domain of f(x) and for all $t \in [0, 1]$, then

$$C_1(t * x_1 + (1-t) * x_2,\ t * y_1 + (1-t) * y_2) \ge t * C_1(x_1, y_1) + (1-t) * C_1(x_2, y_2) \tag{36}$$

It is assumed, without the limitation of generality and knowing, that the function C(x, y) is symmetric

$(C_1(x, y) = C_1(y, x))$ that for every $t \in [0, 1]$ and every $x_1 \le x_t \le x_2$, $y_1 \le y_t \le y_2$ that $x_t = t * x_1 + (1-t) * x_2$ and $y_t = t * y_1 + (1-t) * y_2$. Thus, substituting in relation (36) we obtain the following:

$C_1(x_t, y_t) \leq t * C_1(x_1, y_1) + (1-t) * C_1(x_2, y_2)$. Now the substitute from relation (35) and obtain:

$$t * C_1(x_1, y_2) + (1-t) * C_1(x_2, y_1) \leq t * C_1(x_1, y_1) + (1-t) * C_1(x_2, y_2) \tag{37}$$

Relation (37) stands for every t ∈ [0, 1], so for t = 0.5, we obtain the following:

$$(0.5) * C(x_1, y_2) + (0.5) * C(x_2, y_1) + (0.5) * C(x_1, y_1) + (0.5) * C(x_2, y_2).$$

Multiply by two, and finally

$$C_1(x_1, y_2) + C_1(x_2, y_1) \leq C_1(x_1, y_1) + C_1(x_2, y_2).$$

This is the third property needed to satisfy for C_1(x, y) to be a copula. □

Remark 3. *In addition, it should be noted that the copula constructed above matches both the symmetric and the prefix property.*

And that is because

$$C_1(x,\ y) = g\left(g^{-1}(x) * g^{-1}(y)\right) = g\left(g^{-1}(y) * g^{-1}(x)\right) = C_1(y, x)$$

also

$$C_1(C_1(x,y), w) = g\left(g^{-1}\left(g\left(g^{-1}(x) * g^{-1}(y)\right)\right) * g^{-1}(w)\right) = g\left(g^{-1}(x) * g^{-1}(y) * g^{-1}(w)\right)$$

And

$$C_1(x,\ C_1\ (y,\ w)) = g\left(g^{-1}(x) * g^{-1}\left(g\left(g^{-1}(y) * g^{-1}(w)\ \right)\right)\right) = g\left(g^{-1}\ (x) * g^{-1}(y) * g^{-1}(w)\right)$$

thus

$$C_1(C_1(x,y)\ , w) = C(x, C_1(y,w)).$$

Example 4. *Let the function g(x) =* $\sqrt{x}$ *when* $0 \leq x \leq 1$*, then,* $g^{-1}(x) = x^2$ *when* $0 \leq x \leq 1$*. So, we construct the copula* C_1 *(x, y) =* $\left(\sqrt{x} * \sqrt{y}\right)^2$*. Let us check the three conditions:*

(1) $C_1(t,0) = \left(\sqrt{t} * \sqrt{0}\right)^2 = 0 = \left(\sqrt{0} * \sqrt{t}\right)^2 = C_1(0,t)$

(2) $C_1(t,1) = \left(\sqrt{t} * 1\right)^2 = 0 = \left(\sqrt{1} * \sqrt{t}\right)^2 = C_1(1,t)$

(3) *The function g(x) is productive, so it is relatively easy to prove the third property, provided that the derivative*

$$\frac{\partial^2 C_1(x,y)}{\partial xy} \geq 0 \Leftrightarrow$$

$$\frac{\partial C(x,y)}{\partial x} = \left(\frac{1}{\sqrt{x}} * \sqrt{y}\right)\left(\sqrt{x} * \sqrt{y}\right) = y \text{ and } \frac{\partial^2 C(x,y)}{\partial xy} = 1\ \geq 0\ .C_1 \text{ is a copula.}$$

In the next theorem, we will try to combine the construction of the fuzzy implication that we have already constructed with the construction of the last copulas.

Theorem 5. *Let the function* $g : [0,1] \to [0, +\infty)$ *continuous, strictly increasing and convex, g(0) = 0, g(1) = 1 and* g^{-1} *continuous. The function* $C : [0,1]^2 \to [0,1]$*, when*

$$C(x,y) = max\left\{g\left(g^{-1}(x) * y\right), g\left(g^{-1}(y) * x\right)\right\} \text{ is a copula.} \tag{38}$$

Proof of the Theorem 5.

(1) $C(t,0) = C(t,0) = max\{g(g^{-1}(t) * 0), g(g^{-1}(0) * t)\} = max\{g(0), g(0 * t)\} = max\{g(0), g(0)\} = max\{0,0\} = 0$
$C(0,t) = max\{g(g^{-1}(0) * t), g(g^{-1}(t) * 0)\} = max\{g(0 * t), g(0)\} = max\{0,0\} = 0$, which proves that $C(t,0) = C(t,0) = 0$

(a) $C(t,1) = C(t,1) = max\{g(g^{-1}(t) * 1), g(g^{-1}(1) * t)\} = max\{g(g^{-1}(t)), g(t)\} = max\{t, g(t)\} = t$.
and that is because $g(x)$ is convex, which means that $g(t) \leq t$.

(b) $C(1,t) = C(1,t) = max\{g(g^{-1}(1) * t), g(g^{-1}(t) * 1)\} = max\{g(t), g(g^{-1}(t))\} = max\{g(t), t\} = t$. So, $C(1,t) = C(t,1) = t$.

(2) Let $g^{-1}(x) * y = u$ and $g^{-1}(y) * x = w$, which means that C(x, y) is either equal to $g(u)$ or $g(w)$. It has already been proven before that if the function $g(x)$ is convex, the third property of the copulas is settled. So, there is no need to prove again, as the proof is obvious. □

Example 5. *Let the function* $g(x) = \frac{x}{3-2x}$ *for every x in the interval* $0 \leq x \leq 1$ *be continuous, strictly increasing and convex, with* $g^{-1}(x) = \frac{3x}{2x+1}$ *continuous and strictly increasing. We will prove the following:*

The function $C(x,y) = max\{ \frac{\frac{3x}{2x+1}y}{3-2\frac{3x}{2x+1}y}, \frac{\frac{3y}{2y+1}x}{3-2\frac{3y}{2y+1}x}\}$ *is a copula.*

(1) $C(x,0) = max\{\frac{\frac{3*x}{2x+1}0}{3-2\frac{3x}{2x+1}0}, \frac{\frac{3*0}{2*0+1}x}{3-2\frac{3*0}{2*0+1}x}\} = max\{0,0\} = 0$

$C(0,y) = max\{ \frac{\frac{3*0}{2*0+1}y}{3-2\frac{3*0}{2*0+1}y}, \frac{\frac{3y}{2y+1}0}{3-2\frac{3y}{2y+1}0}\} = max\{0,0\} = 0$

(2) $C(x,1) = max\{ \frac{\frac{3x}{2x+1}1}{3-2\frac{3x}{2x+1}1}, \frac{\frac{3*1}{2*1+1}x}{3-2\frac{3*1}{2*1+1}x}\} = max\{x, \frac{x}{3-2x}\} = x$ *because* $x \geq \frac{x}{3-2x}$.

$C(1,y) = max\{ \frac{\frac{3*1}{2*1+1}y}{3-2\frac{3*1}{2*1+1}y}, \frac{\frac{3y}{2y+1}1}{3-2\frac{3y}{2y+1}1}\} = max\{\frac{y}{3-2y}, y\} = y$ *again because* $y \geq \frac{y}{3-2y}$.

(3) *As for the third property, we just have to prove that g(x) is convex. We can easily check that* $g'(x) = \frac{3}{(3-2x)^2} \geq 0$ *and* $g''(x) = \frac{4}{(3-2x)^3} \geq 0$, *so g(x) is convex and the third property is automatically proved.*

4. Discussion

The primary main goal of this paper is to present fuzzy negations, fuzzy implications and copulas through a common construction process, using very simple functions with certain properties. In fact, by studying the paper in its entirety, one can see that the present constructions could be performed using a single function.

In an attempt to detail the role played in these constructions by the formula $\mathbf{f}\left(\mathbf{f}^{-1}(\mathbf{y}) * \mathbf{x}\right)$, the following points should be emphasized: f(x) is strictly decreasing, f(0) = 1 and $f^{-1}(y) > 0$. Going ahead with the constructions, some additional properties are given to f(x), such as it is convex, and f(1) = 0. These additional properties do not negate the previous constructions but merely come to complement them. In Section 3 where the constructions are presented, a reference to two functions is made, since, in addition to the decreasing function f(x), there is also in use an increasing function g(x) with almost similar properties. To be precise, one can easily assume that g(x) = f (1−x). So, what is achieved? The achievement is to represent all of the above constructs by means of a single formula $f\left(f^{-1}(y) * x\right)$ and a single function f(x). Recall also that strong negations were constructed with the help of the use of the equilibrium point. Negations that help to calculate exactly what the equilibrium point will be. In addition to that, a very interesting construction is presented that is proved to be a copula, the $C_1(x, y) = g(g^{-1}(x) * g^{-1}(y))$. This copula formula is very similar to the other formula presented in Section 3 ($C(x,y) = max\{g(g^{-1}(x) * y), g(g^{-1}(y) * x)\}$). A very detailed proof is given concerning the fact that if the function g(x) is convex, $C_1(x, y)$ will always be a copula.

If we try to talk about the consequences of, for example, applying some of the copulas proved in Section 3 to domains of fuzzy logic such as AI and robotics, this will be a significant prospect. Other areas, such as "Control synthesis for discrete-time T-S fuzzy systems based on membership function-dependent H∞ performance" [27] or "Finite-Time Membership Function-Dependent H∞ Control for T-S Fuzzy Systems via a Dynamic Memory Event-Triggered Mechanism" [28] will have results that could be some of the below:

1. Uncertainty Handling: Copulas can be used to model the dependency between different uncertainties in the system. By incorporating copulas into the T-S fuzzy model, one can more accurately capture the interdependencies between different sources of uncertainty, leading to more robust control designs.
2. Performance Enhancement: Copulas can help in designing membership function-dependent H∞ controllers by accurately modeling the joint behavior of the system's uncertainties. This leads to better performance metrics, such as improved disturbance rejection and enhanced stability under varying operating conditions.
3. Event-Triggered Mechanisms: The use of copulas can optimize event-triggering conditions by better predicting the evolution of system states and disturbances. This optimization can lead to more efficient control actions, reducing unnecessary computations and communications while maintaining desired performance levels.

- Modeling Dependencies: Both papers focus on enhancing control synthesis by considering the dependencies between uncertainties. Copulas offer a sophisticated way to model these dependencies, leading to improved controller performance.
- Robustness and Adaptivity: By using copulas, controllers can be designed to be more adaptive to varying conditions and more robust against disturbances, aligning with the goals of H∞ performance and finite-time stability.
- Efficiency in Control: In event-triggered mechanisms, copulas can optimize the conditions for control actions, leading to more efficient system operation without compromising performance.

In essence, copulas provide a powerful tool to enhance the modeling and control of T-S fuzzy systems by accurately capturing the dependencies between uncertainties, thus improving the robustness and efficiency of control strategies discussed in both papers.

5. Conclusions

Fuzzy negations are necessary in many areas and especially in generating new fuzzy implications. In this article, there have been proposed some novel construction methods of strong fuzzy negations. This is achieved using a specific type of formula to construct at the same time strong fuzzy negations, fuzzy implications and Copulas in an attempt to bring those mathematical concepts a bit closer. Two theorems are presented in negations, one in implications and two theorems in copulas. All of the above are accompanied by their own proofs. Furthermore, there is presented one very interesting proof in the third property of the copulas regarding how one non-productive function g(x) constructs a copula only if it is convex.

The above constructions are intended to provide the mathematical community with the following information:

(a) All of the above constructs can be represented by means of very simple functions, common among the concepts used.
(b) A formula is presented that participates in all three mathematical concepts discussed in this article.
(c) A proof in the area of copulas is presented.

All of the above is intended to bring all the mathematical concepts discussed in this article closer together, from a mathematical point of view, and to give ground for future analysts to build on it and further investigate the convergence and application of these concepts.

6. Patents

The formula $f\left(f^{-1}(y) * x\right)$, which can generate strict fuzzy negations, strong fuzzy negations, fuzzy implications and copulas for a strictly decreasing, positive function, convex with

f (0) = 1 (in some cases f(1) = 0 also).

Author Contributions: Methodology, P.G.M.; Supervision, B.P. All authors have read and agreed to the published version of the manuscript.

Funding: This research received no external funding.

Data Availability Statement: Data are contained within the article.

Acknowledgments: Special thanks to all three reviewers for their notes and comments on this article.

Conflicts of Interest: The authors declare no conflicts of interest, financial or otherwise.

References

1. Bustince, H.; Campión, M.J.; De Miguel, L.; Induráin, E. Strong negations and restricted equivalence functions revisited: An analytical and topological approach. *Fuzzy Sets Syst.* **2022**, *441*, 110–129. [CrossRef]
2. Bedregal, B.C. On interval fuzzy negations. *Fuzzy Sets Syst.* **2010**, *161*, 2290–2313. [CrossRef]
3. Gupta, V.K.; Massanet, S.; Vemuri, N.R. Novel construction methods of interval-valued fuzzy negations and aggregation functions based on admissible orders. *Fuzzy Sets Syst.* **2023**, *473*, 108722. [CrossRef]
4. Pradera, A.; Beliakov, G.; Bustince, H.; De Baets, B. A review of the relationships between implication, negation and aggregation functions from the point of view of material. *Implic. Inf. Sci.* **2016**, *329*, 357–380. [CrossRef]
5. Baczynski, M.; Jayaram, B. QL-implications: Some properties and intersections. *Fuzzy Sets Syst.* **2010**, *161*, 158–188. [CrossRef]
6. Baczynski, M.; Jayaram, B. (U, N)-implications and their characterizations. *Fuzzy Sets Syst.* **2009**, *160*, 2049–2062. [CrossRef]
7. Durante, F.; Klement, E.P.; Meriar, R.; Sempi, C. Conjunctors and their residual implicators: Characterizations and construction methods. *Mediterr. J. Math.* **2007**, *4*, 343–356. [CrossRef]
8. Massanet, S.; Torrens, J. An overview of construction methods of fuzzy implications. In *Advances in Fuzzy Implication Functions*; Studies in Fuzziness and Soft Computing; Springer: Berlin/Heidelberg, Germany, 2013; Volume 300, pp. 1–30. [CrossRef]
9. Baczynski, M.; Jayaram, B.; Massanet, S.; Torrens, J. Fuzzy implications: Past, present, and future. In *Springer Handbook of Computational Intelligence*; Springer Handbooks; Springer: Berlin/Heidelberg, Germany, 2015; pp. 183–202. [CrossRef]
10. Baczynski, M.; Jayaram, B. On the characterization of (S, N)-implications. *Fuzzy Sets Syst.* **2007**, *158*, 1713–1727. [CrossRef]
11. Massanet, S.; Vicente, J.; Clapes, R.; Aguilera, D.R. On fuzzy polynomials implications. In Proceedings of the 2015 Conference of the International Fuzzy Systems Association and the European Society for Fuzzy Logic and Technology (IFSA-EUSFLAT-15), Gijón, Spain, 30 June–3 July 2015. [CrossRef]
12. Rapti, M.; Papadopoulos, B. A Method of Generating Fuzzy Implications from n Increasing Functions and n+1 Negations. *Mathematics* **2020**, *8*, 886. [CrossRef]
13. Daniilidou, A.; Konguetsof, A.; Souliotis, G.; Papadopoulos, B. Generator of Fuzzy Implications. *Algorithms* **2023**, *16*, 569. [CrossRef]
14. Baczynski, M.; Jayaram, B. *Fuzzy Implications*; Springer: Berlin/Heidelberg, Germany, 2008. [CrossRef]
15. Bustince, H.; Pagola, M.; Barrenechea, E. Construction of fuzzy indices from fuzzy DIsubsethood measures: Application to the global comparison of images. *Inf. Sci.* **2007**, *177*, 906–929. [CrossRef]
16. Bogiatzis, A.C.; Papadopoulos, B.K. Local thresholding of degraded or unevenly illuminated documents using fuzzy inclusion and entropy measures. *Evol. Syst.* **2019**, *10*, 593–619. [CrossRef]
17. Bogiatzis, A.C.; Papadopoulos, B. Global Image Thresholding Adaptive Neuro-Fuzzy Inference System. Trained with Fuzzy Inclusion and Entropy Measures. *Symmetry* **2019**, *11*, 286. [CrossRef]
18. Bogiatzis, A.C.; Papadopoulos, B.K. Producing fuzzy inclusion and entropy measures and their application on 277 global image thresholding. *Evol. Syst.* **2018**, *9*, 331–353. [CrossRef]
19. Betsakos, D. *Introduction to Real Analysis*; Afoi Kyriakidi: Thessaloniki, Greece, 2016.
20. Baczyński, M.; Grzegorzewski, P.; Mesiar, R.; Helbin, P.; Niemyska, W. Fuzzy implications based on semicopulas. *Fuzzy Sets Syst.* **2017**, *323*, 138–151. [CrossRef]
21. Mesiar, R.; Kolesarova, A. Copulas and fuzzy implications. *Int. J. Approx. Reason.* **2020**, *117*, 52–59. [CrossRef]
22. Durante, F.; Sempi, C. *Principles of Copula Theory*; Chapman and Hall/CRC: New York, NY, USA, 2015. [CrossRef]
23. Nelsen, R.B. *An Introduction to Copulas*, 2nd ed.; Springer: New York, NY, USA, 2006.

24. Giakoumakis, S.; Papadopoulos, B. Novel transformation of unimodal (a)symmetric possibility distributions into probability distributions. *Fuzzy Sets Syst.* **2024**, *476*, 108790. [CrossRef]
25. Baczynski, M.; Jayaram, B. (S, N)-and R-implications; a state-of-the-art survey. *Fuzzy Sets Syst.* **2008**, *159*, 1836–1859. [CrossRef]
26. Giakoumakis, S.; Papadopoulos, B. An Algorithm for Fuzzy Negations Based-Intuitionistic Fuzzy Copula Aggregation Operators in Multiple Attribute Decision Making. *Algorithms* **2020**, *13*, 154. [CrossRef]
27. Yang, D.; Xie, X. Relaxed H∞ control design of discrete-time Takagi–Sugeno fuzzy systems: A multi-samples approach. *Neurocomputing* **2016**, *171*, 106–112. [CrossRef]
28. Hou, Q.; Dong, J. Finite-Time Membership Function-Dependent H∞ Control for T-S Fuzzy Systems via a Dynamic Memory Event-Triggered Mechanism. *IEEE Trans. Fuzzy Syst.* **2023**, *31*, 4075–4084. [CrossRef]

MDPI AG
Grosspeteranlage 5
4052 Basel
Switzerland
Tel.: +41 61 683 77 34

Mathematics Editorial Office
E-mail: mathematics@mdpi.com
www.mdpi.com/journal/mathematics

www.ingramcontent.com/pod-product-compliance
Lightning Source LLC
LaVergne TN
LVHW072351090526
838202LV00019B/2517
* 9 7 8 3 7 2 5 8 3 4 5 3 2 *